Guide to Manuscript Revision

ab	......	Spell out abbreviation (M6b)
adv	......	Use adverb form (U2b)
agr	......	Make verb agree with subject (or pronoun with antecedent) (U1c, U4a-b)
ap	......	Use apostrophe (M4b)
cap	......	Capitalize (M4a)
coh	......	Strengthen coherence (C2c-d)
coll	......	Use less colloquial word (U3a)
cs	......	Revise comma splice (M2a-b)
d	......	Improve diction (W3)
dev	......	Develop your point (C1b)
div	......	Revise word division (M6a)
dm	......	Revise dangling modifier (U4c)
frag	......	Revise sentence fragment (M1a)
FP	......	Revise faulty parallelism (U4e)
gr	......	Revise grammatical form or construction (U1-2)
awk	......	Rewrite awkward sentence (U4)
lc	......	Use lower case (M4a)
mm	......	Shift misplaced modifier (U4c)
p	......	Improve punctuation (M1-4)
¶	......	New paragraph (C1)
no¶	......	Take out paragraph break (C1)
ref	......	Improve pronoun reference (U4b)
rep	......	Avoid repetition (U4)
shift	......	Avoid shift in perspective (U4d)
sl	......	Use less slangy word (U3)
sp	......	Revise misspelled word (M5)
st	......	Improve sentence structure (U4)
t	......	Change tense of verb (U1b)
trans	......	Provide better transition (C2d)
w	......	Reduce wordiness (U4)

American English Today

The American English Today Series:

Exploring English

Our Common Language

The Tools of English

The World of English

The Uses of Language

Our Changing Language

American English Today

General Editor and Senior Author: *Hans P. Guth*

Contributing Author, 7–9: Edgar H. Schuster

Third Edition

WEBSTER DIVISION/McGRAW-HILL BOOK COMPANY
New York   St. Louis   San Francisco   Dallas   Atlanta

Editorial Development: *John A. Rothermich*
Managing Editor: *Hester Eggert Weeden*
Design: *Bennie Arrington*
Production: *Judith Tisdale*

Acknowledgments—see page 446

Library of Congress Cataloging in Publication Data

Guth, Hans Paul, date
    The tools of English.

    (His American English today; [3])
    Includes index.
    1. English language—Composition and exercises.
    2. English language—Grammar—1950-   I. Schuster, Edgar Howard,
date joint author.
II. Title.
PE1408.G933   1980 vol. 3   808'.042s   [428'.2]   79-4066
ISBN 0-07-025019-7

Copyright © 1980, 1975, 1970 by McGraw-Hill, Inc. All rights reserved. Printed in the United States of America. No part of this publication may be reproduced, stored in a retrieval system, or transmitted, in any form or by any means, electronic, mechanical, photocopying, recording, or otherwise, without the prior written permission of the publisher.

The Authors

HANS P. GUTH

General Editor and Senior Author

Dr. Guth is a widely published teacher-scholar who writes about effective communication with the authority that comes from successful practice. His first book on the discipline of English, *English Today and Tomorrow,* was widely praised and hailed as a "milestone with no equal in its field." His second book, *English for a New Generation,* offered a "most lucid" discussion of the basic responsibilities and commitments of English teachers. Through his college textbooks —especially the widely used rhetoric handbook, *Words and Ideas* (Wadsworth)—Dr. Guth has become today's most prominent and effective teacher of language and composition. He has lectured at numerous conferences and institutions for teachers and has taught the language course in the NDEA institutes sponsored by Stanford University.

EDGAR H. SCHUSTER

Contributing Author, Grades 7–9

Dr. Schuster is Language Arts Coordinator for the Allentown (Pa.) School District. He has taught English in both urban and suburban high schools in the Philadelphia area. He has also taught at the college level. He has written articles for professional journals, including the *Clearing House,* the *English Journal,* and *Educational Leadership.* Dr. Schuster has been a Master Teacher at Harvard University and is a recipient of a Lindback Foundation Award for Distinguished Teaching. He is the principal editor of *American Literature,* the Grade 11 text of McGraw-Hill's *Themes and Writers* anthology series.

Consultants and Contributors

Student Writing	**Gabriele Rico,** *San Jose State University*
Cultural Minorities	**Carol Kizine,** *Kansas City Public Schools*
Teaching Suggestions	**Barbara Johnston,** *San Jose State University*
Testing and Measurement	**William Kline,** *California Test Bureau*
Graphics	**Herbert Zettl,** *San Francisco State University*

The Authors and the Publishers also thank the following teachers who evaluated manuscript, provided hundreds of examples of student writing, and tried out *American English Today* in their classrooms:

Marge Archer, Lawrenceville, New Jersey
James Conway, St. Louis, Missouri
Jeanne Irwin, Los Angeles, California
Cherry Mallory, Kansas City, Missouri
Donald Mayfield, San Diego, California
Virginia McCormick, Allentown, Pennsylvania
Jane McGill, Chula Vista, California
Janet Minesinger, Columbia, Maryland
Nancy Mitchell, Lakewood, California
Richard E. Roberts, Clinton Corners, New York
Margaret Timm, Bay City, Michigan
Marilyn Walker, Salem, Oregon

To the Teacher

American English Today, Third Edition, offers solid productive work in the basic areas of language and composition. Its aim is to provide materials that are intelligible, workable, and motivating for today's students. The following are key features of the new Third Edition:

1. More varied, effective, and interesting exercises than any competing series.

2. A functional, plain-English approach designed to help students defeated by awkward, elaborate terminology or theory.

3. Streamlined, compact presentation for efficient study and reference.

4. A positive, constructive teaching program systematically developing the students' skills and proficiencies.

5. Frequent provision for measurement of student achievement, with new unit review exercises, diagnostic tests, and achievement tests. A new section on how to take tests, complete with sample tests, appears in the resource chapter of each volume.

6. High-interest materials designed to help teachers overcome students' resistance to English as a subject.

7. Effective use of charts and other visuals designed to help students take things in at a glance.

8. A positive, habit-building program for teaching standard English.

9. Proven step-by-step instruction in the process of composition.

10. Special attention to familiar trouble spots and problem areas for students.

Chapter Table of Contents

Chapter 1
    WORDS   Your Word Resources   1

Chapter 2
    SENTENCES   Writing Better Sentences   55

Chapter 3
    COMPOSITION   Writing for a Reader   141

Chapter 4
    USAGE   Using Standard English   239

Chapter 5
    MECHANICS   The Written Page   307

Chapter 6
    ORAL LANGUAGE   The Brief Talk   379

Chapter 7
    RESOURCES   The Library, Study Skills, Taking Tests   403

TABLE OF CONTENTS

Chapter 1
WORDS: Your Word Resources   1

     W1   Learning New Words   4

     W2   Word Building   10
         a   Going to the Roots   11
         b   Our Changeable Prefixes   14
         c   Adding Suffixes   17

     W3   The Right Word   21
         a   Using Specific Words   21
         b   Synonyms and Antonyms   23
         c   Using Figurative Language   28

     W4   Using the Dictionary   32
         a   Finding Words   34
         b   Words and Their Meanings   39
         c   Word History   43
         d   Pronunciation Guide   45

     For Further Study: Language Around the World   51

Chapter 2
SENTENCES: Writing Better Sentences   55

     S1   Words in a Sentence   59
         a   Recognizing Nouns   60
         b   Recognizing Pronouns   64
         c   Recognizing Verbs   67
         d   Recognizing Adjectives   73
         e   Recognizing Adverbs   79
         f   Recognizing Connectives and Prepositions   83

S2	**The Complete Sentence**		87
	a	Subject and Verb	88
	b	Verb and Object	91
	c	Linking Verb and Noun	94
	d	Linking Verb and Adjective	97
	e	The Indirect Object	100
S3	**Adapting the Simple Sentence**		103
	a	Requests and Questions	104
	b	The Passive	106
S4	**Building Combined Sentences**		110
	a	How Coordination Builds Sentences	111
	b	How Subordination Builds Sentences	114
	c	How Relative Clauses Build Sentences	118
	d	How Noun Clauses Build Sentences	120
S5	**Expanding Our Sentence Resources**		123
	a	Using Infinitives	123
	b	Using Participles	127
	c	Using Appositives	131

For Further Study: The Exception to the Rule   134

Chapter 3
COMPOSITION: Writing for a Reader   141

C1	**Writing the Paragraph**		145
	a	Gathering Material	146
	b	Writing the Topic Sentence	148
	c	Giving Examples	153
	d	Comparison and Contrast	156
	e	Giving Reasons	159
C2	**Writing a Short Paper**		161
	a	Gathering Material	163
	b	Supporting a Central Idea	166
	c	Outlining the Paper	169
	d	Helping Your Reader Follow	175

C3	**Writing for a Purpose**		180
	a Describing a Scene		181
	b The Story with a Point		187
	c Explaining a Process		196
	d Persuading Your Reader		203
C4	**Writing a Letter**		209
	a How Business Letters Look		209
	b What Business Letters Say		216
	c Writing a Personal Letter		220
C5	**Writing and Reading**		221
	a The Summary		222
	b The Book Report		225

For Further Study: Writing and Imagination   229

Chapter 4

USAGE: Using Standard English   239

U1	**Standard English: Basics**		243
	a Plurals of Nouns		244
	b Verbs and Time		248
	c Verbs and Number		253
	d Auxiliaries		258
U2	**Standard English: Finer Points**		260
	a Standard Pronouns		261
	b Adjectives and Adverbs		264
	c Other Nonstandard Expressions		266
U3	**Formal and Informal**		271
	a Informal Words		272
	b Pronoun Case		275
	c Adverb Forms		278
	d A Guide to Formal English		281

U4	**Revising Written Sentences**		287
	a	Agreement	287
	b	Pronoun Reference	291
	c	Position of Modifiers	294
	d	Shifts	297
	e	Parallel Structure	300

For Further Study: Folk Speech and Slang   303

Chapter 5
MECHANICS: The Written Page   307

M1	**End Punctuation**		311
	a	Sentences and Fragments	311
	b	Questions and Exclamations	315
M2	**Linking Punctuation**		317
	a	Commas with Coordinators	317
	b	Semicolons with or without Connectives	319
	c	Commas and Dependent Clauses	323
M3	**Inside Punctuation**		327
	a	Commas for Modifiers	327
	b	Commas for Minor Breaks	330
	c	Colons, Dashes, and Parentheses	334
M4	**Capitals and Special Marks**		337
	a	Using Capitals	337
	b	Using Apostrophes	343
	c	Using Quotation Marks	348
	d	Using Hyphens	352
	e	Using Italics (Underlining)	354
M5	**Spelling**		356
	a	Commonly Misspelled Words	357
	b	Spelling Rules	363
	c	Confusing Pairs	368

M6		**Manuscript Form**	372
	a	Dividing Words	374
	b	Abbreviations	375
	c	Numbers	376

Chapter 6
ORAL LANGUAGE: The Brief Talk   379

O1		**The Speaker's Resources**	381
	a	Using Your Voice	381
	b	Talking with Your Hands	384
O2		**Preparing a Brief Talk**	387
	a	The Informative Talk	388
	b	The Personal Viewpoint	390
	c	The Commentary	391
O3		**The Interview**	393

For Further Study: Acting Things Out   397

Chapter 7
RESOURCES: The Library, Study Skills, Taking Tests   403

R1		**Using the Library**	404
	a	Finding Library Materials	404
	b	Using the Card Catalogue	408
	c	Finding Magazine Articles	413
	d	Using Reference Materials	415
R2		**Improving Study Skills**	419
R3		**Taking Tests**	421
	a	Vocabulary Tests	422
	b	Tests of Written English	431

PROSE MODELS

C3   Writing for a Purpose

    C3a   Describing a Scene
        PROSE MODEL 1
        LOREN EISELEY, *The Pigeons of the El*   185

    C3b   The Story with a Point
        PROSE MODEL 2
        LOIS PHILLIPS HUDSON, *A Silver Dollar*   195

    C3c   Explaining a Process
        PROSE MODEL 3
        NORMAN B. WILTSEY, *The Doomed Buffalo*   199

    C3d   Persuading Your Reader
        PROSE MODEL 4
        PAUL EHRLICH, *The End of the Ocean*   205

To the Student

Language is around us everywhere. Much of the work of the world is done by language. People doing a job use words to give directions and to ask for help. People in business use language to order a product, to advertise it, and to bill the customer. Our society would come to a standstill if telephones, letters, and books no longer carried information.

Words help us live together as people. We use language to talk things over. We use it to complain and to make requests. We use it to show that we are happy or dissatisfied.

How can you learn to put language to good use?

This book is designed to help you make the most of your language potential. The materials in this book will help you develop your language ability in three important ways:

(1) *Know your language.* The more you learn about the way language works, the more you will be able to use it with confidence.

(2) *Learn from experience.* Listening and reading are only one-half of your work in an English class. The other half is added when *your turn* comes to speak and write. Use all opportunities to speak up or to put something down on paper.

(3) *Profit from advice.* No one likes to be corrected or criticized. But the advice you receive from your English teacher and from your textbook is not designed to put you down. It is designed to help you develop your potential.

Chapter 1

Words
Your Word Resources

W1 **Learning New Words**

W2 **Word Building**
    a Going to the Roots
    b Our Changeable Prefixes
    c Adding Suffixes

W3 **The Right Word**
    a Using Specific Words
    b Synonyms and Antonyms
    c Using Figurative Language

W4 **Using the Dictionary**
    a Finding Words
    b Words and Their Meanings
    c Word History
    d Pronunciation Guide

For Further Study: Language Around the World

Chapter Preview 1

IN THIS CHAPTER:
- How to read clues that help us to understand and use new words.
- How to recognize the building blocks our language uses in word-making.
- How to choose the word that is right for the purpose.
- How to make full use of a dictionary.

Learn how to make new words your own.

Words help us find our way in the world in which we live. We use words to give directions. We use words to explain our problems. In training for a career, students learn the language of their trade. Studying history, they read about words that were once fighting words in our nation's past. Studying chemistry or electronics, they learn words that modern science has made "household words."

As you learn about the world in which you live, you build up your **vocabulary.** You build up your word resources. Look at the following preview exercises. They will make you think about words that you make your own as you move into a new field of study or a new area of interest.

PREVIEW EXERCISE 1

THE LANGUAGE OF NATURE LOVERS Many voices have warned us that we are wasting the natural resources of this planet. We are polluting our natural environment. Are people learning to value the landscape and the wildlife that remain? The following words might come up in a conversation with a lover of nature. Select five of them. Explain them to people who have spent all their lives in the city.

rodent	predator	humus	vegetation
habitat	foliage	fawn	pollination
hibernate	ravine	fern	pod

Your Word Resources

LANGUAGE IN THE WORLD OF WORK People doing a job have to be able to talk about the tools and materials of their trade. How well do you understand the language of one of the following occupations? Choose one of them, and explain the words listed there to an outsider.

PREVIEW EXERCISE 2

builder:	insulation, foundation, vent, solar heating
mechanic:	carburetor, flywheel, traction, radiator
farmer:	pesticide, irrigation, germinate, incubator
office worker:	duplicate, discount, endorse, ditto sheet
banker:	deposit, interest, account, mortgage
jeweler:	carat, facet, gem, setting
retailer:	discount, wholesale, receipt, inventory
reporter:	headline, feature, interview, columnist
lawyer:	brief, felony, objection, tort
programmer:	computer, terminal, print-out, bug

LANGUAGE IN SOCIETY Words tell us what we can do and what we should do as members of society. Words make us understand the rights and obligations we have as citizens. Read the following sentences. How many of the italicized words do you know? Where have you seen or heard them used? State the meaning of each in a few words of your own.

PREVIEW EXERCISE 3

1. The people leading the protest asked everyone to *boycott* British goods.
2. Her parents had been born in Japan and were *naturalized* citizens of the United States.
3. A well-known lawyer, Elizabeth Baker, ran against the *incumbent* governor and unseated him.
4. All our neighbors signed a *petition* that asked for a traffic light at the school crossing.
5. The two kidnappers were sentenced to life in prison without the possibility of *parole*.
6. The employer promised to listen to the *grievances* of the employees and to correct the problems if possible.
7. According to the latest *census,* the number of families with only one child or with none was increasing.
8. Because of the youngster's age, a different court had *jurisdiction* in the case.
9. Voters in the state used to be given a *literacy* test before they were allowed to register.
10. Under the new law, old people were *eligible* for improved benefits.

Words

W1 LEARNING NEW WORDS

Learn to read the clues that tell us the meaning of unfamiliar words.

We learn new words all the time. We see a word in action, and the second or third time we encounter it, we say to ourselves: "I'm beginning to see what this word means and how it is used." Look at the way Mark Twain uses the word *transient* in the following passage. In how many ways does the passage help you to see what the word means?

> When I was a boy, there was but one permanent ambition among my comrades in our village on the west bank of the Mississippi River. That was, to be a steamboatman. We had *transient* ambitions of other sorts, but they were only *transient*. When a circus came and went, it left us all burning to become clowns. The first minstrel show that ever came to our section left us all suffering to try that kind of life. Now and then, we had a hope that, if we lived and were good, God would permit us to be pirates. These ambitions faded out, each in its turn. But the ambition to be a steamboatman always remained.—Mark Twain, *Life on the Mississippi*

Here are some of the clues that help us tell the meaning of *transient* in this passage:

- One ambition was "permanent." It "always remained." The others (the transient ones) were different.
- Transient ambitions had something to do with things that came and went (like the circus). They were the kinds of ambitions that came "now and then."
- Transient ambitions "fade out," each in its turn.

From these clues, we gather that *transient* means passing, not permanent, just "passing through." When we look for clues such as these, we look at the way a word is used in a sentence or in a paragraph. The passage that the word fits into is its **context**. We often say: "Let's look at this word *in context*." In order to understand a word, we have to look at what goes with it. We have to see how it fits in. Look especially for the following clues when you examine the way a word is used:

(1) SITUATION. Often what is happening is clear from the situation. Look at the following sentence:

Learning New Words

The ship tied up at the *quay*.

A *quay* must be some sort of dock or pier. Ships tie up only at such places.

(2) **EXPLANATION.** Often a writer or speaker explains in more detailed words the idea that the key word sums up. Look at the word *prominent* in the following passage. Can you see how it sums up the idea that the person was "known, liked, and feared"? Obviously, prominent people are not unknown. They are known; they stand out.

> The town marshal of Yellow Sky, a man known, liked, and feared in his corner, a *prominent* person, had gone to San Antonio. (Stephen Crane)

(3) **EXAMPLE.** What kind of behavior is shown in the examples in the following passage? If this is the way the comedian W. C. Fields really acted, what would we mean by calling his behavior *neurotic?*

> Fields' distrust of doctors and lawyers was *neurotic*. Bankers were even worse, he held. In order to outwit them, he deposited small sums of money in banks scattered all over the world, even stepping off a train to open an account in a small town while the engine was taking on water. (Corey Ford)

(4) **COMPARISON.** Sometimes we can tell what a word means when we see what the writer compares it to. To judge from the following passage, something is *inevitable* when no one can stop it from happening:

> Growing up may seem to take a long time, but it is as *inevitable* as the coming of spring or the falling of the leaves in autumn.

(5) **CONTRAST.** Often we can tell what a word means when a writer contrasts it with something that is its opposite. To judge from the following passage, *shambling* is a kind of walking that is the opposite of "carrying yourself tall" and walking "a straight line." It must be a stooped-over, slumping kind of walk:

> People drooped and *shambled,* but the girls carried themselves tall and walked a straight line, as befitted young heiresses on their afternoon promenade. (Dorothy Parker)

Words

LANGUAGE IN ACTION

THE WILD HORSES OF THE WEST

Which of the three choices is *closest* to the right meaning of the italicized word? After the number of the sentence, write the letter for the right choice. (If you don't know the meaning of the word, what helps you guess?)

1. Eighty years ago, two million wild horses *roamed* the West.
   a. left   b. ranged over   c. came to
2. Horses, deer, and antelopes shared the same *habitat*.
   a. living space b. food   c. climate
3. Spaniards on horseback had explored vast *tracts* of America.
   a. mountains   b. stretches of land c. river valleys
4. The Indians learned to *domesticate* the animals.
   a. tame   b. capture   c. breed
5. But thousands of horses *reverted* to wild ways.
   a. yearned for   b. resisted   c. went back to
6. In our century, the mustangs were almost *exterminated*.
   a. driven out   b. stamped out   c. bought up
7. Thousands were captured and *converted* to chicken feed.
   a. compared to   b. traded for   c. turned into
8. Hunters in airplanes *panicked* the animals.
   a. pursued   b. spotted   c. stampeded
9. Hunters in trucks herded the animals into *concealed* corrals.
   a. hidden   b. open   c. closed
10. A few thousand mustangs survived in *inaccessible* places.
    a. hard to get to b. unknown   c. high up
11. Newspapers started to report the mustangs' *plight*.
    a. price   b. flight   c. predicament
12. Congress was *inundated* with mail.
    a. bombarded   b. flooded   c. threatened
13. A law was *enacted* in 1971.
    a. proposed   b. made official   c. abolished
14. Some ranchers have *designated* limited areas as reserves.
    a. extended   b. set aside   c. offered
15. Wild horses still live free in *remote* areas of Nevada.
    a. distant   b. dry   c. wet

EXERCISE 1

Look at the italicized word in each of the following passages. How does the rest of the passage help you understand what the word means? What clue (or clues) does it provide? Explain how the *context* helps you understand the word.

Learning New Words

1. "We will be married now. Kino has said so." She looked at the neighbors for *confirmation,* and they nodded their heads solemnly. (John Steinbeck)

2. Even with the glasses, Billie Jean had trouble seeing. The frames blocked certain areas from *vision,* creating blind spots on both sides. To make things worse, sweat tended to run down the lenses during a game, and heat caused them to fog over. (Francene Sabin)

3. Now one of the fire warning lights was misbehaving. . . . Some *malfunctioning,* which the engineers had so far been unable to correct, caused them to light up across the instrument panel like a crazy pinball machine. (Ernest K. Gann)

4. The only difference between the programs was that in some the shooting was done out of doors and often from horses and that in others it was done in hotel rooms, bars, or apartments. The first *category* was called Western and was considered a wholesome fight between good men and bad men in healthy country. The second was called Crime and Detective. (Marya Mannes)

5. He trembled with each shock of *turbulence,* watched his wing tips bend too much, waiting for the rending sound that would signal he had pushed things too far. Those were an uneasy few seconds, but a thousand feet over the water the air became smooth as glass. (Walter S. Ross)

EXERCISE 2

Look at each of the following words in context. Which of the three meanings listed best fits the context? Write the letter for the most likely meaning after the number of the word. Explain in class how the rest of the sentence helped you choose the right meaning for the word.

1. **initial** Less than a month after he graduated from West Point in 1861, General Custer made his *initial* contact with war during the battle of Bull Run.
   a. first   b. frightening   c. frequent

2. **distinguished** In 1863, Custer *distinguished* himself by daring acts at Gettysburg.
   a. stood out   b. became unpopular   c. retired

3. **decisive** Custer took part in many *decisive* cavalry actions which were to hasten the defeat of the Confederacy.
   a. important   b. minor   c. unsuccessful

Words

4. **assigned** After the war, he was *assigned* to Kansas, and arrived in that territory in 1866.
   a. traded   b. released   c. transferred

5. **expeditions** He took part in several *expeditions* against the Cheyenne.
   a. trade trips   b. campaigns   c. rescue trips

6. **leisurely** Custer spent five rather *leisurely* years, and even found time to write a book entitled *My Life on the Plains*.
   a. wasted   b. hurried   c. unhurried

7. **dispatched** In the year 1873, Custer was *dispatched* to fight against the Sioux in Dakota and Montana.
   a. reprimanded   b. promoted   c. sent

8. **junction** Custer's force arrived at the *junction* of the Big Horn and Little Big Horn rivers on June 24, 1876.
   a. meeting point   b. time   c. riverbed

9. **segments** Told that a small force of Sioux was in the area, General Custer divided his troops into three *segments*.
   a. tasks   b. shapes   c. groups

10. **estimated** The size of the Sioux band was incorrectly *estimated*, and Custer and 226 men were killed when they rode into the midst of the enemy.
    a. guessed   b. defeated   c. mentioned

EXERCISE 3   Which of the three meanings listed for each word best fits the context? Write the letter for the most likely meaning after the number of the word. Be prepared to explain in class how the rest of the sentence helped you choose the right meaning for the word.

1. **invisible** The planet Neptune, *invisible* to the naked eye, can be viewed only through a telescope.
   a. unseeable   b. misty   c. apparent

2. **remote** This *remote* world is over two thousand million miles from the Earth.
   a. far away   b. unknown   c. strange

Learning New Words

3. **estimate** — Of course, astronomers can only guess Neptune's temperature, which they *estimate* to be 330° below zero.
   a. calculate   b. know   c. guess

4. **worshiped** — Neptune is named after the god of the sea, *worshiped* by the ancient Romans.
   a. invented   b. adored   c. feared

5. **prior** — *Prior* to Neptune's discovery in 1846, no one was sure it existed.
   a. before   b. because of   c. in spite of

6. **suspected** — But beginning as early as 1830, some astronomers *suspected* the planet's presence.
   a. revealed   b. assumed   c. denounced

7. **observed** — They had *observed* that something was disturbing the movement of the planet Uranus.
   a. seen   b. remembered   c. announced

8. **calculated** — Using mathematical formulas, a French astronomer *calculated* Neptune's position.
   a. guessed   b. figured   c. scorned

9. **proclaimed** — At exactly the same time, a British astronomer *proclaimed* that he too had discovered Neptune.
   a. attempted   b. announced   c. kept secret

10. **previously** — Both men had discovered the *previously* unknown planet at the same time.
    a. before   b. always   c. never

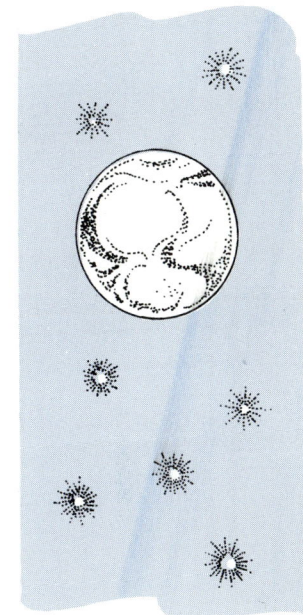

For each italicized word, choose the meaning that fits best. Write the letter for the right meaning after the number of the word.

UNIT REVIEW EXERCISE

1. our *initial* success
   a. at the end   b. at the beginning   c. in the long run
2. a *transient* ambition
   a. passing   b. permanent   c. hidden
3. a *remote* area
   a. crowded   b. rocky   c. far away
4. a *malfunctioning* signal
   a. working badly   b. shut off   c. warning
5. a *decisive* victory
   a. unexpected   b. very important   c. doubtful
6. *enacted* in 1980
   a. acted out   b. made official   c. canceled

Words

7. a *concealed* camera
   - a. hidden
   - b. very small
   - c. smuggled
8. the *inevitable* collapse
   - a. expected
   - b. unbelievable
   - c. unstoppable
9. the *plight* of the survivors
   - a. threatened state
   - b. good luck
   - c. story
10. excellent *vision*
    - a. direction
    - b. sight
    - c. control
11. *estimated* attendance
    - a. guessed
    - b. paid
    - c. recorded
12. unexpected *turbulence*
    - a. stalling
    - b. choppy air
    - c. spoiled food
13. an *exterminated* tribe
    - a. unknown
    - b. converted
    - c. wiped out
14. an *inaccessible* valley
    - a. fertile
    - b. unreachable
    - c. dried out
15. a *prominent* speaker
    - a. well-known
    - b. very tall
    - c. long-winded
16. *domesticated* animals
    - a. tamed
    - b. raised for food
    - c. taught tricks
17. unequal *segments*
    - a. rewards
    - b. parts
    - c. treatments
18. *previously* identified
    - a. too late
    - b. right away
    - c. earlier
19. waiting for *confirmation*
    - a. agreeing it's true
    - b. apology
    - c. hardening
20. the *habitat* of the buffalo
    - a. hunting
    - b. dying out
    - c. living space

W2 WORD BUILDING

Recognize the building blocks that can help you understand and use words.

When we want to see how a clock works, we take it apart. By taking it apart, we learn how it was put together. We see what went into it to make it work. By taking words apart, we learn what went into them. Look at what happens when we take apart a word like the following:

invisible   The *vis–* in this word has something to do with vision, with seeing. The last part of the word, *–ible*, often shows that something can be done. (Ed*ible* food can be eaten.) The first part of the word, *in–*, often shows that something is *not* true. When we put the three parts together, the word *invisible* tells us: "It cannot be seen."

Word Building

The building blocks that we find in words are of three major kinds:

(1) The part that gives us the *core meaning* of a word is its root. Look at the following set of words:

liberty   liberate   liberation

All of these words have grown from a common root: *lib–*. This root means "free": Liberty is "freedom." To liberate is to "set free." Liberation is the freeing of a city or the setting free of a prisoner.

(2) The kind of interchangeable part that we can attach *in front* of many familiar word roots is a **prefix**. A prefix is something "attached ahead." Look at the words in the following set:

mispronounce   misspell   mistake

Each time, the prefix *mis–* adds the idea that something is done *wrong*. Something is "amiss."

(3) The kind of interchangeable part that we can attach *at the end* of many word roots is a **suffix**. Look at the words in the following set:

hopeless   childless   penniless

Each time, the suffix *–less* adds the idea that we have to do *without* something. Hopeless people suffer from a *loss* of hope.

Study familiar word roots shared by many different words.

W2a Going to the Roots

Words with the same root share a common ancestor. Words like *liberty* and *liberate* go back to the Latin word the Romans used to show that somebody was free and not a slave. For a long time, to become educated meant to study Roman law and Roman history and the arts and sciences of the Greeks. Therefore, much of our language of education, of politics, and of science uses words that came into English from Latin and Greek.

Study the Latin and Greek word roots that appear in the following sample words on the next page. In each case, what is the meaning of the second or third word in each set?

Words

ROOT	MEANING	EXAMPLES
capt-	take	When we *capture* someone, we take a prisoner. A *captive* is ———————. An artist who *captivates* an audience knows how to ————.
ceed-	go	If you *proceed,* you go on; you go forward. If you *exceed* the speed limit, you ————.
dict-	say	If you *predict* something, you say something ahead of time—before it happens. If you give a *benediction,* you say "good wishes"—you give a blessing. If you *contradict* somebody, you ————.
duct-	lead	A *conductor* leads the members of an orchestra. The Romans used *aqueducts* to ————.
fac-	make	A *factory* is a place for making things. A *facsimile* is ————. Things that are *manufactured* abroad are ———— in foreign countries.
fer-	carry	When we *transfer* money, we carry it to some other account. A *reference* to a book carries us to a part of that book. A *referral* ————————.
graph-	write	A *biography* is the written account of someone's life. An *autograph* is ————————.
miss-	send	A *mission* is a task that we are sent out to accomplish. A *missionary* is ————————. A *missile* is ————.
port-	carry	A *portable* radio can be carried easily. *Exports* are ————————. *Imports* are ————————.
scrib-, scrip-	write	A *description* is written about something. A *script* is ————————.
vis-	see	Something that is *visible* can be seen. A *visual* check is ————. An *invisible* film is ————.

Word Building

W2a

LANGUAGE IN ACTION

THE WORLD OF NUMBERS

In our civilization, one of the most common questions is, "How many?" "How much?" Our language uses many different words that in one way or another deal with numbers. Look at the words in each of the following sets. The words in each set are concerned with the same basic number. How is each word different from the other words in the same set?

1. **ONE**   unique   unilateral   solo   singular
2. **TWO**   double   twin   duet   dual   duplicate
3. **THREE**   triple   triplicate   triplet   trinity   trio
4. **FOUR**   quartet   foursome   quart   quadrangle
5. **FIVE**   pentagon   quintuplets
6. **TEN**   decimal   decade   decathlon
7. **HUNDRED**   centennial   centigrade   percent
8. **THOUSAND**   millimeter   millennium

EXERCISE 1

In each of the following sentences, use one of the word roots you have studied to complete the half-finished word. Write the completed word after the number of the sentence. (Write on a separate sheet of paper.)

1. Evidence we can see is _____ual evidence.
2. Someone who leads the wrong kind of life is accused of miscon-_____.
3. When we see to it that someone is led somewhere safely, we arrange safe-con_____.
4. When you carry a canoe around waterfalls or across land, you _____age it.
5. When you write carelessly or messily in small letters, you are _____bling.
6. A weapon that can be used to send warheads halfway around the world is a _____ile.
7. The invention that enabled people to send written messages by Morse code was the tele_____.
8. The announcement that says what a jury has determined is the ver_____.
9. People can carry you back to your childhood when they re_____ to your hometown.
10. Priests sent to Mexico and California from Spain built _____ion churches.

13

Words

11. Wild animals that have been taken to zoos live in _____ivity.
12. A book telling the story of the writer's life is an autobio_____y.
13. When goods are carried out of the country and sold abroad, they are ex_____ed.
14. When soldiers attempt to retake a town, they try to re_____ure it.
15. To bring their ideas together, people hold a con_____ence.

EXERCISE 2

How much does your knowledge of word roots help you when you encounter words like the following? After the number of each word, fill in the letter of the description that fits it best. (Write on a separate sheet of paper.)

1. A visionary _____.
2. A seismograph _____.
3. A reporter _____.
4. A dictator _____.
5. A prescription _____.
6. A duct _____.
7. Deportation _____.
8. Emissions _____.
9. A captive audience _____.
10. Proceeds _____.

Descriptions:
  a. writes down measurements for earthquakes.
  b. is a written request for medicine.
  c. leads from one part of a building to another.
  d. carries undesirable people out of the country.
  e. are profits that go to somebody or somewhere.
  f. are sent out by an engine.
  g. sees far ahead into the future.
  h. carries back news.
  i. is taken and held so that it cannot get away easily.
  j. says something and everybody else has to do it.

W2b
Our Changeable Prefixes

Study the way familiar prefixes change the meaning of words to which they are attached.

A prefix is an attachment that we can put in front of many different words and that changes the meaning of each in a very similar way. Some common prefixes have been in our language since the oldest times:

Word Building

PREFIX	MEANING	EXAMPLES
mis–	wrong	"Miscalculate" means to calculate *wrongly* or incorrectly. A "misdeed" is a *wrong* action.
over–	too much, beyond	If an item is "overpriced," it costs *too much*. A river that "overflows" rises *beyond* its banks.
un–	not	A person who is "unconscious" is *not* awake. If a railroad car is "uncoupled," it is *not* connected to another car.

But many common prefixes came into English from Latin and Greek:

PREFIX	MEANING	EXAMPLES
ad–	to, toward	An "advance" is a movement *toward* a place. "Adhesive" tape sticks *to* something else.
con–	together	A "congregation" is a group of people who meet *together*.
de–	down	If a supply of something "decreases," it goes *down*. A "deflated" balloon has gone *down* in size and air pressure.
dis–	not, away	Someone who is "disliked" is *not* liked. A person who is "dismissed" is sent *away*.
ex–	out of	To "expel" is to push *out*.
in–	in, into	An "injection" is something put *into* our bloodstream.
in–	not	An "incorrect" answer is *not* correct. That which is "invisible" can*not* be seen.
pre–	before	If you "preview" a movie, you see it *before* it is released to the general public.
pro–	forward	A "propellant" is a fuel that drives a vehicle *foward*. If you "promote" a cause, you push it *forward*.
re–	again, back	If you receive a "refund," you get money *back*.

Words

EXERCISE 1

Answer the following questions:
1. In each of the following, what is done "together"?
   convoy   concert   conspiracy
2. What goes "out" in each of the following examples?
   exhale   exempt   exhaust
3. What goes "in" in each of the following?
   inhale   invade   inscription
4. What goes "forward" in each of the following?
   propeller   projector   progress
5. In each of the following, what is going "back"?
   recall   reduce   retreat
6. In each of the following, what is done "ahead of time"?
   prefabricated   preview   premeditated
7. In each of the following, what goes "away"?
   disband   disinherit   discourage
8. What kind of "going down" is described by each of the following?
   decline   descent   deduction
9. What can*not* be done in each of the following?
   insoluble   interminable   inedible
10. In each of the following, how is one thing moved closer "toward" another?
    adapt   adopt   adjoining

EXERCISE 2

Complete each of the half-finished words in the following sentences by using the right prefix. Write each completed word after the number of its sentence.

1. Many of our words have _____ scended from Latin and Greek ancestors.
2. If we _____ cluded Latin words, our dictionaries would be only half-size.
3. Latin words first came into English when Roman armies _____ vanced to the north.
4. Latin survived after the Roman Empire _____ clined.
5. Christian _____ gregations heard Latin when they came together for their religious services.
6. Greek _____ vived when scholars went back to the arts and sciences of ancient Greece.
7. Many Greek words had _____ viously become part of Latin.
8. Modern science started its _____ gress through books written in Latin.
9. For many modern Catholics, the Latin they heard in church had become _____ comprehensible.
10. The church _____ carded much of the Latin that had been used in its services.

Word Building

EXERCISE 3

Prefixes are hard to recognize when they *blend* with the word that follows. For each of the following, what changes in sound or spelling take place when the prefix blends with the rest of the word? Write down the completed word. Be prepared to explain in class what each completed word means.

1. in + legible
2. ad + proximate
3. in + luminate
4. ad + sist
5. con + bination
6. ex + liminate
7. con + pression
8. in + probable
9. in + regular
10. ad + traction

W2c Adding Suffixes

Study what suffixes add to the meaning of words.

Many of the suffixes we add to words are all-purpose. Their exact meaning is hard to pin down. Endings like –*al* or –*able* or –*ic* often simply mean "related to" or "having to do with":

- **–al**   *visual* has to do with sight
  mental is related to the mind

- **–able**   *reasonable* shows the use of reason
  seasonable means fit for the seasons

- **–ic**   *prophetic* is being like a prophet
  fantastic labels things produced by fantasy

Here are suffixes with more definite meanings:

SUFFIX	MEANING	EXAMPLES
–er, –or	one who does something	A *teacher* teaches. A *governor* governs. An *elevator* lifts us up and brings us down.
–escent	growing	A *convalescent* is getting well.
–fy	make	To *satisfy* means to make content. To *amplify* is to make more ample.
–ling	small, low	A *duckling* is a small duck. A *hireling* is a low, base person hired for dirty work.
–ize	make	To *sterilize* means to make sterile. To *modernize* is to make modern.
–en	come about, or bring about	To *weaken* means to turn weak. To *darken* means to make dark.

Words

EXERCISE 1

Look at the italicized words in the following sentences. In each set of two sentences, the italicized words share the same suffix. Do you know the words in each pair? Choose the meaning that best fits the context. Write the letter after the number of the sentence.

1. Henry Ford was an *innovator* who built the first assembly line.
   a. loves tradition   b. starts new things   c. makes excuses
2. The lifeguard rushed a *resuscitator* to the beach.
   a. revives people   b. counts money   c. prevents burns
3. The balloonists started their *hazardous* journey.
   a. swift   b. everyday   c. dangerous
4. There were *ominous* cracks in the front wall of the house.
   a. frightening   b. familiar   c. unimportant
5. The tourists enjoyed the *picturesque* old city.
   a. dirty   b. forgotten   c. pretty
6. The rain dancers wore *grotesque* masks.
   a. smiling   b. weird   c. expensive
7. *Adolescent* readers like the story of Helen Keller's childhood.
   a. reluctant   b. growing up   c. hurried
8. The *convalescent* patient was beginning to walk again.
   a. getting better   b. badly injured   c. complaining
9. Good microscopes *magnify* a picture many times.
   a. reflect   b. make larger   c. light up
10. We had to *justify* all our requests for money.
    a. refuse   b. joke about   c. give reasons for
11. The leading contender suffered a *fracture* of her wrist.
    a. taping   b. waving   c. break
12. We were looking for the *puncture* in the flat tire.
    a. hole   b. repair   c. break
13. The school did not *authorize* absences for pleasure trips.
    a. teach about   b. approve   c. record
14. Absences *jeopardize* a student's grades.
    a. improve   b. do not affect   c. endanger
15. An hour after the accident, traffic had still not returned to *normal*.
    a. the main highway   b. the usual   c. the off ramp
16. Sick and weak old people often still have all their *mental* faculties.
    a. in the mind   b. in the body   c. in the heart
17. *Innumerable* buffaloes roamed the prairies.
    a. can't be counted   b. huge   c. hard to find
18. We expected a *reasonable* finder's fee.
    a. can be argued   b. within reason   c. usual
19. Songs by the glee club *enliven* our reunions.
    a. make lively   b. interrupt   c. entertain
20. The bad news will *dampen* their spirits.
    a. affect   b. lower   c. raise

W2c

Word Building

EXERCISE 2

Choose a suffix to add to each incomplete word below: *-ade, -cide, -ee, -esque, -ette, -ish, -some*. Write the completed word after the number of the sentence.

EXAMPLE: She is the least self_____ person I know.
(Answer) *selfish*

1. A drink made from oranges is called orange_____.
2. A person employed by someone else is an employ_____.
3. A small kitchen may be called a kitchen_____.
4. A person being trained is a train_____.
5. A street that makes a pretty picture is pictur_____.
6. A task that is a heavy burden is burden_____.
7. A chemical that kills insects is an insecti_____.
8. Someone who is like a devil is devil_____.
9. Someone who has been appointed is an appoint_____.
10. Farmers get rid of pests by using a pesti_____.
11. Water that flows slowly is slugg_____.
12. The official in charge at a game or contest is the refer_____.
13. A person who looks impressive, like a statue, is statu_____.
14. Trying to take one's own life is attempted sui_____.
15. Many families buy a din_____ set for everyday meals.

UNIT REVIEW EXERCISE

For each of the following words, which of the three meanings given is *closest*? (What helps you make the right choice?)

1. **promote**   a. push up   b. push back   c. hold still
2. **visionary**   a. talker   b. doer   c. seer
3. **premeditated** a. planned   b. unplanned   c. accidental
4. **retract**   a. push in   b. take back   c. push down
5. **amplify**   a. make thin   b. make big   c. check out
6. **conduct**   a. lead   b. follow   c. investigate
7. **proceed**   a. look back   b. stay put   c. go forward
8. **biography**   a. life story   b. experiment   c. travel
9. **captive**   a. imaginary   b. prisoner   c. pursuer
10. **dismiss**   a. send away   b. accuse   c. search
11. **inscription** a. invitation   b. tale   c. writing
12. **predict**   a. prohibit   b. allow   c. foretell
13. **extricate**   a. pull out   b. pull ahead   c. pull aside
14. **deport**   a. collect   b. carry away   c. write about
15. **converge**   a. come off   b. come back   c. meet
16. **visual**   a. by eye   b. by ear   c. by mouth
17. **convalescent** a. being well   b. being sick   c. getting well
18. **terrify**   a. make afraid   b. be afraid   c. be numb
19. **disqualified** a. not let in   b. entered   c. overpriced
20. **adhesive**   a. can stretch   b. sticks well   c. folds up

19

WORDS ARE AROUND US EVERYWHERE

W3 THE RIGHT WORD

Learn to choose the right word for the job.

Have you ever heard anyone say: "There must be a better word for it"? Usually, in talking about anything, we have a choice. If our language really provided only for the bare necessities, we might be able to manage most of our activities with maybe 800 or 1,000 words. But even a small dictionary includes 20,000 or even 60,000 actual English words. We do not have only one single word for *rock*. We can choose from words like the following:

> **rock**   **stone**   **boulder**   **pebble**

How do we choose from such a set of possible words? What makes people say: "That is exactly the right word"?

W3a Using Specific Words

Learn to use specific words to take us in for a close-up view.

We need different words depending on how *close* we want to get to a subject. **General** words take in the whole scene. They cover much ground. The word *tool* takes in every conceivable kind of tool. To get closer, we need more **specific** words like *hammer, drill, saw, screwdriver, pliers, file*. To get really close, we need even more specific words like *hacksaw, jigsaw, bow saw*, and the like.

Here are some ways specific words help us communicate:

(1) *Specific words help us locate and identify things.* Someone working in a clothing store needs specific words like *velvet, corduroy, denim, plaid, satin, linen*, and the like.

(2) *Specific words enable us to pack in added information.* What does each of the specific words in the following sets add to the more general word at the beginning?

GENERAL	SPECIFIC		
rock	boulder	pebble	slab
ship	trawler	barge	tug
horse	pinto	mare	pony
house	cabin	shack	mansion
cask	keg	barrel	tub
board	plank	stave	slat
hit	slap	punch	poke

Words

(3) Specific words help us get close to the actual sights and sounds of experience. We can use specific words to make a listener (or a reader) say: "I can see it in front of me!" or "I can hear it now!" Words like *totter, stagger,* and *stumble* are very *visual* words—they make us see a person staggering or stumbling. Words like *hiss* or *swish* make us hear the sounds they stand for. We call words that seem to appeal directly to one of our five senses **concrete** words.

EXERCISE 1 List five specific words that would help newcomers find their way around one of the following:

1. a store that sells equipment for fishing;
2. the section of a hardware store that stocks hardware needed by carpenters;
3. a book that teaches different kinds of needlework;
4. a store that sells auto parts;
5. a bicycle repair shop.

EXERCISE 2 How good are you at finding the specific word that is just right for the job? For each description below, give a *single* specific word that gives the same information.

1. a thick heavy cup: _____
2. a young horse: _____
3. a simple three-legged seat with no back and a round surface to sit on: _____
4. an artwork made up of pasted-up parts of pictures, posters, and the like: _____
5. what blood itself does to stop bleeding: _____
6. the lumps that form in milk as the first step toward forming cheese: _____
7. the kind of furnace in which potters bake and glaze their earthenware: _____
8. in a forest, a spot that has no trees or shrubs: _____
9. the hard hollow stem of a bird's feather: _____
10. long, sharp animals' teeth: _____
11. a hastily constructed, temporary barrier thrown up in the streets during a riot or revolt: _____
12. a wheel on which to roll up fishing line or movie film: _____
13. what we do to an egg when we cook it in hot water without its shell: _____
14. a wooden hammer used by stonecutters, for instance: _____
15. to sell goods, especially inexpensive ones, from door to door: _____

The Right Word W3b

16. a small ship used to tow bigger ones: _____
17. an individual piece or particle of something like sand or salt: _____
18. a huge mass of snow tumbling down a mountain: _____
19. a huge structure for sheltering airplanes: _____
20. a flat kitchen utensil for turning over pancakes: _____

EXERCISE 3

Words that are specific enough can make us see. They can create a vivid picture of what each word stands for. Choose *three* of the following sets. Can you *act out* what each word stands for? Make us *see* what the word means. (Your teacher may ask you to team up with two classmates to act out each set of words.) Later, explain in your own words what makes each word *different* from the other words in the same set.

1. grab—tug—haul
2. sip—drink—slurp
3. sway—totter—stagger
4. fall—trip—collapse
5. shake—tremble—jerk
6. smile—grin—sneer
7. weep—sob—bawl
8. creep—crawl—slither
9. leap—hop—lunge
10. doze—sprawl—snore

EXERCISE 4

Write one sentence each on *five* of the following topics. Use as many specific and concrete words as you can. Use words that take your readers to the scene—words that make them see, hear, smell, taste, feel.

EXAMPLE: a storm
(Answer) *The breakers, piled high by the jostling winds, crashed onto the craggy shore.*

1. a race
2. a waterfall
3. a nervous person
4. a skier
5. a jet plane
6. a machine
7. a hungry person
8. a boat
9. a typist
10. an athlete

Choose the synonym with the right shade of meaning.

W3b
Synonyms and Antonyms

Many words have almost exact doubles—often not just one but two or three:

car	auto	automobile	motor vehicle
jail	prison	penitentiary	lockup
vacation	leave	furlough	time off

Words that have the same meaning, or almost the same meaning, are **synonyms.** They "name something together."

Words

Many synonyms are interchangeable. When the weather bureau gives us an educated guess about the weather, we can call it a *prediction* or a *forecast*. But often synonyms are only *partly* the same. They cover much common ground, but each branches out in a slightly different direction. *Strength, force,* and *power* all have the same basic meaning. But *strength* often fits best when we talk about physical strength, or when it is applied to something that is beneficial or harmless. *Force* fits best for strength that compels others to do something *against* their will—and often not for their benefit. *Power* often means political power—power that is organized and works through institutions.

What shades of meaning set apart the synonyms in each of the following sets? In each case, explain how the third word differs from the other two.

exhibit—display—expose
    We *exhibit* something when we present it for public view.
    We *display* it when we try to show it to advantage.
    We *expose* it when ———————————————— .

predict—project—conjecture
    We *predict* something after careful study of the problem.
    We *project* when we have definite figures and trends to go by.
    We *conjecture* when ———————————————— .

surrender—abandon—discard
    We *surrender* something after a struggle.
    We *abandon* something that was once valuable, with or without pressure.
    We *discard* something ———————————————— .

overlook—neglect—ignore
    We excusably *overlook* something.
    When we *neglect* something, we are to blame.
    We *ignore* something ———————————————— .

continue—last—endure
    Something that *continues* simply goes on.
    Something that *lasts* goes on longer than expected.
    Something that *endures* ———————————————— .

intentional—deliberate—willful
    When we do something *intentionally,* we do it on purpose.
    We do something *deliberately* with full knowledge of what is involved.
    We do something *willfully* ———————————————— .

The Right Word

W3b

quarrel—conflict—strife
   A *quarrel* can be petty, dealing with a minor matter.
   A *conflict* is likely to be more serious and longer lasting.
   Strife _____ .

We often use a synonym to help someone understand the meaning of a difficult word. We sometimes use an **antonym** for the same purpose. An antonym gives us a meaning that is roughly the opposite of the original word: *young* for *old;* or *ugly* for *beautiful.* Can you see how the following antonyms could help someone understand unfamiliar words?

- *lively* is an antonym of *apathetic;*
- *rebel* is an antonym of *conform;*
- *pure* is an antonym of *contaminated.*

EXERCISE 1

How good are you at explaining the difference between words that are almost the same—but not quite? Choose *five* of the following pairs. Is there any difference? Explain the difference in your own words.

1. penalty and punishment
2. worker and laborer
3. farmer and rancher
4. barter and trade
5. sing and chant
6. tidy and snug
7. trip and voyage
8. attack and assault
9. disaster and catastrophe
10. work and toil

EXERCISE 2

Which of the choices listed after each word is closest to it in meaning? (Which could be used as a synonym for it in the right situation?) Write the letter for the possible synonym after the number of the word.

1. **division** a. movement b. separation c. awareness d. convenience
2. **mutiny**   a. reason   b. completeness c. beginning d. rebellion
3. **alter**   a. change   b. normal   c. complete   d. startle
4. **plan**   a. development b. project c. movement d. request
5. **guard**   a. protect   b. require   c. eliminate d. assure

25

Words

6. **vague**   a. valuable   b. hazy   c. available
                   d. pleasant
7. **cunning**   a. handsome   b. acceptable   c. sly
                   d. cute
8. **liberate**   a. free   b. increase   c. reward
                   d. open
9. **implicate**   a. discover   b. renew   c. complicate
                   d. involve
10. **ponder**   a. dig   b. construct   c. meditate
                   d. enrich
11. **strange**   a. easy   b. eccentric   c. usual
                   d. demanding
12. **banish**   a. exile   b. bargain   c. negotiate
                   d. undergo
13. **imposing**   a. inadequate   b. beneficial   c. magnificent
                   d. fair
14. **sharp**   a. mighty   b. short   c. tense
                   d. intense
15. **extreme**   a. fatal   b. accidental   c. direct
                   d. utmost
16. **memory**   a. mention   b. recollection c. phase
                   d. mystery
17. **obliterate** a. erase   b. rebuild   c. straighten
                   d. produce
18. **generous**   a. kind   b. bountiful   c. careful
                   d. proper
19. **evident**   a. free   b. open   c. proven
                   d. available
20. **forbid**   a. entangle   b. progress   c. shrink
                   d. prohibit

EXERCISE 3

Each of the following sentences has a blank space and is followed by three possible synonyms. Choose the one that *best fits the context*. Write its letter next to the appropriate number. (Your teacher may ask you to consult the dictionary in working this exercise.) Be prepared to explain and defend your choice in class.

1. The officer who acted as an agent of the enemy was eventually convicted of _____ acts.
   a. traitorous   b. faithless   c. false
2. The general, after long and careful study, _____ that the enemy would attack the bridge first.
   a. guessed   b. conjectured   c. concluded

The Right Word

3. The intense pain was almost impossible to _____, but somehow or other John managed it.
   a. suffer   b. tolerate   c. endure
4. The _____ cowhand was never at ease in company.
   a. naïve   b. unsophisticated   c. natural
5. His greed drove him to _____ more and more land.
   a. possess   b. own   c. have
6. The child had managed to _____ the furniture badly.
   a. hurt   b. mar   c. harm
7. The group planned to _____ the chief of state.
   a. assassinate   b. execute   c. kill
8. The Senator's _____ forced her to take an extremely unpopular stand on the issue.
   a. beliefs   b. convictions   c. opinions
9. The court had the _____ to determine guilt or innocence.
   a. strength   b. force   c. power
10. Their attitude _____ anger in everyone with whom they came in contact.
    a. provoked   b. stimulated   c. excited

EXERCISE 4

Which of the choices listed after each word is a possible antonym? Pick the one that is closest to being opposite in meaning. Write the letter of the antonym after the number of the word.

1. **display**   a. investigate   b. hide   c. show
                  d. know
2. **cherish**   a. organize   b. seek   c. neglect
                  d. value
3. **strife**   a. peace   b. noise   c. plan
                  d. excurison
4. **apathetic** a. endless   b. weird   c. lively
                  d. short
5. **polluted**   a. infiltrated   b. pure   c. questioned
                  d. recorded
6. **conform**   a. listen   b. shape   c. answer
                  d. rebel
7. **deliberate** a. accidental   b. crooked   c. sly
                  d. new
8. **conflict**   a. departure   b. agreement   c. ban
                  d. arrival
9. **discard**   a. keep   b. sell   c. borrow
                  d. loan
10. **obliterate** a. divide   b. preserve   c. ask
                   d. ignore

Words

W3c
Using Figurative Language

Use figurative expressions to add life and color to language.

Figurative expressions can create vivid pictures in our minds. But these pictures are borrowed from something else. Look at the following examples:

> He was a bear of a man.
> We saw a barrel-chested woodcutter by the side of the road.
> The news spread like fire through the small village.

These sentences are not really about a bear, a barrel, and a fire. But they make us *think* of a bear or a barrel to help us imagine huge people. The third sentence makes us think of a fire to make us see how fast the news spread.

When we see the words *man* and *chest* here, they really stand for a man or his chest. They are used with their **literal** meanings. But when we see the words *bear* and *barrel* here, we are using them **figuratively**. We use words figuratively when we are really comparing one thing to another. We borrow the big hulking shape of a bear or the big round shape of a barrel to show what a really big person looks like.

Most figurative expressions take one of the following forms:

(1) Simile. A **simile** is a stated comparison that uses the words *like* or *as*. The following are similes:

> He was as helpless *as a rudderless ship in a storm*.
> The house looked *like a castle*.
> Over and over above them, innumerable little roundworms crawl . . . slender *as threads*. (Rachel Carson)

(2) Metaphor. A **metaphor** moves one step further than a simile. A metaphor simply pretends that one thing is another. The listener or reader must fill in the words *like* or *as*. A *thundering* voice is not really made up of thunder. It just sounds as loud or startling as thunder. The following are metaphors:

> She was *a mountain of strength*.
> He was buried under an *avalanche of complaints*.

(3) Personification. **Personification** talks about non-human things as if they were human—as if they could talk and feel:

> The evening wind *whispered* in the trees.
> My brother's car *died* on the steep hill.

The Right Word

W3c

LANGUAGE IN ACTION

WEEPY CROCODILES AND OTHER ANIMALS

Many popular expressions draw on the animal world for vivid comparisons. How many of the following examples can you explain in your own words?

1. What are crocodile tears?
2. What is a swan song?
3. How do we ape someone?
4. What is a kangaroo court?
5. What is a stag dinner?
6. What do we do when we lionize a person?
7. How do we ferret something out?
8. What goes on when someone is weaseling?
9. What happens to someone who is outfoxed?
10. What kind of a legendary animal was the phoenix?
11. When can someone be rightly called a drone?
12. What is someone doing who stays in a cocoon?
13. What happens to someone who becomes a guinea pig?
14. What do you do when you get on your high horse?
15. What kind of person is called a snake in the grass?

Figurative expressions can make us say: "Now I see what it is like!" But when we hear the same expression too often, we begin to feel: "Everybody says that—I wonder what this is *really* like." Figurative expressions that have become trite are called **clichés.** Many people have heard expressions like the following too many times:

Put your shoulder to the wheel.
Let the cat out of the bag.
Stand up and be counted.
It rained cats and dogs.
Use some elbow grease.

EXERCISE 1

In each of the following pairs, one statement is literal, the other figurative. After the number of each pair, write the letter for the *figurative* expression. (Be prepared to explain what the figurative expression *adds* to the literal meaning. What *kind* of comparison does the figurative expression use in each case?)

1. (a) The jet roared down the runway.
   (b) The jet took off right away.
2. (a) Clouds galloped across the sky.
   (b) Clouds moved across the sky.

Words

3. (a) The mob melted away when the police arrived.
   (b) The mob disbanded when the police arrived.
4. (a) The roof withstood the weight of the snow.
   (b) The roof labored beneath the weight of the snow.
5. (a) The tulips announced the coming of spring.
   (b) The tulips bloomed when spring came.
6. (a) The old bridge creaked beneath the weight of the traffic.
   (b) The old bridge groaned beneath the weight of the traffic.
7. (a) Everyone knew when the boxer would punch.
   (b) The boxer telegraphed his punches.
8. (a) Henderson launched his career forty years ago.
   (b) Henderson began his career forty years ago.
9. (a) A gentle breeze moved the branches.
   (b) A gentle breeze caressed the branches.
10. (a) The officer pieced together the circumstances of the crime.
    (b) The officer understood the circumstances of the crime.
11. (a) The sergeant shouted commands.
    (b) The sergeant barked commands.
12. (a) Two giant elms stood at the entrance to the driveway.
    (b) Two giant elms guarded the entrance to the driveway.
13. (a) The floodlight conquered the darkness.
    (b) The floodlight lit up the darkness.
14. (a) Snow carpeted the fields.
    (b) Snow covered the fields.
15. (a) Her remark made him feel unhappy.
    (b) Her remark crushed him.

EXERCISE 2

Choose five of the following tired comparisons. For each, write down a better, fresher one that can really make us see what it is like.

1. When the riots started, the principal immediately *took the bull by the horns*.
2. In her classes, the school bully was *as meek as a lamb*.
3. When asked to give up an old habit, Grandfather was *as stubborn as a mule*.
4. When the *cat is away, the mice will play*.
5. A parent of teenagers must have *the patience of a saint*.
6. By this time we were so hungry *we could have eaten a horse*.
7. To make the program successful, we will have to *put our shoulders to the wheel*.
8. In the evenings the whole troop was *dog-tired*.
9. He had been *on pins and needles* all during his first job interview.
10. The underpaid workers *led a dog's life*.

The Right Word

EXERCISE 3

How many different figurative expressions can you find in each of the following passages? What does each figurative expression add that a more literal expression would lack? In each case, what is being compared with what?

1. The cracking whips bit and horses plunged and tugged. The white-topped wagons strained and stumbled like fat sheep. —Stephen Crane, *The Red Badge of Courage*

2. We were only four degrees of latitude from the North Pole, the sun was slightly below the horizon, and the sky was heavily overcast. The Skate was surfaced in a frozen lead whose sides were marked by heavy hummocks of pressure ice—the black shadows I had seen through the periscope. The ice on the lead was covered with perhaps half an inch of snow and looked as smooth as a tabletop.—James Calvert, *Surface at the Pole*

3. Rivers perhaps are the only physical features of the world that are at their best from the air. Mountain ranges, no longer seen in profile, dwarf to anthills. Seas lose their horizons. Lakes have no longer depth but look like bright pennies on the earth's surface. . . . But rivers, which from the ground are usually seen in cross sections, like a small sample of ribbon—rivers stretch out ahead as far as the eye can reach.—Anne Morrow Lindbergh, *North to the Orient*

UNIT REVIEW EXERCISE

In each of the following sentences, one word has been left out. Of the two possibilities given after each sentence, which is the better choice? Choose the word that is

- more specific than a general word;
- more accurate than another synonym; or
- more vivid than a literal word.

Write the letter after the number of the sentence.

1. The reporters _____ employees who stole from parking meters.
   a. exposed   b. displayed
2. Coal came up the river in _____ towed by small tugs.
   a. ships   b. barges
3. The team was met by the usual _____ of well-wishers.
   a. crowd   b. avalanche
4. He skillfully turned over the eggs with the _____.
   a. spatula   b. utensil
5. People used to sharpen goose _____ for use as pens.
   a. quills   b. stems
6. The crowd had _____ away when the principal came out.
   a. gone   b. melted

31

Words

7. The police had no hard facts, so the report was mostly _____.
   a. prediction   b. conjecture
8. From the plane, the lakes looked like bright _____ on the Earth's surface.
   a. pennies   b. circles
9. A _____ of small yellow flowers stretched across the meadow.
   a. cover   b. carpet
10. The tribe _____ the hides for salt and blankets.
    a. bartered   b. sold
11. The outcome was decided by a _____ in the closing minutes.
    a. punishment   b. penalty
12. The angry driver, red in the face, _____ toward the accuser.
    a. moved   b. lunged
13. Fortunately, the lifeboat carried a _____ of water.
    a. keg   b. container
14. The players _____ to their positions on the field.
    a. went   b. trotted
15. Daffodils are among the first _____ of spring.
    a. messengers   b. signs
16. At the end of the war, the ship had to be _____ to the enemy.
    a. surrendered   b. discarded
17. She accused us of _____ failure to obey orders.
    a. intentional   b. willful
18. Their proud ancestors had _____ many years of slavery.
    a. tolerated   b. endured
19. The visitor had apparently _____ the attack from the usually friendly animal.
    a. provoked   b. excited
20. The newspaper had _____ out the source of the rumor.
    a. ferreted   b. found

W4 USING THE DICTIONARY

Turn to your dictionary for information on words.

The dictionary is for the word watcher what the atlas is for the geographer. The reader interested in words can keep turning page after page and explore a world of words and meanings.

Remember that there are many kinds of dictionaries:

SCHOOL DICTIONARIES

Thorndike Barnhart Advanced Dictionary
Webster's New Students Dictionary
The Macmillan Dictionary
The American Heritage School Dictionary

Using the Dictionary

WHAT'S IN A DICTIONARY?

just plain words

thim ble (thim′bl), *n*, **1.** a small metal cap worn on the finger to protect it when pushing the needle in sewing. **2.** a short metal tube. **3.** a metal ring fitted in a rope, to save wear on the rope. [OE *thӯmel* < *thūma* thumb]

thimble

new words for new things

mi cro film (mi′krō film′), *n*. film for making very small photographs of pages of a book, newspapers, records, etc., to preserve them in a very small space. —*v*. photograph on microfilm.

old words for things of the past

Con es to ga wagon (kon′is tō′gə), a covered wagon with broad wheels, formerly used for traveling on soft ground or on the prairie. [from *Conestoga*, Pa.]

Conestoga wagon

technical words

ig ni tion (ig nish′ən), *n*. **1.** a setting on fire. **2.** a catching on fire. **3.** apparatus for igniting the explosive vapor in the cylinders of an internal-combustion engine.

unusual words

pol y glot (pol′ē glot), *adj*. **1.** knowing several languages. **2.** written in several languages. —*n*. **1.** person who knows several languages. **2.** book written in several languages. [< Gk. *polyglottos* < *polys* many + *glotta* tongue]

Your Turn: Choose *five* of the following words or expressions. For each, write one sentence that would help a dictionary maker explain what the word means:

crash helmet	dribble (a ball)	landing strip	thermostat
gusher	shuttle bus	commuter	re-entry
jet lag	compact		

Words

COLLEGE DICTIONARIES
Webster's New World Dictionary
The Random House College Dictionary
The American Heritage Dictionary
Webster's New Collegiate Dictionary
Standard College Dictionary

UNABRIDGED REFERENCE DICTIONARIES
Webster's Third New International Dictionary
Funk and Wagnalls New Standard Dictionary
The Random House Dictionary: Unabridged Edition

W4a Finding Words

Learn how to find information in your dictionary quickly and efficiently.

Two *guide words* are given at the top of a dictionary page. The one on the left is the first word on the page. The one on the right is the last word on the page. If the word you are looking for falls alphabetically between the two guide words, it will be on that page. The words under *a* or *b* or any other letter are alphabetized according to their second letter, third letter, or whichever letter is the first to be different. In these words the fifth letter establishes the order: *trombone, trommel;* in these, the sixth letter: *truckage, trucker, truck farm.*

Remember the following about word entries:

(1) An entry word is usually the plain form of a word. However, a dictionary will give later in the entry any forms of the word that are irregularly formed or spelled. For example, a regular plural formed by adding –*s* or –*es* will not be given, but irregular plurals like *wolves, feet,* and *ladies* will be shown.

Notice how many related forms are given along with the plain form of the word *slim* in the following entries:

> ¹**slim**\\'slim\\ *adj* **slim·mer; slim·mest** [D, bad, inferior, fr. MD *slimp* crooked, bad; akin to MHG *slimp* awry] **1** : of small diameter or thickness in proportion to the height or length : SLENDER **2 a** : MEAN, WORTHLESS **b** : ADROIT, CRAFTY **3 a** : inferior in quality or amount : SLIGHT **b** : SCANTY, SMALL < a ~ chance **syn** see THIN **ant** chubby (of *persons*) — **slim·ly** *adv* — **slim·ness** *n*
> ²**slim** *vb* **slimmed; slim·ming** *vt* : to make slender ~ *vi* : to become slender
>
> —*Webster's New Collegiate Dictionary*

Using the Dictionary

(2) Look-alike or sound-alike words are listed separately. Words like *seal* (on a document) or *seal* (the animal) are spelled the same but have different meanings and origins. A dictionary will list such **homonyms** as separate entries, with numbers to show that they are different words. There may also be separate entries for different *uses* of the same word:

¹seal *n.* (the animal)
²seal *v.* (hunting the animal)
³seal *n.* (the stamp on a document)
⁴seal *v.* (using the stamp)

(3) Dictionaries show word divisions. Some dictionaries leave a space between parts, others use a dot. These show where a word should be divided at the end of a line:

in ten tion al
in·ter·cept

(4) Some dictionaries have a separate biographical section. Here they list the names of people important in history, arts, science, and so on. This section is usually found in the back of the book. Remember, however, that names of fictional people, mythical characters, ancient heroes, etc., usually appear in the main body of a dictionary. Entries like the following will be found there: *John Doe* or *Jane Doe* (parties to a legal proceeding whose real names are unknown), *Arthur* (legendary king of Britain), *Zeus* (the chief Greek god), *Juno* (queen of the gods).

(5) Some dictionaries have a separate section for geographical names (usually called the Gazetteer). Again, fictional names like *Atlantis, Shangri-la,* or *Hades* will be in the main body of the dictionary.

Remember: Many sounds are spelled several different ways:
• A beginning *k* sound *may* also be spelled with *c,* as in *cabin* or with *ch* as in *chorus.*
• The sound of *s* at the beginning of a word may be spelled with *c* rather than with *s,* as in *civilize.*

Study the chart of possible spellings on page 36. Point out several words that might be hard to find in an alphabetical listing. Explain why.

SOME POSSIBLE SPELLINGS OF FAMILIAR SOUNDS

VOWELS

a (as in *lane*)	also	*ai:*	vain, constrain, maid
		ei:	vein, sleigh, weigh
		ay:	bray, clay, stray
		ey:	they, whey
		ea:	break, steak
e (as in *me*)	also	*ee:*	deed, creed, keen
		ea:	beam, team, steam
		ei:	receive, ceiling, leisure
		ie:	believe, retrieve
i (as in *hit*)	also	*y:*	hymn, gymnasium
		ui:	build, guild
i (as in *hide*)	also	*ai:*	aisle
		ei:	height, stein
		ey:	eye
		uy:	buy, guy
		y:	sky, defy, rye
o (as in *tone*)	also	*oa:*	toad, shoal, foal
		ou:	soul, though
		ow:	low, crow, stow
u (as in *use*)	also	*eu:*	feud, queue
		ew:	few, curfew, dew
		iew:	view, review

CONSONANTS

f (as in *father*)	also	*ph:*	phone, phrase, emphatic
		gh:	laugh, cough, enough
g (as in *go*)	also	*gh:*	ghost, ghastly
		gu:	guess, guest, brogue
h (as in *hot*)	also	*wh:*	whole, who
j (as in *jam*)	also	*g:*	gypsy, oxygen, logic
		dg:	budget, knowledge, grudge
k (as in *kin*)	also	*c:*	castle, account, coat
		ch:	chemist, chlorinate, chrome
		qu:	clique
n (as in *noon*)	also	*gn:*	gnat, gnarled, gnash
		kn:	knife, knave, knight
		pn:	pneumonia
r (as in *run*)	also	*rh:*	rhythm, rhapsody, rhubarb
		wr:	wrong, wrangle, wry
s (as in *sit*)	also	*c:*	cent, decide, decimate
		sc:	scent, descent, science
		ps:	psychology, psalm, pseudonym
sh (as in *shine*)	also	*ch:*	machine, chef
		ci:	special, vicious, delicious
		si:	impression, possession, tension
		ti:	notion, imagination
		sci:	conscious, conscience
z (as in *zero*)	also	*x:*	xylophone

Using the Dictionary

W4a

EXERCISE 1

Each pair of guide words listed in boldface type below is followed by a series of words. Number your paper from 1 to 15. Choose the words that would fall between the pair of guidewords and write them on your paper next to the appropriate number.

1. **Olympics—oneself** omnibus, omen, olive, Oliver, once
2. **hawk—head** hawthorne, hayseed, health, headline, hazard
3. **sleet—slip** slink, sleuth, sleek, slingshot, slate
4. **bother—bow** bowling, bout, botulism, bovine, bowie knife
5. **dedicatory—defense** default, decree, dedicate, defection, deface
6. **interwove—introduce** intrigue, intolerance, intersect, intolerable
7. **hour—how** housefly, hound, hovel, howl
8. **misread—mistral** missile, mismatch, mistaken, misled, misspell
9. **overarch—overheat** overgrown, overact, oval, overhear, overdraft
10. **pathfinder—pattern** patronage, paternal, patio, patchwork, petunia
11. **angelic—angry** angina, animal, angle, Angola, animate
12. **heavy—heel** hedge, heir, heaven, hectic, help
13. **scarlet—schedule** scent, scavenge, scene, scepter, scheme
14. **spelunker—spice** sperm whale, spiceberry, spent, spinach, spell
15. **quart—Quebec** quarter, queen, quay, quarry, quartz

EXERCISE 2

Write down your answers to the following questions:

1. How many different words does your dictionary list that are all spelled *rook?* What does each mean?
2. How many different entries are there for *palm* and for *pitcher?* What is the difference in meaning between the different words?

Words

3. You have heard about a tool that sounds as if it might be spelled "neu-matic" drill. You cannot find the word under *n* in your dictionary. Where do you find this word? How is it spelled? What does it mean?

4. For each of the following, write down a word that has exactly the same sound but a different spelling:
   a. wry   b. dew   c. by   d. soul   e. Jim
   f. night   g. scene   h. way   i. sent   j. rap

5. You have heard about a game that sounds as if it were spelled "sha-rade." Where do you find the word in your dictionary? How is it spelled? What do you learn about the game?

6. Each of the following first gives the meaning of a word. Then, in parentheses, it gives another word that the word sounds like. Write down the correct spelling under which the word is listed in the dictionary. If necessary, use the chart on page 36 to help you find the dictionary spelling of each word below:
   a. a passageway between seats in a theater (I'll)
   b. a line outside a theater (cue)
   c. a religious song (him)
   d. a nice smell (cent)
   e. a weight on a line (plum)
   f. a channel between two bodies of water (straight)
   g. money to set a person free (bale)
   h. to quote (sight)
   i. a metal (steal)
   j. a hunted animal (pray)
   k. to put on a scale (way)
   l. the middle of your body (waste)
   m. to rule (rain)
   n. the opposite of war (piece)
   o. the inside part of a nut (colonel)

7. Find the following three words in which the *f*- sound at the beginning is spelled *ph*-:
   a. a drugstore specializing in medicines
   b. a wild bird similar to a chicken
   c. a doctor of medicine

8. Find the following words in which the *k*- sound at the beginning is spelled *ch*-:
   a. a large group of people singing together
   b. a religion
   c. a word for utter confusion and disorder
   d. a silver-white metal often used as a decoration on automobiles

W4b Using the Dictionary

EXERCISE 3

Which of the following names can you find in your dictionary? Where do you find them? Whom or what does each name? If the name is a combination, under what part is it listed?

1. De Soto
2. Romeo
3. Von Braun
4. O'Keeffe
5. Machu Picchu
6. Okefenokee
7. Goliath
8. Queen Victoria
9. St. Francis
10. Joan of Arc

EXERCISE 4

Look up *ten* of the following words. Show where they could be *divided* at the end of a line. Using hyphens, show all of the possible breaks for each word.

1. plebiscite
2. retrenchment
3. revelation
4. shrubbery
5. unabridged
6. photoelectric
7. battery
8. bazooka
9. ozone
10. overwork
11. huckleberry
12. oleomargarine
13. fantastic
14. gaudy
15. gauge
16. laboratory
17. poetry
18. saturation
19. valuable
20. contaminate

Explore the full range of meanings of a single word.

W4b Words and Their Meanings

Many of our words cover a whole *range* of meaning. They started out with some basic core meaning, and then they branched out. A *foot* is basically the lower part of the leg; it gives us something to stand on. Then the word *foot* extended its range. It came to mean the "lower part" of many other things. So we talk about the foot of a mountain or the foot of the stairs. Then people began to measure things by saying, "This is about a foot long. It stretches about as far as a human foot." So the word *foot* came to mean a twelve-inch unit of *measurement*.

For most words, a dictionary lists *several different* meanings to show how the word has branched out. Often a word simply branches out from what it means to other things like it:

> **fork** (fôrk), *n.* **1.** instrument with a handle and two or more long, pointed parts at one end. A small fork is used to lift food. A much larger fork, called a pitchfork, is used to lift and throw hay. See pitchfork for picture. Another kind is used for digging. **2.** anything shaped like a fork. The place where a tree, road, or stream divides into branches is a fork.

Words

With many words, there is more of a jump from one meaning to the next. Can you see how the word *canvas* developed from "a strong cloth made of cotton . . . used to make tents and sails" to "oil painting"?

> **can vas** (kan′ves), *n.* **1.** a strong cloth made of cotton, flax, or hemp, used to make tents and sails. **2.** something made of canvas. **3.** sail or sails. **4.** piece of canvas on which an oil painting is painted. **5.** an oil painting.

Can you see that the last meaning listed in the following entry goes far afield from the basic meaning of the word?

> **cap** (kap), *n., v.,* **capped, cap ping.** —*n* **1.** a close-fitting covering for the head with little or no brim. **2.** a special head covering worn to show rank, occupation, etc.: *a nurse's cap.* **3.** anything like a cap. The top of a mushroom is called a cap. **4.** the highest part; top. **5.** a small quantity of explosive in a wrapper or covering.

—all from *Thorndike Barnhart Dictionary*

Remember the following points about how dictionaries list meanings:

(1) Abbreviations show how the word is used in a sentence. For instance, *n.* stands for noun. It shows that the meanings listed apply to the word used as a noun, like *the cap,* or *a cap.* The abbreviation *v.* stands for verb. The following meanings all stand for something we can do:

> —**v. 1.** put a cap on. **2.** put a top on; cover the top of: *Whipped cream capped the dessert.* **3.** do or follow with something as good or better: *Each clown capped the last joke of the other.*

(2) Abbreviations show that a word is in some way limited in its use. The abbreviation *dial.,* for example, is a **usage label.** It shows that a word is used mainly in a regional dialect. It might sound "countrified" to people outside that region:

> ¹**lar·rup** \′lar-əp\ *vb* [perh. imit.] *vt* **1** *dial* : to flog soundly : WHIP **2** *dial* : to defeat decisively : TROUNCE ~ *vi, dial* : *to move indolently* or clumsily : SLOUCH
> ²**larrup** *n. dial* : BLOW

—*Webster's New Collegiate Dictionary*

(3) Dictionaries often give the meaning of familiar expressions. For instance, your dictionary will first list various meanings of the word *way,* listed as a single word. But then it may also show what the word means in familiar combinations like "by the way," "give way," "make one's way," or "see one's way clear." We often call such familiar combinations **idioms.**

Using the Dictionary

EXPLANATION OF DICTIONARY ENTRIES

Key to the parts of a dictionary entry

① the entry word, printed in boldface type; often called *main entry* or simply *entry* (shows how the word is spelled and divided in writing)

an them (an′thəm), *n.* **1.** song of praise, devotion, or patriotism: *"The Star-Spangled Banner"* is the national anthem of the United States. **2.** piece of sacred music, usually with words from some passage in the Bible. [< VL *antefna* < LL < Gk. *antiphona* antiphon.]

② the pronunciation, in parentheses; often called the *respelling*

③ grammatical label, abbreviated, in italic type

④ any irregular forms, in small boldface type

⑤ the word's meanings (special phrases in boldface type)

buy (bī), *v.,* **bought, buy ing,** *n.–v.* **1.** get by paying a price: *You can buy a pencil for five cents.* **2.** buy things. **3.** bribe: *It was charged that two of the jury had been bought.* **4. buy off,** get rid of by paying money to. **5. buy out,** buy all the shares, rights, etc., of. **6. buy up,** buy all that one can of; buy. –*n.* **1.** *Informal.* thing bought; purchase. **2.** *U.S. Informal.* a bargain. [OE *bycgan*]
Syn. *v.* **1. Buy, purchase** mean to get something by paying a price. **Buy** is the general and informal word: *A person can buy anything in that store if he has the money.* **Purchase** is used in more formal style and suggests buying after careful planning or by business dealings or on a large scale: *The bank has purchased some property on which to construct a new building.*
Buy is used with *from,* not *off of: He bought it from a stranger he met on the street.*

⑥ usage label such as *informal, slang, dialectal*

⑦ the origin of the word, in square brackets

⑧ synonyms keyed by number to the definition to which they apply

pro tec tive (prə tek′tiv), *adj.* **1.** being a defense; protecting: *the hard protective covering of a turtle.* **2.** preventing injury to those around: *a protective device on a machine.* **3.** guarding against foreign-made goods by putting a high tax or duty on them: *a protective tariff.* **—pro tec′tive ly,** *adv.* **—pro tec′tive ness,** *n.*

⑨ usage notes dealing with words frequently confused and similar problems

⑩ words derived from the entry word; often called *run-on entries* or simply *run-ons*

protective coloring, a coloring some animals have that makes them hard to distinguish from the things they live among, and so hides them from their enemies.

—*Thorndike Barnhart Dictionary*

Words

EXERCISE 1

Find *two* different meanings for each of the following words. Does your dictionary list the two different meanings that would fit best in the two possible situations listed for each word? After the number of each word, write down the two meanings.

1. **circle**
   a. in geometry
   b. in social life
2. **admission**
   a. in a court of law
   b. at the box office
3. **solution**
   a. on the label of a bottle
   b. in discussing a scheduling conflict
4. **tune**
   a. in talking about a radio
   b. in talking about a piece of music
5. **beat**
   a. as part of a cook's job
   b. as part of a police officer's job
6. **position**
   a. at an employment office
   b. in rearranging furniture
7. **occupation**
   a. in a history of World War II
   b. in applying for a driver's license
8. **condition**
   a. in talking about a patient
   b. in talking about a contract
9. **receiver**
   a. in football
   b. as part of a telephone
10. **record**
    a. in a filing cabinet
    b. in a music store
11. **ruler**
    a. of a country
    b. in drawing
12. **letter**
    a. in a mailbox
    b. in a word
13. **country**
    a. opposed to city
    b. in talking about citizenship
14. **demonstration**
    a. of new equipment
    b. against a new law
15. **save**
    a. from drowning
    b. at a bank

EXERCISE 2

Do you ever encounter a familiar word that does not make sense the way it is used? Sometimes a familiar word is used with an unfamiliar meaning. Sometimes it is really a *different* word that happens to be spelled the same way. For each of the italicized words, find a meaning that would help you make sense of the sentence. Write this meaning after the number.

1. The last chief of the tribe had died without *issue*.
2. We were looking for someone to *chair* the meeting.

3. A papal *bull* had arrived with grave news.
4. The *packet* had brought his granddaughter up the river.
5. They refused to *credit* the story.
6. She quoted the old *saw* about letting sleeping dogs lie.
7. They were two adventurers of the same *kidney*.
8. They succeeded in stealing a *march* upon the enemy.
9. We saw all *manner* of fish in the aquarium.
10. Their favorite sport was putting the *shot*.

Can you find the meaning of the following familiar expressions in a dictionary? List the meaning for each expression.

EXERCISE 3

1. hold a candle to
2. take to heart
3. give and take
4. do a Houdini
5. do the honors
6. ride circuit
7. head off
8. puppet government
9. eat crow
10. part company

Look at the way word history helps us understand current meanings and current uses.

W4c
Word History

Words have a history. Our word for *street* goes back to the Latin word for "paved road." The English and the Germans took over this Latin word from the Romans because the Romans were the first to build paved roads in their part of the world. We call the history of a word its **etymology**—a Greek word for "going to the roots." Dictionaries give a brief summary of a word's history to help us understand how it acquired its current meaning or meanings. In some dictionaries, this brief summary appears immediately following the pronunciation. In other dictionaries, the etymology of the word appears at the end of the entry. Familiar abbreviations are used again and again:

O.E.   for the oldest form of English—a word has been part of the English language for over a thousand years

M.E.   for Middle English—a word has been part of English for at least five hundred years

F.   a word was borrowed by the English from the French

L.   a word came into English from Latin (many of these came into English by way of French—the French borrowed them first and then passed them on to the English)

Gk.   a word goes back to ancient Greek

<   "goes back to"

Words

Look at the following examples of etymologies from a high school dictionary. Can you see how these words developed from their roots to their modern meanings?

> **con cord** [< F < L *concordia*, ult. < *com*-together+*cor* heart]

(Concord is harmony among people, a "coming together of hearts.")

> **mar shal** [< OF *mareschal* < LL *mariscalcus* groom < Gmc., literally, horse servant]

(Among the Germanic tribes, the marshal was at one time the person who took care of the king's horse. The word then came into late Latin and the oldest kind of French.)

LANGUAGE IN ACTION

THE WINDS THAT BLOW

English at one time was the language of small farming communities with a few scattered trading centers. Most people never got very far away from their native village or their native town. But in later centuries, English-speaking people ranged all over the world. Their language took in words for the many new things travelers and explorers encountered on their way around the world.

How many of the following questions can you answer without any help? For how many of them would you have to turn to a dictionary for help?

1. Where would you expect the following winds to blow? Where were they first named, and by whom?

   monsoon   hurricane   tornado   zephyr

2. From whom and from where did we get the following names for places with much water?

   sound   fjord   gulf   delta   river

3. In what language was a geyser first called a geyser? Or a volcano a volcano? Or a plateau a plateau?

4. Who were the people who first built or named the following?

   aqueducts   basilicas   minarets   galleons

5. Where did people first dance (or name) the following?

   jig   polka   waltz   tango   mazurka

Using the Dictionary

EXERCISE 1

How much does your dictionary tell you about the history of the following words? Choose *ten* of these. Write the story behind each word in a sentence or two.

1. Thursday
2. candidate
3. pretzel
4. melancholy
5. daisy
6. companion
7. agony
8. amateur
9. dandelion
10. villain
11. vaccine
12. hooligan
13. magazine
14. money
15. disaster

EXERCISE 2

Many of our words have been part of English for as long as our language has been spoken. Many other words have come from a few major sources, such as French and Latin. From what other languages has English borrowed words? After the number of each word, write the language that it is traced back to in your dictionary.

1. admiral
2. yam
3. chocolate
4. bamboo
5. tea
6. scarlet
7. emerald
8. ketchup
9. coffee
10. bungalow
11. raccoon
12. tiger
13. sable
14. polka
15. shamrock
16. waltz
17. slogan
18. tackle
19. flamingo
20. petunia
21. gong
22. oasis
23. tomato
24. renegade
25. million

W4d
Pronuncuation Guide

Use the dictionary as a guide to how words are pronounced.

Dictionaries provide a guide to pronunciation of almost every word. As soon as we have seen how the word is spelled, a dictionary usually shows how the same word *sounds*. The guide to the pronunciation of the word usually appears in parentheses or between slashes:

con clu sion (kən-ʹklü-zh ən)

con sec u tive \kən-ʹsek-(y)ət-iv\

The second spelling of each word is a **phonetic** spelling. It is closer to the actual *sounds* of a word than English spelling normally is. Here are some of the things dictionaries do to help bring the phonetic respelling closer to the sounds of actual speech:

(1) Silent letters are simply left out:

psalm (säm)   **debt** (det)   **home** (hōm)

45

Words

(2) The same letters always stand for the same sounds:

• The letter *c* is never used in phonetic respelling. Since *c* has the sound of either the letter *s* or the letter *k*, one of these letters will be used in the pronunciation to show which sound occurs in a given word:

cabin (kab ən)   **space** (spās)

• The letter *x* is never used in phonetic respelling. Since it is pronounced as *ks*, those letters are used instead (**fix**—fiks).

• The letters *kw* are used to show the pronunciation of *qu* (**quit**—kwit).

• The letter *y* is used only when it has the consonant sound as in *yellow* (yel′ō). As a vowel, *y* has either the short or the long *i* sound, or the long *e* sound:

tryst (trist)   **try** (trī)   **baby** (bā-bē)

• When *g* is used in phonetic respelling, it represents the "hard" sound as in *got*. When *g* has the soft sound, *j* is used to represent the sound (**gym**—jim).

(3) Added marks help us tell apart the different sounds represented by the same letter (as in bit and bite). These added marks are called **diacritical** marks. Here are some "marked up" letters showing the sounds in familiar words:

meet (mēt), **mate** (māt), **mule** (mūl)
spoke (spōk), **light** (līt)
dare (dăr)
far (fär), **mute** (myüt)
could (kủd)
four (fôr)

In addition to these marks, some dictionaries use a ligature (or "tie") to show that two letters have a single sound:

s͡h shoe   c͡h chief

(4) Dictionaries show which syllables are stressed. Stress makes a syllable stand out in pronunciation. Some dictionaries put the stress signal *before* the stressed syllable—a high signal for the strongest, a low signal for the second strongest:

pen·man·ship \ˈpen-mən-ˌship\   **ra·di·a·tion** \ˌrād-ē-ˈā-shən\

Other dictionaries put the stress signal *after* the stressed syllable—dark signal for strongest, lighter signal for second strongest:

pen·man·ship (pen′mən ship′)   **ra·di·a·tion** (rā′dē ā′shən)

Read the following words in their phonetic respellings. Write the usual spelling after the number of the word.

EXERCISE 1

1. (sû′kəl)   5. (blaṅg′kit)   9. (luks′sẖō re)
2. (pan′trē)   6. (yo͝orz)   10. (lo͞os)
3. (hī′jak′)   7. (kwôr′tər)
4. (c̱hild′līk′) 8. (päm)

Sometimes a dictionary lists two current pronunciations for the same word. One way of saying the word may be more common in one part of the country, or in one occupation, than the other way. Read the two different pronunciations for each of the following words:

EXERCISE 2

1. **roof** (rüf *or*ru̇f)
2. **bath** (bath *or* bäth)
3. **cor ri dor** (kôr′ə dər *or* kôr′ə dôr)
4. **i o dide** (ī′ə dīd *or* i′ə did)
5. **na ta to ri um** (nā′tə tô′rē əm *or* nā′tə tō′rē əm)
6. **de tail** (di tāl′ *or* dē′tāl)
7. **an gi na** (an jī′nə *or in medicine often,* an′jə nə)
8. **top sail** (top′sāl′ *or nautical* top′sl)
9. **il lus trate** (il′əs trāt *or* i lus′trāt)
10. **Ros a lind** (roz′ə lind *or* roz′ə līnd)

Each dictionary provides a pronunciation key that explains how it uses letters, diacritical marks, and other special symbols. Study the two keys reprinted on page 48—the first from a high school dictionary, the second from a college dictionary. Point out anything that you would have to get *used* to—anything that might be unexpected or hard for the layperson. Point out four or five sounds that the two dictionaries handle differently.

EXERCISE 3

Words

PRONUNCIATION KEY A

a	hat, cap	f	fat, if	o	hot, rock	u	cup, butter
ā	age, face	g	go, bag	ō	open, go	u̇	full, put
ã	cave, air	h	he, how	ô	order, all	ü	rule, move
ä	father, far			oi	oil, voice	ū	use, music
		i	it, pin	ou	house, out	v	very, save
b	bad, rob	ī	ice, five			w	will, woman
ch	child, much			p	paper, cup	y	young, yet
d	did, red	j	jam, enjoy	r	run, try	z	zero, breeze
		k	kind, seek	s	say, yes	zh	measure, seizure
		l	land, coal	sh	she, rush		
e	let, best	m	me, am	t	tell, it	ə represents:	a in about
ē	equal, be	n	no, in	th	thin, both		e in taken
ėr	term, learn	ng	long, bring	TH	then, smooth		i in April
							o in lemon
							u in circus

—*Thorndike Barnhart Dictionary*

PRONUNCIATION KEY B

						p	pot, supper, stop
						r	read, hurry, near
a	act, bat, marry	i	if, big, mirror, furniture	s	see, passing, miss
ā	aid, cape, way			sh	shoe, fashion, push
â(r)	air, dare, Mary	ī	ice, bite, pirate, deny	t	ten, butter, bit
ä	alms, art, calm			th	thin, ether, path
b	back, cabin, cab	j	just, badger, fudge	th	that, either, smooth
ch	chief, butcher, beach	k	kept, token, make		
d	do, rudder, bed	l	low, mellow, all	u	up, love
		m	my, simmer, him	û(r)	urge, burn, cur
e	ebb, set, merry	n	now, sinner, on	v	voice, river, live
ē	equal, seat, bee, mighty	ng	sing, Washington	w	west, away
				y	yes, lawyer
ēr	ear, mere	o	ox, box, wasp	z	zeal, lazy, those
f	fit, differ, puff	ō	over, boat, no	zh	vision, mirage
		ô	ought, ball, raw		
g	give, trigger, beg	oi	oil, joint, joy	ə	a in alone
		oo	book, poor		e in system
h	hit, behave, hear	oo	ooze, fool, too		i in easily
hw	white, nowhere	ou	out, loud, prow		o in gallop
					u in circus

—*The Random House Dictionary*

Using the Dictionary

UNIT REVIEW EXERCISE

This review exercise tests your ability to interpret information from widely used school dictionaries. Study the sample entries carefully and answer the questions that follow them. On your paper put the letter for the right answer after the number of the question.

A. **i tin er ar y** (ī tin′ər er′ē or i tin′ər er′ē), *n., pl.* **-ar ies,** *adj.* —*n.* **1.** route of travel; plan of travel. **2.** record of travel. **3.** guidebook for travelers. —*adj.* **1.** of traveling or routes of travel. **2.** itinerant.
—*Thorndike Barnhart Dictionary*

itin·er·ary \ī-'tin-ə-,rer-ē, ə-\ *n, pl* **-ar·ies** **1** : the route of a journey **2** : a travel diary **3** : a traveler's guidebook —**itinerary** *adj*
—*Webster's New Students Dictionary*

1. In the alphabetical listing, this word would come after all of the following words *except*
   a. issue
   b. Italian
   c. ivory
   d. itemize
2. The main stress is on which syllable?
   a. first
   b. second
   c. third
   d. fourth
3. How is the first syllable pronounced?
   a. always like *eye*
   b. often like *eye*
   c. never like *eye*
4. Each dictionary gives three numbered meanings for the use of this word as a
   a. noun
   b. verb
   c. adjective
   d. adverb
5. According to these entries, the following is *not* one of the meanings of this word:
   a. travel plan
   b. travel record
   c. route of travel
   d. travel agent

B. **mav er ick** (mav′ər ik), *n. U.S.* **1.** calf or other animal not marked with an owner's brand. **2.** *Informal.* one who refuses to affiliate with a regular political party. [Am.E; probably named after S. *Maverick,* Texan who did not brand his cattle]
—*Thorndike Barnhart Dictionary*

mav·er·ick \'mav-(ə-)rik\ *n* [after Samuel A. *Maverick* d 1870 American pioneer in Texas who did not brand his calves] **1** : an unbranded range animal; *esp* : a motherless calf **2** : a person who refuses to follow the leadership of his political party or conform with his group and sets an independent course
—*Webster's New Students Dictionary*

W4d

Words

6. In the alphabetical listing, this word would come before all of the following *except*
   a. mayor
   b. maze
   c. mature
   d. mawkish
7. To judge from these entries, the meaning of the word went through all of the following stages *except*
   a. a person's name
   b. a label for an animal
   c. a meat cutter's word
   d. a word used in politics
8. Which of these two entries provides usage labels?
   a. both
   b. the first
   c. the second
   d. none
9. The *a* in the first syllable should be pronounced like the vowel in
   a. mat
   b. mate
   c. mar
   d. mug
10. Both entries for this word show
    a. one stress
    b. two stresses
    c. three stresses
    d. no stress

C. **can·di·date** \\'kan-də-,dāt, -dət\\ *n* [L *candidatus*, lit., one clothed in white, fr. *candidus* white; so called fr. the white toga worn by candidates for office in ancient Rome] : one who offers himself or is proposed by others for an office, membership, right, or honor < a gubernatorial candidate >   —*Webster's New Students Dictionary*

11. The *a* is pronounced as in *mate* in
    a. first and third syllables
    b. always in the third syllable
    c. often in the first syllable
    d. often in the third syllable
12. The strongest stress is on which syllable?
    a. first
    b. second
    c. third
13. The word goes back to
    a. French
    b. Latin
    c. Lithuanian
    d. Greek
14. To judge from the context, a toga is
    a. a document
    b. a poster
    c. an article of clothing
    d. a political office
15. The word *candidate* fits best if someone wants to
    a. leave an organization
    b. belong to a club
    c. found a new organization
    d. take time off

Your Word Resources

FOR FURTHER STUDY

LANGUAGE AROUND THE WORLD

Languages do not exist in isolation. Often they are members of a family of languages, descended from a common parent language. Thus, French, Italian, and Spanish are close cousins. They are modern forms of what once was the language of the Roman Empire—Latin. Between existing languages, there are many possible kinds of contact. War, trade, or immigration helps words move from one language to another. The following assignments will give you a chance to explore some of the relations and contacts between the English language and other languages of the world.

ACTIVITY 1

Over the centuries, English has borrowed words from almost every major language around the globe. What languages are represented in the following list? For each word in the list below, find out the language from which it originally came.

1. aficionado
2. blitz
3. kimono
4. luau
5. boulevard
6. touché
7. kibbutz
8. kayak
9. smorgasbord
10. pyramid
11. algebra
12. kibitzer
13. guru
14. vodka
15. pentagon

ACTIVITY 2

When we check the meaning of a word in a dictionary, we often find that there is a story behind it. When we call a bullet a "lethal" bullet, we mean that it was fatal, deadly. In ancient Greek legend, Lethe was the name of the river that flowed through the land of the dead. Those who drank from the river lost all memory of their former existence.

Tell the story behind five of the following words:

cereal
plutocrat
titanic
panic
fortune

marital
Europe
lunar
echo
January

Words

ACTIVITY 3

Study the following Greek and Latin roots. Can you think of more words for each root? List several other words that seem to go back to the same common ancestor. What seems to be a common meaning that fits all or most of the words in each set?

1. **spec–**   spectator
2. **mote–**   remote
3. **tract–** attract
4. **pel–**   repel
5. **struct–** construct
6. **rupt–**   interrupt
7. **meter–** thermometer
8. **sect–**   intersect
9. **pend–**   suspend
10. **audi–** auditorium

ACTIVITY 4

The people who came to this country often brought with them the memory of things that were good to eat. Teaching others how to appreciate and prepare the foods they liked, they often passed on the *words* for these foods as well as the recipes and customs that went with them. How much could you contribute to a "Dictionary of Cooking"? Study the following questions to find out.

1. From what country did immigrants bring a taste for *goulash* and *paprika?*
2. What is your ethnic background likely to be if the word *schmaltz* reminds you of your grandmother's cooking? Or if you remember *blintzes* and *borscht?*
3. What part of the world are your ancestors likely to have come from if your family likes *haggis, black pudding, scones,* and *potted head?* What are these things?
4. In what kind of neighborhood would you look for a store that sells *wonton* dough and *soy* sauce?
5. What kind of accent would you be likely to hear in a place where people love *liverwurst, knockwurst,* and *pumpernickel?*
6. What kind of restaurant would you go to to eat *pepperoni, ravioli,* or *prosciutto?*
7. From what part of the world did *shishkebab* and *baklava* come?

ACTIVITY 5

The American tourist in France notices many familiar English words that have been taken over by the French in recent years. Americans in turn have always added new

Your Word Resources

French words to their language. Below is a list for each of these categories of borrowed words. As you study them, ask yourself: To judge from these words, in what areas do the French tend to follow the American (or British) lead? In what areas are Americans strongly influenced by the French?

FRENCH BORROWINGS FROM ENGLISH: jazz, jet, best seller, dancing, snack, weekend, teenager, baby-sitter, jeep, gangster, knockout, parking

ENGLISH BORROWINGS FROM FRENCH: hors-d'oeuvres, cologne, sauté, rosé, revue, Roquefort, console, liqueur, deluxe, discothèque, lingerie, au gratin, canapé, cul-de-sac, valet

ACTIVITY 6

The vocabulary of bullfighting is *Spanish,* since bullfighting is popular in Spanish-speaking countries. Much of the vocabulary of skiing is *German,* since skiing is a sport much cultivated in the German-speaking parts of the Austrian and Swiss Alps. The vocabulary of cricket is *British English,* usually new and strange to American ears. Study the vocabulary of one such sport that requires the knowledge of terms borrowed from another language, or from another variety of English. (Your teacher will tell you whether to present your findings in a short paper or as an oral report.)

ACTIVITY 7

Many Americans are *bilingual.* In New York City, or Texas, or California, many students hear Spanish at home, while the language of school, radio, and television for them is English. In California or Hawaii, many students hear Japanese at home. Your parents may have grown up in an immigrants' community where the first language of many was Polish, or German, or Armenian. In neighborhoods or communities where there is much such bilingualism, words from the other language are likely to be taken over into English. Report on your own observation of such borrowings—either from one language, or from several.

Chapter 2

Sentences
Writing Better Sentences

S1 Words in a Sentence
  a Recognizing Nouns
  b Recognizing Pronouns
  c Recognizing Verbs
  d Recognizing Adjectives
  e Recognizing Adverbs
  f Recognizing Connectives and Prepositions

S2 The Complete Sentence
  a Subject and Verb
  b Verb and Object
  c Linking Verb and Noun
  d Linking Verb and Adjective
  e The Indirect Object

S3 Adapting the Simple Sentence
  a Requests and Questions
  b The Passive

S4 Building Combined Sentences
  a How Coordination Builds Sentences
  b How Subordination Builds Sentences
  c How Relative Clauses Build Sentences
  d How Noun Clauses Build Sentences

S5 Expanding Our Sentence Resources
  a Using Infinitives
  b Using Participles
  c Using Appositives

For Further Study: The Exception to the Rule

Chapter Preview 2

> **IN THIS CHAPTER:**
> - How to recognize the basic building blocks that make up an English sentence.
> - How to recognize a complete English sentence.
> - How to expand and adapt the basic sentence patterns.
> - How to build combined sentences from simple source sentences.
> - How to develop your sentence potential by drawing on special sentence resources.

Make full use of the resources of the English sentence.

The sentence is the most basic tool of every speaker and writer. When we speak and write, we put words together in sentences. When we study sentences, we are learning how to make fuller use of the resources of our language. We ask: "How are sentences put together? How do they carry as much freight as they do? How do we put them to use?"

Sentence study helps you become more familiar with your tools as a speaker and writer. Productive sentence practice helps you put these tools to effective use.

PREVIEW EXERCISE 1

How does our language work? Today English is a language spoken in many countries around the world. But suppose English had remained the language of a small island nation cut off from other countries. Suppose you were a member of a team that had arrived from the outside world to learn the islanders' language. What are some of the first things you would learn about the language they speak?

You would soon recognize words like *tree, door, house, open, walk,* and *cook*. Some of these come with possible attachments like *–d* or *–ed*. These are often action words. They stand for something we can do: *walked, opened, cooked*. You would soon realize that the *–d* or *–ed* often signals a change in time: We walk *now*. We walked *yesterday*. Look at the following

Writing Better Sentences

sample sentences. How many action words can you find in them by putting the word *yesterday* at the beginning of each sentence? After the number of each sentence, write down all the action words that would change to past time, adding –d or –ed at the end. Write down the form for past time.

1. Our neighbors plant vegetables in their own garden.
2. They light a fire and cook a meal.
3. We look at the instructions again carefully.
4. We fell trees, saw the trunks, and cart the wood home.
5. The campers dress early and hike up the mountain.
6. They enter the building after I open the door.
7. Volunteers help the workers when flood waters threaten the dam.
8. They travel in the morning but rest in the afternoon.
9. People close their windows and lock the door.
10. The workers ask for a vacation, but the bosses turn them down.
11. The campers rest, dance, or play games in the evening.
12. The leaders of the group call an emergency meeting.
13. The members of our team defeat all those who challenge them.
14. The spectators cheer our victory.
15. Words of praise encourage those who work hard.
16. The judges announce the winners after each contest.
17. The neighbors complain because our dogs bark.
18. Firefighters rescue people from the building.
19. Our friends organize team sports and conduct a raffle.
20. Special barriers protect the animals from the visitors.

PREVIEW EXERCISE 2

As you study the islanders' language, you would often encounter "map words." Such words help people map out the world in which they live. They help them find their way. As people explain a rough map of part of their island to you, they might say:

This mark stands for a _____ .

Write down ten English words that would fit into this statement. (Each time use a single word.) The same kind of word is used for things that are too small to show on a map but that might appear on a list of equipment. If a team of campers were to ask for supplies, they might send this message:

Please send a _____ .
Please send several _____ .

Write down ten English words that would fit into one of these messages. (Each time use a single word.)

THE ENGLISH SENTENCE
A Bird's-Eye View

WORD CLASSES:

Noun:	cars, trees; a bird, the roof, this world
Pronoun:	I, me, my; he, him, his; we, us, our
Verb:	ask, will arrive, stalled, had driven
Adjective:	successful, very sweet, quite true
Adverb:	easily, soon, there, well
Connective:	and, but, if, because, although
Preposition:	of, at, for, on, by, through

BASIC SENTENCE PATTERNS:

S–V	The boys are swimming.
S–V–O	The dog chased the squirrel.
S–LV–N	Amy became my friend.
S–LV–Adj	Your friend seems lazy.
S–V–IO–O	Jim gave his fiancée a present.

ADAPTING THE SIMPLE SENTENCE:

Request:	Tell the truth.
	Drive carefully.
Question:	Will he be late?
	Did he arrive later?
Passive:	Gerald was hit by a car.
	The squirrel was chased by the dog.

SENTENCE BUILDING:

Coordination:	We had planned a picnic for Saturday, *but* unfortunately it rained.
Subordination:	The horses started to panic *when* the storm broke.
Relative Clause:	We caught the men *who* had robbed the train.
Noun Clause:	She knew *that* the bus had left.

ADDED SENTENCE RESOURCES:

Infinitive:	The guard asked him *to leave*.
	We decided *to drive* to the beach.
Participle:	The *burning* structure collapsed.
	She raked up the *scattered* leaves.
Appositive:	Wilma, *the runner-up*, shook her hand.

Words in a Sentence

Recognize the major word classes that help us build the English sentence.

In an English sentence, we use the same kinds of building blocks over and over again. Look at the following requests. They make use of four major **word classes** that we draw on again and again in building a sentence:

1	2	3	4
Lift	heavy	packages	slowly.
Read	important	instructions	carefully.
Greet	angry	people	politely.
Pat	big	dogs	cautiously.

Each slot in these sentences is made for a different kind of word:
- In the first slot, we can put words that ask people to do something. We use such words when we ask people to *lift* an object, *read* a book, *open* a door, *close* a window, *say* hello. We call such words verbs.
- In the third slot, we can put words for things and people that we can do something *to*. We can lift a *package*. We can mail it, open it, shelve it. We can read *instructions*. We can write them, change them, forget them. The words that fit the third slot are nouns.
- The words in the second slot tell us more about the words in the third slot. Some packages are *heavy*, some *light*. Some people are *angry*, some *happy*. Some dogs are *big*, others *little*. These words tell us which one or what kind. We call them adjectives.
- The words in the fourth slot tell us how something is done. We call them adverbs.

In addition, almost every sentence uses different kinds of words that help the sentences run smoothly. "Friend—drive—car" can tell us who is going to drive. But "A friend *will* drive *the* car" runs much more smoothly. Words like *a, the,* and *will* are part of the sentence machinery. Their function is to help tie the major parts of the sentence together and to help them do their jobs. We call the "little words" **function words.** In the following sections, you will look at some of the things that help us tell one major word class from another. You will also look at some of the function words that help the major sentence parts do their work.

Sentences

S1a
Recognizing Nouns

Know the signals that help us recognize nouns.

Nouns are map words. Just as the markings on a map stand for churches, streets, and schools, so nouns stand for things in the world around us. All the names of places and things that you see on your way to school would be nouns: *a car, an intersection, a tree*. When a noun stands for one example of a whole group of things, it is an ordinary noun, or **common** noun. When it is the name of just one thing or person or place, we call it a **proper** noun: *Jack, Mississippi, the Titanic*.

COMMON NOUN: church, school, truck, highway, river, dog
PROPER NOUN: Juanita, Ohio, the Potomac, the *Enterprise*

Nouns do not always stand for things we can touch or point out. People also have qualities of body and mind: *courage, health, hope*. We call such names of qualities and ideas **abstract** nouns—nouns for things "beyond our touch."

ABSTRACT NOUN: courage, strength, freedom, illness, spirit

Know the signals that help us recognize nouns:

(1) Most English nouns have a special plural form.   Most English nouns stand for things we can count. To show that we mean "more than one," we can add the ending *–s* or *–es*. *Match* refers to one single match. We call it the **singular** form. *Matches* refers to "more than one." We call it the **plural** form. How would you change the following words to indicate "more than one"?

toothbrush   boot   sock   flashlight   sweatshirt   comb

See U1a for more on plural forms.

(2) Nouns often come after function words that serve as noun signals.   Nouns often follow a word like *the, this,* or *my*: *the* island, *this* tree, *my* hut. These words are like signals that tell us: "Noun coming." We call these signals **noun markers.** Three kinds of noun markers are used in English sentences:

ARTICLES: the, a, an
POINTING PRONOUNS: this, these; that, those
POSSESSIVE PRONOUNS: my, your, his, her, its, our, their

The noun does not always follow the noun marker immediately. One or more other words may come between the noun and its marker. In the following, the noun comes last:

the early *bird* | that horrible *noise* | our only real *friend*
a certain *smile* | this happy *family* | your broken-down *tricycle*

Words in a Sentence

(3) *Many nouns have special noun-making endings.* Even in their singular forms, many nouns already have endings that help show that the word is a noun. For instance, many nouns have the ending *–th.* People want *strength, health,* and *wealth.* Objects have *depth, width,* and *breadth.* Endings like the *–th* help us turn other words into nouns or make new nouns from old. Here is a list of familiar endings that help us make nouns:

–er/–or	farmer, tailor, operator
–ist	biologist, scientist, specialist
–ism	heroism, communism, Catholicism
–ment	agreement, government, argument
–ness	happiness, numbness, thoroughness
–tion/–sion	creation, permission, invitation

WHAT'S MY LINE?

Nouns enable us to label a person's occupation. All of the italicized words below are nouns that people might use to show what kind of work they do. All of the nouns listed here have familiar noun-making endings: very common ones like *–er* or *–or,* or less common ones like *–ician.* Describe each person's job in your own words.

1. In the world of music, what is the difference between a *composer* and an *arranger*?
2. In the world of medicine, what is the difference between a *physician,* a *pediatrician,* and an *obstetrician*? (What other occupations use the same noun-making ending?)
3. What do the following people do: a *projectionist,* a *contortionist,* a *conservationist*? (What other names of occupations use the same ending?)
4. In what kind of office would you expect to find a *designer,* a *dispatcher,* or a *distributor*?
5. What functions are performed by a *monitor,* a *moderator,* and a *coordinator*?
6. In our courts, what is the function of a *prosecutor*?
7. Where would you expect the following people to be working: a *chauffeur,* a *restaurateur,* a *coiffeur*? (What other formerly French nouns use the same *–eur* ending?)
8. What kind of occupation would you guess at if someone were called a *scavenger,* a *collier,* or a *purser*?
9. What is the difference between a *trainer* and a *trainee*?
10. What does a *navigator* do?

LANGUAGE IN ACTION

Sentences

EXERCISE 1

Find nouns of your own choice to fill in the blanks in all of the following:

1. If you could have your wish, what would be your five most valuable possessions? My _____, my _____, my _____, my _____, and my _____.
2. List five things you remember about the characters in a book or movie: his _____, her _____, her _____, his _____, and her _____.
3. List five qualities that people would need to survive on a desert island: _____, _____, _____, _____, _____.
4. List five things that you feel there might not be enough of in the world of the future: _____, _____, _____, _____, _____.
5. Usually, the names of countries do not follow a noun marker: *England, Canada, Italy*. List the names of three countries that do: the _____, the _____, the _____.

EXERCISE 2

How many of the following words are nouns standing for the things we can *count?* Try to add –*s* or –*es* to each word. Does the ending change the meaning of the word from "one" to "more than one"? Write the plural form of each such noun after its number. If the word cannot be made plural, write *No* next to its number.

EXAMPLES: change   (Answers) *changes*
           beautiful   *No*

1. hope
2. sidewalk
3. happy
4. honest
5. excellent
6. rocket
7. argument
8. fierce
9. ran
10. race
11. admire
12. admirer
13. second
14. college
15. duplicate
16. transistor
17. gooey
18. groggy
19. ocean
20. travel

EXERCISE 3

In each sentence, find all the nouns that are signaled by *noun markers*. Write all such nouns after the number of the sentence. (Include the marker with the noun.) Remember that the noun is not always the first word after the marker.

EXAMPLE: The ballad existed before the invention of the book.
(Answers) *the ballad, the invention, the book*

1. Our ballads have always charmed their listeners.
2. These songs tell us about our outlaws.
3. A ballad often tells the story of a hero or an important event.

Words in a Sentence

4. Often these songs have come to our country from England.
5. "Barbara Allen" is an old example.
6. Perhaps a local version of this song can be found in your state.
7. This ballad tells of a woman who could not save her lover from his death.
8. According to a famous ballad, Robin Hood lived in the forest with his friends.
9. The sheriff swore he would bring those outlaws to their deserved end.
10. Read this ballad in one of its many versions to see if that prediction came true.

EXERCISE 4

A. In each sentence, find all nouns that use a familiar noun-making ending. Write all such nouns after the number of the sentence. (A plural–s may follow the noun-making ending.)

1. Our discussion about happiness turned into an argument.
2. Scientists seldom get rich through their achievements.
3. The speaker made statements about their patriotism.
4. The specialist helped the sailor regain consciousness.
5. Many parishioners came for the baptism.
6. The computer made accurate predictions.
7. The announcer and the moderator helped the panelists.
8. Dizziness and congestion are signs of the infection.
9. Moviegoers watched the tough inspector hunt the gangsters.
10. The producer fired the writer, the director, and the actors.

B. Turn each word listed on the left into a noun. Use a familiar noun-making ending to fit the word into the blank in its sentence. Write the new noun after the number of the sentence. (Adjust sound or spelling where necessary.)

EXAMPLE: happy   Words cannot describe their _____.
(Answer) *happiness*

11. **adopt**   Her parents told her about the _____.
12. **final**   She had been a _____ in the Winter Olympics.
13. **clumsy**   They complained about my _____.
14. **fiddle**   He had been a _____ in their band.
15. **disappoint**   The movie was a terrible _____.
16. **excavate**   The _____ produced ancient treasures.
17. **exterminate**   The _____ knew all about rodents.
18. **eager**   Their _____ showed in their faces.
19. **burn**   The kettle had been left on the _____.
20. **divide**   We were learning long _____.

Sentences

EXERCISE 5

Look at the numbered words in the following passage. Which of them are nouns? If the word is a noun, write it after its number. If it is not a noun, write *No* after its number. All nouns in this passage are identified by one or more of the familiar noun signals.

Eight hundred (1) **years** ago, the (2) **Normans** conquered England. Before this (3) **time**, Anglo-Saxon names were (4) **popular**. (5) **Boys** were called Edgar or Alfred. A (6) **girl** might be called Ethel. The new (7) **government** brought many (8) **changes**. The (9) **conquerors** liked (10) **names** like William or Richard. John was the most popular of the more (11) **recent** names. Mary and Ruth are names from the (12) **Bible**. The (13) **expression** "Christian name" (14) **probably** can be traced to the common (15) **use** of Biblical names. William was the name of the (16) **king** who had led the (17) **invasion**. Thomas was the name of an (18) **archbishop**. He was (19) **killed** in his (20) **cathedral** and became a (21) **saint**. For (22) **centuries**, (23) **pilgrims** would come to Canterbury and (24) **see** his (25) **shrine**.

S1b Recognizing Pronouns

Recognize the pronouns that can replace a noun.

Pronouns are shortcut words. They help us avoid repetition. We do not want to repeat the names in a sentence like the following: "*Sue* smiled at *Fred* when *Fred* showed *Sue* the letter." We use *he* and *her* instead: "Sue smiled at Fred when *he* showed *her* the letter." *I, you, he, she, it, we,* and *they* are our **personal pronouns**. They can take the place of a noun, along with any noun marker:

NOUN:	*The spectators* cheered.	*The Erskines* admire loyalty.
PRONOUN:	*They* cheered.	*We* admire loyalty.

Pronouns have different forms for different uses:

(1) Pronouns change depending on the person they point to. *I* and *we* point to "Number One." We call them **first person** pronouns. *You* points to a "second party"—the person, or persons, we are talking to. We call *you* a **second person** pronoun. *He, she, it,* and *they* point to a "third party." They point to people we are not talking *to*—we are talking *about* them. We call these words **third person** pronouns.

Third person pronouns change further depending on a person's *sex*. *He* is the "masculine" pronoun. *She* is the "feminine" pronoun. *It* is "neuter"—we use it when sex is irrelevant.

Words in a Sentence

PRONOUNS—A Summary

	Plain Form	Object Form	Possessive
Singular	I	me	my
	you	you	your
	he	him	his
	she	her	her
	it	it	its
Plural	we	us	our
	you	you	your
	they	them	their

(2) *Pronouns change depending on the number of people (or things) involved.* Like nouns, they have forms for singular (one of a kind) and plural (more than one):

SINGULAR: I, you, he, she, it ‖ PLURAL: We, you, they

See U3d for indefinite pronouns like *anybody, somebody,* and *nobody*.

(3) *Pronouns change depending on their position in the sentence.* We use *I, he, she, we,* and *they* when we talk about what a person does: *I* talk, *he* shouts, *she* smiles, *they* applaud. We often use *me, him, her, us,* and *them* when we talk about what is happening *to* a person. The pronoun then stands for the "object" or *target* of the action:

DOER: *I* called the dog. *He* stole my wallet.
OBJECT: The dog bit *me.* The thief robbed *him.*

For uses of the object forms, see U3b.

(4) *Pronouns change depending on the function they serve.* We use a special set of **possessive** pronouns as noun markers. *I* then changes to *my. You* changes to *your. He* changes to *his. She* changes to *her.* These forms show where or to whom something belongs:

I mind *my* own business.	She knows *her* way.
Put *your* house in order.	We put *our* shoulders to the wheel.
He kept *his* powder dry.	They played *their* cards right.

Sentences

EXERCISE 1

After the number of each sentence, write all the nouns (with any noun markers) that you can find in the sentence. After each noun, put in parentheses a pronoun that you could substitute for the noun in the original sentence.

EXAMPLE: The cab picked up the passengers.
(Answer) *the cab (it), the passengers (them)*

1. The Bergdamas are a tribe.
2. These people live in Africa.
3. The tribe often listens to storytellers.
4. Often their stories teach a boy or a girl about the world.
5. Children often ask questions.
6. A girl might ask about fire.
7. A boy might ask about animals.
8. The storytellers might tell the youngsters about fire.
9. At first, people lived without fire.
10. Families suffered from the cold.
11. A chieftain visited the lions.
12. The lions were sitting around a fire.
13. The animals offered the stranger a meal.
14. The stranger snatched a brand from their fire.
15. He threw the cubs into the flames.
16. The mothers saved a son or a daughter.
17. The man escaped because of the confusion.
18. The chief brought fire to his followers.
19. Did your father or your mother tell stories?
20. Did an aunt or an uncle tell you about the world?

EXERCISE 2

The following sentences give you a chance to put pronouns through their paces. Rewrite each sentence, substituting the appropriate pronoun for each italicized noun. Be prepared to label the pronouns in class discussion—"plain," "object," or "possessive," as well as singular or plural.

1. *John* loves *Emily*.
   Emily loves *John*.
2. *Visitors* hate *our dog*.
   Our dog hates *visitors*.
3. *John* looks like *John's* mother. *Joan* looks like *Joan's* father.
   The children look like *the children's* parents.
4. *Buffalo Bill* attracted *crowds*.
   His sharpshooters included *Annie Oakley*.
   Spectators loved *the Wild West Show*.
5. *Robin* robbed *travelers*. *Robin's* friends helped *Robin*.
   The forest sheltered *the outlaws*.

S1c Recognizing Verbs

Know the signals that help us recognize verbs.

Verbs help us talk about actions or events. They make us "time conscious." There is usually something built into a verb that says "now" (he *works* hard), or "in the past" (she *worked* hard), or "in the future" (they *will work* hard).

Know the signals that help us recognize verbs in a sentence:

(1) Verbs can take us from the present to the past by a change in the word itself. The technical term for the different kinds of time shown by verbs is **tense.** The biggest single difference between nouns and verbs is that verbs have separate forms for present and past tense. The most familiar form of the verb is the simple or plain form: *look, miss, tell, breathe, want, suspect, televise, dignify*. We use this form for actions and events that happen at the **present** time. They may be happening right now, or they may happen all the time:

PRESENT: I *miss* you. (now)
They *tell* stories. (all the time)
We *breathe*. (all the time)

The form for the present adds *–s* or *–es* when we are talking about *one* third party (**third person,** singular):

THIRD PERSON: He *misses* us. (now)
She *tells* stories. (all the time)
A whale *breathes*. (all the time)

Almost all verbs have a third form that takes us from the present to the **past.** With most verbs, we simply add *–d* or *–ed* to show past time. We call such verbs **regular** verbs: *asked, missed, suspected, arrived, completed, organized*. With other verbs, we show past time by making a change in the word itself. We call such verbs **irregular** verbs: *tell/told; write/wrote; bring/brought; know/knew*.

PRESENT: I *miss* you. (now)
PAST: I *missed* you. (then)

PRESENT: The officer *suspects* George. (now)
PAST: The officer *suspected* George. (then)

PRESENT: We *write* to him. (now)
PAST: We *wrote* to him. (then)

Sentences

PRESENT: The train *arrives* on time. (now)
PAST: The train *arrived* on time. (then)

PRESENT: Sarah *completes* the story. (now)
PAST: Sarah *completed* the story. (then)

PRESENT: We *bring* our lunch. (now)
PAST: We *brought* our lunch. (then)

PRESENT: They *know* the answer. (now)
PAST: They *knew* the answer. (then)

**VERBS help us talk about things to do.
How many verbs can you find in these photographs?**

Words in a Sentence

> For standard forms of regular and irregular verbs, see U1b-1d.

(2) *The main verb is often preceded by verb markers called auxiliaries.* These **auxiliaries** are "helping verbs." They help us make up other forms of the verb. One common helping verb is *have,* which has two additional forms: *has* and *had.* It helps us make up the **perfect** tenses of a verb. These auxiliaries often tell us about something that has happened recently, or that still matters:

PERFECT: The rain *has stopped.*
                      The parcels *have arrived.*
PAST PERFECT: She *had written* to her parents.
                      Phil *had brought* the food.

Another common helping verb is *be.* It has many different forms: *am, is, are, was, were, been.* We use it with forms like *asking* and *writing* to make up the **progressive** forms of a verb. These show that something is currently going on, or "in progress":

PROGRESSIVE: I *am pedaling* as fast as I can.
                     The engine *is running* smoothly.
                     My mother *was painting* the den.
                     Her friends *were waiting* for us.

A special set of helping verbs includes *can (could), may (might), shall (should), will (would),* and *must.*

You *can tell* me.	We *will miss* you.
Suddenly he *could walk.*	He *would suspect* us.
They *might want* it.	I *must go* now.

Note: More than one auxiliary may come before the main verb:

    She *should have called* first.
    These tribes *may have come* from Polynesia.
    The bus *has been waiting* for us.

(3) *Even in their plain form, many verbs already have endings that help show they are verbs.* The words *organize, specialize,* and *serialize* all have the typical verb ending *–ize.* The words *simplify, magnify,* and *justify* all have the typical verb ending *–fy.* We can use these endings to turn other words into verbs. *Specialize* comes from the familiar word *special. Simplify* comes from the familiar word *simple.*

Sentences

	SOME COMMON ENGLISH VERBS		
REGULAR:	I walk she walks we walked they have walked you were walking	you work he works they worked it had worked I was working	they complain he complains we complained she has complained they are complaining
IRREGULAR:	I write he writes they wrote I have written she is writing	we think she thinks they thought I had thought I am thinking	I begin it begins they began it has begun it was beginning

EXERCISE 1

A. Fill in the form for the past in each of the following. What past forms simply use –d or –ed? Which use some other way of taking us from the present to the past? Each time use the same single word in a changed form. Write the changed form after the number of the sentence.

1. **(give)**   The officer _____ the motorist a ticket.
2. **(pass)**   The car _____ a truck.
3. **(invent)**   A German inventor _____ the Diesel engine.
4. **(build)**   Henry Ford _____ the Model T.
5. **(win)**   An Italian driver _____ the race.
6. **(lose)**   The second car _____ a wheel.
7. **(collect)**   An ambulance _____ the injured.
8. **(reassure)**   The announcer _____ the crowd.
9. **(drive)**   Aunt Martha _____ the tractor.
10. **(follow)**   We _____ the other car.

B. Use –ize or –fy to turn each of the words on the left into a verb. You may have to drop part of the original word, or make some other change in sound or spelling, to make the ending fit. After the number of the sentence, write down the plain or present form of the new verb. (Make sure your new verb would fit into the sample sentence.)

11. **(memory)**   Actors _____ long speeches.
12. **(identity)**   Witnesses _____ suspects.
13. **(ample)**   Loudspeakers _____ sound.

Words in a Sentence

S1c

14. (penalty)   Referees _____ players.
15. (pure)   Communities _____ their water.
16. (public)   Social groups _____ their events.
17. (standard) Governments _____ measurements.
18. (vapor)   Steam engines _____ water.
19. (glory)   Nations _____ their heroes.
20. (serial)   Some magazines _____ novels.

EXERCISE 2

The following sets of sentences give you a chance to put some typical English verbs through their paces. In each set, use the *−s* form of the verb (third person, singular) in one of the three sentences. Use the past tense form of the verb in another sentence. Use the *−ing* form after the auxiliary in the remaining sentence. (Write on a separate sheet of paper.)

EXAMPLE: drive   a. Carol _____ eighty miles yesterday.
                  b. Carol _____ very well.
                  c. Carol is _____ to Connecticut tomorrow.

(Answers) *a. drove   b. drives   c. driving*

1. **ask**   a. Tom _____ foolish questions.
               b. He _____ one yesterday.
               c. He is _____ one now.
2. **solve**   a. I _____ that problem a month ago.
               b. Meg _____ problems easily.
               c. They are _____ the problem right now.
3. **choose** a. The senate _____ a new leader today.
               b. The onlookers were _____ sides.
               c. Lincoln _____ his words carefully.
4. **work**   a. Jake was _____ there last summer.
               b. He _____ there for three years.
               c. My father _____ six days a week.
5. **talk**   a. Michael _____ all the time.
               b. She _____ about him last week.
               c. The students were _____ among themselves.
6. **listen** a. The children were _____ carefully.
               b. They _____ to their transistors yesterday.
               c. He _____ regularly to Station WIGB.
7. **travel** a. The Jones family _____ every summer.
               b. The band is _____ to Chicago.
               c. We _____ across the country last year.
8. **finish** a. He _____ the letter last night.
               b. She is _____ the job.
               c. Fred always _____ his work first.

Sentences

LANGUAGE IN ACTION

> **THE EXPERT HAS A VERB FOR IT**
>
> The verb-making endings –*fy* and –*ize* come in handy whenever we need new verbs to name a process or a technique. When you study a technical subject, do you notice how many words you encounter ending in –*fy* or –*ize*? How many of the following examples do you know? Answer each question in a few words to a fellow student.
>
> 1. What happens to something when it becomes *ossified?*
> 2. What happens to something when it becomes *petrified?*
> 3. What is a *rarefied* atmosphere?
> 4. What verb ending in –*fy* could you use to show that something is turning into a liquid?
> 5. What verb ending in –*fy* refers to the opposite of "turning into a liquid"?
> 6. What has been done to a metal plate that has been *galvanized?*
> 7. What do we do when we *visualize* an accident?
> 8. What does a state do when it *legalizes* gambling?
> 9. What does a government do when it *socializes* an important industry?
> 10. What has happened when opinions on an important issue have become *polarized?*

9. **take** a. Quality work _____ time.
  b. The firm was _____ a survey.
  c. The voyages of Columbus _____ months.

10. **give** a. A good Christian _____ to the poor.
  b. Our last Thanksgiving dinner _____ me indigestion.
  c. The company was _____ everyone free samples.

EXERCISE 3

Find the verb in each of the following sentences. After the number of each sentence, write the complete verb, including any auxiliaries.

EXAMPLE: The early settlers learned many Indian words.
(Answer) *learned*

1. Every young American knows Indian words.
2. These words came into English in the New World.
3. The early settlers were living close to the Algonquin tribes.

Words in a Sentence

4. The earliest arrivals had borrowed words like *tomahawk*.
5. The pioneers might have called it a war ax.
6. But they must have heard the Indian word many times.
7. Strange new animals were roaming the forests.
8. The settlers called them Indian names.
9. They could use words like *moose* and *raccoon*.
10. They saw wigwams in Indian villages.
11. They heard words like *squaw* and *papoose*.
12. Some words must have bothered the settlers.
13. Few people can pronounce words like *askutasquash*.
14. This word later became *squash*.
15. Other words changed in similar ways.
16. Only a specialist would recognize them today.
17. Other languages have borrowed Indian words.
18. Maybe we should call corn by its original name.
19. Then we would be calling it maize.
20. The Spaniards had learned this word in the West Indies.

S1d Recognizing Adjectives

Know the signals that help us recognize adjectives in the English sentence.

Adjectives are words that tell us which one or what kind. We use a noun to point out a glass. We use an adjective to say whether it is full or empty. The adjective "tells us more" about the noun. It adds to, or narrows down, its meaning. We say that the adjective **modifies** the noun.

In each of the phrases in the list below, an adjective modifies a noun:

a *full* glass
an *empty* bottle
the *narrow* street
a *wonderful* day
this *shaggy* dog
a *tremendous* explosion
a *helpless* feeling
complete instructions
high prices
the *ideal* car

Know the signals that help us recognize adjectives in a sentence:

(1) Many adjectives can show a change in degree by a change in the word itself. We can add the ending *–er* to many

Sentences

ADJECTIVES
 tell us what kind.

Words in a Sentence

adjectives to add the meaning "more so." We then get the **comparative** form of an adjective:

PLAIN: I am *tall*.
COMPARATIVE: She is *taller*. (She is "more so.")

PLAIN: My parents were *poor*.
COMPARATIVE: My grandparents had been *poorer*.

These same adjectives can add the ending *–est* to add the meaning "more so than anything else." We then get the **superlative** form of an adjective. We use superlatives when something stands out above anything else:

SUPERLATIVE: She was the *tallest girl* on the team. (more so than anybody else)
SUPERLATIVE: They were the *poorest* family in town. (more so than anybody else)

With many other adjectives, *more* and *most* (instead of the endings *–er* and *–est*) show changes in degree:

My gift was *expensive*.
His gift was *more expensive*.
Their gift was the *most expensive* of all.

My call was *important*.
Her call was *more important*.
The *most important* call came next morning.

Still other adjectives change the whole word to produce comparative and superlative forms:

PLAIN	COMPARATIVE	SUPERLATIVE
good	better	best
bad	worse	worst
far	farther	farthest
little	less	least

(2) *Most adjectives fit in after words like* very. *Very, quite, rather, really,* and *extremely* are called **intensifiers**. (A very hot stove produces intense heat.) *Very* and the other intensifiers work as adjective signals in the following sentences:

She is *very* polite.
John was always a *very* honest boy.
Your answer was *quite* true.
We'll have a *really* good show tonight.

Sentences

LANGUAGE IN ACTION

FROM THE OLD NEWSPAPER FILE

For each of the following sentences, do two things: (1) In your own words, explain briefly what the italicized adjective means. (2) Find any *additional* adjectives hidden in the sentence.

1. A recent book about *notorious* criminals tells the story of John Dillinger.
2. Dillinger was an average boy who became our *classic* bank robber.
3. He came from a humble *rural* past.
4. He had been a *precocious* student with good grades.
5. His father firmly disciplined the unruly, *defiant* youngster.
6. The boy had an *asymmetrical* face, with the eye higher on the more irregular side.
7. Like other *conspicuous* bandits, Dillinger had a high opinion of himself.
8. He acquired a *formidable* reputation as the result of spectacular robberies.
9. Dillinger and his *desperate* mob had terrorized Wisconsin.
10. His end was *inevitable* after the government offered a large reward for his capture.

Note: A few adjectives do *not* change to show degree. They do not fit in after *very*. They do not have comparative or superlative forms. Words like *daily* or *annual* tell us more about a newspaper or a celebration: a *daily* newspaper, an *annual* celebration. But these adjectives do not change in degree. Something cannot be *more* daily or *more* annual than something else.

(3) Many adjectives have typical adjective endings like –ful, –less, –like, *and* –ous. These endings help us turn other words into adjectives. Can you see that all of the following adjectives have been made from nouns?

–ful   wonderful, hopeful, truthful
–less   senseless, timeless, careless
–like   childlike, businesslike, lifelike
–ous   poisonous, ruinous, disastrous

Other typical adjective endings are –ic, –ish, –able, –ible: *basic, purplish, washable, digestible.*

Words in a Sentence

S1d

EXERCISE 1

In the following sentence, a student used many adjectives to tell people about himself. Use this sentence as a model. Fill in three of the frames that follow it with adjectives of your own choice. Use only words that would fit in after *very:* very *patient,* very *humble.* Write on a separate sheet.

MODEL: As a basketball player, I am *fast, quick, patient, smooth, sharp, sensible, magnificent, great, unbeatable, outstanding, outgoing, fantastic, marvelous,* and *humble.* (Jesse F. Kingsberry)

YOUR TURN:
1. As a student, I am _____
   but also sometimes _____.
2. As a friend, I am _____
   but also sometimes _____
   _____.
3. As a member of a group, I am _____
   but also sometimes _____
   _____.
4. As a _____, I am _____
   _____ but also sometimes _____.

EXERCISE 2

All of the adjectives in the following list fit in after an intensifier like *very.* Find all adjectives in the list. Test each word to see if it would fit into the following test pattern:

He (she) (it) was very _____.

Write *Adj.* after the number of each word that fits into the pattern. Write *No* after the number of each word that does not fit.

EXAMPLE: *dark*   Test: It was very *dark.*
(Answer) *Adj*

EXAMPLE: *table*   Test: It was very *table.*
(Answer) *No*

1. generous
2. table
3. sit
4. handsome
5. capable
6. suspicious
7. kind
8. again
9. card
10. bring
11. easy
12. animal
13. song
14. lazy
15. careful
16. type
17. hero
18. heroic
19. crime
20. criminal
21. smart
22. workable
23. golden
24. school
25. short
26. good
27. heavy
28. thin
29. scientific
30. science
31. healthy
32. capsule
33. brick
34. intelligent
35. colorful
36. brave
37. light
38. anxious
39. newspaper
40. sincere

Sentences

EXERCISE 3

A. In the following sentences, find all the adjectives that have one of the typical adjective endings: *–ful, –less, –like, –able, –ible, –ic, –ish, –ous*. After the number of each sentence, write all the adjectives that have one of these adjective endings.

1. Horror movies create awful sights for their fans.
2. Toothless mummies scare foolish grave robbers.
3. Horrible creatures rise from cavernous depths.
4. Fantastic new horrors are possible as the result of wonderful new inventions.
5. Powerful machines transmit live bodies like radio waves.
6. One machine prepared bodies for transmission in a metallic chamber.
7. A luckless scientist entered the chamber along with a cheerful little fly.
8. A regrettable accident happened during transmission.
9. A manlike body appeared with the gigantic head of a fly.
10. A microscopic fly buzzed around with a pitiable human head.

B. Turn each of the words on the left into an adjective. Use one of the typical adjective endings. (You may have to drop part of the original word or change its spelling.) Make sure each new adjective would fit into the blank in its corresponding sentence. Write the adjective after the number of the sentence.

EXAMPLE: (dispose) We used only _____ plates.
(Answer) *disposable*

11. **(use)** The weird new invention was _____ .
12. **(renew)** The contract was not _____ .
13. **(sense)** You have made a _____ decision.
14. **(depend)** We need _____ workers here.
15. **(realist)** The new plans were more _____ .
16. **(poison)** The woods were full of _____ snakes.
17. **(child)** This is another of his _____ pranks.
18. **(war)** The Apaches were _____ people.
19. **(sugar)** The dentist recommended _____ gum.
20. **(beauty)** We drove through _____ scenery.

EXERCISE 4

All of the adjectives in the following passage are identified by one of the following clues: (1) They appear after an intensifier, like *very*. (2) They use a comparative or superlative form. (3) They use a typical adjective ending. If one of the num-

Words in a Sentence

bered words is an adjective, write *Adj.* after its number. If a numbered word is not an adjective, write *No.*

The (1) **warlike** Normans came to England from France. They became (2) **masters** of England and (3) **remained** masters for a very (4) **long** time. Because they ruled the (5) **country,** they left a very (6) **deep** (7) **impression** on the language. Nearly all of our words about (8) **government** and the (9) **highest** administration are borrowed from the French. The most (10) **familiar** (11) **exceptions** are *king, queen, lord,* and *lady.* These are quite (12) **English.** These words are (13) **useful** and extremely (14) **important.** But they are less (15) **numerous** than the words we (16) **borrowed** from the Normans, such as *govern, state,* and *authority.* The Normans also had (17) **control** of the army and navy. Many words about (18) **fighting** were (19) **introduced** by them at a very (20) **early** date. Examples (21) **include** *battle, navy,* and *soldier.* The Normans (22) **also** controlled the (23) **courts** and (24) **laws.** A (25) **greater** number of the words we (26) **use** in court are French than are English. Very (27) **common** and quite (28) **simple** words like *court* and *judge* are of French (29) **origin.** The (30) **higher** classes also (31) **controlled** the Church. Their (32) **priests** had a (33) **powerful** effect on the language of (34) **religion.** The (35) **lower** classes looked up to the higher. It is quite (36) **natural** that the English (37) **imitated** their French (38) **masters.** The influence of the French (39) **language** became (40) **stronger.**

S1e Recognizing Adverbs

Know the signals that help us recognize adverbs.

Adverbs tell us how, when, and where. When a verb says what is happening, we can add an adverb that says how, when, or where. The word *adverb* itself means "added to the verb." We say that the adverb modifies the verb:

How? He answered *politely.*
  The motor ran *quietly.*
  The plane tilted *dangerously.*

When? He called us *early.*
  The fair starts *tomorrow.*
  We are leaving *now.*

Where? The children played *outside.*
  She is sleeping *upstairs.*
  She never comes *here.*

Sentences

Know the signals that help us recognize adverbs in a sentence:

(1) Many adverbs have the –ly ending. Adverbs share many features with adjectives, and they are often made from adjectives. Most English adverbs are simply an adjective like *careful* with the ending *–ly* added:

ADJECTIVE: The drivers were *careful*.
ADVERB: They drove *carefully*.

ADJECTIVE: We need a *cautious* manager.
ADVERB: She managed our business *cautiously*.

ADJECTIVE: The umpire was *unfair*.
ADVERB: He penalized our team *unfairly*.

ADJECTIVE: The writing was *careless*.
ADVERB: He wrote *carelessly*.

ADVERBS tell us how, when, and where.

Remember that many of the adverbs showing when or where do without the *–ly* ending:

When? now, then, later, often, today, yesterday, tomorrow, soon
Where? outside, inside, upstairs, here, there, away, everywhere

Sometimes adjective and adverb are exactly the same. Sometimes they are completely different:

ADJECTIVE: I like a *fast* train.
ADVERB: She was driving too *fast*.

ADJECTIVE: Susan was a *good* pitcher.
ADVERB: Susan pitched *well*.

See U2b and U3c for standard forms of adverbs.

(2) *Like adjectives, many adverbs can show changes in degree.* They fit in after *very* and other intensifiers:

They left *very suddenly*.
Jim visited us *quite often*.
We had bought the place *rather cheaply*.

Many adverbs use the *–er* or *–est* endings or the words *more* and *most* in comparisons:

The plane will arrive *sooner*.
Water boils *more rapidly* at high altitudes.
He drove *most cautiously* of the three.

With some adverbs, we have to change the whole word to show changes in degree:

PLAIN	COMPARATIVE	SUPERLATIVE
well	better	best
badly	worse	worst

(3) *Adverbs can move in a sentence more freely than other kinds of words.* In how many different places would each of the following adverbs fit into its sample sentence?

suddenly	The animal moved.
unexpectedly	The ship changed course.
repeatedly	His friends had warned him.
gracefully	The skaters moved across the ice.
clumsily	He climbed down from the upper bunk.
immediately	You should have called the police.
here	The people never slow down.

Sentences

Note: In addition to modifying verbs, adverbs can also modify adjectives and other adverbs. Intensifiers like *very* and *extremely* are themselves adverbs. They modify adjectives and adverbs:

very *kind,* extremely *sudden,* quite *suddenly*

EXERCISE 1

Use each italicized word as an adverb in the sample sentence that follows it. Most of the words you can turn into adverbs by adding the ending *–ly*. Some words are ready to use as adverbs without any added ending. A few can be made into adverbs by added adverb endings that are more rarely used, such as *–wise* (in *counterclockwise*), or *–ward* (in *forward* and *backward*). You may have to change or omit some final letters to make the endings fit. Write the added adverb after the number of the sentence.

1. *neat* — He folded his clothes _____ .
2. *silent* — Her father listened _____ .
3. *handsome* — The duke rewarded his followers _____ .
4. *reluctant* — We entered the cave _____ .
5. *eager* — The natives rowed out to the ship _____ .
6. *downtown* — We did our shopping _____ .
7. *length* — The pole might fit in _____ .
8. *intelligent* — The guide answered all questions _____ .
9. *sensible* — The trapped climbers behaved _____ .
10. *intense* — The fallen army hated the invaders _____ .
11. *heaven* — He turned his eyes _____ .
12. *abroad* — Eugene met his wife _____ .
13. *outside* — Delbert parked his new car _____ .
14. *abrupt* — The truck stopped _____ .
15. *furious* — The owner waved his arms _____ .
16. *courageous* — She answered her questioners _____ .
17. *happy* — The released prisoners were shouting _____ .
18. *good* — Everyone except Colin behaved _____ .
19. *upstairs* — Laurel and Hardy moved the piano _____ .
20. *side* — We moved the box into the trunk _____ .

EXERCISE 2

Find the adverb in each of the following sentences. Write it after the number of the sentence. Make sure each word you choose tells us how, when, or where something was done.

1. The group should have met sooner.
2. Eagles rarely visit this state.

Words in a Sentence

3. Lassie followed her new owner everywhere.
4. The car jumped forward with a roar.
5. We crouched uncomfortably in our hideaway.
6. The truck sank deeper into the mud.
7. Wilma answered fastest of the three contestants.
8. Prices of food have jumped considerably.
9. Athletes are now training for the Olympics.
10. We will try a different experiment tomorrow.
11. The train later stalled in deep snow.
12. The secret agent performed her mission well.
13. The guards checked doors and windows routinely.
14. We worked hard for low wages.
15. Applause has regularly interrupted their performance.
16. An ambulance arrived on the scene immediately.
17. An ex-champion has seldom regained the title.
18. The trailer suddenly veered to the right.
19. Our troop had left several stragglers behind.
20. The explorers well knew the penalty for failure.

Learn to recognize connectives and prepositions.

When we speak or write, words from the major word classes carry most of our message. Nouns help us put labels on things and ideas. Verbs help us talk about actions and events. Adjectives help us explain which one or what kind. Adverbs help us explain how, when, and where. But in addition to these major kinds of words, almost everything we say also uses other words to join them together. Here are four kinds of words that help us join the major parts of a statement:

S1f
Recognizing Connectives and Prepositions

DETERMINERS: Sister lent   friend   bicycle
               My sister lent *her* friend *the* bicycle.

AUXILIARIES: Doris   worn mittens
               Doris *should have* worn mittens.

CONNECTIVES: Colin   Brian tried   failed
               Colin *and* Brian tried *but* failed.

PREPOSITIONS: We met   Detroit   accident
               We met *in* Detroit *by* accident.

Study the way connectives and prepositions help us join words in a statement or to a statement:

(1) We use several different kinds of connectives to join several parts of the same kind. **Connectives** are joining words.

Sentences

For instance, *and, or,* or *but* can join two nouns: butter *and* bread, liberty *or* death. They can join two verbs: skipped *and* jumped, tried *but* failed. The same connectives can join not just single words but groups of words, or whole statements:

> The settlers could arrive *by land* or *by water.*
> We *raised the window* and *looked at the snow.*
> *We asked our neighbors,* but *they refused.*

See S4 for kinds and uses of connectives.

(2) *We use prepositions to join an additional noun to the rest of a statement.* **Prepositions** "come before" a noun (and its noun marker):

in the rain	*with* luck
by accident	*without* a map
for a friend	*on* the table
at night	*from* memory
through the gate	*of* our town
to the door	*into* the car

COMMON PREPOSITIONS
A checklist

The following words may all be used as prepositions. Many point out relationships in *time* or in *space:*

about	before	for	through
above	behind	from	to
across	below	in	toward
after	beneath	into	under
against	beside	like	until
along	between	of	up
among	beyond	off	upon
around	by	on	with
as	during	over	within
at	except	since	without

The following *combinations* are also used as prepositions:

aside from	instead of
as to	in view of
as well as	on account of
because of	on behalf of
due to	out of

Words in a Sentence

Find all the prepositions in this picture.

Many prepositions help us show where things are in time or space: *before, after, during, on, under, below, above, between, across, to, among*. Sometimes two words act together as a preposition.

He acted *out of* spite.
She quit *because of* ill health.
We saw a musical *instead of* a play.

When several words combine in a group to fill a slot in a sentence, we call them a **phrase**. A preposition and what it joins to the rest of a sentence together make up a **prepositional phrase**.

What link is missing from each of the following sayings? Write the missing connective after the number of the sentence.

EXERCISE 1

1. A fool _____ his money are soon parted.
2. Time _____ tide wait for no man.
3. Fish _____ cut bait.
4. The rain falls alike on the just _____ the unjust.
5. Make hay _____ the sun shines.
6. All is fair in love _____ war.

85

Sentences

7. Nobody knows you _____ you are down and out.
8. You can lead a horse to the water, _____ you can't make him drink.
9. Hope for the best _____ prepare for the worst.
10. Sticks and stones may break my bones, _____ words can never hurt me.

EXERCISE 2

Find a preposition that would fill the blank for each of the following sentences. Write the complete prepositional phrase after the number of the sentence.

EXAMPLE: The winner collapsed _____ the race.
(Answer) *after the race*

1. They served the lunch _____ a tray.
2. We found the exit _____ accident.
3. He gave us pesos _____ our dollars.
4. We missed the end _____ the program.
5. The candy _____ the package was stale.
6. Gliders are aircraft that fly _____ engines.
7. He had secretly recorded the conversation _____ tape.
8. A play _____ Shakespeare was on the reading list.
9. Paroled prisoners are released _____ jail.
10. The slaves rebelled _____ their masters.
11. Strong currents run _____ the surface.
12. Workers today expect vacations _____ pay.
13. The only way out is _____ the tunnel.
14. Customers _____ shoes were not allowed in the restaurant.
15. The train was traveling _____ reduced speed.
16. We had a short recess _____ classes.
17. At night the count turned _____ a werewolf.
18. There might be valuable pieces _____ these coins.
19. You should type your name _____ your signature.
20. Planes often climb _____ the clouds.

UNIT REVIEW EXERCISE

Look at each numbered word in the following sentences. After the number of the word write the abbreviation that shows how the word is used in the sentence. Use the following abbreviations:

N	Noun
Pro	Pronoun
V	Verb (or part of a complete verb)
Adj	Adjective
Adv	Adverb
Prep	Preposition

The Complete Sentence

The astronauts had (1) **traveled** (2) **through** space for many (3) **years.** Their (4) **trip** was coming (5) **to** an end. The (6) **spaceship** (7) **approached** a very (8) **distant** planet. (9) **It** (10) **carried** a (11) **team** of highly trained specialists. Its (12) **navigator** could (13) **find** a (14) **needle** in a very (15) **big** haystack. The radio operator could (16) **interpret** (17) **signals** (18) **from** the stars. The archeologist had (19) **unearthed** forgotten (20) **civilizations.** The (21) **astronauts** set their (22) **ship** down (23) **cautiously** in a very (24) **large** garden. (25) **They** were greeted by a very (26) **intelligent** being. (27) **It** looked like a very (28) **large** turtle. It (29) **moved** (30) **slowly** on chubby hind legs. It uttered (31) **intelligible** sounds (32) **in** a low (33) **whisper.** Each of these (34) **creatures** had survived (35) **countless** centuries. They lived (36) **peacefully** as (37) **vegetarians.** They were (38) **looking** (39) **at** their visitors (40) **curiously.**

S2 THE COMPLETE SENTENCE

Know the basic patterns of the complete sentence.

What makes a complete sentence? In the normal English sentence, two or more basic sentence parts work together to make a statement. Though actual sentences come in many different shapes, they use a limited number of basic designs. We can see the same basic pattern repeated again and again in many sentences.

Look at the following sentences:

"DOER"	ACTION	TARGET
The railroad	reached	the Pacific.
The champion	defeated	every challenger.
Lightning	had struck	the tree.

Though these sentences differ in detail, the basic pattern in each is the same. They first point to somebody or something that is in action. The sentences then move through the verb to the target.

The same type of jet plane, though equipped differently, will still have its same basic design. One design may have four engines, two to each wing. Another may have three engines together toward the rear of the plane. The same way, sentences may be equipped with various additional parts and still follow the same basic design. Know the most basic patterns we use as basic designs of the complete English sentence.

Sentences

S2a Subject and Verb

Write and expand the basic subject-verb sentence.

A bare-minimum sentence in English needs only two basic parts. These are like the two pillars that hold up an arch. The first basic part of the structure is a noun, with or without its noun marker. (Or it may be a pronoun that has taken the place of a noun.) The first basic part is the **subject** of the sentence. The subject points to something as if to say: "Here—I want to say something about this."

The man _____. (What about him?)
Babies _____. (What about them?)
They _____. (What about them?)

The second basic part is a verb that makes a statement about the subject:

Subject-Verb (S-V):   The man *disappeared*.
Subject-Verb (S-V):   Babies *cry*.
Subject-Verb (S-V):   They *suffered*.

The part of the sentence that says something about the subject is the **predicate.** In a Pattern One sentence, the verb alone can serve as the complete predicate. The following two-part statements are all Pattern One sentences:

God exists.	Speed kills.	The sun rises.
Airplanes fly.	Power corrupts.	My head hurts.
Frogs croak.	Cities grow.	The dust settled.

Just as the subject of a Pattern One sentence may be a noun with its markers, so the predicate may be a verb with its auxiliaries:

SUBJECT	VERB
My friends	*are leaving.*
Your plan	*could work.*
The children	*must have been running.*
A taxpayer	*had complained.*
The pilot	*could have been sleeping.*

Remember these points about Pattern One sentences:

(1) The verb in a Pattern One sentence can make a complete statement. We call such verbs **intransitive** verbs. They are "not in transit" to anywhere. They are not going anywhere. By themselves, they tell the whole story. When someone says, "He gargled," we do not ask, "He gargled—*what?*" or "He gargled—*to whom?*"

The Complete Sentence

S2a

(2) The Subject–Verb pattern can be expanded in various ways. We can work in adjectives that tell us more about the subject. We can work in adverbs that modify the verb, telling us how, where, or when:

SUBJECT	VERB
The *sleepy* lifeguard	dozed *peacefully*.
The *alert* lifeguard	responded *immediately*.
The *angry* lifeguard	walked *away*.

(3) Groups of words as well as single words may serve as modifiers in Pattern One sentences. Prepositional phrases often take the place of adverbs. In the sentences below, notice how the prepositional phrases modify the verb:

The sleepy lifeguard dozed *in the sun*.
The alert lifeguard responded *to the call*.
The angry lifeguard walked *with a limp*.

At other times, prepositional phrases replace adjectives. They modify the subject:

The stranger *from Chicago* arrived unexpectedly.
The stranger *on the platform* lied repeatedly.

EXERCISE 1

The verbs in Pattern One sentences can tell us what people do, how people act, and how things move. The verb alone can give us the complete message. The verb can "tell all." In each of the following blanks, fill in a *single* word—a verb that by itself could complete a Subject–Verb sentence. (Write on a separate sheet of paper.)

1. A monkey can _____, _____, _____, and _____.
2. A penguin can _____, _____, _____, and _____.
3. A hydroplane can _____, _____, _____, and _____.
4. Robots can _____, _____, _____, and _____.
5. A friendly person will _____, _____, _____, and _____.
6. An unmannerly person will _____, _____, _____, and _____.
7. Dishonest people _____, _____, _____, and _____.
8. Lawyers _____, _____, _____, and _____.
9. Dancers _____, _____, _____, and _____.
10. Comedians _____, _____, _____, and _____.

Sentences

EXERCISE 2 Each of the following sentences has as its core a Subject–Verb (S–V) pattern. After the number of each sentence, write down the bare-bones pattern. Include only the two basic parts: (1) the noun or pronoun that serves as subject (including any noun marker); (2) the complete verb (including any auxiliaries).

EXAMPLE: My whole family travels in the summer.
(Answer) *My family travels*

1. The vacation had started early.
2. The whole family went on a trip.
3. They traveled through the hills of South Dakota.
4. They soon arrived in the Badlands.
5. The children slept in a small tent.
6. Their parents stayed in the trailer.
7. Indians live on a reservation nearby.
8. The little town of Wounded Knee lies to the south.
9. Rain falls frequently in the summer.
10. Little vegetation grows in the Badlands.
11. Fossils are waiting for young explorers.
12. Tourists wander through the museum.
13. A huge hide is hanging on the wall.
14. A herd of buffalo is grazing on the plains.
15. These awesome animals fortunately remain at a distance.
16. My family often travels to a park.
17. Sometimes we stay at home.
18. We relax in our backyard.
19. Lucky people fly to Hawaii.
20. Vacations end very quickly.

EXERCISE 3 Put each of the following sentences through its paces. Each sentence is a bare-minimum sentence. Write *two* expanded versions of each. Each time build up the basic structure with your choice of adjectives, adverbs, or prepositional phrases.

EXAMPLE: The campers slept.
(Answer) *The young campers slept soundly at night.*
          The campers from Detroit slept in their tents.

1. A truck arrived.
2. The people were cheering.
3. The hoboes walked.
4. The dog was barking.
5. The audience laughed.

The Complete Sentence

S2b

Write and expand sentences that include an object.

S2b
Verb and Object

In a second basic pattern, the verb alone does not carry the complete message. The action described by the verb goes on to a target or a result. Each Pattern Two sentence has three basic parts:

"DOER"	ACTION	TARGET
Our cat	scratched	the furniture.
Pepito	found	the dime.
That snake	crushes	people.
The arrow	had pierced	his coat.

"DOER"	PROCESS	RESULT
Susan	was writing	a letter.
That factory	makes	bricks.
The Smiths	had baked	a cake.

Remember:

(1) In a Pattern Two sentence, a third basic part is needed to complete the basic structure. The sentence goes on to a target or a result that we call the **object** of the verb. The object in a Subject–Verb–Object sentence is not something we can add or leave out as we please. It is needed to complete the basic pattern; it is needed as a "completer." The more technical name for such completers is **complement.** Removing the object from a Subject–Verb–Object sentence is like removing the third wheel from a tricycle. The missing object makes the following sentences sound unfinished:

SUBJECT	VERB	OBJECT	
Dorothy	mailed	———	(what?)
Dorothy	mailed	her letter.	
Pepito	found	———	(what?)
Pepito	found	the dime.	

(2) The verb in a Pattern Two sentence is a transitive verb. A **transitive** verb "keeps going." It is aimed at something—usually something *other than* the subject. The object that the transitive verb aims at is a second noun (or pronoun). The verb locks this second noun into the basic structure of the sentence without the need for any further connecting link.

Sentences

(3) The Subject−Verb−Object pattern can be expanded in many ways. Adjectives can tell us more about both the subject and the object. Adverbs may tell us how, where, or when. Prepositional phrases may do the work of either adjectives or adverbs. In each of the following sentences, look at what has been added to the basic S−V−O pattern:

The *small* bird ate a *large* worm.
The *expert* gambler *never* cut the deck *fairly*.
His *new* game *soon* wore our patience *down*.
The girls *from Chicago* met the boy *from Detroit*.
The driver *of the truck* reported the accident *immediately*.
A student *in my class* invented a *new* thermometer.
Dorothy mailed her letter *at the post office*.
Pepito found the *shiny, new* dime *on the sidewalk*.

Note: The object of the verb in an S−V−O sentence is *not* preceded by a preposition. Be sure you know the difference between an S−V sentence expanded by a prepositional phrase and an S−V−O sentence.

    S   V
Marcia ran *to the store*.
(S−V with prepositional phrase)

    S   V   O
Marcia ran *a mile*.

EXERCISE 1

What transitive verb could fill the blank in each of the following sentences? Each completed statement will fit the S−V−O pattern. After the number of each sentence, write *three* different verbs that could fill the blank in the sentence. Use a single word each time.

EXAMPLE: Grocers _____ merchandise.
(Answer) *sell, advertise, bag*

1. Mechanics _____ cars.
2. Cooks _____ meat.
3. Barbers _____ hair.
4. Plumbers _____ pipes.
5. Employers _____ workers.
6. Artists _____ pictures.
7. Teamsters _____ trucks.
8. Pilots _____ planes.
9. Gardeners _____ trees.
10. Dishwashers _____ dishes.
11. Grooms _____ horses.
12. Doctors _____ patients.
13. Counselors _____ students.
14. Reviewers _____ books.
15. Guards _____ buildings.
16. Coaches _____ athletes.
17. Cashiers _____ money.
18. Secretaries _____ letters.
19. Farmers _____ wheat.
20. Musicians _____ music.

The Complete Sentence

S2b

The object in a S–V–O sentence is locked into the sentence directly. It does not follow a connecting link like a preposition: *in, on, at, by, over, for, through, with,* and the like. Which of the following are S–V–O sentences? Which are Subject–Verb sentences, expanded by means of prepositional phrases?

After the number of each S–V–O sentence in the legends below, write the object (including any noun markers, but without modifiers). After the number of each Subject–Verb sentence, write S–V.

EXERCISE 2

EXAMPLE: The Arapaho tribe told a legend about the porcupine.
(Answer) *a legend*

A.
1. The porcupine climbed a tree.
2. A woman went after him.
3. She wanted his quills.
4. Near the top, the tree suddenly lengthened.
5. The woman climbed into the sky.
6. She married the porcupine.
7. The strange couple lived in a house in the sky.
8. In the fall, the woman was digging for potatoes.
9. The woman accidentally struck a hole in the sky.
10. She lowered her body back to earth.

B.
11. A father had raised a family of seven sons.
12. They were constantly quarreling over little things.
13. A wise old man helped the father.
14. He set a task for the sons.
15. He asked for a bundle of sticks.
16. Perhaps a giant could have broken the sticks in the bundle.
17. The sons made the attempt in vain.
18. The old man put single sticks in their hands next.
19. The boys broke the individual pieces easily.
20. Strength comes from unity.

For each of the following transitive verbs, write a short Pattern Two sentence using the verb as part of the S–V–O pattern. Include modifiers for either the subject, verb, or object, if you wish.

EXERCISE 3

1. construct
2. eliminate
3. destroy
4. argue
5. deliver
6. regulate
7. amaze
8. negotiate
9. design
10. alter

Sentences

S2c Linking Verb and Noun

Write and expand the Subject–Linking Verb–Noun sentence.

Like Pattern Two, Pattern Three has a noun after the verb. But this time, the noun is not a target or a product. Instead, it points *back* to the subject:

SUBJECT	LINKING VERB	NOUN
I	am	Tarzan.
Lassie	is	a dog.
Gorillas	are	apes.

Remember:

(1) The verb in a Pattern Three sentence is a linking verb. A **linking verb** is a special kind of intransitive verb. It does not carry action from one noun across to the other. Instead, it provides a link between two different ways of talking about the same thing. The most common linking verb is *be,* with its various forms: *am, are, is, was, were, will be, have been,* etc. Two other linking verbs that fit the S–LV–N pattern are *become* and *remain.* Look at the following links:

SUBJECT	LINKING VERB	NOUN
The books	*were*	novels.
Lucy	*remained*	his friend.
My dog	*became*	her companion.
I	*am*	the master.
They	*will remain*	enemies.
Gonzales	*must have been*	a dictator.
The Lord	*is*	my shepherd.

(2) The added noun in a Pattern Three sentence is a label we pin on the subject. The additional noun provides a label or a name for the subject. Can you see that the third part of the following sentences is still talking about the subject?

PERSON	LINK	SAME PERSON
Washington	was	*a general.*
Many Presidents	have been	*lawyers.*
James Carter	was	*a farmer.*
President Truman	had been	*a haberdasher.*
President Johnson	had been	*a teacher.*
Vice Presidents	may become	*Presidents.*

The Complete Sentence

Like the object in a Pattern Two sentence, the added noun in a Pattern Three sentence serves as a "completer" (or complement). It is part of the basic structure. It is needed to complete the sentence.

(3) The Subject–Linking Verb–Noun pattern can be expanded in various ways. Various kinds of modifiers may help build up the subject, the verb, or the added noun. Look at the modifiers used to build up the S–LV–N pattern in the following sentences:

Their *new* dog was a poodle.
The *brown* bear is *generally* a *peaceful* animal.
The book *on the desk* is his *favorite* novel.
My grandfather was *always* the master *in his own business*.

EXERCISE 1

The labels we place on people and things depend on our point of view. They show what we think of somebody, or whether we like something or not. For each of the following, find a noun that would complete a Subject–Linking Verb–Noun sentence. Each time fill in a single noun that shows your point of view. (Change *a* to *an* if necessary.)

EXAMPLE: A stingy person is a _____ .
(Answer) *miser*

1. A broken-down car is a _____ .
2. A hated ruler is a _____ .
3. An undesirable dog is a _____ .
4. A brave person becomes a _____ .
5. A misbehaving child is a _____ .
6. Unwanted plants are _____ .
7. An admired Indian was a _____ .
8. Water from a swollen river becomes a _____ .
9. Lack of rainfall becomes a _____ .
10. Cockroaches are _____ .
11. An unexpected gift of money is a _____ .
12. Without water, land remains a _____ .
13. People without any faults at all are _____ .
14. A very successful book may become a _____ .
15. Unknown actors may become _____ overnight.
16. A very lush forest may still remain a _____ .
17. Roosevelt remained the _____ for a third term.
18. A very evil person is a _____ .
19. Many famous American artists have been _____ .
20. A sweet little child is a _____ .

PET

Sentences

EXERCISE 2

Which of the following sentences are S–LV–N sentences? Which of the following sentences are S–V–O sentences? Write the right abbreviation after the number of the sentence.

EXAMPLE: Elephants are intelligent animals.
(Answer)   *S–LV–N*

1. The instrument was a gyroscope.
2. The city council had banned the movie.
3. Hitler might have remained an obscure politician.
4. Canada could have become a part of the United States.
5. The animal trainer always dressed her performing chimpanzees in cute clothes.
6. The settlers in the valley had been Mormons.
7. The manager fired the unsuccessful coach.
8. The evil magician put a spell on the unlucky prince.
9. Her favorite horse was a white stallion.
10. The people in the cabins were growing their own corn.
11. Slim was runner-up in the Ugly-Man Contest.
12. The institute was training dogs for blind people.
13. The favorites of the audience were a pair of robots.
14. His grandmother had been a priestess of the tribe.
15. Nancy bought the bicycle with her own money.
16. The land will remain the property of the state.
17. The king summoned his faithful followers.
18. The hikers should have chosen a different route.
19. Our present governor will be the incumbent in the next election.
20. The boy from the log cabin became the sixteenth President of the republic.

EXERCISE 3

Put each of the following S–LV–N sentences through its paces. Write *two* expanded versions of each. Each time build up the basic structure with your choice of adjectives, adverbs, or prepositional phrases.

EXAMPLE: Nations can become friends.
(Answer)   *Hostile nations can become warm friends.*
           Nations in different continents can become excellent friends.

1. Students are people.
2. The potato is a food.
3. A boy became king.
4. The United States remained a country.
5. The mayor had been a lawyer.

The Complete Sentence

S2d Linking Verb and Adjective

Write and expand the Subject–Linking Verb–Adjective sentence.

Pattern Four, like Pattern Three, does not go on to a target or a product. The completer again points back to the subject. But this time the completer is not a noun but an adjective. The adjective "tells us more" about the subject. What does the adjective in each of the following sentences tell us about its subject?

SUBJECT	LINKING VERB	ADJECTIVE
The flaps	were	detachable.
The judge	had been	lenient.
The silence	was	ominous.
Attendance	will be	compulsory.
The wings	are	retractable.

Remember:

(1) Pattern Four sentences use additional linking verbs. Like Pattern Three, Pattern Four uses forms of *be (am, is, are, was, were, been, will be)*. Pattern Four also uses words like *become* and *remain*. But in addition, Pattern Four sentences use linking verbs that show how things look, sound, feel, smell, or taste:

The room *remained* dark.
His face *turned* red.
The survivors *looked* tired.
Their friends *sounded* happy.
The surface *felt* rough.
The food *smelled* good.
The bread *tasted* fresh.

To make sure that the word that follows the verb is an adjective, you can try to fit it in before the noun:

the *dark* room	their *happy* friends
his *red* face	the *rough* surface
the *tired* survivors	the *good* food

(2) The Subject–Linking Verb–Adjective pattern can be expanded in various ways. Modifiers may help us build up the subject, the verb, and also the adjective. Notice that various kinds of *intensifiers* may appear with the adjective. Look at what has been added to the basic structure in the sentences on the following page:

97

Sentences

The sailors *on deck* seemed hostile.
Her *low* voice sounded *very* innocent.
The islands *in the gulf* had remained independent *for centuries*.
The villain *in a melodrama* should be *extremely* ugly.
The soup *in our dishes* smelled *rather* odd.
A *pink* elephant would *probably* look horrible.

EXERCISE 1

Look at the linking verbs in each of the following examples. For each blank space, find *two* different adjectives that would complete a S–LV–Adj sentence. To make sure you are using adjectives, choose only words that would fit in after *very*.

EXAMPLE: Mr. Hyde looked ―――――.
(Answer) *restless, different*

1. Camels look ―――――.
2. Knights were ―――――.
3. His hair had turned ―――――.
4. Sirens sounded ―――――.
5. Italian food tastes ―――――.
6. India has remained ―――――.
7. Diamonds are ―――――.
8. Movie stars look ―――――.
9. Sharks look ―――――.
10. Cartoons have become ―――――.
11. Space travel was ―――――.
12. Life on other planets is ―――――.
13. Flowers smell ―――――.
14. The paper had turned ―――――.
15. Chemicals are often ―――――.
16. Foreign cars are often ―――――.
17. Jokes can be ―――――.
18. Friends should be ―――――.
19. A job can be ―――――.
20. Robots may seem ―――――.

EXERCISE 2

What is the basic pattern for each of the following sentences? After the number of the sentence, write S–V, S–V–O, S–LV–N, or S–LV–Adj.

EXAMPLE: The pilot was unconscious.
(Answer) *S–LV–Adj.*

1. English is our common language.
2. The girls danced well.
3. Our new neighbors seemed apprehensive.

The Complete Sentence

S2d

LANGUAGE IN ACTION

THE WORD FOR TODAY

Study the following sayings. In each of these, a simple basic pattern has been expanded. What was the simple pattern? After the number of each sentence, put the right abbreviation: S–V, S–V–O, S–LV–N, or S–LV–Adj.

1. The leopard cannot change its spots.
2. A jest breaks no bones.
3. A day of battle is a day of harvest for the devil.
4. The advice of fools is worthless.
5. A little rebellion is a good thing. (Thomas Jefferson)
6. One must never turn his back on life. (Eleanor Roosevelt)
7. Love conquers all things.
8. Honesty is the best policy.
9. Bad luck has no friends.
10. One man's meat is another man's poison.
11. Actions speak louder than words.
12. A little learning is a dangerous thing. (Alexander Pope)
13. The early bird gets the worm.
14. All cats look gray in the dark.
15. In the kingdom of the blind, the one-eyed man is king.
16. The grass is always greener on the other side of the fence.
17. The watched pot never boils.
18. Too many cooks spoil the broth.
19. Hunger is the best cook.
20. Beggars can't be choosers.

4. Their pies looked delicious.
5. The police questioned the suspect for eight hours.
6. Her arm felt good in a sling.
7. Jane sings beautifully.
8. Bill developed an infection in his eye.
9. The wound must have been very painful
10. Their new president is Gustavo Real.
11. The name on the sign was unfamiliar.
12. A general became the new foreign minister.
13. Jan wrote a story for our magazine.
14. Unemployment remains a serious problem.
15. A steak has never smelled better to me.
16. He cultivated his garden every spring.
17. The pear tasted strange.
18. The line seemed straight.
19. The play began smoothly.
20. The material felt smooth to the touch.

Sentences

EXERCISE 3 Put each of the following S–LV–Adj sentences through its paces. Write *two* expanded versions of each. Each time build up the basic structure with modifiers and intensifiers.

1. Pizza is good.
2. Manners are important.
3. My skill is obvious.
4. Dogs are nice.
5. Life can be beautiful.
6. Winter is cold.

S2e The Indirect Object

Write and expand sentences that include an indirect object.

A sentence may have not just three but *four* basic parts. Each of the four parts, like the four legs of a chair, helps to hold the structure up. We often use a four-part pattern with verbs like *give, send,* or *bring.* Such verbs raise *two* questions in our minds. The first is: *"What* did somebody give, or send?" The answer to this question is an ordinary object:

SUBJECT	VERB	OBJECT
The uncle	gave	a dime.
Chubby	sent	roses.
Pedro	had brought	a pizza.

We often ask a second question: *"Where* is the dime going? *Who* will receive the roses?" We can insert the answer to this second question *between* the verb and the object:

The uncle	gave	*his nephew*	a dime.
Chubby	sent	*his mother*	roses.
Pedro	had brought	*us*	a pizza.

Remember:

(1) A sentence may "go out of its way" to show us the destination *before it fills in the object.* We call the noun (or pronoun) that shows the destination the **indirect object** (IO). The S–V–IO–O pattern does not head "directly" for the object. It goes to the indirect object first. Look at the way the indirect object shows destination in the following examples:

S	V	IO	O
Sergei	gave	*the cabdriver*	directions.
The amulet	will bring	*you*	luck.
The preacher	told	*the congregation*	the truth.

The Complete Sentence

(2) The verbs that fit this pattern all tell us about some kind of transfer. Something goes to somebody (or something). Typical "transfer verbs" are *give, send, show, teach, lend, offer, sell, ask, tell, hand, grant,* and *pass:*

Vactioners *send* their friends postcards.
We *offered* the stranger a sandwich.
Susan *passed* Sondra the ball.
The witness *had told* the court the truth.

(3) Sentences with an indirect object can be expanded in various ways. Look at the modifiers that have been added to each of the following examples:

The *cooperative* prisoner told his captors the *whole* truth.
Grandfather had sent his *future* bride his proposal by *stagecoach*.
Her *untimely* death caused her friends *great* pain.
He always sent the children *shiny* toys *for Christmas*.

EXERCISE 1

After the number of each sentence, write a verb that would fill the blank and complete an S–V–IO–O pattern. Use as many *different* verbs as you can. (Include auxiliaries if you wish.)

EXAMPLE: An assistant _____ the announcer the envelope.
(Answer) *handed*

1. Bankers _____ borrowers money.
2. Publishers _____ parents encyclopedias.
3. The experience _____ the climbers a lesson.
4. The governor _____ the prisoners a pardon.
5. The warden _____ the lion raw meat.
6. My aunt _____ the children a lullaby.
7. We _____ the conductor our tickets.
8. My sister _____ me questions.
9. Jim _____ the guest the butter.
10. Her grandmother _____ the mayor a long letter.
11. My aunt _____ her cats liver.
12. The boys _____ their friends success.
13. God _____ us our sins.
14. The church _____ sinners salvation.
15. His eagerness _____ him a promotion.
16. We _____ the puppies a different home.
17. The operator _____ her the telegram.
18. Grandmother _____ us a cake.
19. The agency _____ the applicant a job.
20. The millionaire _____ her housekeeper a fortune.

Sentences

EXERCISE 2 What is the basic pattern of each of the following sentences? After the number of each sentence, write S–V, S–V–O, or S–V–IO–O.

1. Newspapers offer their readers a choice.
2. They print straight news.
3. They give their readers stories about celebrities.
4. People can read about sports.
5. Columnists teach cooks new recipes.
6. Famous experts discuss foreign events.
7. Reporters may give us the highlights.
8. Some articles tell the reader important details.
9. Most readers read the headlines first.
10. Headlines often exaggerate.
11. They get our attention.
12. Advertisers send their customers messages.
13. Ads give newspapers financial support.
14. Newspapers grant their advertisers ample space.
15. Many people read the classified section.
16. Want ads offer people jobs.
17. Many advertisers promise their customers quick results.
18. Advertising may mislead the reader.
19. Laws now offer the consumer protection.
20. Honest advertisers tell us the truth.

EXERCISE 3 Put each of the following S–V–IO–O sentences through its paces. Write two different versions of each. Each time, build up the basic structure with modifiers of your own choice.

1. My uncle sent his relatives gifts.
2. The daughter wrote her parents a letter.
3. The princess told the prince a secret.
4. The astronaut gave the robot instructions.
5. The scientist taught the assistant the formula.

UNIT REVIEW EXERCISE What is the basic pattern of each of the following sentences? After the number of each sentence, write S–V, S–V–O, S–LV–N, S–LV–Adj, or S–V–IO–O.

EXAMPLE: Books sometimes become famous overnight.
(Answer) *S–LV–Adj*

1. Nature is the mother of all life.
2. Countless creatures live in the ocean.
3. The forests shelter animals.
4. Rachel Carson wrote a book about our natural environment.

Adapting the Simple Sentence

5. She gave her readers food for thought.
6. The book described a cheerless future.
7. The hens brooded on the farms.
8. The chicks would never hatch.
9. The apple trees were blooming everywhere.
10. The bees were avoiding the blossoms.
11. The roadsides were silent.
12. The streams were now lifeless.
13. They told the visitor a sad story.
14. The fish had died.
15. Patches of a white powder had formed in the gutters of the houses.
16. An invisible enemy had silenced the sounds of life.
17. The enemy was the thoughtlessness of human beings.
18. Their poisons kill the natural life around us.
19. The voices of spring are dead in many places.
20. Rachel Carson gave us her thoughts in *Silent Spring*.

S3 ADAPTING THE SIMPLE SENTENCE

Study simple ways to adapt the basic sentence.

If we needed language only to report simple facts, the basic sentence patterns would serve us well. We would use them to say things like these:

> Father has boiled a chicken.
> The soup is ready.
> Potatoes are fattening.
> Aunt Bertha is a good cook.

But many of the things we say are not simple statements of fact. We *adapt* the simple statement patterns so that they can serve other purposes. For instance, we can change a statement so that it becomes a question or a request. Here are some of the things we do to adapt or adjust the simple sentence:

(1) We may **rearrange** *the parts of a sentence:*

SIMPLE: |Jim| (was) late.
ADAPTED: (Was) |Jim| late?

(2) We may **leave out** *parts of a sentence:*

SIMPLE: |You will| write a letter.
ADAPTED: Write a letter!

(3) We may **add** *new parts to a sentence:*

SIMPLE: The officials canceled the game.
ADAPTED: The game |was| canceled |by| the officials.

Sentences

The technical name for such adjustments or adaptations is **transformations.** When we "transform" a sentence, we change or reshuffle its parts to serve a different purpose.

S3a Requests and Questions

Study the way we change statements to requests and questions.

One of the most common ways we use language is to ask other people to do something. We make requests; we give instructions or directions. Another common use of language is to ask for information. We are constantly asking people "Why?" and "How?" Our language has simple mechanisms for turning statements into requests or questions:

(1) Many requests leave out the subject of the sentence and start with the verb. We can turn each of the following statements into a request by removing the subject and the helping verb:

STATEMENT	REQUEST
You will run away. →	Run away!
You will open the door. →	Open the door!
You should remain my friend. →	Remain my friend.
You should be nice. →	Be nice!

In writing, a strong request or an order is followed by an exclamation mark. The technical term for the request form of the verb is the **imperative.** Though the subject has been dropped from the original sentence, we usually know from the situation *who* is asked to do something. We say that "you" is understood as the subject of such a sentence.

(2) We can turn many statements into questions by making all or part of the verb trade places with the subject. If the verb is a single form of *be,* we can move it out from behind the subject and make it go out in front. *Is, am, are, was,* and *were* switch places with the subject in the following examples:

STATEMENT	QUESTION
It *is* raining. →	*Is* it raining?
I *am* right. →	*Am* I right?
The experiment *was* safe. →	*Was* the experiment safe?
The polls *were* wrong. →	*Were* the polls wrong?
You *are* all right. →	*Are* you all right?

Adapting the Simple Sentence

If one or more auxiliaries are part of the complete verb, the first auxiliary trades places with the subject:

The rain *has stopped*. →	*Has* the rain *stopped?*
Faith *can move* mountains. →	*Can* faith *move* mountains?
He *should have asked*. →	*Should* he *have asked?*

(3) Many questions use *a form of* do. If the verb has no auxiliary, we bring one into the sentence: *do, does,* or *did*. Then, the form of *do* trades places with the subject:

Statement:	The trains *leave* on time.
Step One:	The trains *do leave* on time.
Step Two:	*Do* the trains *leave* on time?
Statement:	He really *loves* her.
Step One:	He really *does love* her.
Step Two:	*Does* he really *love* her?
Statement:	The rain *stopped*.
Step One:	The rain *did stop*.
Step Two:	*Did* the rain *stop?*

EXERCISE 1

Which of the following *signs* use the ordinary statement patterns? Which are examples of the kind of request that has dropped the subject? After each number, write *S* (for "Statement") or *R* (for "Request").

1. FASTEN BELT BEFORE TAKEOFF
2. EMPLOYEES WILL USE SERVICE DOOR
3. TAKE THIS RAMP TO MAIN STREET
4. TWIST CAP FOR EASY REMOVAL
5. CUSTOMERS SHOULD WAIT IN LOUNGE
6. LEAVE CAMERAS AT DESK
7. MOVE TO UTAH AT OUR EXPENSE
8. DOUBLE YOUR READING SPEED IN ONE WEEK
9. MAIL THIS COUPON TODAY
10. LEFT LANE MUST EXIT
11. VISITORS MUST CHECK THEIR COATS AND BAGS
12. EXTINGUISH CIGARETTES AT THE ENTRANCE
13. USE OUR EASY CREDIT PLAN
14. GUESTS MAY USE THE POOL
15. KEEP QUIET
16. CLOSE GATE AT NIGHT
17. OUR TRAINED PERSONNEL WILL ASSIST YOU
18. PEDESTRIANS HAVE RIGHT OF WAY
19. SHUT MOTOR OFF IN GARAGE
20. INSERT COIN

Mail this coupon today.

Move to Utah at our expense

DOUBLE YOUR READING SPEED IN ONE WEEK!

Sentences

EXERCISE 2

Make the necessary changes in word order to turn each of the following statements into a question. Add a form of *do* where it is needed, but add no other words.

EXAMPLE: You know the way.
(Answer) *Do you know the way?*

1. The train was early again.
2. Lindbergh crossed the Atlantic alone.
3. The Smiths have always lived here.
4. A President needs a majority in Congress.
5. The police should arrest suspicious characters.
6. They sent you the right books.
7. Al Capone died in bed.
8. Eighteen-year-olds have the vote.
9. Newspapers print only the bad news.
10. These mushrooms are poisonous.
11. Einstein had lived in Germany.
12. The aborigines are the original inhabitants.
13. Rats make good pets.
14. The results of the operation will be known soon.
15. He would have made a good President.
16. The price includes the sales tax.
17. The post office is closed on Saturdays.
18. The people in Brazil speak Portuguese.
19. The museum will be open during the holidays.
20. They understood the instructions.

S3b The Passive

Study the way we change an active sentence to a passive sentence.

We call a sentence a **passive** sentence when its subject is not "doing" anything. Instead, things *happen* to the subject. A passive person is someone who does not act. Someone who is passive lets things happen. In a passive sentence, the subject is acted upon instead of active:

ACTIVE: The police caught up with the motorist.
PASSIVE: The driver was given a ticket.

ACTIVE: A big sign warned the hikers.
PASSIVE: Trespassers would be prosecuted.

We can turn an active into a passive sentence by going through the following steps:

(1) The object of the original sentence becomes the subject of the new sentence. We turn the usual order of subject and

Adapting the Simple Sentence

object around; subject and object trade places. We put *by* in front of the original subject:

ACTIVE: Tom caught the ball.
PASSIVE: The ball _____ *by* Tom.

ACTIVE: Applause interrupted her speech.
PASSIVE: Her speech _____ *by* applause.

(2) We change the verb to its passive form. The passive forms of a verb include a form of *be* followed by the form of the verb that we normally use after *have: was stolen, could be changed, had been broken, will be caught, were seen.*

PASSIVE: The ball *was caught* by Tom.
PASSIVE: Her speech *was interrupted* by applause.

(3) We sometimes omit the original subject altogether. In the short passive, the original subject has been left out.

SHORT PASSIVE: The ball was caught.
SHORT PASSIVE: Her speech was interrupted.

We often use the short passive when whoever performed the action is unimportant or unknown:

PASSIVE: The train was delayed.
(We may not know *what* caused the delay.)

PASSIVE: Several American Presidents have been assassinated.
(The victims are more important than the assassins.)

When we start from the S–V–IO–O pattern, two passives are possible, depending on which object we pull out in front:

ACTIVE: My uncle left the family a fortune.
FIRST PASSIVE: *The family* was left a fortune by my uncle.
SECOND PASSIVE: *A fortune* was left the family by my uncle.

Note: The passive highlights the target of the action:

PASSIVE: *Slaves* were often separated from their families by slave traders. (Our sympathy centers on the slaves.)

But when *who or what* did something seems the most important part of the sentence, it may then be better to go back to the original active statement:

WEAK PASSIVE: Many crimes were committed by Jim McCracken.
BETTER: *Jim McCracken* committed many crimes.

WEAK PASSIVE: The complaints will be investigated by the principal.
BETTER: *The principal* will investigate the complaints.

Sentences

EXERCISE 1

A. Change each of the following from active to passive. Write down the complete passive each time. If a sentence has two objects, write down *both* possible passives.

1. An earthquake leveled the town.
2. The government ran the trains.
3. A special crew will do the repairs.
4. Strong winds had damaged the antenna.
5. The police offered the highjackers safe conduct.
6. Millions have read his books.
7. The new management has spent millions on improvements.
8. The new government granted political prisoners an amnesty.
9. Many countries banned DDT.
10. A special ceremony could have honored the winners.

B. Change each of the following from passive to active.

11. The play was booed by the disappointed audience.
12. The runner-up should have been picked by the judges.
13. The campsite was prepared by our tired little group.
14. The tickets will be sold by local merchants.
15. Many complaints have been received by the principal.
16. The crime is being investigated by the local police.
17. The sidewalk was swept by my sister and brother.
18. Special favors had been granted his relatives by the mayor.
19. A special meeting has been announced by the troop leader.
20. The operation will be performed by a specialist.

EXERCISE 2

Which of the following sentences are active? Which are passive? Write *A* for active or *P* for passive after the number of each sentence. (Reconstruct in class the basic pattern from which each passive was made.)

EXAMPLE: Stories were told by ancient storytellers.

(Answer) P
          Ancient storytellers told stories.
          (S–V–O)

1. An Apache tribe was threatened by savage animals.
2. Hunters were trampled by a giant elk.
3. Children were attacked by huge eagles.
4. The tribe prayed for help.
5. A deliverer was appointed by the gods.
6. His arrows had been given him by the wife of the sun.
7. A gopher offered his help against the elk.
8. He gnawed the hair from a spot on its hide.

Adapting the Simple Sentence

S3b

9. The bare spot marked the heart of the animal.
10. The elk was mortally wounded by an arrow.
11. The arrow had been carefully aimed.
12. The hero escaped through a tunnel.
13. The tunnel had been burrowed by the gopher.
14. The dying elk plowed up the earth with his antlers.
15. Next the hero was carried away by a giant eagle.
16. He was dropped into the nest.
17. He beat the young eagles with the antlers of the dead elk.
18. Their growth was stunted by the assault.
19. People would be protected from their attacks.
20. The story of the deliverer was told by the Apache.

UNIT REVIEW EXERCISE

Which of the following are ordinary statements? Write *S* after the number of each statement that is an active sentence and follows one of the simple sentence patterns. In which of the following has a simple sentence been adapted to produce a request, a question, or a passive sentence? For each such adapted sentence, write down the original statement from which it was adapted.

EXAMPLE: Did you recognize the face?
(Answer)   *You recognized the face.*

1. The Cherokees started their long trek.
2. The ball was hit by the player.
3. Did he apologize for his mistake?
4. *Black Boy* was written by Richard Wright.
5. Joel had been sent on a fool's errand by a prankster.
6. The neighbors had grown the tulips in their own garden.
7. The demonstrators protested against the new airport.
8. Wrong directions were given the boys by the police officer.
9. Have her parents changed their minds about John?
10. California was first settled by Spaniards.
11. My aunt always sends me long letters.
12. The torch was brought to the stadium by a chain of runners.
13. Drive carefully on the far right side of the street.
14. Does Puerto Rico really mean "rich port"?
15. Talk during lunch was not allowed by the rules.
16. The French people of Quebec love their traditional language.
17. Can different races live together in peace?
18. The chiefs signed the treaties in good faith.
19. Write a letter to your representative.
20. Always look in the rearview mirror first.

Sentences

S4 BUILDING COMBINED SENTENCES

Combine several related statements in a larger sentence.

Often, two statements are closely related. We frequently combine two such statements, each with its own subject and verb, in a larger sentence. When we combine two statements in a larger sentence, we call them **clauses.** The words that help us join the two statements are **connectives,** words like *and, but, if, because,* and *although.*

In each of the following combined sentences, a familiar connective joins two clauses:

The guard opened the gate, *and* the truck drove through.
Pat was our treasurer, *but* she resigned.
We lost the fish *because* the hook was too small.

Connectives build sentences that say more than one thing at a time. They show how two ideas go together.

PREVIEW EXERCISE

Why do we need combined sentences? We combine two statements when the information in one of them would not really be complete. We need the second statement to help people see the whole picture. Fill in material that would help complete the second statement in each of the following combined sentences.

1. Sharks are fish, but whales _____.
2. Communities build bicycle paths so that _____.
3. Lumber companies plant seedlings after the trees _____.
4. The Aztecs were people who _____.
5. A coach changes pitchers when the other team _____.
6. Athletes may be disqualified because they _____.
7. Ordinary tapes record sound, and videotapes _____.
8. In many countries, people bow when _____.
9. Teenagers often ask why they _____.
10. The jury could not agree, so the accused _____.
11. Many people like big cars, although _____.
12. Vandals are people who _____.
13. German shepherds are dogs that _____.
14. A store will refund your money if _____.
15. Nominees are people who _____.
16. Young people are minors until they _____.
17. Student drivers learn how they should _____.
18. Many Canadians speak English, but many others _____.
19. Cars will not start unless _____.
20. Floods happen when _____.

110

Building Combined Sentences

Build combined sentences through coordination.

S4a
How Coordination Builds Sentences

Railroad workers use the couplings at each end of a railroad car to hook up two boxcars as part of a train. People putting sentences together use connectives to hook up related ideas as part of a larger train of thought. The simplest connectives are words like *and, but, for, or, yet,* and *so.* These are **coordinating** connectives, or **coordinators** for short. When two teams of rescuers coordinate efforts, they work together so that their efforts will add up. Coordinators make the parts they join add up.

The coordinator shows us the relationship between the two clauses. It shows *how* they fit together:

(1) **ADDITION.** *And* tells us: "Here is something else of the same kind, or along the same line."

He walked out, *and* she followed him.
The tables were grimy, *and* the doughnuts were stale.

(2) **CONTRAST.** *But* and *yet* tell us: "This points *the other way.*"

The building had been condemned, *but* we used it anyway.
She is often mean to me, *yet* I love her very much.

(3) **EXPLANATION.** *For* tells us: "This will help you understand why."

We ignored the forecast, *for* it was often wrong.
We rushed to the store, *for* prices had been slashed.

(4) **RESULT.** *So* tells us: "The following happened as a result."

He wanted the job, *so* he cut his hair.
His father had died, *so* he lived with an uncle.

(5) **CHOICE.** *Or* gives us a choice.

May I go now, *or* do you need my help?
Open the door, *or* shut the engine off.

Compared with other connectives, a coordinator joins two clauses loosely. We say that the two clauses are joined but **independent.** Each *could* stand by itself. No permanent changes are made in either statement. Though typically there is a comma between the two clauses, there *could* be a period.

For punctuation with coordinators, see M2a.

111

Sentences

EXERCISE 1

In each of the following, complete the second statement. Make sure you fill in at least a verb. The result will be two independent clauses joined by a coordinator. (On a separate sheet of paper, write your complete second clause after the number of the sentence.)

1. Reporters gather news, *and* editors ⎯⎯⎯⎯⎯⎯⎯⎯.
2. Architects design buildings, *and* contractors ⎯⎯⎯⎯⎯⎯⎯⎯.
3. Owls are birds, *but* bats ⎯⎯⎯⎯⎯⎯⎯⎯.
4. Burglaries are common, *so* people ⎯⎯⎯⎯⎯⎯⎯⎯.
5. Judges may jail an offender, *or* they ⎯⎯⎯⎯⎯⎯⎯⎯.
6. Einstein became famous, *for* he ⎯⎯⎯⎯⎯⎯⎯⎯.
7. Mars has an atmosphere, *but* it ⎯⎯⎯⎯⎯⎯⎯⎯.
8. The ground is frozen, *yet* Eskimos ⎯⎯⎯⎯⎯⎯⎯⎯.
9. Smallpox was a common disease, *so* doctors ⎯⎯⎯⎯⎯⎯⎯⎯.
10. The immigrants stayed in New York, *or* they ⎯⎯⎯⎯⎯⎯⎯⎯.

EXERCISE 2

Join the sentences in each of the following pairs. Each time use a coordinator to hook up the two statements in a larger combined sentence. *Which coordinator* would fit best in each pair? (Write your combined sentences on a separate sheet of paper.)

1. A myth is a story about the gods.
   It may also be a story about a hero.
2. One story may describe the creation of the world.
   Another story may explain the origin of fire.
3. These stories are often obscure.
   They go back to very early times.
4. Many tribes told their myths only by word of mouth.
   The Greeks wrote them down.
5. The Greek gods were immortal.
   They quarreled like human beings.
6. Zeus was the king of the gods.
   Hera was his wife.
7. The Greeks told stories about the origin of humankind.
   These stories did not agree.
8. People emerged from the water.
   They were born of Mother Earth.
9. In a different story the gods created people.
   They created the animals at the same time.
10. They gave the animals strength.
    They gave them courage.
11. Little remained for humanity.
    The best gifts had already been granted.

S4a Building Combined Sentences

12. Prometheus was sorry for us.
    He offered help.
13. He lit a torch.
    His torch brought fire to earth.
14. Human beings became the masters of the earth.
    Fire frightened the strongest animals.
15. Zeus was very angry.
    He punished Prometheus cruelly.

EXERCISE 3

Coordinators do not always join two complete clauses. They may also join parts *within* a single clause. After the number of each of the following sentences, write *Yes* if the coordinator joins two clauses. Write *No* if the coordinator joins parts of one clause. Each time, write down the coordinator in parentheses.

EXAMPLE: The music had stopped, and we changed the record.
(Answer) *Yes (and)*

1. We hurried to the station, but the train had left.
2. Oil and truth never drown. (Jamaican proverb)
3. We rang the bell, and a stranger came to the door.
4. Women and elephants never forget. (Dorothy Parker)
5. It was cold in the living room, so I did my homework in the kitchen.
6. Their voices were soft and gentle.
7. You shall know the truth, and the truth shall make you free. (New Testament)
8. I never forget a face, but in your case I will make an exception.
9. The outfit was perfect but very expensive.
10. Blessed are the meek, for they shall inherit the earth. (New Testament)
11. We were running hard but still falling behind.
12. They asked for shorter assignments or more time.
13. Weeping may endure for a night, but joy comes in the morning. (Old Testament)
14. A neighbor may report a fire, or a passing motorist may notice it first.
15. A smile or a friendly word can work wonders.
16. The temperature was rising, so the ice was becoming treacherous.
17. My brothers cleaned the room and vacuumed the rug.
18. We had only one job, yet dozens of people applied.
19. She stated her complaints politely but firmly.
20. A shot rang out, and thousands of birds rose into the air.

Sentences

S4b
How Subordination Builds Sentences

Build combined sentences through subordination.

When we hook a trailer onto the family car, we know that the trailer could not do without the car. It depends on the car for its usefulness. **Subordinating** connectives, or **subordinators,** hook a second statement to the first the way we hook a trailer to the family car. Something is subordinate when something else ranks higher in authority or in importance. When a subordinator hooks a second statement to the first, the first one becomes the **main** clause. The second becomes the **dependent** clause.

Typical subordinators are *if, when, while, because,* and *although*. They help us answer questions that might arise in the reader's or the listener's mind:

SIMPLE: The man with a new idea is a crank.
(But what if the new idea succeeds?)
COMBINED: The man with a new idea is a crank *until the idea succeeds*. (Mark Twain)

SIMPLE: Nero fiddled.
(What's wrong with that?)
COMBINED: Nero fiddled *while Rome burned*.

SIMPLE: The nobles lived in luxury.
(But what about the peasants?)
COMBINED: The nobles lived in luxury, *although the peasants were starving*.

Subordinators help us show almost every possible connection between two related ideas. They help us answer questions like when, where, how, why, and on what condition:

(1) **TIME:** *after, as, before, when, whenever, while, since, until*

Before he took the exam, he had a good night's sleep.
I haven't seen you since you were a little girl.

(2) **PLACE:** *where, wherever*

They are going where the action is.
Kathy brings joy wherever she goes.

(3) **MANNER:** *as, as if*

She did the job as she was told.
Carla walked into the room as if she were a queen.

Building Combined Sentences

(4) **CAUSE:** *because, as, since*

The tribes migrated because the drought was killing their herds.
Since you are under eighteen, you need your parents' consent.

(5) **CONDITION:** *if, unless*

The radiator boils over if you idle the motor.
The house will be sold unless we raise the cash.

(6) **CONTRAST:** *although, though*

We started across the ice, though visibility was poor.
Although the rules forbid it, we will make an exception.

(7) **PURPOSE:** *so that*

He asked for silence so that the speaker could be heard.

As these examples show, subordinators start clauses that give us the same kind of information as adverbs that tell us how, when, or where. We therefore call such clauses **adverbial** clauses. Remember:

• An adverbial clause can *switch places* with the main clause. The dependent clause then *precedes* the main clause. Here are examples with the dependent clause first:

Until the idea succeeds, the man with a new idea is a crank.
While Rome burned, Nero fiddled.
Although the peasants were starving, the nobles lived in luxury.

You can use this "switch-the-clause" test as a way of telling subordinators apart from coordinators. The two clauses joined by a coordinator cannot be switched:

RIGHT ORDER: He insulted the police, *so they arrested him.*
WRONG ORDER: *So they arrested him,* he insulted the police.

• Some subordinators can be used *only* as subordinators. But words like *before* and *after* may be either subordinators or prepositions. They are subordinators when they are followed by full sentences. They are prepositions when they are followed by something *less* than full sentence patterns —a word or a phrase:

SUBORDINATOR: He talked to us *before the meeting started.*
PREPOSITION: He talked to us *before the meeting.*
SUBORDINATOR: The coach resigned *after the game was canceled.*
PREPOSITION: The coach resigned *after the game.*

For punctuation with subordinators, see M2c.

Sentences

EXERCISE 1 Complete the following sentences. Each time, add a clause with at least its own subject and verb. Each time the result will be a main clause followed by an adverbial clause. (Write your complete adverbial clause after the number of the sentence.)

1. People climb mountains because _____ .
2. A player is a natural for basketball if _____ .
3. Champions often endorse commercial products after _____ .
4. A referee may stop a fight when _____ .
5. Coaches ask for time out so that _____ .
6. The crowd at a football game will be quiet until _____ .
7. The second string sits on the bench while _____ .
8. Swimmers have little chance in competition unless _____ .
9. Soccer was little known in this country, although _____ .
10. People in Japan love baseball as if _____ .

EXERCISE 2 After the number of each sentence, write a subordinator for the blank space. (Discuss in class *other* possible subordinators that might fit the same space.)

1. We were followed by a secret agent _____ we went.
2. We will stay outside the cave _____ you come with us.
3. He tightened our bonds _____ we could not flee.
4. _____ the tribe had warned him, Aaron entered the forbidden city.
5. He held them as prisoners _____ the ransom was paid.
6. He escaped his enemies _____ he designed masterful disguises.
7. The onlookers screamed _____ the door gave way.
8. The exhausted Ahmed slept _____ his trusted friend kept watch.
9. We face a terrible fate _____ our plans are discovered.
10. We continued our exhausting march _____ our guide had deserted us.
11. He cleaned his weapons with care _____ he started on his journey.
12. She walked down the dark street _____ she feared no danger.
13. They wore gloves _____ their hands would leave no fingerprints.
14. _____ the flames spread, panicky pilgrims rushed through the gates.
15. _____ he became a fan of adventure stories, Cyril saw shadowy figures everywhere.

Building Combined Sentences

LANGUAGE IN ACTION

HOW CATS BRING GOOD LUCK

After the number of each sentence, first write the connective. Then write *Co* or *Sub* to indicate whether the connective is a coordinator or a subordinator.

1. You will have good luck after a cat follows you home.
2. You should never cut a baby's fingernails, for the child will become a thief.
3. The weather will turn bad unless you clear your plate.
4. If you plow on Good Friday, the ground will bleed.
5. Bring an old broom when you move into a new house.
6. You shook out the tablecloth after sunset, so you will never marry.
7. Clean the table at night, or the children will sleep badly.
8. Your tongue is sore because you have told a lie.
9. When your lips itch, someone is slandering you.
10. If three girls look into a mirror, the oldest marries first.
11. You sweep a broom over your husband's feet, and he will run off.
12. When you put on shoes, put your right shoe on first.
13. You may leave on a trip with itchy feet, but the trip will be unlucky.
14. Although a chimney sweep brings good luck, you should never walk under his ladder.
15. A girl will turn into a boy if she kisses her toes.

EXERCISE 3

Look at the italicized word in each of the following sentences. Write *Sub* after the number of the sentence if the word is used as a subordinator. Write *Prep* if it is used as a preposition.

1. We stayed *until* the party ended.
2. His friends had waited for him *since* early morning.
3. We blew out the candles *before* we went to sleep.
4. The coach always gave them a long talk *before* an important game.
5. The population had dwindled *since* the sawmill closed down.
6. The company owned the machines *until* the last payment.
7. He arrived in town *after* a scary journey through the desert.
8. Jim had signed on *as* our new plant manager.
9. The crew looked on helplessly *as* the tent collapsed.
10. The suspect complained to the mayor *after* her car was searched.

S4c
How Relative Clauses Build Sentences

Build combined sentences using relative clauses.

Relative clauses help us work information into a sentence in many different ways. Look at the way information has been added to the following statements. Each of the clauses starting with *who, which,* or *that* is a **relative clause:**

BARE: The men escaped.
COMPLETE: The men *who robbed the train* escaped.

BARE: The photograph showed a friend.
COMPLETE: The photograph *that he lost* showed a friend.
The photograph, *which she kept under her pillow,* showed a friend.

Who (whose, whom), which, and *that* are **relative pronouns.** They serve a double function. Like other connectives, they help us join two clauses in a larger sentence. But, at the same time, they work like pronouns. They take the place of a noun. *Who* substitutes for a person. *Which* substitutes for a thing or idea. *That* may take the place of either.

Look at the way the two statements in each of the following pairs are combined. The two statements in each pair *share* a noun. The relative pronoun takes the place of the shared noun in the added statement:

STATEMENT: We cheered *the girl*.
ADDED SOURCE: *The girl* won the race.
RESULT: We cheered the girl *who won the race*.

STATEMENT: I borrowed *the book*.
ADDED SOURCE: Everyone was reading *the book*.
RESULT: I borrowed the book *that everyone was reading*.

STATEMENT: *My uncle* is my favorite relative.
ADDED SOURCE: *My uncle* lives in Dayton.
RESULT: My uncle *who lives in Dayton* is my favorite relative.

Like the clauses introduced by a subordinator, relative clauses are dependent clauses. They cannot easily be unhooked from the main statement. They cannot normally stand by themselves.

FRAGMENT: Our schools need teachers. *Who know Spanish.*
COMPLETE: Our schools need teachers *who know Spanish.*

See M2c for punctuation of relative clauses.

S4c

Building Combined Sentences

Complete each of the following statements. For each statement, the material you fill in together with the relative pronoun that precedes it will make a complete relative clause.

EXERCISE 1

1. The American West fascinates people who _____ .
2. Fans all over the world know the expressions that _____ .
3. A posse is a group of people who _____ .
4. People who _____ are called outlaws.
5. A deputy is a person who _____ .
6. A ghost town is a town that _____ .
7. Prospectors look for ores that _____ .
8. Mines in the West yielded silver, which _____ .
9. Every town had a saloon in which _____ .
10. Every cowboy carried a Colt, which _____ .

Combine the two statements in each of the following pairs in a single larger sentence. Each time, turn the second statement into a relative clause. Be careful where you place each clause. Remember that sometimes a relative clause may have to be *inserted* into the first statement instead of simply following it. Read over the combined sentence to see if you have captured the sense of the original pair.

EXERCISE 2

1. The sheriff was talking to the woman.
   The woman had witnessed the accident.

2. The painting was a great treasure.
   The painting had been stolen.

3. The team had a perfect record.
   The team defeated us.

4. An English composer had written the song.
   She liked the song.

5. The gloves didn't fit her.
   She recently bought the gloves.

6. Miriam is a person.
   A person can be trusted.

7. *The Yearling* is a novel.
   The Yearling was written by Marjorie Kinnan Rawlings.

8. The man wants his money.
   The man is standing at the door.

9. We sent flowers to the children.
   The children were injured in the accident.

10. The truck spilled thousands of oranges onto the highway.
    The truck turned over.

Sentences

EXERCISE 3

Who, which, and *that* are relative pronouns. But they also have other uses. We use *who* and *which* to ask questions: *Who* called? *Which* side is up? We use *that* as a noun marker: Close *that* door. Which of the following sentences have a relative clause that starts with a relative pronoun? Write the relative clause after the number of each such sentence. Write *No* if the sentence does not have a relative clause.

EXAMPLE: The tracks that we saw in the snow looked fresh.
(Answer) *that we saw in the snow*

1. The bus that goes to the hospital does not stop here anymore.
2. Students who play the piano do finger exercises.
3. I had many friends whose parents were both working.
4. When the electricity goes off, whose fault is it?
5. The crowd, which had been cheering the champion, turned silent.
6. People who steal from a small grocery are seldom caught.
7. In an emergency, who will be in command?
8. You should take that escalator to the upper floors.
9. I am looking for the switch that turns off the fan.
10. Which bus goes past the auditorium?
11. They built a glider that could be pedaled like a bicycle.
12. She keeps hamsters, which make interesting pets.
13. The seats in that row are already reserved.
14. The people that rode the wagon looked starved.
15. In your opinion, who would make the better leader?
16. The seals on that island were safe from hunters.
17. The horse would throw off riders who seemed inexperienced.
18. The people in that family have very little in common.
19. The family whose mansion we visited had met a strange fate.
20. Bagels, which are popular in New York, are like doughnuts.

S4d
How Noun Clauses Build Sentences

Build combined sentences using noun clauses.

When we work a **noun clause** into a sentence, we do not simply add something to the original sentence. We take something out, and we replace it with something else. The noun clause fills a slot that would normally be filled by a noun:

NOUN:	She reported *the accident.*
NOUN CLAUSE:	She reported *what had happened.*
NOUN:	I repeated *the information.*
NOUN CLAUSE:	I repeated *what I had learned.*
NOUN:	Linda knew *the place.*
NOUN CLAUSE:	Linda knew *where the family lived.*

S4d

Building Combined Sentences

Noun clauses fill in the missing information in a sentence like "Somebody said—what?" "Everyone knows—what?" They follow verbs like *say, know, tell, ask, report, wonder,* and *deny.* The noun clause itself often starts with a question word like *who* (whom), *what, where, when, why,* and *how.* These are then used as special connectives starting a noun clause:

The priest asked *why the door was open.*
Robert knew *when the store would close.*
My sister told me *who had called.*

That is often used as a relative pronoun. But it is also often used as a special connective starting a noun clause:

NOUN: The girl denied *the accusation.*
NOUN CLAUSE: The girl denied *that she knew the code.*

Like other clauses, each noun clause has its own subject and complete verb. Note that *who* and *what* can serve as the subject of the noun clause they start. Other noun clauses need their own subject after the connective.

EXERCISE 1

Fill in a noun clause to complete each of the following sentences. Write down your complete noun clause after the number of the sentence. Make sure your noun clause has its own subject and verb.

1. Columbus thought that _____.
2. A water witch tells us where _____.
3. Scientists have discovered that _____.
4. Manuals explain how _____.
5. People often wonder why _____.
6. Superstitious people believe that _____.
7. Birdwatchers know where _____.
8. Teachers know who _____.
9. Considerate people ask their guests what _____.
10. An encyclopedia can tell us when _____.

EXERCISE 2

Which of the sentences on the following page contain a noun clause? After the number of each such sentence, write the special connective that starts the noun clause. If there is no noun clause, write *No* after the number of the sentence.

EXAMPLE: Tell the judge what you saw.
(Answer) *what*

Sentences

1. We realized what had gone wrong.
2. The water in the reservoir had almost disappeared.
3. Dorothy knew where her aunt had hidden the will.
4. She would not tell us why the meeting had been canceled.
5. The coach gave us a long lecture after the game.
6. We wondered how the prisoner had escaped.
7. We were inside when the storm broke.
8. Manuel denied the rumors that we had heard.
9. Scientists had decided that the chemical was highly toxic.
10. Light from the stars travels through space for many years.
11. The owner announced that she was selling the ranch.
12. The police knew who had stolen the car.
13. The weather report had said that the skies would clear.
14. The witness could not remember what the letter said.
15. They described the unidentified objects that they had sighted.
16. You would never guess who won the award.
17. A young man had run from the building before the fire started.
18. The producer denied that the show was rigged.
19. The driver told us when the bus would leave.
20. The victim reported what had been stolen.

UNIT REVIEW EXERCISE

Study the following combined sentences. After the number of each sentence, put the right abbreviation:

Co — if two clauses are joined by a coordinator;
Sub — if two clauses are joined by a subordinator;
Rel — if two clauses are joined by a relative pronoun;
NC — if a special connective links a noun clause to the rest of the sentence.

EXAMPLE: People who like poetry remember Robert Frost.
(Answer) *Rel*

1. Many Americans live in cities, but they dream of a simpler life.
2. They like poets who write about life in the countryside.
3. Many readers remember that Robert Frost wrote about country life.
4. He wrote about tramps who pass by a farm in the springtime.
5. In another poem, he asked why people like fences.
6. Frost, who was perhaps our best-known poet, wrote poems about New England.
7. Although he lived in New England, he was born in San Francisco.
8. His parents admired Robert E. Lee, so they named their boy after the general.
9. When the father died, the mother took the boy to New Hampshire.

10. They came to the East because the father had wanted a New England burial.
11. The mother, who was a teacher, then stayed in New England.
12. When he finished school, young Robert gave the farewell address for his class.
13. He went on to college, but he did not stay long.
14. After he worked on a country newspaper, he taught school.
15. He discovered that the publishers did not like his poems.
16. He and his wife owned a farm until they left this country for England.
17. *A Boy's Will,* which was his first book of poems, was published in England.
18. Robert Frost returned to America after his poems made him famous.
19. He read his poems to many audiences, who loved the sound of his voice.
20. Many readers remember what his poems tell us about the sights and sounds of country life.

S5 EXPANDING OUR SENTENCE RESOURCES

Learn to draw on the full resources of the English sentence.

If we always used only the most familiar sentence machinery, we could make our sentences do many of the jobs that are necessary. But we would be using one plodding sentence after another. Much of the *real* potential of the English sentence would remain unused. The following sections encourage you to draw on the resources that give the English sentence its full range and variety. Study these resources. Experiment with them; learn to put them to good use.

S5a Using Infinitives

Study the many jobs infinitives can do in a sentence.

The **verbal** is a kind of all-purpose tool in our language. We all know the kind of pocketknife that has several different blades and other attachments. It can be used for cutting, chiseling, prying off bottle tops, pulling corks. Verbals can do many different jobs in a sentence. A verbal looks like a verb, and in some ways it acts like a verb. But at the same time it also acts like a modifier or a noun.

The most simple verbal is the *to* form. We produce this form by simply putting *to* in front of the plain form of a verb.

Sentences

The more technical name for the *to* form is the **infinitive.** All of the following are infinitives:

| to solve | to talk | to like | to look | to ask |
| to write | to speak | to throw | to do | to say |

The *to* forms are the most versatile of our verbals. They can do almost any job in a sentence—except that of a true verb:

(1) We can use infinitives to **replace** *major sentence parts.* They can take over almost all of the jobs usually done by nouns:

NOUN: *Blood* is thicker than *water.*
INFINITIVE: *To walk* is cheaper than *to ride.*

NOUN: His aunt taught him *the alphabet.*
INFINITIVE: His uncle taught him *to read.*

NOUN: *Complaints* were useless.
INFINITIVE: *To complain* was useless.

(2) We can use infinitives to **modify** *major sentence parts.* An infinitive may go with a noun and tell us more about the noun:

They were looking for a place to stay.

The thing to say was yes.

(3) An infinitive may go with a verb and tell us why:

He lied to save himself.

The waiter lingered to get a tip.

(4) An infinitive may go with an adjective:

The problem was impossible to solve.

The dogs were eager to get free.

Note: Often the infinitive in turn brings other materials along with it. It carries along its *own* object or its *own* modifier. The infinitive together with the material it brings along is called an **infinitive phrase.** Here are some more examples of infinitive phrases:

His mistake was *to move the king.*
The sleepers started *to stir in their beds.*
To fight off an angry bear is not easy.

Expanding Our Sentence Resources

S5a

FOR SENTENCE PRACTICE

IN THE FOOTSTEPS OF THE GREAT

Much of what we learn, we learn by *imitation*. We watch someone who knows how, and then we do likewise. Use each of the following as a model sentence. Each time, write a similar sentence on a topic of your choice. Use your own words, but follow the sentence structure of the original as closely as you can. Pay special attention to how the *to* forms are used in these model sentences. For each original, write *two* different imitations.

1. MODEL: All men by nature desire to know. (Aristotle)
   IMITATION: All animals by instinct try to survive.
   YOUR TURN: _____

2. MODEL: Life has loveliness to sell. (Sara Teasdale)
   IMITATION: Bankers have money to loan.
   YOUR TURN: _____

3. MODEL: Fools rush in where angels fear to tread. (Alexander Pope)
   IMITATION: Rock music drowns out what parents have to say.
   YOUR TURN: _____

EXERCISE 1

How would you complete each of the following statements? Each time, fill in a single word or a group of words. Together with the infinitive marker *to*, the result will be an infinitive or an infinitive phrase. (Write on a separate sheet of paper.)

1. At 32 degrees, water begins to _____.
2. Portable radios are easy to _____.
3. We use insecticides to _____.
4. Beavers look for places to _____.
5. We vaccinate people to _____.
6. A radiologist's job is to _____.
7. Edible roots are fit to _____.
8. Eligible bachelors are expected to _____.
9. Suffrage is the right to _____.
10. To disenfranchise somebody means to _____.
11. To _____ is human.
12. Radar is one way to _____.
13. Bicycling is a good way to _____.
14. Stowaways try to _____.
15. A hangar is a place to _____.

Sentences

16. If there was no bridge across a river, travelers had to _____.
17. An anniversary is something to _____.
18. A reconditioned engine is ready to _____.
19. Whales surface to _____.
20. Bats leave their caves to _____.

EXERCISE 2

Can you see how the infinitives do their work in the following sentences? Where does the *to* form *take the place* of a noun? (Write *N* after the number of the sentence.) Where does the *to* form *modify* a noun or another sentence part? (Write *Mod* after the number of the sentence.)

1. To complain was useless.
2. Toddlers are learning to walk.
3. It was a day to remember.
4. Laura taught her parrot to talk.
5. My favorite dishes are easy to cook.
6. The person to see is the supervisor.
7. The boys were ready to leave.
8. To do his duty was his only aim.
9. The lions taught their cubs to hunt.
10. To establish law and order was not easy in frontier towns.
11. The time to watch television is later.
12. We need a law to stimulate foreign trade.
13. The safe method is to put all promises in writing.
14. To give up now would be foolish.
15. Good students are always eager to learn.
16. The astronauts remained quiet to conserve oxygen.
17. The carrier came to deliver the letter.
18. He was happy to announce the winner.
19. To criticize is easy.
20. The family refused to vacate the building.

EASY TO BUY ❀ EASY TO COOK ❀ EASY TO DIGEST

EXERCISE 3

Use the following sentence frames for a sentence-stretching exercise. Fill in *five* things for each frame. Start with a simple infinitive to fill the blank in the sentence frame. The next four times, stretch the sentence frame by adding longer (and longer) infinitive phrases.

FRAME: To _____ takes patience.
EXAMPLES: *To wait* takes patience.
To thread a needle takes patience.
To build a ship in a bottle takes patience.
To *learn to speak a Chinese dialect* takes patience.

Expanding Our Sentence Resources

1. To _____ takes courage.
2. To _____ takes money.
3. To _____ is only human nature.
4. To _____ is boring.
5. To _____ is dangerous.

Study the way participles help us build sentences.

S5b
Using Participles

The *to* form is not the only way we can help a verb perform other duties in a sentence. Two other verb forms are also used as **verbals**—as forms derived from verbs but used for other purposes. The first of these forms always ends in *–ing*. We can simply call it the *–ing* form: *asking, looking, talking*. The second form is the one that fits in after *have*. It often ends in *–ed* or *–en:* had *looked,* has *spoken,* have *written*. We can call the second form the *–en* form. (It does not always actually end in *–en*. It just fits in where forms like *spoken* and *written* also fit in.)

A more technical term for *–ing* forms and *–en* forms is **participles**. The *–ing* form is called the *present* participle. The *–en* form is called the *past* participle. Can you tell from the following sentence why one is labeled *present* and the other *past?*

His *trembling* fingers picked up the *broken* pieces.
We saw the *flying* banners of the *defeated* army.
Her *scheming* friends hid the *stolen* goods.

Here are the three different verbals for several common English verbs:

INFINITIVE	PRESENT PARTICIPLE	PAST PARTICIPLE
to solve	solving	solved
to write	writing	written
to talk	talking	talked
to speak	speaking	spoken
to like	liking	liked
to throw	throwing	thrown
to look	looking	looked
to do	doing	done
to ask	asking	asked
to say	saying	said

In the ordinary simple sentence, the *–ing* form and the *–en* form are used as *part* of the complete verb. When they

Sentences

are so used, they lean on auxiliary verbs. They need an auxiliary like *am* or *have* before they can make a complete statement as a complete verb:

I *am solving* the problem.
Sue *is writing* a letter.
My parents *were talking* to the principal.

I *have solved* the problem.
Sue *has written* a letter.
My parents *have talked* to the principal.

We can lift such *–ing* or *–en* forms out of their usual place after an auxiliary, or helping, verb. We can then use them to add information to another sentence:

STATEMENT: The waves battered the coast.
ADDED SOURCE: The waves were *roaring*.
RESULT: The *roaring* waves battered the coast.

STATEMENT: The boy replaced the window.
ADDED SOURCE: The window *had been broken*.
RESULT: The boy replaced the *broken* window.

STATEMENT: The entertainer bowed to the audience.
ADDED SOURCE: The audience *is applauding*.
RESULT: The entertainer bowed to the *applauding* audience.

Notice that the verbal that we have lifted out of the added source comes into the other sentence as a modifier:

The roaring waves battered the coast.

The entertainer bowed to the applauding audience.

Participles do not always come into a sentence as single words. Often, the participle brings along a modifier or an object of its own. It brings along other material. The participle together with the material it carries along is called a **participial phrase:**

STATEMENT: The person was the music teacher.
ADDED SOURCE: The person *was standing at the door*.
RESULT: The person *standing at the door* was the music teacher.

STATEMENT: We removed the boxes.
ADDED SOURCE: The boxes *were blocking the hallway*.
RESULT: We removed the boxes *blocking the hallway*.

Expanding Our Sentence Resources

Note: The *–ing* form of the verb can be used to *replace* a noun. We then call it a **verbal noun**.

NOUN: *Sports* can be dangerous.
VERBAL NOUN: *Diving* can be dangerous.
NOUN: The club stopped *the sales*.
VERBAL NOUN: The club stopped *selling tickets*.

EXERCISE 1

Fill in the blank spaces in the following sentences. Start each one with an *–ing* form. Write *two* versions of each sentence, filling in a different participial phrase each time.

EXAMPLE: The man stepped out into the road, _____ing _____ .

(Answer)   The man stepped out into the road, *waving his arms excitedly at the approaching car.*

1. The Zulus attacked, _____ing _____ .
2. The rescue party found his body, _____ing _____ .
3. The picture showed the wild horses, _____ing _____ .
4. Martians emerged from the capsule, _____ing _____ .
5. The women had banded together, _____ing _____ .

EXERCISE 2

From the following pairs of sentences make single sentences containing participles or participial phrases. In each pair, make the first sentence the main statement and the second statement your added source.

1. The boys were afraid of the dark.
   The boys were whistling.
2. The trees were carried away.
   The trees had fallen.
3. She was interrupted by the telephone.
   The telephone was ringing.
4. The new tenant repairs watches.
   The watches were broken.
5. We watched the sun.
   The sun was sinking in the west.
6. The judge is very young.
   The judge is hearing the case.
7. The spectators were running from the bull.
   The bull was charging with lowered horns.
8. She was sitting by the window.
   She was thinking sad thoughts.
9. The songs were old favorites.
   The songs were sung by the quartet.

Sentences

10. The speech was the best.
    The speech was given by the principal.
11. The boys were held up in traffic.
    The boys were hurrying to catch a train.
12. The company hired thirty new workers.
    The company had been awarded the contract.
13. The captain spotted a trawler.
    The trawler was fishing about three miles to the west.
14. The college was established in the wilderness.
    The college was founded by the pioneers.
15. The plane was donated to a museum.
    The plane was flown by Lindbergh.
16. The town received aid from the government.
    The town had been hit by the tornado.
17. We never encountered the rain.
    The rain had been predicted.
18. The army retreated from the city.
    The army had been defeated.
19. Nancy was a member of the team.
    The team was winning.
20. The person is a good friend.
    The person is running the meeting.

EXERCISE 3

In each sentence, a participle or participial phrase is used as a modifier. Write the participle or phrase after its number.

1. The shaking boy had just come from the ocean.
2. We listened to the murmuring breezes.
3. The frightened thief ran off.
4. In the water, we saw a bent stick.
5. The man running after the bus is Tom's father.
6. The scout bitten by the snake was taken to the hospital.
7. Laughing, she waved at the boys.
8. Words spoken in anger are often regretted.
9. The lookout reported soldiers approaching the camp.
10. The committee voted for the plan suggested by the secretary.
11. The prisoner jumped from the moving train.
12. Torn pages littered the grounds.
13. He showed me a picture taken at the party.
14. The club, organized three years ago, doubled its membership.
15. The police chased the speeding car.
16. Working furiously, Sue finished the job.
17. The students looked with amazement at the leaning tower.
18. The critics called it a fascinating movie.
19. By 1750, Boston was an established city.
20. Joe was aware of the quickening beat of his heart.

Expanding Our Sentence Resources

S5c Using Appositives

Use the appositive to work added information into a sentence.

An **appositive** is an additional noun that is put next to one of the original nouns in a sentence. We simply put it there without any link. By just being there, it provides further information about the other noun. It *modifies* that noun.

Look at the way an appositive comes into each of the following sentences:

STATEMENT:	Rin-Tin-Tin was one of the first animal stars.
ADDED SOURCE:	Rin-Tin-Tin was *a dog*.
RESULT:	Rin-Tin-Tin, *a dog,* was one of the first animal stars.
STATEMENT:	James Carter was elected President.
ADDED SOURCE:	James Carter was *a former naval officer*.
RESULT:	James Carter, *a former naval officer,* was elected President.
STATEMENT:	They went up the Amazon.
ADDED SOURCE:	The Amazon *is the longest river in the world*.
RESULT:	They went up the Amazon, *the longest river in the world*.
STATEMENT:	Mark Twain told the story of Jim.
ADDED SOURCE:	Jim was *the runaway slave*.
RESULT:	Mark Twain told the story of Jim, *the runaway slave*.

In each of these examples, we have lifted a noun out of the second sentence. (Sometimes, we lift other material along with it.) We then insert this noun next to one of the original nouns. Usually, commas set the appositive off from the rest of the sentence. An appositive in the middle of a sentence is like a wedge inserted between the more basic sentence parts:

Her dog, *a collie,* barked all night.

Jim Greeley, *our mayor,* always has a friendly smile.

The appositive itself is often *in turn* modified by other material. The wedge inserted into the original sentence then becomes larger:

James Baldwin, *a black writer,* is well known in Europe.

The defect, *a crack in the metal,* was hardly noticeable.

Sentences

An appositive need not always be wedged in between other parts of a sentence. Sometimes the appositive appears at the very end of the sentence:

She had attended Columbia, *an Ivy League college.*

See M3a for punctuation of appositives.

EXERCISE 1

Below are ten pairs of sentences. Make a single sentence out of each pair by turning the second sentence into an appositive. Write the new sentence after the number of the pair.

EXAMPLE: Sherlock Holmes turned to Watson.
          Watson was his trusted assistant.
(Answer) *Sherlock Holmes turned to Watson, his trusted assistant.*

1. Her sister explained the will to us.
   Her sister was a lawyer.
2. Quincy fell asleep watching the late show.
   The show was an old movie.
3. John is the best player on our team.
   John is our defensive right halfback.
4. Mount McKinley is in Alaska.
   Mount McKinley is the highest peak in the United States.
5. Mrs. Martin called a meeting for Tuesday morning.
   Mrs. Martin is the new owner.
6. Thomas Dooley devoted his life to the unfortunate.
   Thomas Dooley was a retired naval officer.
7. Sam introduced us to his friend.
   His friend is a visitor from Hong Kong.
8. Buenos Aires is one of the largest cities in South America.
   Buenos Aires is the capital of Argentina.
9. Mr. Kurath was born in Austria.
   Mr. Kurath is a famous American linguist.
10. In London the cabdrivers speak Cockney.
    Cockney is a dialect not easily understood by Americans.

EXERCISE 2

What label, description, or explanation would you fill in to add information to each of the following sentences? Each word or group of words you fill in, together with the noun marker already provided, will be an appositive. Write your appositive after the number of the sentence.

EXAMPLE: Scientists are studying Venus, our _____.
(Answer) *our sister planet*

Expanding Our Sentence Resources

1. No life exists on the moon, a _____ .
2. The sun, a _____ , is too hot for living things.
3. Mars, a _____ , shows no reliable signs of life.
4. The Earth has a life-giving atmosphere, a _____ .
5. Oxygen, a _____ , is necessary for animals.
6. Carbon, a _____ , is necessary for plants.
7. Our earthly life forms, our _____ , would die on Venus.
8. Humans are looking for life in outer space, the _____ .
9. The astronauts, our _____ , will explore the universe.
10. Maybe there is life in the other galaxies, the _____ .

EXERCISE 3

Study the way appositives bring information into the following sentences. Write the complete appositive after the number of each sentence. Write *No* if the sentence does not contain an appositive.

1. Robin Hood, a famous outlaw, was the hero of many ballads.
2. With his friends, he lived in Sherwood Forest, his hiding place.
3. For many years, he hid from his old enemy, the sheriff.
4. In many countries, outlaws are among famous popular heroes.
5. The story of an outlaw often becomes a legend, a folk tale.
6. Martha Canary, a sharpshooter, was a real person.
7. Most people know only her nickname, Calamity Jane.
8. To cross her might produce a disastrous result, a calamity.
9. Ballads are not always about outlaws.
10. John Henry, the railroad worker, won a contest with a machine.
11. Ballads are often about a familiar figure, the jealous lover.
12. Another colorful figure, the gambler, may also play a role.
13. In the American West, many ballads told about life on the trail.
14. Often the cowboy was alone with his best friend, the horse.
15. The ballads of today are often sad songs about love.

UNIT REVIEW EXERCISE

What resources were used in the following to help build up a bare-bones sentence? After the number of each sentence, write *Inf* for infinitive, *Part* for participle, or *App* for appositive. Each of these may carry additional material.

1. Firefighters rescued people from the burning house.
2. He stood on his toes to catch a glimpse of the queen.
3. We staged only one play, a disaster.
4. Our mail carrier, a dreamy-eyed young man, was always late.
5. Barking at all comers, his huge dogs terrorized the neighborhood.
6. The archeologist patiently assembled the broken vase.
7. The candidate to watch is the son of the incumbent.
8. In July, she worked at Swan Lodge, a summer camp.

Sentences

9. Wally seemed eager to resume our friendship.
10. The man heckling the speaker was hustled out of the auditorium.
11. The water seeping through the canvas had spoiled our provisions.
12. He lay on the bed, staring at the ceiling.
13. She had been the first woman to fly a commercial plane.
14. Smiling politely, she turned down our request.
15. Eileen, our treasurer, explained the deficit.
16. Paul Bunyan, the lumberjack, was invented by a writer.
17. The courthouse was the first building to use nuclear energy.
18. We saw the Concorde, a supersonic plane.
19. Birds trapped by the oil littered the beaches.
20. Marcia knew the right number to call.

FOR FURTHER STUDY

THE EXCEPTION TO THE RULE

When we study language, our first question naturally is: "How are things *usually* done? What are the *routine* procedures that make our language work?" At the same time, we know that our language must be flexible enough to handle special problems and special cases. The following assignments explore some of these special cases.

ACTIVITY 1

In headlines, space is at a premium. The people who write headlines condense their messages as much as they can. Sometimes they omit *too much,* and we are lucky if we guess at the right meaning. Each message below could have two different meanings, depending on what we think has been omitted. For instance, we may not be sure whether the message is a statement or a request, or whether it gives us directions or a report. Write two *complete* versions of each message, filling in the sentence parts that would help us see the two possible meanings.

1. TEACHERS PAY UP
2. SHIP SAILS TODAY
3. POLICE ARRESTS CAUSE OF CONTROVERSY
4. MODEL DRESSES IN THE LIMELIGHT
5. SNOWMAN REMAINS A MYSTERY
6. PAPER DEMANDS CHANGE
7. PLANE DELAYS A NUISANCE
8. PLAN MOVES SLOWLY
9. AIR FORCE REJECTS CHARGE
10. SUPPORT INCREASES FOR FIRE FIGHTERS

ACTIVITY 2

If you were to list the words from a book page or a magazine page in four columns headed noun, verb, adjective, and adverb, several words would appear in more than one column. They do double (and perhaps triple) duty. They are versatile, like a person who teaches music during the day, drives a cab at night, and plays in a band on weekends.

In each of the following pairs, the same word is used twice. First it is used with a plural –s that says "more than one"—it is used as a noun. Then it is used with the ending –d (or –ed) that says "past time"—it is used as a verb:

NOUN: The citizens hid *arms* in their houses.
VERB: The citizens *armed* themselves.

NOUN: Mother stacked the *cans* on the shelf.
VERB: Mother *canned* her own tomatoes.

Look at the italicized double-duty words in the following sentences. If the word is used as a noun, write another short sentence in which the word is used with the –d (or –ed) ending as a verb. If the word is used as a verb, write another short sentence in which the word is used with the plural –s (or –es), as a noun.

1. We could see the *light* from his window.
2. You should *book* your passage now.
3. Our *climbs* were always eventful.
4. The sentries would *sound* the alarm.
5. My *alarm* woke up the neighbors.
6. The detective *noticed* a suspicious stain.
7. The machine could *duplicate* documents exactly.
8. The Wright brothers *designed* a flying machine.
9. We received the *supplements* to the dictionary.
10. Olive trees will *flourish* in a warm climate.

ACTIVITY 3

The ordinary English noun fits in after the noun markers *a* (or *an*) and *the*. Either one of these articles could fill the blanks in sentences like the following:

_____ girl slowly put _____ cup on _____ table.
_____ hawk circled over _____ field.
_____ ship was tied up at _____ pier.

Sentences

But in some situations we find that only *one* of these articles is really right in front of a noun—or *neither* of them.

After the number of each of the following sentences, write *one*:

the/*a*   if either would fit;
the   if required;
a   if required;
No   if there should be no article.

1. We saw _____ car turn into the driveway.
2. Modern scientists believe that our earth circles around _____ Sun.
3. His grandfather had gone down with _____ *Titanic*, a luxury ocean liner.
4. The two exhausted and hungry men were finally rescued by _____ freighter.
5. Her father had been an air force sergeant in _____ Germany.
6. The Japanese planes torpedoed _____ battleship.
7. Japanese planes sank _____ *Arizona*.
8. They were planning a trip to _____ Japan.
9. Americans were in a race to _____ moon with the Russians.
10. The expedition reached _____ North Pole after incredible hardships.
11. Day after day the battered but sturdy ship plowed through _____ water.
12. We piled into our ancient car and crossed the border into _____ Arizona.
13. Several of the guards were assigned to keep an eye on _____ *Mona Lisa*.
14. At weddings, he always kissed _____ bride.
15. France exports wines to the United States and to _____ Canada.
16. The Air Force always paid the fares for both the serviceman and _____ wife.
17. We spent hours looking for _____ well.
18. The Russians had just sent an unmanned spacecraft to _____ Mars.
19. He had personally shaken hands with _____ Queen Elizabeth.
20. The ship tied up at the pier was _____ *Queen Elizabeth*.

ACTIVITY 4

Not *all* words that have the −*ly* ending are adverbs. At least *some* words with the −*ly* ending are adjectives. After the number of each sentence, write *Adv* if the italicized word is an adverb. Write *Adj* if the italicized word is an adjective. As you have seen, adverbs can usually be made by adding −*ly* to an adjective. In the examples below, what has the −*ly* been added to in order to make an *adjective* instead?

1. A *friendly* police officer knocked at the door.
2. My father *firmly* answered "No."
3. Alice encountered a *cowardly* lion.
4. Odysseus *foolishly* opened the sack full of winds.
5. His ships were *immediately* blown out to sea.
6. The *manly* Odysseus encountered many misfortunes.
7. A *saintly* hermit lived in the forest.
8. The ship finished its *leisurely* trip.
9. Odysseus *suddenly* felt very sleepy.
10. The gas company had sent us our *monthly* bill.

Bonus: How many *additional* adjectives can you find that use the −*ly* ending? Try to find additional words that would fit into a frame like the following:

a very _____ly person   a very _____ly thing

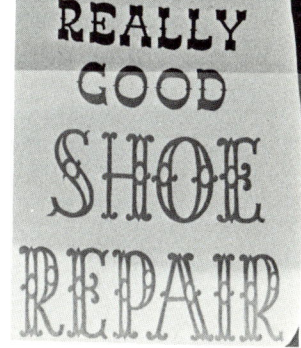

ACTIVITY 5

The five most common basic sentence patterns are S−V, S−V−O, S−LV−N, S−LV−Adj, and S−V−IO−O. Have you encountered special cases that do not follow one of these basic models? Among the following sentences, find all those that do not fit one of the five basic patterns. What is the pattern they share? Describe the new pattern you discover in as much detail as you can.

1. His parents had bought a new house.
2. Elmwood Park was an integrated neighborhood.
3. Uncle Joe always gave the family free advice.
4. Aunt Rachel had called my father a liar.
5. We elected Muriel treasurer.
6. Refreshments were free.
7. The whole trip had been a disaster.
8. We considered his behavior a disgrace.
9. The opposition called the election a farce.
10. Grandmother always sent the children a Christmas parcel.

Sentences

11. The club made John secretary.
12. The men were hunting bear in Alaska.
13. The leader should set us an example.
14. We painted the shutters.
15. The principal called the incident an exception.
16. We are changing the rules.
17. The court freed the prisoner.
18. White musicians adapted the blues.
19. The President named his friend Secretary of War.
20. The boy scout called the lady a taxi.

ACTIVITY 6

Our language makes many words do double duty. Words used as coordinators also have *other,* special uses. In which of the following sentences are *but, for, so,* and *yet* being used as coordinating connectives? (Write *Co* after the number of each such sentence.) In which do the words have other uses? (Write *No* after the number of each sentence.)

In these sample sentences, count words as coordinators only if they were used to connect two related sentences, each with its own subject and verb. Can you discover for yourself what the other uses of these words are?

1. Everyone left the class *but* the boys in back of the room.
2. Ned bought a new knife, *for* he had broken the blade on his old one.
3. Leonore had never looked *so* happy.
4. Her mother called her, *so* she stopped reading.
5. Uncle Tim bought a kite *for* the boys.
6. Tom knew the answer, *but* he didn't say anything.
7. I had never felt *so* stupid in my life.
8. Everyone else left the class, *but* the boys in the back of the room stayed.
9. The teacher was waiting *for* an answer.
10. He put everything in the salad *but* the salt.
11. The shipment had not *yet* arrived.
12. He called for help, *yet* the passersby ignored him.

ACTIVITY 7

In writing sentences, as in mapping out a hike, some shortcuts are safe to take. Some signals are safe to leave out. The message will come through anyway. When the circumstances are right, we can *omit* the relative pronoun

Writing Better Sentences

from a relative clause. In each of the following sentences, a relative pronoun that would normally link a relative clause to the rest of the sentence has been left out. *Where would you insert the missing link?*

After the number of each sentence, write the relative clause. Include the missing link.

EXAMPLE: The meal they had cooked was delicious.
(Answer) *that they had cooked*

1. Home was the place he liked best in the whole world.
2. The suitcase he had left on the doorstep had disappeared.
3. Sue showed us a clock her mother had brought from England.
4. I never met a man I didn't like. (Will Rogers)
5. The bicycle you borrowed was mine.
6. He inherited the clothes his father had worn as a boy.
7. The money our friends had lent us soon ran out.
8. The directions she had given us were incomplete.
9. Irma gave people she liked a big smile.
10. The rolls we had put in the oven had burned to a crisp.

Chapter 3

Composition
Writing for a Reader

C1 **Writing the Paragraph**
    a Gathering Material
    b Writing the Topic Sentence
    c Giving Examples
    d Comparison and Contrast
    e Giving Reasons

C2 **Writing a Short Paper**
    a Gathering Material
    b Supporting a Central Idea
    c Outlining the Paper
    d Helping Your Reader Follow

C3 **Writing for a Purpose**
    a Describing a Scene
    b The Story with a Point
    c Explaining a Process
    d Persuading Your Reader

C4 **Writing a Letter**
    a How Business Letters Look
    b What Business Letters Say
    c Writing a Personal Letter

C5 **Writing and Reading**
    a The Summary
    b The Book Report

For Further Study: Writing and Imagination

Chapter Preview 3

IN THIS CHAPTER:

- How to present and support a single major point in a paragraph.
- How to write paragraphs that develop a comparison or give reasons why.
- How to present and support a major point in a paper of several paragraphs.
- How to write for a special purpose: description, narration, explanation, and persuasion.
- How to write an effective letter.
- How to present information in a summary and in a book report.

Write to answer questions that might be on your reader's mind.

Writing is for readers. When you write something, you must be able to make your readers feel: "This tells me something that is good to know. This answers a question on my mind. This will be worth my while." Much successful writing answers questions that are natural for one person to ask of another:

"What was it like?"
"What do you think?"
"How does it work?"
"What lies ahead?"
"Why is it important?"

Writing a paper is in some ways like serving as a tourist guide to a city. As a guide, you would have to get your listeners' attention and make them welcome. You would ask yourself what parts of the city you know best. You would ask yourself what would most interest your audience—the buildings, the theaters, the parks, the churches, the schools. You would ask yourself what they already know, and what would be new. As a writer, you have to ask yourself questions that are very similar: What do you have to offer your readers? How can you serve their interests and needs?

C

Writing for a Reader

PREVIEW EXERCISE 1

We often write to make our readers share in something they missed. It is as if we were turning to them to say: "This is how it was. If you had been there, this is what you would have seen. This is what you would have heard." In the following poem, a student writer tells us "what it was like." What has the writer done to satisfy the reader's curiosity? What has the writer done to get the reader into the spirit of the thing? (Read the poem out loud. Then tell us in your own words "what it was like.")

Midday

Midday!
Sunshine streaming in a window
Falls on people—
Few girls, mostly guys.
Newspapers,
Timetables,
Coke bottles,
Strewn everywhere.
Sport scores lie flat,
Hiding between columns of words.
Above them the sound
Of Radio Baseball Blaring.
Answered by
Oh!   Yea!   All right!
Gosh!
Six!
Gee!
Laughs.
In comes bat, ball, and glove.
Are you going to play?
Come on!   Let's practice.
Spring fever or spring training?
We have a potentially good team—
According to Charlie Brown.
The Cubs are on their way!!

Your Turn: Write a poem or other short piece of writing. Help your reader get in the spirit of some favorite sport, hobby, or other activity. Concentrate on a scene or event that shows "what it is like." Make your readers see what they missed by not being there.

Composition

PREVIEW EXERCISE 2

What interests readers? Newspapers and magazines have always made a special effort to attract their readers' attention.

Study the following sample newspaper headlines. What is interesting about each one? What kind of reader would find each headline interesting? Look at recent newspapers. Collect ten attention-getting or interest-creating headlines.

> **Radiation in Drinking Water**
>
> **National Honors For Scouts**
>
> **Burglar Caught Napping at Job**
>
> **The Spider That Died In Orbit**
>
> **Boat Capsizes-- 250 Feared Dead**

PREVIEW EXERCISE 3

In much of the writing people do, they communicate their thoughts and feelings. When we read this kind of writing, we feel that we are getting to know the writer as a person. What kind of person wrote each of the following short pieces? What do you learn about the person's thoughts and feelings? After you read these personal messages, write a similar piece that tells something about what kind of person *you* are.

Hats

I have always loved hats since I was a little kid. My parents always told me that I used to go nowhere without some type of hat on my head. It could have been a baseball cap, a plastic army helmet, mouseketeer's ears, a cowboy hat, a wool hat, or a pirate hat. I didn't care. Just this past summer I bought two hats, one a purple flop hat, and the other an Indian hat. You should know what they look like because it's the hat that the Indians wear on T.V. who say, "he went that-a-way." So far, this year, I have bought two more hats. One is a green sports car hat and the other a brown sports car hat. I think for as long as I live I will love hats because I have grown up with a hat on my head. To me, someone with a hat on, no matter what it looks like, is a distinguished person.

Writing the Paragraph

These Things Are Good

These things are good:
The bird in the wood,
The wind in the trees,
The small crawling things,
The child and her mother,
The love of a brother,
These things are good.

Your Turn: Choose one:

1. Write a short piece of writing that starts "I have always (loved) (hated) (_____). . . ." (Fill in a word of your own choice.)

2. Write a poem or other short piece of writing that starts "These things are good" or "These things are sad" or "These things are _____." (Fill in a word of your own choice.)

Learn to write paragraphs that answer the questions in your reader's mind.

C1
WRITING THE PARAGRAPH

The paragraph is a short unit of writing that we use to satisfy an imaginary listener. We first make a statement. We make our point. Then we imagine the listener getting ready to ask us questions. We imagine someone asking us for details. We then use three or four *follow-up* sentences that answer the questions of our imaginary listener.

Suppose a writer wanted to tell the reader: "The oceans are getting saltier all the time." The imaginary listener would say things like: "Why? How does it happen? Tell me how it works!" Here is a sample paragraph that tells us how it works:

SAMPLE PARAGRAPH

The oceans are getting saltier all the time. The reason is simply that rivers carry into the oceans vast quantities of salt washed out of the land. The fresh, salt-free water that leaves the ocean and enters the atmosphere each year by evaporation returns, for the most part, to the earth as rain. It is estimated that rain-fed rivers and streams bring into the sea each year about 2¾ billion metric tons of dissolved salts. There is now sufficient salt in the sea to cover all the land areas of the world to a depth of 500 feet.

Composition

Look at the following statements. Pretend you are the imaginary listener. What questions would you like to ask the writer? For each statement, jot down two or three questions that you would like to see answered in a short paragraph.

"Human beings will not reach any of the planets beyond the moon in our lifetime."

"In some contests, people can win a free trip to Florida or to Hawaii."

"Creatures of the sea that once provided a rich catch for whole fishing fleets have disappeared along our shores."

"Soccer is as different from football as day is from night."

"For those who hate the city and the factory, there are still occupations that allow them to work in the great outdoors."

C1a

Gathering Material

Learn how to gather material for a paragraph.

The first and most basic step in writing on any topic is to gather material. The first need of a writer is for *content*—something to talk about. A writer has to learn to prime the pump, to make sure the well does not run dry. Learn to do the following:

(1) Pull together what you already know about a topic. We do not give our writing content by moving on quickly from one thing to the next. Learn to focus on one thing at a time. Bring to mind what you already know. Ask yourself questions like:

- Where can we find it?
- For what is it used?
- How does it work?
- Are there different kinds?

The following sample paragraph brings together some of the things the writer remembered about roots:

SAMPLE PARAGRAPH 1

All About Roots

Plants need roots to feed them. Roots collect water and minerals from the soil and carry them to the leaves and blossoms of the plant. Roots can be very thick and wooden, but they can also be like very fine hair. Taproots may grow many feet straight

Writing the Paragraph

down. The roots of some plants are the part we eat. Potatoes, carrots, and beets are the roots that store food for the rest of their plants.

(2) Be a good observer. Learn to take in what there is to see and to hear. Trust your own eyes and ears. Good writers are not always talking and writing. They are often people who know how to stand still and how to notice things. Here is what one successful writer noticed when she walked through a bazaar in her native India:

SAMPLE PARAGRAPH 2

An Indian Bazaar

To me an Indian bazaar is a source of endless delight and excitement. It is usually a series of plain wooden stalls on which are piled brightly colored fruits, vegetables, spices, gleaming silver jewelry, brilliant silks and cottons, or painted wooden toys. The vendors who can't afford a stall sit on the sidewalk outside the market, their baskets stacked behind them, their wives in vivid cotton saris crouching in the shade. In front of them are spread carpets of scarlet chillies drying in the sun, small hills of saffron, turmeric, coriander, ginger, cinnamon— all the magical names from the old days of the spice trade with the Indies. With a worn stone mortar and pestle the vendor or his wife will grind your spices for you, blending them according to your particular taste, and weigh them in tiny brass scales strung on twine and balanced delicately in one hand.—Santha Rama Rau, *Return to India*

(3) Pay attention to things as they happen. To write about an event or a process, we have to trace things as they develop. We have to be able to follow something step by step. In the following sample paragraph, a mountain climber tries to trace a difficult part of a climb step by step:

SAMPLE PARAGRAPH 3

In front of me was the rock wall, vertical but with a few promising holds. Behind me was the ice-wall of the cornice, glittering and hard but cracked here and there. I took a hold on the rock in front and then jammed one of my crampons hard into the ice behind. Leaning back with my oxygen set on the ice, I slowly lowered myself. Searching feverishly with my spare boot, I found a tiny ledge on the rock and took some of the weight off my other leg. Leaning back on the cornice, I fought to regain my breath. Constantly at the back of my mind was the fear that the cornice might break off, and my nerves were taut with suspense.

Composition

But slowly I forced my way up—wriggling and jambing and using every little hold. In one place I managed to force my crampons into a crack in the ice . . . then I found a solid foothold in a hollow in the ice, and the next moment I was reaching over the top of the rock and pulling myself to safety.—Edmund Hillary, *High Adventure*

EXERCISE 1   Write a paragraph in which you bring together what you already know about one of the following topics. Choose one:

- all about leaves;
- all about bands;
- all about summer;
- all about snow;
- all about buses.

EXERCISE 2   Write a paragraph about your favorite store. What would a good observer see and hear? Include the sights and sounds that for you make it a good place to be.

EXERCISE 3   Write a paragraph that traces something as it happens. For instance, trace step by step a high dive, a key play in a recent game, a winning routine at a gymnastics meet, a series of steps or movements in ballet or in a cheerleader's routine.

C1b Writing the Topic Sentence

Sum up the major point of your paragraph in a topic sentence.

Cars come in all shapes and sizes. But the typical car still has four wheels and an engine up in front. A typical paragraph has the main point up in front and four or five sentences to back it up. We call the sentence "up front" the **topic sentence.** It sums up what we are trying to say. The rest of the paragraph then shows the reader what we mean in detail.

What makes a good topic sentence? A good topic sentence is *the end result of a process*. We look at something carefully, and we take in various details. We then *funnel* them into a conclusion. Look at how the funneling process works in the following examples. In each case, the conclusion at the bottom of the funnel would make a good topic sentence:

Writing the Paragraph

C1b

DETAILS:
- Part of the front porch had caved in.
- Shingles had been blown from the roof.
- The paint was blistered.
- The siding was ripped.
- Several windowpanes had been broken.

CONCLUSION: The house had a much-neglected look.

DETAILS:
- In a recent crash test conducted at the legal speed, car doors flew open.
- Motor mounts broke loose.
- Door handles and instruments inflicted possible injuries.
- Some seat belts tore loose from their bolts.

CONCLUSION: Cars still are not as safe as they should be.

In the finished paragraph, we usually turn the funnel *upside down*. We put the conclusion first, then the details after it. The conclusion becomes the topic sentence of the finished paragraph. Here are the finished paragraphs, with the topic sentences in italics:

SAMPLE PARAGRAPH 1

The house had a much-neglected look. Part of the front porch had caved in. Several shingles had been blown from the roof. The chimney, minus a few bricks, held a badly bent and rusted television antenna. The front steps were broken. The paint was marred by bubbles and blisters. The window frames held either broken glass or no glass at all. Missing sections of siding exposed the tar paper underneath to the elements. A side door clung to its post on a single hinge.

SAMPLE PARAGRAPH 2

Cars still are not as safe as they should be. Potentially fatal defects were registered in recent crash tests conducted at legal speeds. Some car doors flew open, greatly increasing the risk of passengers being thrown from the car. Motor mounts broke loose, throwing the heavy engine into the laps of the front-seat passengers. Door handles and instrument controls proved to be hazards. Some seat belts tore loose from their bolts.

Composition

EXERCISE 1

Study each of the following groups of sentences. Each pulls together things a writer might have learned or observed about one limited topic. How would you add up the statements in each set? Draw the conclusion that could serve as the topic sentence of a paragraph. Write your topic sentence after the number of each group. (Write on a separate sheet.)

1. TOPIC SENTENCE: _____.
Every Saturday, teenagers in my neighborhood work on their cars.
They wash their cars and clean the floors and seats.
They remove grease from the engine.
They let the motor idle, listening for a misfiring sparkplug or a slipping fan belt.

2. TOPIC SENTENCE: _____.
Fish need oxygen, and an aquarium often has an air pump that pumps fresh air through the water.
Tropical fish, especially, need the right temperature to ensure their survival.
Many fish do not do well in dirty water, and an aquarium often has a water filter to help keep the water clean.

3. TOPIC SENTENCE: _____.
Some eels stun their prey with electric shocks.
The moray eel lies in wait and then strikes.
The speedy barracuda dashes through the water to hunt down its food.
Some kinds of whales and sharks sift tiny animals and plants from the water with many comblike teeth.

4. TOPIC SENTENCE: _____.
A palace in England is haunted by the ghost of a queen who was beheaded on the order of her husband.
Another well-known English ghost is that of a nun who was buried without a proper funeral.
In Wayne County, New York, an old wooden house was haunted by the ghost of a wandering peddler who had been murdered on the property.

5. TOPIC SENTENCE: _____.
In a very popular science-fiction movie, the true hero of the audience was a midget-size computerized robot with flashing lights and strange whistling noises.

Writing the Paragraph

Another audience favorite was a fussy golden robot who looked and walked like a dummy from a window of a department store.

Also very popular was a huge hairy copilot who looked like a huge cuddly ape.

6. TOPIC SENTENCE: _____.

Every second commercial seems to be about a toothpaste that promises whiter teeth.

Many commercials are about shampoos and hairsprays that will give us softer, fluffier, and more glamorous hair.

Many commercials advertise clothes that will make the wearer look youthful and carefree.

7. TOPIC SENTENCE: _____.

People who lived on the American frontier had no building contractors to build their homes for them.

They had no supermarkets to offer them every kind of food.

They had to grow their own food and raise their own livestock.

They had to be their own doctors and teachers.

8. TOPIC SENTENCE: _____.

Telecasts of the Olympics have made gymnastics a favorite sport of many viewers.

The popularity of soccer has grown tremendously in recent years.

Skiing has been discovered by thousands of young people as their favorite winter sport.

9. TOPIC SENTENCE: _____.

On most of today's passenger trains, the vending machine has replaced the dining car.

The trains often run half an hour or an hour late.

During the cold weather, there is often either no heat or heat enough to roast the passengers.

Some cars look as if they have not been cleaned for years.

Railroads will sidetrack passenger trains while freights pass.

10. TOPIC SENTENCE: _____.

Contrary to popular belief, wolves do not attack people.

Wolves serve nature by tracking down and eliminating weak and sick animals of other species.

Wolves usually stay far from people, prowling the prairies and forests for their prey.

The howls that frighten people in the wilds are usually not those of the wolf but those of the coyote.

Composition

EXERCISE 2

Study the two statements in each pair. Which is the *more* general statement—the one that would make a good topic sentence? Which is the *less* general statement—the kind that could have led up to the more general conclusion? Write the letter for the topic sentence after the number of each pair.

EXAMPLE: *(a)* It was a beautiful day.
(b) The temperature was a comfortable 75 degrees.

(Answer)   *a*

1. *(a)* The cliff blocked our progress.
   (b) The cliff rose at an angle of 55 degrees.
2. *(a)* The lawn was in a state of neglect.
   (b) Large patches of dirt spotted the lawn.
3. *(a)* An astronaut must spend long hours in silence.
   (b) An astronaut must be a special kind of person.
4. *(a)* The cost of living is rising.
   (b) The price of butter recently went up 10 percent.
5. *(a)* Mr. Saunders has much leisure time.
   (b) Mr. Saunders attends three baseball games each week.
6. *(a)* The Volkswagen is an economical car to operate.
   (b) Her Volkswagen averages 27 miles to a gallon.
7. *(a)* Bill never appears without a jacket.
   (b) Bill is a conservative dresser.
8. *(a)* The boy continually bit his fingernails.
   (b) The boy was nervous.
9. *(a)* Growing flowers takes patience.
   (b) A poppy requires as many as 300 days from seed to flower.
10. *(a)* The Western villain usually wears a black hat.
    (b) Western movies seem to be the same in some ways.
11. *(a)* Goldfish thrive in cold water.
    (b) Common aquarium fish have special requirements.
12. *(a)* My brother's car is a wreck.
    (b) Every fender on my brother's car is dented.
13. *(a)* Jules Verne was ahead of his time.
    (b) In *20,000 Leagues Under the Sea,* Jules Verne introduced the submarine.
14. *(a)* Harbor pilots have to memorize shifting channels.
    (b) Harbor pilots need a thorough knowledge of the harbors they work.
15. *(a)* Painting takes time.
    (b) A painter can spend two hours on one window.
16. *(a)* There were eighty-three complaints about the cafeteria.
    (b) The workers were dissatisfied.

Writing the Paragraph

17. *(a)* The rainfall was 6 inches below average.
    (b) It was a bad spring.
18. *(a)* The *Titanic* was a large ship.
    (b) The *Titanic* weighed 46,328 gross tons.
19. *(a)* Alice had a valuable stamp collection.
    (b) A 1923 airmail stamp alone was worth more than $200.
20. *(a)* Most of his snapshots had a washed-out look.
    (b) Joe wasn't much of a photographer.

Back up your main point with related examples.

C1c
Giving Examples

In the most basic kind of paragraph, we try to satisfy the reader who says, "Give me an example." We make a statement more convincing by adding examples like the following:

STATEMENT: Tropical fish require care.
EXAMPLE: The water in which tropical fish live must be kept at a temperature between 70 and 75 degrees.

STATEMENT: When I was young, girls and boys shared the work of adults.
EXAMPLE: In North Dakota, I had worked on our farm—trampling hay, driving a team of horses, fetching cows, feeding calves and chickens. (Lois Phillips Hudson)

STATEMENT: Quite often boys would run away from the orphanage.
EXAMPLE: A boy named Nuttsy Perry became a sort of hero when he hid out in an old rusted car body in the woods next to the orphanage for ten days before giving in and coming back. He had a girl in the dining room who sneaked peanut butter and bread to him over the fence every night.

The most basic all-purpose paragraph starts with a statement that gives the main point. It then goes on to give several examples. If the examples are convincing, the reader will say: "I see what you mean. I see that you have a point." Here is a sample paragraph that gives several examples:

(Topic Sentence)   *Words fill our lives.* Students listen for much of the day to teachers, principals, and counselors.
(Example 1)   When they come home, many of them listen to hours of television drama, interrupted by eager
(Example 2)   voices selling soft drinks, detergents, and shampoos. The average American home receives a

Composition

(Example 3)
(Example 4)

(Example 5)

daily newspaper that has fifty or sixty closely printed pages. In addition, the mail often brings magazines and direct-mail advertising. When we drive down the highway, billboards beckon to us with messages that keep up the never-ending stream of words.

Study the following sample paragraphs. For each, state the main point in your own words. Then, in your own words, identify three major examples that are given in the paragraph.

SAMPLE PARAGRAPH 1

Cecil was a small, brown-skinned man of perpetual motion and tremendous spirit. I admired the way he kept the paper going from the cramped and disordered space he called his office. He wrote the editorials, sports, news and society columns, hustled ads and kept his numerous creditors at bay with fast talk and sincere promises.... He didn't have much money to offer his few employees, but the titles he handed them were of Herculean stature. If you wanted to be a correspondent instead of a reporter that was your prerogative. If you wanted to be a *foreign* correspondent, then mail back a story on your trip abroad. —Gordon Parks, *A Choice of Weapons*

SAMPLE PARAGRAPH 2

An inexhaustible variety distinguishes the various worlds from one another. On the Moon, for example, there are only twelve days and twelve nights in a year, although the length of the year is the same as ours and ours is divided into 365 days. On Jupiter the year is nearly twelve times longer than ours, while the day is shorter by over a half; so that on Jupiter there are over 10,500 days in a year. On Saturn ... the disproportion is even greater, for its year is twenty-nine times longer than ours and has nearly 25,000 days in it. And what should we say of Neptune, where each year lasts over a century and a half, or 165 of our short years; or of Pluto, whose year is 249 of ours, two centuries and a half?—Camille Flammarion, *The Flammarion Book of Astronomy*

EXERCISE 1

Choose *five* of the topic sentences below. After the number of each sentence, write a sentence that gives an example.

SAMPLE TOPIC SENTENCE: Cafeteria food has been poor.

(Answer) *Yesterday I unwrapped my ham sandwich and found a wafer-thin slice of ham between two stale slices of bread.*

Writing the Paragraph

1. Teenagers have a weird sense of humor.
2. Accidents happen just like that—out of nowhere.
3. Sometimes television news takes us right to the middle of the action, making us feel like a spectator at the scene.
4. The wrong word at the wrong time can really ruin things.
5. Parents of teenagers sometimes lose their tempers.
6. Newspapers are full of gory crimes.
7. Many television comedians joke about the same familiar subjects.
8. Black actors are getting some prominent roles in recent movies.
9. Sometimes a major disaster really lives on in the public memory.
10. Every television viewer recognizes a few familiar types of television French people or television Germans.

EXERCISE 2

Read the two sets of sentences that follow. Each statement in the first set could serve as the topic sentence of a paragraph. Each statement in the second set provides an example or follow-up for one of the topic sentences. After the number of each topic sentence, put the letter for the follow-up passage that fits it best.

TOPIC SENTENCES:

1. Football is still becoming more popular year by year.
2. Sports that are still new to many people, such as skiing or gymnastics, are rapidly reaching a mass audience.
3. Soccer in our area has grown enormously in popularity among young people.
4. Soccer had long been popular in Europe.
5. Parents felt soccer was a fair sport.
6. Unlike traditional football, soccer brought with it the fast growth of girls' leagues.
7. Soccer is a safe sport.
8. Various kinds of activities help raise money to support the soccer leagues.
9. People of all age groups participate in soccer.
10. Players seem to be as interested in trophies for sportsmanship as in winning.

EXAMPLES:

A. Children could play no matter what their size, and the biggest players did not win all the time.
B. Millions of people watch the world's best skiers and gymnasts during the Olympic Games.
C. Injuries are few: In one major area, with 1,100 girls playing in an under-sixteen league, the injuries during the year could be counted on one hand.

Composition

D. Four years ago, 3,000 young soccer players were registered. Right now, there are more than 15,000.
E. The bitterest rivals are often the best of friends between games.
F. One of our coaches had known the game since her childhood in Scotland.
G. Major tournaments have special categories for under-twelve, under-fourteen, and under-sixteen teams. Parents play in the "old folks" league.
H. In traditional football, boys played, and the girls were cheerleaders. In soccer, boys and girls can show equal skills and earn equal respect.
I. Cake sales, raffles, and exhibition games by professional teams help pay travel expenses for regional competition.
J. During the football season, a dedicated football fan can watch several college games and professional games every weekend.

EXERCISE 3

Choose one of the following for a "made-to-order" paragraph. Fill in the examples needed to back up the topic sentence. Use a sentence or more for each separate example. (Write on a separate sheet of paper.)

1. There are three or four kinds of developments on the field that are guaranteed to bring a crowd at a football game to its feet. _____

2. Several television programs have been so popular that their reruns have come back year after year. _____

3. Many new downtown office buildings have common features that make them look like identical twins. _____

C1d

Comparison and Contrast

Use a paragraph to develop a comparison or contrast.

What would be a natural question to ask if someone told you about a revolutionary new engine for cars? You might ask:

"Is it anything like a piston engine?"
"Is it anything like a jet engine?"
"Is it anything like an electric motor?"

Writing the Paragraph

Often when we want to know more about something, we ask how it is *similar* to things we already know. Often we ask how it is different from things we already know. You can use a paragraph for a **comparison**, showing the similarities. Or you can use a paragraph for **contrast**, showing the differences. Or you can do a combination of both.

Look at the following model paragraph which describes the large, luxurious ocean liners that used to sail across the Atlantic Ocean:

(Topic Sentence)	*A great ocean liner was like a large luxury hotel.* It had almost as many crew members as it had passengers (and sometimes more). It carried an army of stewards, waiters, and cooks. The furnishings were expensive and elaborate. Large dining rooms had wooden paneling and gilded mirrors. The food service tried to imitate the service in the best restaurants. The passengers could choose from long menus, and they were offered specialties of every kind.
(First Similarity)	
(Second Similarity)	
(Third Similarity)	

Look at how the following paragraph develops a contrast between then and now:

(Topic Sentence)	*Zoos have changed much in the last twenty or thirty years.* In the past, animals that died in cramped cages could be cheaply replaced with animals caught in the wild. Zoo animals could never live and breed the way they did in their natural setting. In a modern zoo, there is space for animals to move in. Water, vegetation, and temperature are as similar to the natural habitat of the animal as possible. With wild animals hard to obtain, zoos depend more and more on animals that have been born in captivity.
(Conditions then)	
(Conditions now)	

EXERCISE 1

In each set of statements, choose the comparison that to you makes the most sense. Then write a paragraph to develop the comparison that you have chosen. Be sure to include in your paragraph two or three good *similarities*.

1. School is like an army camp.
   School is like a jail.
   School is like an amusement park.
   School is like a big family.
   School is like church.

Composition

2. An election is like a military campaign.
   An election is like a circus.
   An election is like an advertising campaign.
   An election is like a Western movie.
   An election is like a ritual of a primitive tribe.

EXERCISE 2 How good are you at putting your finger on what makes two things different? Select *five* of the following pairs. Write two sentences for each pair—one about each member of the pair. Bring out the contrast between the two things as clearly as you can.

1. a pencil—a pen
2. a canary—a parakeet
3. a library—a laboratory
4. the sun—the moon
5. a car—a motorcycle
6. an apple—a pear
7. velvet—satin
8. steel—aluminum
9. moped—motorcycle
10. airplane—helicopter

EXERCISE 3 How would you finish the following "made-to-order" paragraphs? Each time, fill in the second part of the paragraph to complete the contrast. (Write on a separate sheet of paper.)

1. In some of the most popular sports, there are sudden moments of excitement. In baseball, a big play can make the difference between a win and a loss. In football, a run for long yardage or a goal-line stand can bring a whole stadium to its feet. But in other popular sports, sudden bursts of excitement are either missing or much less important. _____
_____
_____
_____
_____

2. An ocean liner used to be like a small city. It had its own restaurants, movie theater, and library. It had its own chapel, beauty parlors, and barber shops. Passengers could go for long walks on the promenade decks that lined each side of the ship. Just as a town has a mayor and council and other functionaries, so the ocean liner had its captain and officers and crew. But a modern jet plane does not resemble a city at all. _____
_____
_____
_____

Writing the Paragraph

C1e Giving Reasons

Write paragraphs that give your reader reasons why.

We often write to influence someone's judgments or actions. We tell the reader: "This is good." "This is bad." "You should do this." "You should do that." The reader's natural reaction is: "Give me some good *reasons* why I should come around to your point of view. Give me some good reasons why I should do as you say."

Suppose there is a campaign in your community to establish a youth center. But the drive for the center is stalled for lack of money. Few people really care. The following paragraph gets together the reasons why people should get behind the stalled drive. Can you restate the reasons in your own words?

(Topic Sentence) — *This town could profit from a community center.* A community center would give teenagers something to do. It would give young people a place to go, and it would do away with the need for standing on street corners, where the dangers of getting into trouble are great. If a swimming pool and a gymnasium were housed in the building, young people could participate in healthy, community-wide competition. An auditorium would make weekend dances possible and keep young people from roaming through the neighborhood on Saturday nights. Such a center would (Second Reason) also help teenagers realize that they belong to a community. Community organizations could hold their meetings at the center. They could encourage teenagers to take an interest in community affairs.

(First Reason)

In the following paragraph, the writer presents an unusual viewpoint and then offers reasons for thinking as he does:

(Topic Sentence) — *Swimming is a very unnatural sport.* Since our ancestors gave up life in the water some time ago, we have lost almost everything aquatic crea-(First Reason) tures need. We aren't streamlined or finned or gilled, we have no webbing left anywhere. Even (Second Reason) our buoyancy is wrong. If we try to lie on the surface we sink, if we try to lie on the bottom we rise. Our natural level is somewhere in between, where we can't breathe.—John Knowles, "Everybody's Sport," *Holiday*

Composition

EXERCISE 1

From the following statements, select one with which you find yourself in agreement. Write a paragraph that fills in "the reasons why."

1. Hockey is a great spectator sport.
2. We all have to keep some of our thoughts to ourselves.
3. Dogs should be banned in residential areas.
4. A teenager should not own a car.
5. School rules should be enforced by a student court.
6. Vacations can be a bore.
7. Schools should put less emphasis on sports.
8. Attendance in class should be voluntary.
9. A school should not have a dress code.
10. Young people need someone in authority to keep them in line.

EXERCISE 2

Write a paragraph in which you give the reasons why you disagree with *one* of the statements in Exercise 1.

UNIT REVIEW EXERCISE

In each of the following paragraphs, the topic sentence has been left out. Among the three sentences that follow each paragraph, find the one that would make the best topic sentence. Write the letter for the topic sentence of your choice after the number of the paragraph. Then add one of the following in parentheses to show what kind of paragraph it is: (examples) (comparison/contrast) (reasons).

1. _____. In one Disney movie, the hero was a dragon who became a runaway boy's best friend. Fans of Disney movies have watched the adventures of cute elephants and cuddly bears. An all-time favorite is the lovable stray dog.
   a. Disney movies are often about animals.
   b. The animals in Disney movies are often friendly and lovable.
   c. An animal is sometimes a child's best friend.

2. _____. Many aquariums contain plants, which need light so that they can produce oxygen—the way plants in a garden produce oxygen in the sunlight. Fish always need an adequate oxygen supply in the water, or they will suffocate. If the tank is near a window, too much sunlight may overheat the water. Too much light leads to green water, with too many algae and with sickly fish.
   a. Many aquariums need the right kind of light.
   b. Fish need oxygen.
   c. Sunlight is essential for healthy fish.

Writing a Short Paper

3. _____. Almost every football game takes its toll of injuries. There are injured knees, dislocated shoulders, and sprained ankles. Injured players often miss the rest of the season. Hockey also is known as a very dangerous sport. Baseball, by contrast, causes few injuries, if any. Basketball also involves little physical contact, and it causes few injuries to players.
   a. Some sports involve more physical contact than others.
   b. Americans like sports that lead to violence.
   c. Some team sports are more dangerous than others.

4. _____. A hundred thousand humpback whales used to roam the Pacific Ocean. After centuries of hunting, their number is down to about 5,000. In recent years, whaling fleets hunting for sperm whales have been taking whales of smaller size. Few whales have had a chance to grow to full size and old age. Traditional refuges for mother whales and their calves are threatened by traffic and pollution.
   a. Whales have long been an important source of food and fuel.
   b. It is getting more difficult to hunt whales.
   c. Humans are threatening the survival of whales.

5. _____. Children in the foster home used to be taught by teachers who were employed by the institution. Dating was forbidden, except for supervised visits to the girls' building on Sunday afternoon. Today the students in the home go off campus to public schools. They have dates as they wish. Some even have automobiles.
   a. The students in the foster home today enjoy more freedom than in the past.
   b. Growing up in an orphanage can be a sad experience.
   c. Foster homes are not as bad as people might think.

C2 WRITING A SHORT PAPER

Develop several related points in a short theme of three or four paragraphs.

Paragraphs are like the rungs in a ladder or the rooms in a home. They do their job as part of a larger whole. Most topics are too involved to be handled in a single paragraph. Imagine, for instance, that you have taken a trip to New York City. You want to talk about one of the tourist attractions you have seen. Here is your attempt to describe it in a single paragraph:

> When I went to see the famous Guggenheim Art Museum, I really learned what the word *modern* means. The museum has a continuous slanting floor that winds round and round till the

Composition

visitor reaches the top of the building. The first painting that caught my eye showed chopped-up parts of people and animals arranged Picasso-style. Another painting showed a nineteenth-century railway station as one might see it in a strange, surrealistic dream, with people in weird costumes in a spooky atmosphere. But the painting that was furthest from what I expected looked like a piece of old green wallpaper. On it were drawn dozens of grinning moon faces of the kind children draw.

This paragraph will get your audience interested, but it will not satisfy them. They are likely to ask:

1. What's this about a "slanting" floor? In a museum?
2. What do you mean by "Picasso-style"?
3. What gave the painting such a "spooky" atmosphere? What were some of the weird costumes like?
4. Are you joking about those moon faces? What were they supposed to mean?

To answer these questions, you would have to devote one paragraph to each question. Your original single paragraph would develop into four paragraphs, or maybe five. The result would be a short **theme**—a short paper of several paragraphs. Your paper might look like this:

An Unusual Museum

(INTRODUCTION)

When I visited New York City this summer, I went to see the Guggenheim Art Museum, which I had been told was like no other museum in the world. By looking at the building and the paintings inside it, I really learned what the word *modern* means.

(PARAGRAPH 1: The Building)

Even from the outside, the museum looks more like a gigantic, concrete spaceship than like the old-fashioned buildings that surround it. The walls are round rather than straight, with the whole structure wider at the top than at the bottom. The reason for this strange shape becomes clear as the visitor steps inside. The main feature of the museum is a continuous, slanted walkway that winds its way up like a huge spiral along the inside of the building's circular wall....

(PARAGRAPH 2: First Painting)

The first painting that caught my eye reminded me of the strange, geometric shapes of the Spanish painter Picasso. Chopped-up parts of people and animals were arranged in squares and triangles....

(PARAGRAPH 3: Second Painting)

Another painting showed a nineteenth-century railway station as one might see it in a strange, surrealistic dream. A half-hidden moon threw a spooky light on passengers walking around as in a weird masquerade....

(PARAGRAPH 4: Third Painting)

But the painting that was the least old-fashioned did not look like a painting at all at first glance. It seemed like a piece of old green wallpaper put in a frame. The scrawls and squiggles on it turned out to be dozens of grinning moon faces of the kind children draw. Some of these faces were attached to tiny bodies, bunched together like people in a crowded New York subway....

By putting each point in a separate paragraph, you have given it room to grow and expand. One paragraph alone can give only part of the picture. A short theme of three or four paragraphs still cannot "tell the whole story." But it can tell enough of it for the reader to start saying: "I am getting the picture. I can see what you mean."

Learn how to gather material for a short paper.

C2a

Gathering Material

A writer needs materials to draw on. Putting a short paper together is in some ways like building a shelf. We need materials, and we need an overall plan. We can then put the materials together according to our blueprint. The blueprint alone will not do us any good in an empty workshop, without any wood or other resources that can serve as raw material for the finished product. For a writer, as for a carpenter, shopping around for *the right materials* is an important and necessary part of the job.

Do one or more of the following to help you find the material for a short paper:

(1) Draw on what you already know. Draw on the "memory bank" of past experience and past observation. Show the connection between your current topic and your own per-

Composition

sonal experience. Here is the kind of personal experience a writer drew on when he wrote about "How Young People Get a Start in Life":

- When we left school, my friends got jobs as mechanics, optical technicians, and bus drivers.
- They settled down in and around our town.
- As the country grew more prosperous, there were more college scholarships.
- Some of the young people from our neighborhood became dentists, restaurant owners, and business executives.

(2) Draw on close firsthand observation. Learn to use your eyes and ears. How good are you at taking things in? Go to a place where you can be the camera eye. Take a good close look at what there is to see. Take your time—really look around. What do you see? What is going on?

(3) Draw on printed sources and on information from other media. How much do you read about sports or politics? Do you keep up with the news? If someone asked you to provide background for a current event, how much would you know? How much could you find out? Pretend you have been asked to work up background material for an article in a student newspaper or school magazine. The editor in charge has asked you to work on one of the following questions:

TOPIC: "UNITED STATES SWIMMERS—WHAT'S THE SECRET OF THEIR SUCCESS?"

Over the years, United States swimmers and swim teams have done well in international competition. Why? How? To answer these questions, consult sources like the following:

- television coverage of major swimming events;
- articles in *Sports Illustrated* or similar magazines;
- a book or articles about an outstanding United States swimmer.

TOPIC: "WHERE HAVE THE FISH GONE?"

We sometimes read grim predictions that the fish in our waters are being killed off by pollution and other factors. How *is* the fish population faring in our rivers and lakes? What is being done or planned by people concerned with the problem? You could get information from sources like the following:

- newspaper reports;
- recent government pamphlets;
- articles in fishing or outdoor magazines.

Writing a Short Paper

EXERCISE 1

Choose one of the following topics. Write down anything that comes to mind as you think about the topic. Don't try to sort things out. Just let things come to the surface. *Keep writing*—fill the page.

1. Write about a *house* where you spent a large part of your childhood. Talk about the place, the people, and the things that happened there. Put down anything that thinking of the place brings back to your mind.
2. Write about a *street* where you lived for a fairly long time. What was it like? What are your earliest memories of it? What are some of the things that may have happened to change it? What are some of the things that happened there?
3. Write about a *trade or occupation* that you were close to over a number of years. Maybe it was the job of someone in your family or of a friend of the family. Write about what you could observe yourself or about what you heard when people talked about it.

EXERCISE 2

Choose one of the following for a close look. Prepare a set of notes—copy them over, so other people can read them.

1. Visit a large *institutional building:* a hospital, a museum, a large city or county office, or the like. Jot down any striking details and local angles. Don't try to sort things out—just get it all down.
2. Visit a *local factory* or other manufacturing or business place with much varied activity: a busy workshop, a garage, a newspaper plant, or the like. Just rove around. Take in as much as you can of what goes on.
3. Visit a theater, a concert hall, or the like *during rehearsals*. Take notes for a report from "behind the scenes." What goes on? What do the people look like? What do they say and do?

EXERCISE 3

Every so often, the mass media turn the full spotlight on a major current issue. Newspapers have reports on it. The television networks prepare special programs on it. Magazines publish articles on it. Experts and leading public figures are interviewed. Which of the following issues has recently been much in the news? Choose *one* of the issues from the ten listed below. How much background material do you already have for a paper? Get down on paper whatever you have recently heard, read, or watched about your topic.

1. New sources of energy
2. The chances of American athletes in international competition
3. Clean water, or clean air

Composition

   4. Job opportunities for women
   5. Space exploration
   6. Car or highway safety
   7. Racial balance in our schools
   8. Honesty in government
   9. Improving mass transport
  10. Redevelopment in the city

C2b Supporting a Central Idea

Learn how to back up a single major point.

What does it take to pull together the material you have collected for a short paper? Even while collecting material, an experienced writer is thinking about how to make it *add up*. Sooner or later a reader will say:

"This is all very interesting, but what is the point?"

"You have taken a good look—what conclusions have you reached?"

A writer has to be able to say: "*This* is what I am trying to show. *This* is my major point." We call the major point that holds a short paper together the **central idea**. To make a dent, a writer has to learn how to make material add up to one central idea, to one major point.

Remember the following guidelines:

(1) Make sure your central idea will provide the direction for your paper as a whole. The central idea is like a promise: "This is what the rest of the paper will try to show." Here are some examples:

CENTRAL IDEA: In many television cartoons, the same basic situation is repeated over and over.

(The reader will expect several examples of situations that the viewer sees again and again:
  • the wily coyote who tries in vain to catch the roadrunner;
  • the wisecracking rabbit that bests the angry fellow animals who consider the rabbit a pest; and so on.)

CENTRAL IDEA: People who collect stamps learn many things from their hobby.

(The reader will expect to hear in detail what makes stamp collecting educational: What do we learn about distant and little-known countries? What do we learn about famous people and events? What famous places and works of art appear on stamps, and what do we learn from them?)

Writing a Short Paper

(2) Limit yourself to a central idea that you will be able to support. Look at a central idea like the following: "New York City has many tourist attractions unequaled in other parts of the country." Remember that the theme on the unusual museum just barely covered the basic, modernistic design of *one* building and *three* of the paintings hung there. It obviously *left out* many other sights to be seen in this one place. How could the same theme make room for "many other tourist attractions" equally famous?

Narrow down your topic in order to do it justice. For the museum topic, the process might have gone like this:

TOO BROAD:	Tourist Attractions in New York City
STILL TOO BROAD:	Famous Art Museums in New York City
MORE LIMITED:	The Guggenheim Museum
CENTRAL IDEA:	By looking at the building and the paintings inside it, I really learned what the word *modern* means.

EXERCISE 1

The more limited your topic, the better your chance of coming up with a central idea that you can really support. In each of the following sets of topics, find the one that is more limited in scope than the other two. Write it next to the number of the set. Then select *three* of these limited topics. For each write a central idea that you could support in a short paper.

1. Raising Newborn Guppies
   Tropical Fish as a Hobby
   Breeding Tropical Fish
2. Democracy in Action
   A Public Hearing on the School Budget
   Everyone's Viewpoint Should Be Heard
3. Operating a Newspaper Route
   Learning Self-Reliance
   Starting Your Own Business
4. Participating in Sports
   The Quarterback's Responsibilities
   Playing the Backfield
5. Working as a Hospital Volunteer
   Making Yourself Useful
   Teenage Community Contributions
6. Food from the Sea
   Feeding the World's Population
   The Harvesting of Lobsters

Composition

   7. Learning a Process
      Baking a Chocolate Layer Cake
      Following Directions
   8. Growing Lettuce
      Planting a Garden
      Observing Nature
   9. My First Day on the Job
      Growing Up
      Getting Out on Your Own
 10. Learning to Use Your Hands
      Developing Skills
      Learning to Type

EXERCISE 2

The central idea points a paper in one definite direction. It makes us select the examples and the evidence we need to back it up. For each of the following topics, write *two* different central ideas that you could follow up in two different short papers. (Be prepared to discuss in class the two different directions the two papers would take and also the different kinds of supporting material you would need to write the two papers.)

EXAMPLE: The Influence of the Jet Plane
(Answers) (a) *People who live near major airports are not fans of the jet.*
          (b) *The modern jet has tremendously shortened the distance between American cities.*

1. Life in a Small (Large) Town
2. How to Make Good Use of Your Leisure Time
3. Things Parents Should Do with Their Children
4. What Teenagers Like to Read
5. Violence in Movies and Television

EXERCISE 3

Each of the following outlines provides a framework for a short paper that you can "write to order." Choose one of the three topics. Decide upon your central idea by leaving out those choices that in your opinion do not apply. Then fill in three different examples. Write one paragraph for each of the examples.

  1. Central Idea: American doctors seem to be trained to have a (pleasant) (unpleasant) (superior) (understanding) (absentminded) manner with their patients.

Writing a Short Paper

   First Example: _____
   _____

   Second Example: _____
   _____

   Third Example: _____
   _____

2. Central Idea: Today's teachers go out of their way (to ignore) (to humor) (to discipline) (to embarrass) (to help) students who cause trouble.
   First Example: _____
   _____

   Second Example: _____
   _____

   Third Example: _____
   _____

3. Central Idea: Students today want from their teachers (more work) (greater freedom) (a chummy attitude) (more personal interest) (firmer guidance).
   First Example: _____
   _____

   Second Example: _____
   _____

   Third Example: _____
   _____

C2c Outlining the Paper

Arrange your material in an order that makes sense to the reader.

We organize things so that we can find our way. Someone reading your paper is like a driver trying to find an address in a strange city. Suppose the address is "1970 N. 8th Avenue." The place will be easy to find if all the streets of the city are laid out in a clear overall pattern. Perhaps all the streets running north to south are called "avenues," and all streets running east to west are called "streets." But what if streets are named "street," "lane," "avenue," or "boulevard" at random? What if they cross each other at many different angles?

Help readers find their way by giving your paper a clear ground plan. Observe the following guidelines:

(1) Group related details together. The most basic procedure for organizing a piece of writing is **classification:** putting things together that belong together. Looking at a list of details, the writer sorts them in order to put them under three

Composition

or four major headings. In the same way, a post-office worker puts together in the same pigeonhole letters going to the same general destination.

Suppose you have collected the following pieces of advice for the topic "Buying a Used Car":

- get exact price of the car
- check condition of the body
- check the engine
- look at the *Blue Book*
- avoid taxicabs
- make a thorough check of car
- road test the car
- read newspaper ads to compare prices
- check cooling system
- remember: steering important
- avoid late-model car with suspiciously low price
- listen to the transmission
- make an appointment with a mechanic

By looking at the list, you realize that some of these details belong together. For instance, the late-model car and taxicabs are examples of cars to avoid buying. You distribute the pieces of advice into three pigeonholes as follows:

ADVICE ON HOW TO COMPARE PRICES:

- *Blue Book*
- Newspaper ads
- Demand for certain models
- Time of year

Writing a Short Paper

ADVICE ON WHAT CARS TO AVOID:
- Cars used as taxicabs
- Suspiciously low-priced cars
- Those that have been in bad accidents

ADVICE ON HOW TO CHECK MECHANICAL CONDITION OF THE CAR:
- engine
- body
- steering
- transmission
- road test

(2) Use a topic outline as an aid in improving the organization of a paper. An informal working outline helps you sort out and shift things around as needed. A final outline helps someone else see the organization of your paper at a glance. Most outlines simply show the arrangement of topics and subtopics in the finished paper. The following is an example of a final **topic outline** for the paper on the subject of buying a used car:

```
                Buying a Used Car


   I.  Comparing prices
        A.  Sources to check
            1.  Blue Book
            2.  Newspaper ads
        B.  Things to consider
            1.  Time of model year
            2.  Demand for certain models

  II.  Avoiding undesirable cars
        A.  Cars suspiciously low priced
        B.  Cars reconditioned after bad accidents
        C.  Cars used as taxicabs

 III.  Checking the condition of the car
        A.  Mechanical check
            1.  Engine
            2.  Body
            3.  Steering
            4.  Transmission
        B.  Road test
```

Composition

Remember the following points about this sample outline:

• Subdivide a topic only if there are *two or more* subtopics. (We cannot divide something into a single subdivision.) If there is a subtopic *A.*, there has to be a subtopic *B*. If there is a subtopic *1.*, there has to be a subtopic *2*.

• Use similar or parallel wording for a set of topics or subtopics if you can: "Sources *to check*"; "Things *to consider*." Or, "*Comparing* prices"; "*Avoiding* . . ."; "*Checking* . . ."

(3) Know how to prepare a sentence outline. A **sentence outline** shows the organization of a paper. But at the same time, it summarizes the ideas or information in the paper. Study the following example of a sentence outline:

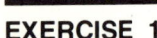

Learning from Stamps

CENTRAL IDEA: Stamp collectors can learn a great deal from the colorful pieces of paper they put in their albums.

   I. Stamps teach us about history.
      A. Stamps show famous political leaders, artists, and scientists.
      B. Stamps show historic sites and famous buildings.
      C. Stamps show artistic masterpieces of all ages.
  II. Stamps teach us geography.
      A. Stamps teach us about lesser-known nations.
      B. Stamps show the natural wonders of the world.
 III. Stamps teach us about papermaking and printing.
      A. Collectors learn about ways of marking paper.
      B. Collectors learn about different kinds of printing.

EXERCISE 1

Study the following list of examples for a paper on "How Birds Got Their Names." Write a central idea that would sum up what we learn from the different examples. Then prepare a topic outline that arranges the examples under several major headings:

• bluebird has mainly blue feathers;
• cuckoo sounds its own name;
• woodpecker taps trees;
• ovenbird builds nests open at the sides like an oven;
• roadrunner moves swiftly;

- chimney swift lives in chimneys;
- greenfinch has green and yellow feathers;
- shrike gives a shriek just before pouncing on its prey;
- the killdeer echoes its name.

EXERCISE 2

The following outline summarizes the advice given in a car-buyers manual on what to look for in buying a used car. Things for the buyer to do have been arranged under five major headings. But the person who sorted out these "tips for the buyer" became confused. Under each major heading, find the advice that does not belong. Put its letter after the number of the heading.

Buyer Beware

I. Inspecting the body
   A. Look for obvious scratches.
   B. Check the top of the hood, the roof, the trunk deck, and both sides for dents.
   C. Look underneath to make sure the frame is not bent out of shape.
   D. Check tires for cuts.
II. Signs of high mileage
   A. Check tire treads for excessive wear.
   B. Inspect for worn armrests, seat covers, floor mats, and pedals.
   C. Check for visibility from driver's seat.
III. Looking under the hood
   A. Run engine and listen for taps and knocks.
   B. Make sure that excessive dirt and grime are not clustered around the air cleaner and carburetor opening.
   C. Inspect windshield wiper blades.
   D. Check battery terminals for corrosion.
IV. Road test
   A. Try the reverse gear.
   B. Be alert for the abnormal vibration of the front end at speeds over 40 miles per hour.
   C. Inspect spark plug wires for wear.
   D. Set parking brake and put car in gear to check for transmission slippage.
V. General maintenance
   A. Check for recent servicing sticker.
   B. Turn on radio.
   C. Inspect engine oil level.
   D. Inspect transmission oil level.

Composition

EXERCISE 3

Choose one of the following frames for a "made-to-order" paper. For each of the three headings, provide the examples or details needed to complete one paragraph.

1. CENTRAL IDEA: Cars are an essential part of the American way of life.

    FIRST CATEGORY: For almost all Americans, the car is a basic means of transportation. _____

    SECOND CATEGORY: For many Americans, the car is a status symbol. It shows how people want others to rank them as members of society. _____

    THIRD CATEGORY: For many Americans, the car is a major hobby. _____

2. CENTRAL IDEA: Television plays a big role in the lives of most Americans.

    FIRST CATEGORY: For many Americans, television is the main source of news about the world. _____

    SECOND CATEGORY: Television is a never-failing source of entertainment and amusement of all kinds. _____

    THIRD CATEGORY: Television brings a constant stream of advertising into every American home. _____

EXERCISE 4

Every person is an individual. But every so often we feel: "I know the type—I've known this type of person before!" Identify *three types* of students (or teachers) that make you feel: "Every school has one!" Some familiar types are the comedian, show-off, teacher's pet, bookworm, and the like. (Can you include some less familiar ones in your description?) Write one paragraph about each of the three types.

Writing a Short Paper

C2d Helping Your Reader Follow

Help your reader follow from one part of your paper to the next.

Your reader needs to see the connection between one part of your paper and the next. Reading a well-written paper is like traveling down a well-marked road. The traveler knows what is ahead. The traveler is prepared for the next turn.

What can you do to help your reader follow? Remember:

(1) Let your reader know what is ahead. Use your **title** and **introduction** to get the reader's attention and steer it in the right direction. The introduction to the following paper prepares the reader for what follows. The title too serves as a preview. How does the paper as a whole live up to the program sketched out in the introductory paragraph?

Cover Up, Comrade Councilor

The greetings and polite expressions used in different languages can tell us much about the people who use them. They can tell us about the history of a country, about its social structure, and about its local customs. . . .

Even if we knew nothing about the history of Soviet Russia, we could tell that at one time Russia was a very religious country. The Russian word for "thank you" originally meant "God save." Similarly, Americans, whether very religious or not, use "Good-bye," which originally was "God be with you". . . .

We can tell much about the social structure of a country by listening to how its citizens address each other. In Germany, a letter to a high school teacher begins: "Greatly honored Mr. Councilor of Studies!" In Russia, even the highest official is still called "Comrade". . . .

The customs of a country are often revealed in amusing ways. According to Mario Pei, someone entering an Arab's house may be greeted by "Cover up!" This was originally a warning to the women of the household that they must cover their faces. . . .

(2) Keep the reader's attention focused on your subject. If you write about the water shortage, we can easily follow if you write about where water comes from, where it goes, and why the demand for water has increased. We can follow easily if there are words and expressions that echo the basic idea: "shortage," "scarcity," "dwindling supplies," and so on.

Look for the "echo effect" in the following passage. How many times is the word *water* actually used? How many other words have to do with water in one way or another?

Composition

A Thirsty World

... In today's world, the need for water has become acute in many areas. In some arid countries the per capita consumption of water, thanks to improved sanitation, has suddenly risen from two or three quarts per day to 20 or 30 or more. Underdeveloped countries seeking to raise their standard of living by industrialization and irrigation find themselves with huge new needs for water supplies. Even our own water-favored country is beginning to be concerned, with many communities already facing shortages. The problem is widespread, not confined to localities such as the drought-stricken Southwest. Since 1900 the U.S. has increased its consumption of water almost sevenfold. By 1975, our water requirement will have nearly doubled again. We shall then be using about 27 percent of the total supply of natural fresh water in our rivers, lakes, springs, and wells. Many areas will have reached the limits of their natural resources. The remaining 73 percent of the total supply, largely stream water, will probably be prohibitively expensive to collect, store, and distribute to the places where it is needed.—David S. Jenkins, "Fresh Water from Salt," *Scientific American*

(3) Use transitional words and expressions to keep the reader on the right track. Transitional expressions are signposts that help the reader move on. They are like signs that say "This way" or "Turn here." Common transitional expressions help us see how events follow each other *in time.* They help things move along in **chronological order.** Here are common expressions that help the reader move along in time:

first	before	the next day
soon	after	just then
later	finally	in the end
next	as soon as	to begin with
then	by the time	the following day

What transitional expressions do we use to show the connection between ideas? Here are some of the signs we can post to show where we are going:

- going on in the same direction to give additional examples or reasons: *also, too, furthermore, moreover*
- changing course to look at the other side: *but, however, on the other hand*
- going on to draw a conclusion: *so, therefore, consequently, as a result*

- moving on to something more important: *more importantly, more basically*
- winding things up: *to summarize, to conclude, in conclusion, finally*

EXERCISE 1

A. The following titles are from a collection of student writing. Which of the papers would you turn to first? Which last? Why? What kind of writing does each title lead you to expect? What kind of person do you think wrote each paper?

The Thought of Leaving Them
The Gift Horse
My Wilting Yellow Rose
My Neighborhood
The Idiot Hero
Politics in the Olympics
Cheerleading
Frightened and Embarrassed
My Mother and I

B. Write three imaginary titles for "Papers I Would Like to Read."

EXERCISE 2

In this passage, which expressions help the reader follow?

The Treasure at the Bottom of the Sea

The next afternoon, we weighed anchor and started in an opposite direction from our goal in case someone should follow us. After a couple of miles we changed direction toward the treasure. We were all excited, and many were the questions we asked one another. What was really in that metal box? Documents of the Fascist regime? But what if it was full of gold? Would we have to smuggle it to Switzerland? With these thoughts we became more fascinated by that iron box resting under seventeen feet of water at the bottom of the sea. As soon as we arrived at the spot I dived and saw that the anchor was lowered about a yard from the treasure. Cesare, wanting to assure himself, put on a mask and came down to hold one of the handles of the box, and both of us tried to move it. But it was all in vain. Cesare returned to the surface crying, "You're right, it is truly a treasure, and it must be full."

We lowered a rope and I passed it around one of the handles. But when we tried to lift it the rope slipped off. I turned the rope several times around the handle and tied it securely, and returned to the surface. Finally, after much heaving, we felt the

Composition

box moving and coming free from the sand. We all cried, "It's coming, it's coming." In my excitement I dived into the water to see it. You can never imagine what depression I felt. That strong box was not a box at all but only the shell of a wheelbarrow used by a road construction gang, which had been thrown in the sea and had landed upside down in the sand. It had a riveted bottom with two side handles which were grasped by the workers when dumping paving material. —Guido Garibaldi, "Autobiography of a Skin Diver," *The Skin Diver*

UNIT REVIEW EXERCISE

Read this model passage, adapted from *The Snow Walker*. Prepare your answers to the questions that follow it.

FARLEY MOWAT

The Snow People

The true people of the snows . . . live only in the northern hemisphere because the land of snow in the southern hemisphere—Antarctica—will not permit the existence of any human life unless equipped with protective devices not far short of what a spaceman needs. The snow people ring the North Pole. They are the Aleuts, Eskimos and Athapascan Indians of North America; the Greenlanders; the Lapps, and related peoples of Eurasia and Siberia. . . .

Snow was these people's ally. It was their protection and their shelter from cold. Eskimos built complete houses of snow blocks. When heated only with simple animal-oil lamps, these had comfortable interior temperatures, while outside the wind screamed unheard and the mercury dropped to fifty degrees or more below zero. Compacted snow provides nearly perfect insulation. It can be cut and shaped much more easily than wood. It is light to handle and strong, if properly used. A snowhouse with an inner diameter of twenty feet and a height of ten feet can be built by two men in two hours. On special occasions Eskimos used to build snowhouses fifty feet in diameter. By linking several such together, they formed true snow mansions.

All of the snow people use snow for shelter in one way or another. If they are folk possessing wooden houses, they bank their homes with thick snow walls in wintertime. Some dig a basement in a snowdrift and roof it with reindeer skins. As long as snow is plentiful, the peoples of the far north seldom suffer serious discomfort from the cold.

Snow also makes possible their transportation system. With dog sleds and reindeer sleds, or afoot on snowshoes or trail skis,

Writing a Short Paper

they can travel almost anywhere. The whole of the snow world becomes a highway. They can travel at speed, too. A dog or reindeer team can move at twenty miles an hour and easily cover a hundred miles a day.

The mobility snow gives them, combined with the way snow modifies the behavior of game animals, ensures that the snow people need not go hungry. Out on the arctic ice, a covering of snow gives the seals a sense of false security. They make breathing holes in the ice, roofed by a thin layer of snow. The hunter finds these places and waits beside them. At a signal from a telltale wand of ivory or wood inserted in the roof, he plunges his spear down into the unseen animal below.

In wooded country, moose, elk and deer are forced by deep snow to "yard" in constricted areas where they can be killed nearly as easily as cattle in a pen. Most important of all, every animal, save those with wings and those who live beneath the snow, leaves tracks upon its surface. From bears to hares, they become more vulnerable to the human hunter as soon as the first snow coats the land.

The northern people are happy when snow lies heavy on the land. They welcome the first snow in autumn, and often regret its passing in the spring. Snow is their friend. —an excerpt from "Snow," in *The Snow Walker*

1. Which of the following statements best sums up the *central idea* of this passage? (Be prepared to explain your choice.)

   A. The true people of the snow live only in the northern hemisphere.
   B. For the true people of the snow, snow is an ally and a friend.
   C. Snow offers the snow people shelter and protection from the bitter cold.

2. Explain in one sentence what the introductory paragraph does. Explain in one sentence what the concluding paragraph does. (What does each add to the passage as a whole?)

3. Write a *topic outline* for the main body of the passage—without the first and last paragraphs. Try to set up three major headings or categories. Include subtopics for one or more of the major categories.

4. Can you see how clearly this passage is focused on the role of snow in the lives of these people? In this passage, find six combinations or word groups that use the word *snow*. Look for words like *snowbound, packed snow, snow barrier, snowed in,* and the like. Then write down two words closely related to snow that also appear several times each in this selection.

Composition

5. Write down the *transitional expression* in each of the following:

   A. Snow **also** makes possible their transportation system.
   B. They can travel at speed, **too**.
   C. **Most important of all**, every animal leaves tracks upon its surface.

C3
WRITING FOR A PURPOSE

Learn how to make your writing serve its purpose.

When we start a piece of writing, we need to know what we are trying to do. We can then choose the right tools for the job. It is one thing to write directions on how to glue together a plastic model of a vintage car. It is another thing to write a letter that will change the principal's mind about how students should dress.

Look at each of the following brief samples of different kinds of writing. From each brief selection, can you tell what kind of writing to expect in the rest of the piece? What is each writer trying to do? What do you think is the main purpose? Describe it in your own words.

1. The octopus has two distinct means of locomotion. . . . Its method of swimming consists of inflating the head with water and jetting the fluid to achieve moderate speed. . . .—J. Y. Cousteau, *The Silent World*

2. Great road cars are made, not born. Look at our new Fastback XLY. It's 428 cubic inches big, giving you enough power to take the measure of a long black line on the salt or to snake over the purple mountains in the distance. . . .

3. My coldest time was training on Lake Ontario in 1974. I was supposed to leave later that day but thought, why waste the time? Why not swim for an hour, just to loosen up? I did a thousand strokes out, then stopped to turn around, empty my goggles, get a sighting onshore. But I realized I hadn't been feeling my legs. I couldn't bring them to the surface. My skin was lobster red. My breath stuck in my throat. I tried to scream to some boys onshore, but nothing came out. I started to swim a slow breaststroke. My hands were so cold I couldn't close my fingers — Diana Nyad, "Mind over Water"

4. Math and physics have a reputation as hard subjects. But a high school student should think twice before passing them up for easier courses. In many everyday jobs, a knowledge of basic math is required. Many careers are closed to students who do not have a background in math and science.

Writing for a Purpose

The following sections of this chapter deal with four major kinds of writing, each with a different major purpose. Study them to see how the difference in purpose helps the writer choose the right tools for the job.

Describe a scene to make it real for the reader.

**C3a
Describing a Scene**

Often a writer turns to us as if to say: "Let me take you to a place I have seen. This is what *you* would have seen if you had been there." Description makes a setting or a scene come to life before our eyes. We see it in "our mind's eye."

What are some of the things that make description come to life? Remember the following guidelines:

(1) Get close enough for a detailed view. In each of the following pairs, the first version gives us only the general picture. The second version moves in for a close-up view. Can you see that the second version has a better chance of making the reader say: "I see it with my mind's eye"?

General:	The train arrived to an accompaniment of noise.
Close-up:	The locomotive entered the station shed. Hissing steam broke from opened valves. The sound of the clanging bell echoed from the walls. Brakes screeched on contact with the slippery surfaces of the drive wheels. The locomotive ground to a stop, the cars banged together, and the throaty loudspeaker announced the train's arrival.
General:	The flood turned the dry creek bed into an angry river.
Close-up:	Near our house, a shallow, sandy bottomed wash, about two feet deep and fifty feet wide, had become a terrifying river which roared and boiled past, slopping over its banks and shipping bits of wood and brush along so fast we could hardly follow them with our eyes. (Bill Mauldin)

(2) Use details that bring all our five senses into play. Use details to help us imagine that we actually see something, or hear, or smell, or taste, or touch it:

Sight:	Every window of the car was crisscrossed with spider web cracks. Chips of dull paint had pulled away from the surface of the hood. In several other places, deep gouges had scarred the finish.

CITY STREET U.S.A.

What would it be like to live here? Tell the story of what you think happens on this street during an ordinary day.

SMALL TOWN U.S.A.

Pretend that you just moved to the town shown in this picture. Write a letter to a friend where you used to live. Tell your friend what this town looks like and what it feels like to live here.

Writing for a Purpose

Sound: Our feet crunched the frosty ground; our powder-horns and shot pouches thumped and rattled at our hips. (Kenneth Roberts)

Touch: My hand passed along the smooth, solid marble. I felt the lack of warmth in the surface, as the chill began to tingle through the tips of my fingers.

(3) Help your reader visualize things by using comparisons. We can imagine what unfamiliar objects and actions are like if they are likened to more familiar ones. Which comparisons below make the description more real for the reader?

We rowed for about an hour up the river against the current. The rainy season was on and the water was high. The muddy river stretched out in channels like arms around an island. Tall trees, the immense kapok with its gray smooth trunk and folds of ingrown roots, and the round umbrella-like mangoes grew at the edge of the banks, with their heavy branches dipping so low they touched the water. Flowering vines were twisted and tangled around them so that they seemed a part of the trees themselves. One was slightly like a dogwood and another like a red camellia and one had petals like the morning glory. Small islands of grass and papyrus seemed to undulate with the waves like a tawny cat stretching its muscles. And here and there, on the fringed tops, a nest of grass swayed, a cradle for the water birds inside.—Charlie May Simon, *All Men Are Brothers*

(4) Make your description add up. Help the reader form an overall picture. Fill in details that support the same **general impression.** In the following passage, how many details add to one general impression: "This place is *dead*"?

It was the most extraordinary dead-looking town I had ever been in. It resembled the set for a rather bad Hollywood cowboy film, and gave the impression that its inhabitants (two thousand, according to the guide-book) had suddenly packed up and left it alone to face the biting winds and scorching sun. The empty, rutted streets between the blank-faced houses were occasionally stirred by the wind, which produced half-hearted dust-devils, that swirled up for a moment and then collapsed tiredly to the ground. As we drove slowly into what we imagined to be the center of the town, we saw only a dog, trotting briskly about his affairs, and a child, crouched in the middle of the road, absorbed in some mysterious game of childhood.—Gerald Durrell, *The Whispering Land*

Composition

EXERCISE 1

For each of the following general statements, write *one sentence* that could become part of a close-up view. On a separate sheet of paper write your close-up sentence after the number of each statement.

1. The school is really deserted on weekends.
2. Museum-goers are a quiet, well-behaved crowd.
3. Without adequate supervision, the locker room can easily turn into a madhouse.
4. Abraham Lincoln had a rugged-looking face.
5. Luxury cars often have a heavy, elaborate grille.
6. A modern electric guitar is a flashy-looking instrument.
7. A dentist's office gives most people an uneasy feeling.
8. A school bus usually does not provide much comfort.
9. Some young people spend hours on the basketball court.
10. A garage is often a place where things accumulate.

EXERCISE 2

The author of the following passage came back from a whale-watching trip eager to share the sights and sounds of the trip with her readers. Point out five words that help us see the shape or appearance of things. Point out five words that help us see different kinds of motion. Point out five words for different sounds.

> The cry goes up: "Dolphins! Porpoises!" and we all dash for the rail as if someone had shouted "Fire!" It's well past sunset, the clouds in the west are a thick blue gray, the sea is in shadow—and here they come, a whole school of the slender Pacific common dolphin, leaping clear of the water toward our starboard bow, curved, compact shapes. Our shouts seem to urge them to higher leaps, and then they slip under the bow to hitch a ride on the compression wave, a favorite game. In the moon's glittering reflection we can barely see them, pale blurs crisscrossing swiftly under water, then dark and shining they break the surface and we hear the chuff of their breathing—and now and then the hair-fine squeak of their speech. We lean down, whoop and holler and whistle, convinced that they hear and appreciate.—Annie Gottlieb, "In the Presence of Whales," *Quest*

EXERCISE 3

Write a brief paragraph that starts with the following sentence: "It was the most _____-looking place I had ever seen." Fill in various details that all help support the same general impression.

Writing for a Purpose

PROSE MODEL 1

The author of the following passage knows how to make a scene real for his readers. Study the passage as an example of descriptive writing. Write down your answers to the questions that follow the passage.

LOREN EISELEY

The Pigeons of the El

Some years ago the old elevated railway in Philadelphia was torn down and replaced by a subway system. This ancient El with its barnlike stations containing nut-vending machines and scattered food scraps had, for generations, been the favorite feeding ground of flocks of pigeons, generally one flock to a station along the route of the El. Hundreds of pigeons were dependent upon the system. They flapped in and out of its stanchions and steel work or gathered in watchful little audiences about the feet of anyone who rattled the peanut-vending machines. They even watched people who jingled change in their hands, and prospected for food under the feet of the crowds who gathered between trains. Probably very few among the waiting people who tossed a crumb to an eager pigeon realized that this El was like a food-bearing river, and that the life which haunted its banks was dependent upon the running of the trains with their human freight.

I saw the river stop.

The time came when the underground tubes were ready. The traffic was transferred to a realm unreachable by pigeons. It was like a great river subsiding suddenly into desert sands. For a day, for two days, pigeons continued to circle over the El or stand close to the red vending machines. They were patient birds, and surely this great river which had flowed through the lives of unnumbered generations was merely suffering from some momentary drought.

They listened for the familiar vibrations that had always heralded an approaching train. They flapped hopefully about the head of an occasional workman walking along the steel runways. They passed from one empty station to another, all the while growing hungrier. Finally they flew away.

I thought I had seen the last of them about the El, but there was a revival and it provided a curious instance of the memory of living things for a way of life or a locality that has long been cherished. Some weeks after the El was abandoned workmen began to tear it down. I went to work every morning by one particular station, and the time came when the demolition crews reached this spot. Acetylene torches showered passersby with

Composition

sparks. Pneumatic drills hammered at the base of the structure, and a blind man who, like the pigeons, had clung with his cup to a stairway leading to the change booth, was forced to give up his place.

It was then one morning that I witnessed the return of a little band of the familiar pigeons. I even recognized one or two members of the flock that had lived around this particular station before they were dispersed into the streets. They flew bravely in and out among the sparks and the hammers and the shouting workmen. They had returned—and they had returned because the hubbub of the wreckers had convinced them that the river was about to flow once more.—from *The Night Country*

READING QUESTIONS

1. Loren Eiseley knows how to fill in the specific details that make a scene real for us. Point out several details he gives us about each of the following:

   - the pigeons;
   - the people buying peanuts;
   - the demolition crews;
   - the blind man.

2. This author often uses comparisons to help us see what something is like. In the first paragraph of this selection,

   a. the railroad is compared to a _____.
   b. the stations of the old railroad are compared to _____.
   c. the pigeons watching someone buy peanuts are compared to _____.
   d. the human passengers of the trains are compared to _____.
   (Write your answers on a separate sheet.)

3. Loren Eiseley usually explains things carefully to the reader. If he uses a word we do not know, its meaning often becomes clear from the explanations that go with it. For each italicized word in the following exercise, choose the meaning that best fits the context of the sentence:

   a. The pigeons *were dependent upon* the railway system.
   (1) lived off   (2) caused trouble for   (3) lived near
   b. They *prospected* for food under the feet of the crowd.
   (1) fought   (2) performed   (3) searched
   c. The traffic was transferred to a *realm* unreachable by pigeons.
   (1) street   (2) track   (3) land
   d. It was like a river suddenly *subsiding* into desert sands.
   (1) springing up   (2) disappearing   (3) spreading out

e. The pigeons thought it was only a *momentary* drought.
 (1) temporary   (2) slight   (3) usual
f. The vibrations had always *heralded* the arrival of a train.
 (1) ignored   (2) followed   (3) signaled
g. The pigeons had been *dispersed* into the streets.
 (1) scattered   (2) lured   (3) pursued

4. The comparison between the railway and a river is carried through all the way to the end of this selection. Point out five different places where the author makes use of it.

5. Loren Eiseley spent much of his life observing the needs and the behavior of living things. State in a few sentences of your own what interested him about the behavior of the pigeons.

WRITING TOPICS

1. How would you describe to inhabitants of a distant planet how things look, taste, and feel on this planet Earth? Describe to them the shape, appearance, taste, and smell of one of the following: an egg, a head of cabbage, an apple, an orange, a pineapple, an artichoke, a banana. Or describe to them some ordinary representative of our animal world: a dog, a cat, a horse, a bird. Use comparisons where you can to help make things clear or real.

2. Write a description of a scene that is not really unusual, but that many people may not pause long enough to take in. For instance, write about one of the following:

   - a sunrise or a sunset;
   - early morning in camp;
   - the first snowstorm of the season;
   - the woods in late fall;
   - a city park in winter.

3. Describe a scene that was strange and new to you: a hospital, a police station, a warehouse, etc. Make your readers see what the place was like. Make them feel what it felt like to be there.

C3b
The Story with a Point

Tell a story that gives your reader something to think about.

Among the oldest kinds of writing is narrative writing. It tells a story. It makes us share in an event or an experience that holds our attention. A good story makes readers say: "I can see it happening in front of me now." It makes them say: "I learned something from the experience."

Composition

Remember the following guidelines for narrative writing:

(1) Follow an event step by step as it happens. When you come to an important part of your story, do not just sum up what happened. Make it happen step by step for your reader. Show how one thing led to another. Look at the following sample passage. The writer could have summed up what happened by saying: "It got very cold, and he made a fire." How many separate steps can you identify in what the author actually wrote?

> There was no mistake about it, it *was* cold. He strode up and down, stamping his feet and thrashing his arms, until reassured by the returning warmth. Then he got out matches and proceeded to make a fire. From the undergrowth, where high water of the previous spring had lodged a supply of seasoned twigs, he got his firewood. Working carefully from a small beginning, he soon had a roaring fire, over which he thawed the ice from his face and in the protection of which he ate his biscuits.—Jack London, "To Build a Fire"

(2) Use words and expressions that mirror action. Some words are static—nothing moves. Other words mirror movement—they can help us create drama or excitement. Point out all the "action words" you can find in the following passages. How many different kinds of action or movement are part of these two accounts?

> The otter rounded the bend carefully, and began his stalk of the trout. He knew it would be lying like a shadow a little above the sandy bottom in the rushing green gloom of the pocket under the great gray rock. It should be facing upstream, and he would gain an advantage by coming up from the rear. He stretched out full length and, paddling gently and slowly with his forepaws, slid through the water like a stealthy shadow, close to the bank and halfway to the bottom. He came to the corner of the rock and paused, sank until his belly softly scraped the sand, and became one with the bottom's shadows. Then, sinuous as a snake, he began to flow around the rock. He saw the trout several yards away, hanging motionless, and tensed for the spring.—Robert Murphy, "You've Got to Learn"

> The forward funnel snaps and crashes into the sea. Its steel tons hammer out of existence swimmers struggling in the freezing water. Streams of sparks, smoke, and steam burst from

Writing for a Purpose

C3b

STORIES IN THE NEWS

Some famous news stories have been told and retold many times: the sinking of the *Titanic;* Charles Lindbergh's first solo flight across the Atlantic; the last flight of the airship *Hindenburg;* the last flight of Amelia Earhart; the bombing of Pearl Harbor; the first landing on the moon. Tell one of these stories as you remember it.

Composition

the after funnels. The ship upends to fifty—to sixty degrees. . . . The *Titanic* stands on end, poised briefly for the plunge. Slowly she slides to her grave—slowly at first and then more quickly—quickly—quickly.—Hanson Baldwin, *R.M.S. Titanic*

(3) Make your reader share the feelings of the people involved. A good story does not just act out scenes and events. The reader shares the fear, or surprise, or joy of the people in it. The authors of the following passages make us share in what it *felt* like to be there:

He drifted to the surface, his face turned up to the air. He was gasping like a fish. He felt he would sink now and drown; he could not swim the few feet back to the rock. Then he was clutching it and pulling himself up onto it.—Doris Lessing, "Through the Tunnel"

I rolled off the bunk and staggered to the door. Dizziness seized me, and my heart turned fantastic somersaults. As from a great distance, I could see the gray fumes of the exhaust smoke curling under the top sill. The upper half of the tunnel, when I entered, was so foggy that I could not see as far as the alcove where the engine lay.—Richard E. Byrd, *Alone*

(4) Use dialogue to help show the personalities of the people in your story. In the following passage, a well-known black playwright retells a conversation he had with a dean while he was a student at Howard University. What does this conversation show about the *characters* of the student and the dean?

A student friend and I were sitting on the campus studying one day and a watermelon truck passed, and I said, "Let's go buy a watermelon." So we bought this watermelon and went to sit on a bench in front of Douglas Hall. Tom Weaver, the boy I was with, had to go to class, and I was left there alone, sawing on the watermelon. The Dean of Men (who might still be the Dean of Men) came up to me and said, "What are you doing?" And I said, "Well, what do you mean? I'm just sitting here." And he said, "Why are you sitting there eating that watermelon?" I said, "Well, I don't know. I didn't know there was a reason for it, I'm just eating it." And he said, "Throw that away, this very instant." And I answered, "Well, sir, I can only throw half of it away, because I only own half. The other part of it is Mr. Weaver's and he's in class, so I have to wait until he comes out and gets it." The Dean, now quite agitated, replied with great emotion, "Do you realize you're sitting right in front of

Writing for a Purpose

the highway where white people can see you? Do you realize that this school is the capstone of Negro higher education? Do you realize that you're compromising the Negro?"—Imamu Amiri Baraka (LeRoi Jones), "Philistinism and the Negro Writer"

(5) *Make your story add up.* A story moves well when it moves *toward* something. It may move toward success or failure in an important attempt. It may move toward the solution of a problem. It may move toward something the writer has learned from the experience. Such a story has a point. It gives the reader something to think about.

Look at how the following student-written story leads up to its point. In your own words, what does it give the reader to think about?

```
              Like Master, Like Dog

     Manard was a German Shepherd and the
friendliest dog on Hayes Street.  Every child
that walked by Manard's residence left aston-
ished, not only by his friendliness, but also
by his size.  He was about four feet tall on
all fours and weighed between 150 and 200
pounds.  He was a beautiful shade of gray and
white.
     Oddly, Manard was friendly with others
but not to his master, a man we called
Scrooge.  Manard felt the same as we did to-
ward Scrooge.  All Manard received was orders.
"Go get the paper.  Get my slippers.  Lie
down.  Sit.  Shake hands."
     He began leaving home when he was let
loose to roam the yard.  He first began to
stay away for two days and from two days to
two weeks.  When he did return home Scrooge
would take him by the collar, drag him awk-
wardly to the rear of his house, and lash him
with a whip.
     Manard was no longer friendly to anyone.
He barked at the children and tried continu-
ously to jump the fence.  People thought to
themselves:  "Two Scrooges.  Like master,
like dog."
```

Composition

EXERCISE 1 Write two different paragraphs about your ordinary trip to school. Do one in a speeded-up version: You are very late; you are hurrying. Do the other in a slow-motion version: You are very tired; you can hardly move. Use as many "action words" as you can to make your reader see the two different kinds of motion.

EXERCISE 2 Study the following two passages, each chosen from a true-life adventure. For each, do the following:

- Show three steps or stages in what is happening.
- Find three words or expressions that show vividly some movement, action, or event.
- Point out several passages that let us share in what the person thought or felt.

1. Amelia's flight had several handicaps, unexpected ones. About four hours out of Newfoundland she saw a tiny flame beginning to creep through a welded joint in the manifold ring. She couldn't turn back, for it would have been impossible to make a landing in the dark. Added to this harrowing discovery was the realization that her altimeter, the instrument that shows the height of the airplane above the surface of the earth, had suddenly failed. She nosed her plane up to the top of the clouds, only to find that in the higher altitude it was picking up ice. To get to warmer air, she came down where she could see the ocean, but the fog came so low she dared not remain there for fear of flying into the water. So she simply "plowed through the soup" till dawn.—Hope Stoddard, *Famous American Women*

2. Just north of Port Franklin, Alaska, we established our position by quick radar sweeps. They showed that we had rounded the corner of the pack and were, at last, aimed directly toward the Barrow Sea Valley, our deep-water gateway to the western Arctic Basin.

    A few hours later, with ice in sight on our port beam and dead ahead, we reached deep water, deep enough to clear even the largest floes. As we planed below the surface, I said to myself: "This is it. Let's go, go, go!" Through the periscope I caught a last glimpse of the sky. It was a lovely clear morning with a full moon. The sun was rising and there was a gentle southerly breeze.

    We set course northeastward, along the Sea Valley, toward very deep water. All sonars were manned, and the operators strained to detect deep-draft ice. I watched the fathometer closely. It revealed that the valley floor was growing deep and wide. I was confident that at last we had it made. Hugging the valley, we took *Nautilus* deep and increased speed to eighteen knots. It was like pulling onto an expressway from a crowded street.—William R. Anderson, *Nautilus 90 North*

EXERCISE 3

Write your own "story with a point." Write a true story that *leads up* to something that you learned from the experience. It might be something that happened to you or to somebody you know well. It might be something that has happened in your family, in your neighborhood, or in your community. Use the *last sentence* of your paper to sum up what you learned from the experience.

PROSE MODEL 2

Study the following passage as an example of a well-told story. Write down your answers to the questions that follow the story. Prepare to discuss your answers in class.

LOIS PHILLIPS HUDSON

A Silver Dollar

One can follow the Yakima River for miles and miles and see nothing but irrigated fields and orchards—and the camps of transient laborers. The workers come like a horde of salvaging locusts, stripping a field, moving to the next. They fill their boxes or crates or sacks, weigh in, collect the bonuses offered to entice them to stay till the end of the season, and disappear again. They spend their days in rows of things to be picked and their sweltering nights in rows of tents and trailers.

We pitched our tent beside the others. . . . The owners and their bristling foremen never smiled at those children who ran through the fields playing games and only occasionally at those who worked beside their parents.

In North Dakota I had worked on our farm—trampling hay, driving a team of horses, fetching cows, feeding calves and chickens—but of course that had all been only my duty as a member of the family, not a way to earn money. Now I was surrounded by grown-ups who wanted to pay me for working, and by children my own age who were stepping up to the pay window every night with weighing tags in their hands and collecting money. I saw that the time had come for me to assume a place of adult independence in the world.

Composition

I made up my mind I was going to earn a dollar all in one day. We were picking hops then, and of all the rows I have toiled my way up and down, I remember hop rows the most vividly. Trained up on their wires fifteen feet overhead, the giant vines resemble monster grape arbors hung with bunches of weird unripe fruit. A man who does not pick things for a living comes and cuts them down with a knife tied to a ten-foot pole so the people below can strip them off into sacks. Hops don't really look like any other growing thing but instead like something artificially constructed—pine cones, perhaps, with segments cleverly cut from the soft, limp, clinging leaves that lie next to the kernels of an ear of corn. A hop in your hand is like a feather, and it will almost float on a puff of air. Hops are good only for making yeast, so you can't even get healthily sick of them by eating them all day long, the way you can berries or peas.

Pickers are paid by the pound, and picking is a messy business. Sometimes you run into a whole cluster that is gummy with the honeydew of hop aphids, and gray and musty with the mildew growing on the sticky stuff. Tiny red spiders rush from the green petals and flow up your arms, like more of the spots the heat makes you see.

The professionals could earn up to six dollars a day. One toothless grandmother discouraged us all by making as much as anybody in the row and at the same time never getting out of her rocking chair except to drag it behind her from vine to vine. My father and mother each made over three dollars a day, but though I tried to work almost as long hours as they did, my pay at the end of the day would usually be somewhere between eighty and ninety cents.

Then one day in the second week of picking, when the hops were good and I stayed grimly sweating over my long gray sack hung on a child-sized frame, I knew that this was going to be the day. As the afternoon waned and I added the figures on my weight tags over and over again in my head, I could feel the excitement begin making spasms in my stomach. That night the man at the pay window handed me a silver dollar and three pennies. He must have seen that this was a day not for paper but for silver. The big coin, so neatly and brightly stamped, was coolly distant from the piled vines and melting heat that had put it into my hand. Only its solid heaviness connected it in a businesslike way with the work it represented. For the first time in my life I truly comprehended the relationship between toil and media of exchange. I saw how exacting and yet how satisfying were the terms of the world. Perhaps because of this insight, I did not want the significance of my

Writing for a Purpose

dollar dimmed by the common touch of copper pettiness. I gave the vulgar pennies to my little sister, who was amazed but grateful. Then I felt even more grown-up than before, because not everybody my age was in a position to give pennies to kids.

That night I hardly slept, lying uncovered beside my sister on our mattress on the ground, sticking my hand out under the bottom of the tent to lay it on the cooling earth between the clumps of dry grass. Tired as I was, I had written post cards to three people in North Dakota before going to bed. I had told my grandmother, my aunt, and my friend Doris that I had earned a dollar in one day. Then, because I did not want to sound impolitely proud of myself, and to fill up the card, I added on each one, "I'm fine and I plan to pick again tomorrow. How are you?"—adapted from *Reapers of the Dust*

READING QUESTIONS

1. What do the following words and expressions mean in the context of the story?

    a. What makes *transient* workers different from other kinds of workers?
    b. What is a *bonus,* and why does it "entice" people to stay until the end of the season?
    c. What are *segments?* How are pine cones divided into segments?
    d. What are *spasms* in a person's stomach? What caused them in this story?
    e. What is a simpler word for *comprehend?* for *toil?* for *media of exchange?*
    f. It takes some doing to get things "exactly" right. If a job or a contract is *exacting,* what is it like?
    g. Why did the author call the extra pennies "copper pettiness" and "vulgar pennies"?

2. Summarize briefly how the migrant workers live and what kind of work they do. Describe briefly the typical work routine in the fields or orchards.

3. The author several times uses comparisons to help her readers see the workers or the hops. Find several of these comparisons in the prose model above.

4. What passage for you best sums up what it felt like to work at picking hops?

5. What did the dollar mean to the person telling the story? What was she trying to prove? What did she learn from the experience?

Composition

WRITING TOPICS

1. In everyone's memory, a few things stand out. Write about something that really made an impression on you when you were younger. It could be a major event, like a fire, a burglary, or a divorce. It could be something like a misunderstanding, a quarrel, or a very special vacation. Tell the story of what happened. Let your reader see what made the event or events special to you, or what you learned from the experience.
2. Everyone has had a first meeting or a *first encounter* with a person, an animal, or a thing that is memorable for one reason or another. You might, for example, remember the first time you saw a giraffe at close range. Or you might recall the first time you rode a train or flew in a jet. Or perhaps there was something memorable about your first encounter with a person unknown to you. From your own experience, write about a first encounter that was important to you in some way.
3. On television, in movies, and in books we meet people who win against overwhelming odds. We read of the ballplayer who comes through in the last half of the ninth inning and wins the game for the team. Yet there are other kinds of victories, ones that average people are more familiar with. There are *small victories* that people have every day. The boy who conquers shyness, the girl who learns to get along with someone whom she really dislikes—these are small victories that are important but not earthshaking. Tell the story of some small victory that you or someone else has enjoyed.

C3c Explaining a Process

Explain a process to make your reader see how something works.

In the most practical kind of writing, a writer explains how something works. Instructions and directions show us how to do something by describing a process. A scientist may describe a process to make us see how something works in the world of nature. A historian may explain to us how something happened in the history of our nation.

What helps a reader understand your explanation of a process? Remember the following guidelines:

(1) Explain one major step at a time. Sort things out so that your readers can concentrate on one thing until it is clear in their minds. Don't move on too quickly from one step to the next. The faster you move on, the better the chance that you will leave your readers behind. Look at the following instructions on what to do when a car starts to skid on a

Writing for a Purpose

slippery road. The author has tried to fix three major steps clearly in the reader's mind:

FIRST STEP: You control a skidding car by using three of your car controls in varying degrees. First is the steering wheel which you use hard. Don't be afraid to swing it fast to get the car under control. Try to point your wheels in the direction you are skidding. This may call for rapid wheel work, as the very nature of a skid often has the car changing its own direction back and forth . . . .

SECOND STEP: Second, you use the throttle. When the skid begins, ease up on the gas pedal but keep your foot right over it. When you feel you have the front wheels pointing in the direction you are skidding, apply a little gas and you should regain control of the car. . . .

THIRD STEP: The third item is your brake pedal, which you do not use until you are absolutely in control of the car, and then you use it gently. . . . —Tom MacPherson, *Dragging and Driving*

(2) *Follow a process through its stages so that the reader can see it as a whole.* To understand something, or to make something work, we have to see how one thing leads to another. We have to see the major stages in a process in the right order. In your own words, describe the major stages in the natural process that is traced in the following sample passage:

The Rock That Burns

Coal is a black rock made from green plants. Many, many years ago, strange-looking trees and giant ferns covered most of the surface of the earth. Lush vegetation grew in a warm and moist climate. When plants died, they fell to the swamp-like ground and were soon covered by mud and by other plants. Over the years the dead plants piled up higher and higher. They rotted together to make a wet, brown mass called peat. In some areas of the world, such as Ireland and parts of Germany, layers of peat are still close to the surface. Peat is then dug up and dried for use as fuel. But in many other parts of the world, the layers of peat were buried deep under sand and mud. Or they were covered by thick layers of rock as the result of great upheavals in the earth's crust. Under the weight of sand and rock, the layers of peat were pressed together and hardened. They gradually turned into rock-hard coal.

Composition

(3) Help your reader with technical terms. Explain words or expressions that only a sailor would know or that only a botanist would use every day. Look at the following description of how a hot rodder modifies a conventional engine. What is the major term that this paragraph helps explain? Can you give a clear explanation of this term in your own words?

> When he opens a network of channels that feed more fuel into the cylinders at a faster rate, the hot rodder creates a need to get the exhaust gases out of the cylinders with equally increased speed. Vapors and gases that linger in the exhaust system create a back pressure that robs the next combustion stroke of some power. So the dragster cuts in a set of pipes he calls "headers." Headers provide each cylinder with its own escape channel. The header leads the exhaust out of the engine with a minimum of bends and without the obstructing baffles found inside a muffler.—Tom MacPherson, *Dragging and Driving*

(4) Compare new or difficult things to things that are familiar. The following passage takes the reader to a site where archeologists are digging for traces of our early human history. How many comparisons does the author use to help us understand what the site is like?

> Olduvai Gorge looks like a miniature Grand Canyon. It has proved perfect for excavation because it comprises four main soil deposits piled on top of each other and undisturbed by earth movements. Imagine a cake upon which a new layer is deposited every million years. If you cut a slice from the cake, you can see each layer as it was before its burial. Since Olduvai is a natural fault in the flat Serengeti Plain, it is like a gash in the cake. Its four layers, or "beds," give us an exact picture of the earth in four different periods.—Adrian Berry, "A Footprint in Olduvai," *Sunday Telegraph*

EXERCISE 1

How good are you at explaining things to the newcomer or to the beginner? Imagine that your audience is an exchange student from another English-speaking country. The person knows English but may know very little about American customs, hobbies, or sports. Write *one sentence* each about five of the following. Give your audience a basic idea of how each is done or how it is produced.

Writing for a Purpose

1. roller derby
2. milkshake
3. rodeo
4. barbecue
5. primary elections
6. stock car race
7. cheerleading
8. square dancing
9. baton twirling
10. surfing

EXERCISE 2

Choose one of the following. Write a paragraph to explain how it works. Try to show the steps involved in its operation in a clear order. Use comparisons if you can to help make things clear. Choose one:

- a piano;
- a modern harvesting machine;
- a carburetor;
- a vacuum cleaner;
- a rifle;
- a tape recorder;
- a blender;
- a radio.

PROSE MODEL 3

In the following model passage, a writer traces a process that stretched over many years. Study the way he explains things that might be new or difficult for the reader. Write down your answers to the questions that follow the passage. Prepare to discuss your answers in class.

NORMAN B. WILTSEY

The Doomed Buffalo

Before the coming of the horse, the Indians hunted buffaloes on foot. Mass kills, designed to secure a winter's meat supply in one operation, were made by driving hundreds of buffaloes over a steep cliff onto rocks below. On the open plains the most productive method was to decoy the buffaloes into corrals where they could be slaughtered with arrow and lance. Braves dressed in fresh buffalo hides lured the slow-witted beasts into the deathtraps.

These wasteful methods were seldom employed by the Indians after the arrival of the horse on the prairie. Riding his well-trained buffalo horse, a hunter could follow a herd for miles, shooting fat cows with arrows or bringing them down with lance thrusts. Forty to fifty kills a day was not an unusual score for the lethal combination of a strong-armed warrior and a good mount. The Indians did not often use firearms in hunting buffaloes until the advent of the repeating rifle on the prairies in the 1860s.

Early-day white explorers regarded the buffalo as a fearsome curiosity, but to the Indian the shaggy giant meant life itself. The whole economy of the plains tribes was based upon the buffalo. Their very existence depended upon it. All parts of the animal were used. To discard any portion of the huge carcass was regarded not only as a sin against the Great Spirit but against the watchful spirit of the buffalo itself. Buffalo skins made up the Indian's winter clothing and his bed and blanket, his tepees, moccasins, leggings and shirts, and provided clothing for his family.

Boats were made from fresh hides stretched taut over green willow or cottonwood hoops. These later became known as the famous "bullboats" of the mountain men. Water buckets were fashioned from the lining of the paunch. Thread and bowstrings were made from the tough back sinews. Spoons, bows, and ornaments came from scraped and polished horn. The massive ribs made excellent runners for dog-drawn sleds. Glue was made from the hoofs. The short, tasseled tails were used as fly swatters. Even the stones found in the gall bladders were used in making "medicine paint."

Pemmican, the first concentrated meat ration, was the invention of the Indian. Buffalo meat was cut into thin strips and dried on racks in the sun. It was then pounded almost to a powder, mixed with boiling buffalo fat, and poured into lengths of buffalo intestines or rawhide boxes. An ideal diet—particularly when mixed with edible berries—it kept the Indian well nourished and free from scurvy. White explorers and later the mountain men learned to make pemmican for themselves. . . .

The mountain men hunted buffaloes primarily for meat and only secondarily for sport. The thought of hunting buffs commercially for their hides never occurred to them until the beaver trade petered out in the late 1830s. Hide hunting developed gradually over the next decade until, in 1845, 90,000 skins were sent to market. Seton estimated that nearly 2,000,000 buffaloes were slaughtered to produce 90,000 marketable robes. True conservationists before the arrival of the white trader with his guns and whiskey and flashy stock of worthless gewgaws, many of the younger tribesmen now killed buffalo for profit rather than food and shelter.

The more intelligent and farseeing among the chiefs clearly foresaw that their avaricious young men were blindly aiding the white men in destroying the tribes' chief source of liveli-

Writing for a Purpose

hood. Councils were held and speeches made in protest, but the chiefs and elders were shouted down by the youthful braves. So the chiefs and headmen lost their battle to exclude the predatory whites from their ancestral hunting grounds, and the buffalo was doomed.—from "The Great Buffalo Slaughter," *Mankind* (1968)

READING QUESTIONS

1. Choose the right meaning for each italicized word:
   a. Mass kills were *designed* to produce the meat supply for the whole winter.
      (1) allowed   (2) banned   (3) planned
   b. The Indians did not hunt with firearms before the *advent* of the repeating rifle.
      (1) banning   (2) arrival   (3) sale
   c. To *discard* any portion of the animals was considered a grave sin.
      (1) throw away   (2) touch   (3) let spoil
   d. *Avaricious* hunters now killed for profit rather than for food and shelter.
      (1) greedy   (2) careless   (3) thrill-seeking
   e. The concerned chiefs had tried their best to keep out the *predatory* whites.
      (1) traveling through   (2) settling   (3) plundering

2. According to the author, no part of the buffalo was wasted by the Indian hunters. Point out as many different uses of parts of the buffalo as you can.

3. Can you explain some of the hunting terms from this passage to someone who knows nothing about hunting? Write one sentence each to explain the following:

   decoy   trap   lance   bow   arrow

4. Over the years, the methods and purposes of hunting the buffalo changed. Sort out the four or five major stages in this process of change. Describe briefly each major stage.

5. The author says that the Native American hunters had been "true conservationists" before the arrival of the white traders. What does he mean? Does he convince you that the statement is true?

Composition

WRITING TOPICS

1. Study the following description of something that happened every day in the days when mail was carried by the pony express. Then write a similar description of a process that is part of an everyday job for many people today:

   - servicing a car that has stopped for gas;
   - taking care of a customer in a cafeteria or fast-food place;
   - washing a car, or the like.

   There was no idling time for a pony rider on duty. He rode fifty miles without stopping, by daylight, moonlight, starlight, or through the blackness of darkness—just as it happened. He rode a splendid horse that was born for a racer and fed and lodged like a gentleman. He kept the horse at his utmost speed for ten miles. And then, as he came crashing up to the station where stood two men holding fast a fresh, impatient steed, the transfer of rider and mailbag was made in the twinkling of an eye. And away flew the eager pair and were out of sight before the spectator could get hardly the ghost of a look.—Mark Twain, *Roughing It*

2. Choose one of the following topics. You be the expert. Tell your audience "how it works."

   - Pretend you are writing for an exchange student from Europe who complains that baseball is a dull game. Describe some exciting moments of a recent game. Explain what happened.
   - Pretend you are providing background material for a group of friends getting ready for their first driving lessons. Explain what a combustion engine is and how it works.
   - Pretend you are writing instructions for someone who is going to be your camp cook. You want to be sure the food is fit to eat. Give instructions on how to fix some basic meals: how to fry eggs, how to fix hamburgers, how to make pancakes.

3. Explain a common process that goes on around us all the time but that may be a mystery to your reader:

   - how some birds live and nest and propagate;
   - how electric power is generated and transmitted;
   - how and why teenagers form clubs or gangs;
   - how butter or bread or some other common food is made;
   - how pottery or some other product is made by the old handicraft methods;
   - how a snake sheds its skin.

Writing for a Purpose

C3d Persuading Your Reader

Learn to help change your reader's mind.

Persuasion aims at results. When we write to persuade our readers, we try to change their minds. We try to change their ways. What does it take to make people change? Remember the following advice:

(1) Know your audience. To change people's minds, we have to know what they are thinking. We have to know something about their needs and desires. Suppose you are a football fan, but the football programs in local schools are under attack. In fact, they may be discontinued altogether. If you wanted to come to the rescue of your favorite sport, what would be some of the arguments you might have to reckon with? What would you be up against? You would need *counter*arguments for some of the following familiar complaints:

- Parents are worried about their children's safety—how many injuries occur each year?
- Teachers will worry about players' academic work—do football players have low grades?
- Some of your friends may worry whether they can make the team—is football merely for the chosen few?
- Why not concentrate on those sports in which everyone can participate on equal terms, such as swimming or tennis?

(2) Use language strong enough to get attention. To persuade anybody, we must make ourselves *heard*. What we say must make an impression on the reader. The following passage is from a book that helped alert many readers to the dangers lurking in the free use of pesticides. How many "strong words" can you point out in the passage?

> It is not my contention that chemical insecticides must never be used. I do contend that we have put poisonous and biologically potent chemicals indiscriminately into the hands of persons wholly ignorant of their potentials for harm. We have subjected enormous numbers of people to contact with these poisons without their consent and often without their knowledge. If the Bill of Rights contains no guarantee that a citizen shall be secure against lethal poisons distributed either by private individuals or by public officials, it is surely only because our forefathers, despite their considerable wisdom and foresight, could conceive of no such problem.—Rachel Carson, *Silent Spring*

Composition

THE ART OF PERSUASION

Maybe you obey stop signs and signals. Some drivers don't. So never assume the right-of-way blindly. Always protect yourself by driving defensively. If someone follows you too closely, don't speed up. Slow down a little and encourage him or her to pass. Remember, being in the right isn't enough. You could be dead right.

This advertisement from the National Safety Council tried to make drivers change their driving habits. How? How successful do you think this ad was in making people think about their driving? Why?

---

(3) Point to consequences and results. Say, "Look—this is what would happen in practice," or, "Look—this could happen to *you!*" Look carefully at the way the following passage brings the dangers of insecticides close to home. Is there something you think would make this passage *especially* persuasive?

The second major group of insecticides, the alkyl or organic phosphates, are among the most poisonous chemicals in the world. The chief and most obvious hazard attending their use is that of acute poisoning of people applying the sprays or accidentally coming in contact with drifting spray, with vegetation coated by it, or with a discarded container. In Florida, two children found an empty bag and used it to repair a swing. Shortly thereafter both of them died and three of their playmates became ill. The bag had once contained an insecticide called parathion, one of the organic phosphates. Tests established death by parathion poisoning. On another occasion two small boys in Wisconsin, cousins, died on the same night. One had been playing in his yard when spray drifted in from an adjoining field where

Writing for a Purpose

his father was spraying potatoes with parathion. The other had run playfully into the barn after his father and had put his hand on the nozzle of the spray equipment.—Rachel Carson, *Silent Spring*

EXERCISE 1

Do you know any expressions or statements that make people angry? What statements or observations anger parents? What expressions or arguments upset your friends? Write down *five* statements that you know would make some people angry. (Be prepared to explain in class why they upset people.)

EXERCISE 2

Have you recently become aware of some danger or hazard that you used to ignore or take lightly? Write a paragraph entitled "It Could Happen to *You*."

PROSE MODEL 4

Writers like Rachel Carson have aroused public opinion to the dangers facing future generations on our planet. The following passage was first written in 1969. The writer was giving an *imaginary* preview of the future. What did he do to persuade his readers?

PAUL EHRLICH

The End of the Ocean

The end of the ocean came late in the summer, and it came even more rapidly than the biologists had expected. There had been signs for more than a decade, starting with the discovery in 1968 that DDT slows down photosynthesis in marine plant life. It was announced in a short paper in the technical journal, *Science,* but to ecologists it smacked of doomsday. They knew that all life in the sea depends on photosynthesis, the chemical process by which green plants bind the sun's energy and make it available to living things. And they knew that DDT and similar chlorinated hydrocarbons had polluted the entire surface of the earth, including the sea.

But that was only the first of many signs. There had been the final gasp of the whaling industry, and the end of the Peruvian anchovy fishery. Indeed, a score of other fisheries had disappeared quietly from over-exploitation and various eco-catastrophes. The term "eco-catastrophe" was coined by a California

Composition

ecologist in 1969 to describe the most spectacular attacks on the systems which sustain human life. He drew his inspiration from the Santa Barbara offshore oil disaster of that year, and from the news which spread among naturalists that virtually all of the Golden State's seashore bird life was doomed because of chlorinated hydrocarbon interference with its reproduction. Eco-catastrophes in the sea became increasingly common in the 1970's. Mysterious "blooms" of previously rare microorganisms began to appear in offshore waters. Red tides—killer outbreaks of a minute single-celled plant—returned to the Florida Gulf coast and were sometimes accompanied by tides of other exotic hues.

It was clear that the entire ecology of the ocean was changing. A few types of phytoplankton were becoming resistant to chlorinated hydrocarbons and were gaining the upper hand. Changes in the phytoplankton community led inevitably to changes in the community of zooplankton, the tiny animals which eat the phytoplankton. These changes were passed on up the chains of life in the ocean to the herring, plaice, cod and tuna. As the diversity of life in the ocean diminished, its stability also decreased.

Other changes had taken place. Most ocean fishes that returned to fresh water to breed, like the salmon, had become extinct, their breeding streams so dammed up and polluted that their powerful homing instinct only resulted in suicide. Many fishes and shellfishes that bred in restricted areas along the coasts followed them as onshore pollution escalated.

The annual yield of fish from the sea was down to 30 million metric tons, less than one-half the per capita catch of a decade earlier. This helped malnutrition to escalate sharply in a world where an estimated 50 million people per year were already dying of starvation.

READING QUESTIONS

1. Explain the italicized terms:

   "*marine* plant life"
   "*sustain* life"
   "*interference* with reproduction"
   "rare *microorganisms*"
   "the entire *ecology* of the ocean"
   "*restricted* areas"
   "*per capita* catch"
   "*escalate* sharply"

2. Point out examples of words that sound the alarm, that warn of *danger*. (Are there any real "scare" words?)

Writing for a Purpose

3. Modern readers are impressed by the authority of *science*. Can you repeat in your own words the author's scientific arguments? What, for instance, is "photosynthesis"? Does the author help us understand terms like these? How?
4. Of all the author's arguments and examples, which makes the strongest impression on you? Why?
5. Write an imaginary letter back to Paul R. Ehrlich from a reader looking at the author's warnings and predictions at the present time.

WRITING TOPICS

1. Have you ever tried being a peacemaker? Take a good look at two groups of people who are hostile or intolerant toward each other. Write a letter to a representative of *one* of the groups. Try to make the group take a less hostile view of the other.
2. Have you ever felt that progress has gone too far? Choose one convenience, invention, or project that you believe you or society could do without. Explain why you feel we would all be better off without it. Try to make your reader say: "Yes, I'll do without. Who needs it?"
3. Can you sell an idea to a *hostile audience?* Write a short paper in which you do *one* of the following:

   - Convince friends that they should do a fair share of the housework.
   - Convince dog owners of the need for a leash law.
   - Convince local business of the need for higher school taxes.
   - Convince your fellow students that teenagers should not be allowed to own cars.
   - Convince motorists that traffic police should be allowed to drive unmarked cars.
   - Convince parents that there should be no restraints on what movies teenagers should be allowed to see.

UNIT REVIEW EXERCISE

Study the two passages that follow. Then answer the questions that follow each passage. After the number of each question, write the letter for the right answer.

A. 7:30 a.m.: Our first whale! John claims to have spotted two blows in the distance and is peering through binoculars when a soft exhaling erupts startlingly close, and *something* gently and deliberately breaks the surface.

   It looks like an island itself: the gray of wet rock, encrusted with barnacles. It is much too big to be alive, but it *is* alive, and with the unmistakable sound of its breath the

Composition

whole expressionless expanse of water has suddenly leaped to life as well. . . .

There she blows! She, or he, is describing a large and leisurely circle around the boat, perhaps investigating us. Now she dives deep, showing first the row of "knuckles" along her spine. Then the tail flukes rise slowly out of the water, astonishingly delicate and graceful, expressive as a human hand and wrist. It's hard to believe they are 10 feet wide. Off at a distance minutes later, the whale (or another one?) breaches twice, driving two-thirds of her thick body's length into the air and slamming down, sending up great sheets of water amid shrieks from the audience, which mingle with the delayed thunderclap of her fall.—Annie Gottlieb, "In the Presence of Whales," *Quest*

1. In this selection, the major purpose of the author is to
   a. tell the story
   b. explain a process
   c. persuade the reader

2. The author mentions an island and a human hand for the purpose of
   a. getting attention
   b. stressing results
   c. comparison

3. *Dive, breach,* and *slam* point to different kinds of
   a. motion   b. sound   c. comparison

4. All of the following words are used to help shape the reader's general impression of the whale:
   a. expressionless, thick, delayed
   b. gently, slowly, leisurely
   c. deep, whole, close

5. A single key word for this passage might be
   a. fear   b. confusion   c. life

B. The immature driver is irresponsible and discourteous. He drives recklessly or in some other show-off way, loses his temper at other drivers, and shows his childish impatience by honking his horn when he is delayed in traffic. There is a story about a woman whose car stalled in traffic. After several attempts, she saw that she couldn't get it started. The man behind her kept honking and honking. Finally, she got out of her car and politely said to him, "I can't get my car to go, but if you'll work with it, I'll keep your horn blasting."
—Maxwell Halsey, *Let's Drive Right*

Writing a Letter

6. The major purpose of the author is to
   a. tell the story
   b. describe a scene
   c. persuade the reader

7. Most of the passage follows up the idea of
   a. recklessness   b. discourtesy   c. traffic jams

8. The following words best show the connecting thread in this passage:
   a. immature, irresponsible, childish
   b. irresponsible, delayed, politely
   c. recklessly, show-off, stalled

9. To achieve his purpose, the author repeatedly uses
   a. words that mirror motion
   b. strong words
   c. comparisons

10. Readers are made to see that the immature driver
    a. endangers other drivers
    b. disobeys traffic laws
    c. annoys other drivers

C4 WRITING A LETTER

Write letters that make a good impression and that do the job.

In the age of the telephone and the electronic media, letters are still one of the most basic means by which people communicate. Letters carry requests, orders, complaints. They ask for information and inquire about jobs. A good letter carries the message. But it also shows that the person who wrote it considered the message important. Make the appearance of your own letters show that you cared about what they say.

C4a How Business Letters Look

Learn to write neat and effective business letters.

In a business letter, as in almost all kinds of writing, appearance counts. The outward appearance of your letter should show that you are serious about the business at hand. It should show that you value the good will of the people to whom you wrote. Lay things out in such a way that your readers can easily find what they want to know. Avoid abbreviations and other shortcuts. Do a letter over when smudges or erasures would cause it to make a poor first impression.

Composition

Observe the following guidelines:

(1) Use unruled white paper—do not use paper from a notebook. Whenever you can, *type* your letter. If your letter is handwritten, make sure your handwriting is easy to read. Use blue or black ink.

(2) *Single-space* each paragraph of a typed letter. Use double-spacing between paragraphs. In many modern business letters, the first sentence of each paragraph starts flush left—it is not indented. But many people still prefer indented paragraphs, as in other kinds of writing. Allow about a one-inch margin on each side.

(3) Put your **return address** at the top of the page, on the right side. Type the date under it. Then write the **inside address** of the person or firm you are writing to—in a block, flush left. Then put the greeting, or **salutation,** followed by a colon. Some people continue to use the traditional *Mrs.* or *Miss.* Others prefer the newer form *Ms.* for either. Use the salutation you feel most appropriate for the person you are addressing.

This is how the introductory part of your letter would look on the page:

```
                                          287 South Fourth Street
                                          San Jose, California  06126
                                          February 7, 1981


Mr. Ralph J. Clark, Jr.
Personnel Manager
San Rafael Independent-Journal
185 Washington Street
San Rafael, California  94947

Dear Mr. Clark:
```

Sample letters in this section are based in part on materials in Marie M. Stewart a. o., *Business English and Communication,* Fifth Edition, McGraw-Hill (1978), and Walter Wells, *Communications in Business,* Wadsworth (1968).

Writing a Letter

Note: We often write to a firm or organization without knowing the name of the person who will read the letter. The traditional greeting for such letters has been "Gentlemen:" or "Dear Sir:" This greeting is now often criticized as inaccurate or misleading. "Dear Sir or Madam:" would be more accurate.

(4) A business firm usually gives its name and address in a **letterhead.** This letterhead is often centered at the top of its business stationery:

```
                    UNION MANUFACTURING COMPANY
                         27840 Park Boulevard
                         Alliance, Ohio 44601




                                                February 7, 1981

   Ms. Linda Cartswin
   178 East Victoria Street
   Birmingham, Alabama   38652

   Dear Ms. Cartswin:
```

(5) The concluding greeting is called the **complimentary closing.** Use "Sincerely," or "Sincerely yours," (another possibility is "Yours truly,"). Type or print your name below your signature.

```
                              Sincerely yours,

                              Lydia Mendez
                              Lydia Mendez
```

Composition

(6) Keep a carbon copy or make a copy of an important letter. Sometimes a letter you receive carries a note like "cc: Gloria Smith." This means that a carbon copy has gone to someone else who should know about the letter. "Encl." means that something has been enclosed with the letter: A price list or a poster, for instance, may have been sent along.

```
                            Sincerely yours,

                            Lydia Mendez
                            Lydia Mendez

cc:  John Miller
Encl.
```

(7) Put your complete return address on the envelope in the upper left-hand corner. Put the complete address of the receiver in the conventional block format. Check names and addresses both in the letter and on the envelope carefully for misspellings and mistakes. (Note one of the advantages of a standard-size business envelope: You need to fold the ordinary full-sized sheet only twice.)

Sample Envelope

```
Joshua Garnett
2349 East Carnegie Lane
Chicago, Illinois  60616
```

```
                    Mrs. Carmen Costagna
                    Manager, Sales Department
                    Hobby Products Inc.
                    3765 North Huron Drive
                    Chicago, Illinois  60603
```

Writing a Letter

EXERCISE 1 Study Sample Letter A. Write a letter back to Cynthia Valdez at the Institute for Business Writing. Thank her for the information about business letters. Tell her briefly what kind of business letters you have seen or received. Ask any questions that you may have about the way business letters should look.

Include all major elements of the standard business letter. Follow either the indented or the block format. (You may want to ask your teacher for his or her preference.)

EXERCISE 2 Study Sample Letter B. Write a letter to Sheila Bialek at Save-Much Electronics. Ask any questions you may have about (a) tape recorders and sound tape; or (b) guarantees and warranties given by business firms. Include all major elements of the standard business letter.

EXERCISE 3 Divide a plain sheet of paper into three sections the size of a standard business envelope. Address each as if it were a business letter ready to be sent out. Address them as follows:

- Send one from your home address to the principal or other chief administrator of your school.
- Send one from your school address to a neighborhood business whose address you know (or can find out).
- Send one from an imaginary local citizen to the President at 1600 Pennsylvania Avenue, Washington, D.C. 20500.

Folding and Inserting Letters

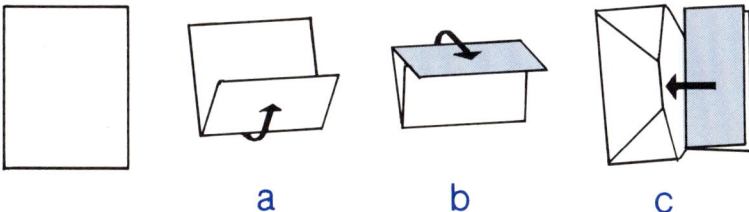

a   b   c

a. Bring the bottom third of the letter up and make a crease.
b. Fold the top of the letter down close to the crease you made in step *a*. Then make the second crease.
c. Put the creased edge you made in step *b* into the envelope first.

SAMPLE BUSINESS LETTER A—Block Format

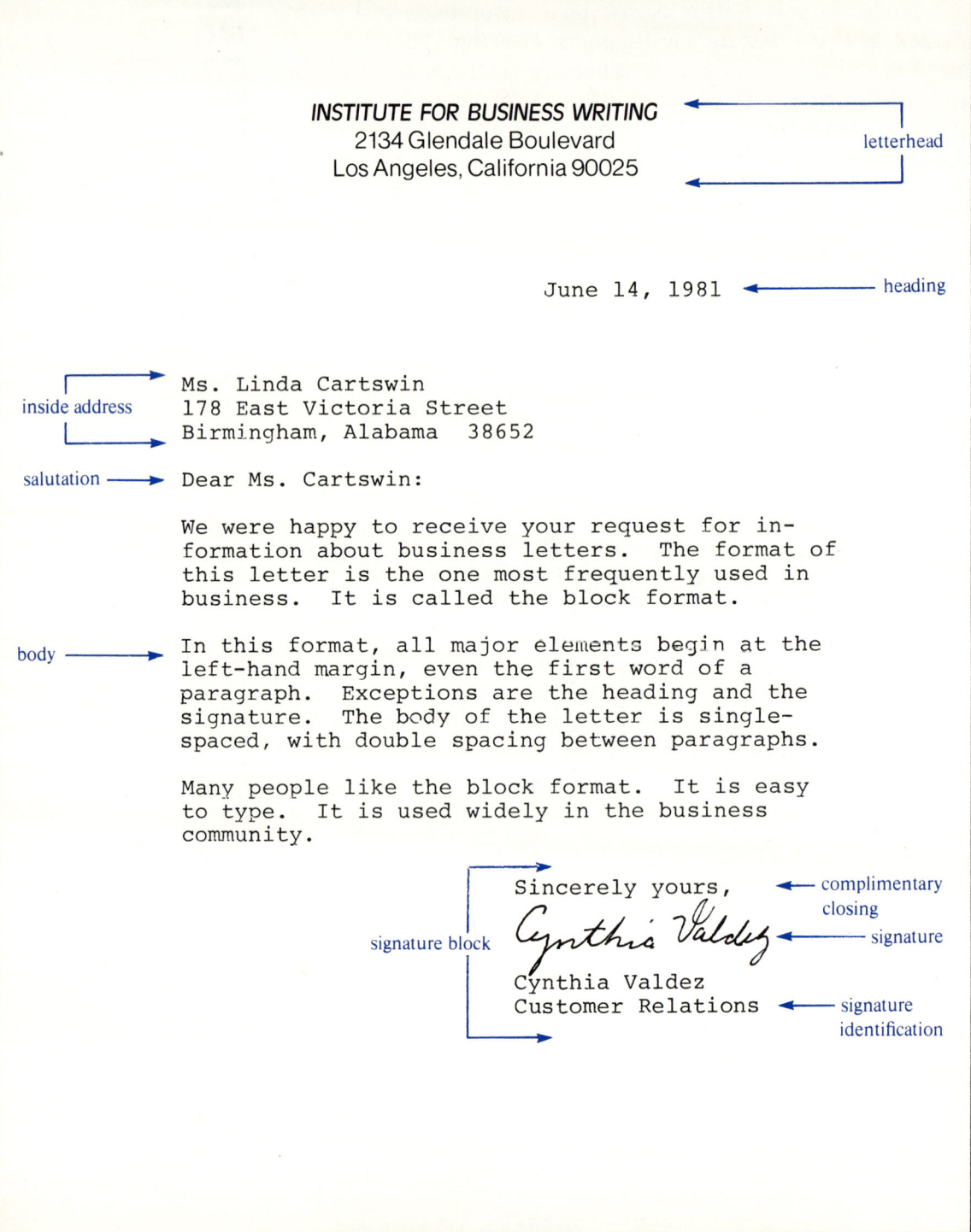

SAMPLE BUSINESS LETTER B—Indented Format

SAVE-MUCH ELECTRONICS
573 Atlantis Street
Boston, Massachusetts 02210

October 30, 1981

Mr. George F. Locke
1282 Daleview Boulevard
Miami, Florida 33171

Dear George:

    We have received your questions about reprocessed sound tape. Many of our customers have been curious about it.

    After investigating this kind of tape, Save-Much Electronics has decided against selling it. We want to be able to guarantee fully any product we put on the market. Reprocessed tape often is outdated tape, and we cannot guarantee its quality. Some of our customers have tried it out and been dissatisfied.

    Our most economically priced tape actually costs little more than reprocessed tape. We feel it is much more dependable.

                                   Sincerely yours,

                                   Sheila Bialek
                                   Sheila Bialek
                                   Customer Service Department

Enclosure: Price List

C4b
What Business Letters Say

Write letters that go straight to the point.

Learn to write letters that are businesslike. Explain clearly what you want or need. Don't go out of your way to flatter or insult your reader. Here are some familiar purposes business letters may serve:

(1) Give clear and complete information when you send orders or requests. Put yourself in the shoes of the reader who says: "What does this person want?" When you order something, give clear information: exact description of the article, size or kind, correct catalogue number, or the like. When you ask for information, help the other person understand your interest in the subject, or your needs. When you ask for a favor, add a personal touch that will make helping you a pleasure for the other person.

Study the following two sample letters. Point out things that help make each a model of its kind:

SAMPLE LETTER C

```
                            583 River Road
                            Bismarck, North Dakota  58501
                            May 1, 1980


Coldbar Publications, Inc.
201 Madison Avenue
New York, New York  10016

Dear Sir or Madam:

     I've searched all around my city for a place
that sells the Weekly Forum, but without success.
Can you tell me if the periodical is distributed
in Bismarck?  If it isn't, can I subscribe to it?
What is the annual subscription rate?  And where
should I send my subscription order?

                            Yours truly,

                            Chris Carlsen
                            Chris Carlsen
```

Writing a Letter

C4b

SAMPLE LETTER D

```
                                    5927 Peachtree Lane
                                    Chamblee, Georgia   30341
                                    October 16, 1980


United World Airlines
378 East 52nd Street
New York, N. Y.  10021

Dear Sir or Madam:

     Last week I was reading a flight magazine published
for your company.  One of the articles mentioned a kit of
materials with luggage stickers, maps, and a set of
"Junior Pilot" wings that your airline gives to youngsters.
I have a younger sister and brother who would very much
enjoy having this kit.  They are very much interested in
planes.  If you could send me two of these kits, I would be
very grateful.

                                    Sincerely,

                                    Joel Cooper
                                    Joel Cooper
```

(2) *Put your best foot forward when asking for a job.* The most important kind of letter that most people write when they get older is the **letter of application.** When you ask for a job, try to include in your letter things that would show any or all of the following:

- you are familiar with the job or the area;
- you have had some previous experience;
- you have skills or training that would help;
- you would like the work;
- you would try to adjust to the employer's requirements concerning time, place, and the like;
- you would make every effort to appear for a personal interview.

Study the model letter on the following page. Put yourself in Mr. Mellow's shoes. Identify three things that he might like about this letter.

Composition

SAMPLE LETTER E

```
                                    3640 Williams Street
                                    Dearfield, Michigan  30742
                                    December 10, 1980




Mr. Thurgood Mellow, Director
Dearfield Young People's Club
5023 Oregon Boulevard
Dearfield, Michigan  30742

Dear Mr. Mellow:

    I would like to apply for a position as counselor
in the Dearfield Young People's Camp this summer.  Last
year, I was in the camp as a camper and really enjoyed
the experience.  I assisted two of the counselors in
planning activities, especially in nature studies.
Both of them encouraged me to apply for a counselor's
position for this year.

    I have enjoyed outdoor life and nature studies
for many years.  For several summers, my family went on
camping trips to the Upper Peninsula.  I very much like
the idea of working with young campers and teaching
them some of the skills of outdoor life.  I could come
in for an interview any time after school, or on a
Saturday.

                                    Sincerely,

                                    *Patricia Phoebes*
                                    Patricia Phoebes
```

(3) Be firm but polite when writing to complain. We often write a letter that asks someone else to correct a mistake. We often write the letter when we are still angry or upset. But the purpose of such a letter is not to insult and blame the guilty party. The purpose is to make the other person feel responsible. We want the other person to do whatever is reasonable to help correct the problem. Try to include any or all of the following:

- sketch out briefly what led up to the problem, or how it came about;

Writing a Letter

- if you can, show the other person's obligation or responsibility;
- suggest specific steps that would take care of the problem.

Here is a sample of the kind of letter of complaint that we all at times *feel* like writing. Use it as a model of a letter *not* to write:

> Just what kind of outfit are you people running? I place a simple order, delivery takes forever, and when it finally gets here, half the pieces are broken. To top it all off, in the same day's mail I get your bill. Some joke!

EXERCISE 1

Write to the Distribution Manager at Coldbar Publications. Ask him or her about a magazine you know, or about a *kind* of magazine you would like to read. Ask about such things as:

- content;
- price;
- how often published;
- where and how to order;
- special bargains at renewal time.

Include all major elements of a standard business letter. (Remember that Coldbar is a fictitious name and address.)

EXERCISE 2

Have you seriously thought about a future job or a future career? Write a letter of application for a possible future job that you have thought about. Write as if you already had some of the training, skills, or experience you hope to have several years from now. Write your letter to a fictitious name and address in the line of work that interests you.

EXERCISE 3

Write a letter that complains about a real-life problem or mistake. Address it to someone with a real responsibility or obligation in the matter. Try to be firm but polite.

Composition

C4c

Writing a Personal Letter

Write personal letters that will be a pleasure to receive.

Most people like to receive personal letters. Many people check their mailbox hoping that someone has thought of them. To make sure your personal letter gives pleasure to the receiver, observe two basic rules: Use neat-looking paper. Take the extra time to write legibly.

Here is an example of a simple thank-you letter:

> 50 Fairway Street
> Wilmington, Delaware 19707
> March 22, 1981
>
> Dear Mrs. King,
>
> I was thrilled with the stamp album you sent me for Christmas. I didn't expect anyone to remember that I collect stamps, and I was planning to buy the type of album you sent me. Now, I will have extra money for stamps with which to start this book. Thank you for a wonderful gift.
>
> Sincerely yours,
> Bruce Carroll

Here are some recommendations:

(1) Use plain stationery and blue or black ink. Until recently, it was considered too businesslike and cold to typewrite a personal letter, but most people now appreciate the legibility of print and do not object to receiving a typewritten friendly letter.

Writing and Reading

(2) Write your address and the date on the right side near the top of the page. (Many people put their address only on the outside of the envelope.) Use a comma or a colon after the greeting. Write your letter in usual paragraph form—indent the first line of your paragraph.

(3) *Sincerely, Sincerely yours, With love,* or *With fond regards* are often used as closings. The signature must be handwritten even if the letter itself is typed.

Here are some ideas for personal letters you could write:

1. Write a thank-you letter for an imaginary gift you would very much like to receive. Write the letter to the imaginary giver.
2. Write letters to relatives or friends of your family. Ask them to help you in your research into family history. Tell them what you already know about the history of your family. Suggest ways they could help you find out more.
3. Write to an imaginary favorite relative. Ask for advice with a problem you have encountered. Explain what the problem is.
4. Write to a pen pal in a foreign country. Tell the person what an American high school is like.
5. Write a letter to your teacher. Help the teacher get to know you better as a person.
6. Write to an imaginary friend in a different part of the country. Tell your friend what it is like to live where you do.
7. Write to a person with whom you share fond memories. Write to remind the person of the experiences you shared.
8. Write to a person you admire. Tell the person about yourself.

WRITING TOPICS

Learn to summarize and to report on the results of your reading.

Writing and reading go together. There are three main ways that reading will benefit you as a writer:

(1) *Reading will improve your writing skills.* Reading makes you more familiar with the resources of language. It acquaints you with the methods and strategies used by successful writers.

(2) *Reading provides information useful in your own writing.* If, for example, you are writing a report on the current airport problem in the United States, you might well begin by checking for current magazine articles that can supply you with information on your topic. You might con-

C5

WRITING AND READING

Composition

sult the latest government statistics on the number of air passengers and local projections for the next few years. You might consult a book by an expert in the field.

(3) Reading enables you to compare your own experience with that of others. Reading what other people have done and thought gives you a basis for comparison. Often you will understand your own problems better when you read how others reacted to similar situations.

Learn to do two things to make good use of the results of your reading in your own writing:

- Collect information and *summarize* it for future use.
- Interpret and *report* on what you read.

C5a The Summary

Condense written material in a summary.

When we summarize, we try to get at the basic meaning of a passage. We omit or condense words, phrases, and sentences that are not essential to the central idea.

The following procedure will help you prepare a summary of written material:

(1) Carefully read the passage that you want to summarize. As you read, try to identify the author's overall purpose. Pick out the main steps in the author's presentation—*outline* it in your mind.

(2) Identify the sentence that comes closest to summing up the passage. A topic sentence or central idea usually is present. Use this sentence, shortening it if possible. Leave out other sentences that restate this key idea in simpler form.

(3) If there are two or three examples, choose the best or clearest one. Omit the others. If there are many statistical figures, select the most essential ones. If an incident or a typical case is discussed in detail, keep only the highlights.

(4) Omit all words and phrases that repeat a similar idea. Wherever you can, make one word do the work of three or four. Put "now" for "at this time," or "maternal grandmother" for "grandmother on his mother's side."

Study the following passage and the summary that follows it. Point out things that have been done to shorten the original. Has anything *essential* been omitted?

Writing and Reading

Original:

When the monumental *Century Dictionary* was prepared late in the last century, the editors very properly considered *garage* a French word which had no place in a dictionary of English. Then came the automobile. The French word *garage* meant any kind of place where bicycles, railroad cars, wagons, or anything of the sort could be stored for protection. It came from French *garer,* to protect; Provençal *garer* and Old High German *warer* had roughly the same meaning as their English cognates *guard, ward*. In the United States and Britain, as in a number of other countries, the word now designates a building for the storage or repair of automobiles. In a half-century the word has become thoroughly acclimated. Most users of it have no notion that it means a place of protection, and they have gone about anglicizing the pronunciation. Some speakers in the United States try to preserve an approximation of the French, and say something like *guh-razh,* but the bulk of the workers in garages, or the patrons of garages do not know French. The growing pronunciation in the United States seems to be that which rhymes with *hodge.* Meanwhile, in England the accent has been shifted to the first syllable, after the conventional English pattern, and the growing pronunciation there seems to be one which about rhymes with *carriage.* —Charlton Laird, *The Miracle of Language*

Summary:

Before 1900, *garage* was a French word for a storage place for any kind of vehicle. *Garage* comes from a word that means "protect" and is related to *guard*. Now the word is thoroughly English and means a place for storing and repairing cars. Some people still imitate the French *guh-razh,* but most Americans make the word rhyme with *hodge*. In England, more and more people make it rhyme with *carriage*.

Note: There is no set length for a summary. If you are summarizing a short paper or article, you might want to devote three or four sentences to each paragraph. If you are summarizing a long article or essay, you might try to condense every paragraph into a single sentence, passing over those that do not contribute importantly to the author's main point.

Composition

EXERCISE 1

Summarize each paragraph below in two or three sentences.

1. The old grammar school P.S. 35 ("Dirty 5's" we called it and with justification) has been replaced by a low, coldly functional arrangement of glass and Permastone which bears its name but has none of the feel of a school about it. The small, grudgingly lighted stores along Fulton Street, the soda parlor that was like a church with its stained-glass panels in the door and marble floor have given way to those impersonal emporiums, the supermarkets. Our house even, a brownstone relic whose halls smelled comfortingly of dust and lemon oil, the somnolent street upon which it stood, the tall, muscular trees which shaded it were leveled years ago to make way for a city housing project—a stark, graceless warren for the poor. So that now whenever I revisit that old section of Brooklyn and see these new and ugly forms, I feel nothing. I might as well be in a strange city.—Paule Marshall, "Reena"

2. The discovery of the throne room in this western section was one of the great thrills of excavation at Cnossus. The first notion the excavator had that the diggers had come upon something exceptional was when the spades struck against the top of the high-backed gypsum throne and its curves began to show above the debris. In great excitement they dug the prize out and cleared the space around it. Nothing in the room had been moved. The big chair still stood in place against the wall. The stone benches on which the counselors had sat still flanked the throne on either side and ran along three sides of the room, the fourth, probably curtained in the great days, opening into an anteroom. On the floor of the throne room lay a shattered, overturned oil jar and some broken libation vessels. An opening in the wall opposite the anteroom led to an inner chamber, which a shrine of the Great Mother Goddess of Crete declared to be a Holy of Holies.—Anne Terry White, *Lost Worlds*

3. The woodchuck's hibernation usually starts about the middle of September. For weeks he has been foraging with increased appetite among the clover blossoms and has grown heavy and slow-moving. Now, with the coming of mid-September, apples and corn and yarrow tops have become less plentiful, and the nights are cool. The woodchuck moves with slower gait, and emerges less and less frequently for feeding trips. Layers of fat have accumulated around his chest and shoulders, and there is thick fat in the axils of his legs. He has extended his summer burrow to a length of nearly thirty feet, and has fastened a deep nestchamber at the end of it, far below the level of the frost. He has carried in, usually, a little hay. He is ready for the long sleep.—Alan Devoe, *Lives Around Us*

Writing and Reading

EXERCISE 2 Find a current newspaper or magazine article on one of the topics that are familiar issues in journalistic writing. If the article runs to several pages, select a passage of about 1,000 words. Write a 300-word summary. Choose an article on one of the following topics:

- long-range prospects for the world's food supply;
- current efforts to make cars safer;
- voter registration efforts for minorities;
- career opportunities for women;
- the future of space exploration;
- job opportunities for teenagers.

C5b The Book Report

Report your reaction to a book you have read.

There are many different types of books that you might choose to report on or that might be assigned to you by your teacher. Most book reports that you write may be about novels. You might, however, report upon a biography, an autobiography, a long essay, a collection of short stories by a single author, or an account of travel or adventure. No matter what type of book you report on, your report can provide answers to the following questions:

PLOT—What *happens* in the book? The reader of your report wants to know what took place in the book you read. Provide at least a brief sketch of the major events. If the book is a novel, summarize the major incidents in the story. If your report is based upon a biography or an autobiography, a travel or an adventure book, summarize the main events. Be brief and to the point. Many students go overboard in reporting the major incidents and wind up retelling the whole story. Remember that explaining what happens is only *a part* of your report.

CHARACTERIZATION—Who are the major *characters* in the book? The reader of your report will be interested in the people who play the major roles in the book. If the book is a novel, identify the main characters and point out their main traits. In a biography or autobiography, the main character will be obvious. But you might want to identify briefly other characters who influenced the subject of the book.

SETTING—*Where* does the story take place? Setting, or the locale, of a book is often important. The surroundings often have an influence upon the characters. Try to show how the setting influences the characters and affects their actions.

Composition

THEME— What is the *major point* of the book? Try to sum up for the reader of your report what the author's major idea seems to be. In a novel, for example, an author might wish to show some basic trait of human nature. A biographer might want to celebrate or criticize a famous person. Authors of a travel book might focus attention upon some feature of the area through which they traveled.

EVALUATION— What is *your reaction* to the book? Why did you react as you did? You will have to support your reaction. Explain what most impressed you about the book, or what you enjoyed most. Explain what was missing that you had hoped to find.

Although a book report will focus primarily upon the actual content of the book, it might be appropriate to present **background material** that will help your reader to understand the book better. You might, for example, know something about the author or the circumstances under which the book was written. Or you might have some additional information about the setting of the story or the historical period in which it takes place. Using such information will help the reader of your report. It will show that you have taken time to investigate beyond the book itself.

In writing book reports, keep these points in mind:

(1) Use short, well-chosen quotations. Use short quotations to show what the characters in the book thought and felt or to show the author's point of view on an important issue.

(2) Explain the role a character or an event plays in the book. When you mention something from the book, give the reader an idea how it "fits in" with the book as a whole.

(3) Do not rely on general labels. Do not just call a book "interesting," or "fascinating," or "exciting." Try to show what *makes* it interesting or exciting.

The following is an example of a book report. Read it carefully. Be prepared to discuss in class how well it answers the questions discussed earlier in this section.

William E. Barrett, The Lilies of the Field

A young man, recently discharged from the Army and happy to be free, is traveling through the western United States in his

Writing and Reading

battered station wagon. He is in no rush to get anywhere. He simply wants to enjoy the life of a civilian again. In a lonely valley, he sees a group of women cultivating the rocky ground and attempting to build a fence. The young man notices that the farm house and its outbuildings on the land are dilapidated and need work. Figuring that he can use the wages from a few days' work, he offers his services to the women. They happen to be a group of Catholic nuns newly arrived from Germany. The Mother Superior of the group feels that the young man has been sent by God to help them build a chapel. Eventually, she persuades the young man to build the chapel. Although he feels that such a task is beyond him, he tackles it and eventually builds a little church. It becomes a religious shrine and a rather famous building.

The young man and main character in this short novel is Homer Smith, who is twenty-four years old, six foot two, and black. Of almost equal importance is Mother Maria Marthe, a headstrong woman who has a dream and who refuses to let go of it. She sees Homer as God's instrument who is going to help the nuns start a school for poor boys from the city. Homer is not too fond of this woman who keeps insisting that he can do what, at first, he has neither the desire nor, in his mind, the ability to do. Moreover, he is rather put off by her commanding attitude. He is annoyed by her constant shouting of "Schmidt!" when she wants to gain his attention.

The chapel serves as the focal point of the story. The chapel enables the author to permit the full development of the characters of Homer Smith and Mother Maria Marthe. Homer believes that the building of the structure is beyond him. In addition, as a practicing Baptist he is not too anxious to build a place of worship for a group of Catholic nuns. Mother Maria Marthe refuses to accept Homer's complaints of not being able to build the structure. She simply knows that he can and believes that he will. Homer does build it and he builds it well. In the process, he learns what he, by himself, can accomplish and develops a tremendous pride in his ability.

The main feature of this story is its simplicity. There are no heroic actions and no moving speeches. There is only the interaction of two strongwilled people who, in the end, give each other something. Mother Maria Marthe gets her chapel and eventually her school. Homer Smith gets confidence in his ability, pride, and a feeling of belonging: "Their smiles made him welcome and Homer felt immediately at ease with them. They did not have any color line; he was just people to them." Homer Smith gives one more thing to the nuns. After he helps them with countless English lessons, they eventually speak with an obvious South Carolina accent.

Composition

EXERCISE 1

What kind of *nonfiction* books does your school library or public library have? Choose a book on one of the topics listed below. Write a book report that would make your friends or classmates want to read the book.

- early explorers on the American continent;
- the building of the railroads;
- pioneers of flight;
- pioneers of modern medicine;
- great discoveries of modern archeology.

EXERCISE 2

What kind of *young adult* novel is popular with teenagers? One student listed books with the following kinds of plots:

- A teenager faces the problem of "finding satisfying relationships with one's peers."
- The central figure is downtrodden or persecuted because of skin color or beliefs. Somehow that person overcomes the obstacles and shows the world that he or she "is valuable."
- A teenager has a serious psychological problem or perhaps is even mentally retarded.
- The leading character has occult powers that make him or her able to communicate with people in another world.

Have you recently read a book in one of these categories? If not, ask a friend, teacher, or librarian to recommend one. Write a report explaining why you would or would not recommend the book.

EXERCISE 3

Books come in all shapes and sizes. Here is a list of books that people over the years have found worth reading. Your teacher might ask you to choose one or more for a book report.

Sheila Burnford, *The Incredible Journey*
Mari Sandoz, *The Horsecatcher*
Arna Bontemps and Jack Conroy, *Anyplace But Here*
Paul Annixter, *Swiftwater*
John Gunther, *Death Be Not Proud*
Suzanne Clauser, *A Girl Named Sooner*
Margaret Craven, *I Heard the Owl Call My Name*
Scott O'Dell, *Island of the Blue Dolphins*
Maia Wojciechowska, *A Single Light*
Majorie Kinnan Rawlings, *The Yearling*
Conrad Richter, *The Light in the Forest*
William Saroyan, *The Human Comedy*
Ray Bradbury, *The Martian Chronicles*

Writing for a Reader

FOR FURTHER STUDY

WRITING AND IMAGINATION

We use our imagination to break through the narrow borders of what we see every day. It can take us to places and times different from our own. It can make us share in the thoughts and feelings of people different from ourselves. An effective writer has to appeal to the readers' imagination to help them understand what is new and unfamiliar. The following projects for reading and writing will give you a chance to use your imagination.

ACTIVITY 1

Some poems are long, but many other poems are very short. Poets *weigh words*—they can say much in a little space. They make each line count. The Japanese *haiku* is a very short kind of poem that makes the poet say something worthwhile in only three short lines. The lines do not rhyme; and they have no regular rhythm, or meter. The requirements are simple: The first line consists of five syllables, the second of seven, and the third of five. Here are examples written by students:

> Deer go through the woods
> swift, but very noiselessly.
> Hunter strikes one down.

> Three very small elves
> took rides on the rainbow slide,
> Now, colorful elves.

> A hot summer day;
> I see no children playing
> —just the butterflies.

Try your hand at writing three examples of *haiku*. Make simple experiences and observations the subjects of your poems. Compare the results with those of your classmates.

ACTIVITY 2

People are not always talking, but they are thinking to themselves all the time. Have you ever tried to write down all the thoughts that were passing through your head at a given time? In the following sample paper, a student writer tells us what it would be like to sit in a small clothing store waiting for customers. How real are the thoughts passing through the person's mind? (What are some of the thoughts that *you* think would have passed through the person's mind?)

```
                    My Store

     My store is small, but equipped with any-
thing a person needs.  Now I have to sit and
wait for that person to come in.  Advertise-
ments are hanging on the wall and boxes are
piled high.  I've satisfied the people's
desire, and now where are the people?  I
ordered several shirts for the man on the
corner, but where is he?  Only one customer,
and he doesn't seem too interested in buying
anything.  Mortgage is going up next week, so
I better get up and attract some customers.
Just ordered a half a dozen jackets that are
popular.  I should make profit enough for go-
ing overseas on my vacation.
```

Do a similar paper telling us the thoughts passing through the mind of *one* of the following:

- a traffic officer;
- someone selling hot dogs at a big stadium;
- someone working in an all-night restaurant;
- a garbage crew working a wealthy neighborhood;
- a parent taking care of several small children;
- a teacher in front of a restless, noisy class;
- a student about to take a difficult exam.

ACTIVITY 3

People have always been curious about the past. How well can you reconstruct in your mind what life was like at some earlier time? Can you imagine how people once thought and felt? Study the following sample entry from an imaginary colonial diary. Does it ring true? Can you picture yourself in a similar situation? Use your imagination to write the next few entries.

Writing for a Reader

Colonial Diary

Friday, December 19, 1650

Dear diary,

I got up earliest of the family this day for to do my chores and fix breakfast for my mother and three brothers. I do this because my mother has fallen ill, like father before he died. There is no doctor in our village so we have to do the best we can on our own.

I woke John and Tim, my older brothers, for it was time to eat and do their chores. I left William to sleep for he is too young to do chores for he is only two years of age.

Round noon of that day John and I rode to town for to help the Charlestons because they just arrived the day before this. While there, we found there were two women on trial for witchery and were to be burned to the stake the day after this.

When we returned, I started a kettle of stew for supper and then fixed lunch. But mother would not eat.

Samantha

As a child, how much attention did you pay to "old-timers"? Pretend you are an old-timer. Tell us about

- life on the family farm;
- building the railroads;
- riding the great trains;
- life in the "old country";
- working in the fields or the factories;
- going to sea;
- serving in the armed forces, old style.

ACTIVITY 4

Can you use your imagination to share in the thoughts and feelings of people with a background different from your own? The passage on the following page is from a story about a boy from a minority background who is trying to become like "everybody else." Can you imagine yourself in his shoes? Read the passage carefully, and answer the questions that follow it.

ACTIVITY 5

Composition

I Rebel Against Being a Mexican

On Monday I borrowed three dollars from my Uncle Rodolfo without telling him what it was for. Miss Rosas hadn't told me what night she wanted me to take her to the movies. But the way she had looked at me made me think that almost any night would do. So I decided on Friday. Waiting for it to come was hard. But I had to keep my mind occupied. So I went to Zamora's newsstand to get the Alma Norteña songbook. Poring through it for the most romantic song I could find, I decided on *La Cecilia.*

All week long I practiced singing it on my way to school and in the shower after basketball practice with the Little Chihuahua Tigers at the Sagrado Corazón gym. But, except for singing this song, I tried not to speak Spanish at all. At home I made my mother mad by saying in English, "Please pass the sugar."

My mother looked at me as though she couldn't believe what she had heard. Since my Uncle Rodolfo couldn't say anything more than "hello" and "goodbye" in English, he couldn't tell what I had said. So my sister Consuelo did.

"May the Dark Virgin with the benign look make this boy well enough to speak Christian again," my mother whispered.

This I refused to do. I went on speaking English even though my mother and uncle didn't understand it. This shocked my sisters as well. When they asked me to explain my behavior, I parroted Miss Rosas, saying "We're living in the United States now."

My rebellion against being a Mexican created an uproar. Such conduct was unorthodox, if not scandalous, in a neighborhood where names like Burciaga, Rodríguez, and Castillo predominated. But it wasn't only the Spanish language that I lashed out against.

"Mother, why do we always have to eat *sopa, frijoles refritos, mondongo,* and *pozole?*" I complained. "Can't we ever eat roast beef or ham and eggs like Americans do?"

My mother didn't speak to me for two days after that. My Uncle Rodolfo grimaced and mumbled something about renegade Mexicans who want to eat ham and eggs even though the Montes Packing Company turned out the best *chorizo* this side of Toluca. My sister Consuelo giggled and called me a Rio Grande Irishman, an American Mister, a gringo, and a *bolillo.* Dulce Nombre looked at me worriedly.
—Amado Muro, "Cecilia Rosas"

Writing for a Reader

1. Explain briefly each of the following: *poring, speak Christian, parroted, unorthodox, scandalous, predominate, grimace, renegade.* Can you explain the Spanish terms used?
2. Pretend you are Uncle Rodolfo. Write a letter to relatives back home telling them what is happening to your nephew.
3. Write a letter offering sympathy, advice, or criticism to the boy. What would you say to someone in his position? Can you imagine yourself in his place?
4. Use the above passage as a model. Write a passage in which you take your classmates to a setting different from their own. Try to make them see and feel how other people in their community or in the larger society live and think.

ACTIVITY 6

In the following passage, a well-known American writer tries to record the way two people *talk* to each other. (The couple has just moved out into the country; and the man has just come back, with a big bag of groceries, from a long walk to the store.) Is there any familiar pattern in the way these people talk to each other? In the original story, the conversation between these two people continues for several more pages. Can you write the next installment—the way it would be if you were to take the story over? (A hint: In the original story, the woman discovers next that the eggs in the grocery bag have been squashed.)

>   Had he brought the coffee? She had been waiting all day long for coffee. They had forgot it when they ordered at the store the first day.
>   Gosh, no, he hadn't. Lord, now he'd have to go back. Yes, he would if it killed him. He thought, though, he had everything else. She reminded him it was only because he didn't drink coffee himself. If he did he would remember it quick enough. Suppose they ran out of cigarettes? Then she saw the rope. What was that for? Well, he thought it might do to hang clothes on, or something. Naturally she asked him if he thought they were going to run a laundry? They already had a fifty-foot line hanging right before his eyes. Why, hadn't he noticed it, really? It was a blot on the landscape to her.
>   He thought there were a lot of things a rope might come in handy for. She wanted to know what, for instance. He thought for a few seconds, but nothing occurred. They

Composition

could wait and see, couldn't they? You need all sorts of strange odds and ends around a place in the country. She said, yes, that was so; but she thought just at that time, when every penny counted, it seemed funny to buy more rope. That was all. She hadn't meant anything else. She hadn't just seen, not at first, why he felt it was necessary.

Well, thunder, he had bought it because he wanted to, and that was all there was to it. She thought that was reason enough, and couldn't understand why he hadn't said so, at first. Undoubtedly it would be useful, twenty-four yards of rope, there were hundreds of things, she couldn't think of any at the moment, but it would come in handy. Of course. As he had said, things always did in the country.—Katherine Anne Porter, "Rope"

ACTIVITY 7

Write a *key scene,* providing action and dialogue, for a science-fiction movie based on one of the following ideas. (You and your classmates may want to *collaborate* and put together several related scenes.)

1. A team of surgeons and scientists are shrunken to bacteria size and are thus able to enter the human body to uncover the secrets of life.
2. Robots have become perfected to the point where people can hardly tell them apart from humans. These robots have infiltrated the command staff of the science-fiction society and seem ready to take over.
3. A group of scientists attempts to explore the ocean depths and finds itself trapped in an incredible underwater world.
4. Scientists experimenting with time have accidentally upset the built-in biological time clock that controls aging in human beings. Everyone is aging at the rate of fifty times normal.
5. A hail of seeds from outer space strikes our planet. These seeds grow into rapidly spreading man-killing plants.
6. A spaceship leaving earth after nuclear war carries hundreds of survivors to an uncontaminated planet. But mysterious changes are beginning to take place in the crew and the passengers as the result of radiation.
7. Scientists are watching a comet coming closer to the earth. Some scientists are beginning to suspect that the comet is actually a body steered and inhabited by life forms looking for a planet to colonize.

Writing for a Reader

8. Someone who has been preserved at very low temperatures is wheeled out of a storage cabinet and unfrozen. All around is the city of the future.

ACTIVITY 8

Sometimes people come to feel that no news is good news. They get tired of hearing solemn warnings on the problems of the day. They turn to someone who can see the funny side of things. Look at the following student-written obituaries. An obituary is written when someone passes away. How have the writers made their subjects seem funny? Write a similar obituary on a subject of your own choice.

1. <u>Mankind Succumbs</u>. Mankind died early this morning as it was fighting a losing battle. It died of cancer. Cancer, as everyone knows, is when the cells multiply at an uncontrollable rate. It was first detected in the early 1900s when the cell count was 1.7 billion. At this stage, doctors started trying everything they knew. They waged war on it twice, but still the cell count kept rising. By the 1970s the count had risen to an all-time high of 3.4 billion. They tried another war that they thought would do it for sure, but in the year 2000 it rose to 7.1 billion. It died at a young age of 2001 and had no surviving relatives.

Composition

> 2. <u>John Automobile</u> (1910-1980) died yesterday from an acute case of starvation. He drank and ate until there was no tomorrow and it eventually ran out (the fuel and oil). Basically, he was a good thing; he just didn't know his limits. His accomplishments over the years included pollution, millions of accidents, and noise. The deceased leaves behind countless roads, highways, and smog-filled cities.

Guide to Manuscript Revision

ab	Spell out abbreviation (M6b)
adv	Use adverb form (U2b)
agr	Make verb agree with subject (or pronoun with antecedent) (U1c, U4a-b)
ap	Use apostrophe (M4b)
cap	Capitalize (M4a)
coh	Strengthen coherence (C2c-d)
coll	Use less colloquial word (U3a)
cs	Revise comma splice (M2a-b)
d	Improve diction (W3)
dev	Develop your point (C1b)
div	Revise word division (M6a)
dm	Revise dangling modifier (U4c)
frag	Revise sentence fragment (M1a)
FP	Revise faulty parallelism (U4e)
gr	Revise grammatical form or construction (U1-2)
awk	Rewrite awkward sentence (U4)
lc	Use lower case (M4a)
mm	Shift misplaced modifier (U4c)
p	Improve punctuation (M1-4)
¶	New paragraph (C1)
no¶	Take out paragraph break (C1)
ref	Improve pronoun reference (U4b)
rep	Avoid repetition (U4)
shift	Avoid shift in perspective (U4d)
sl	Use less slangy word (U3)
sp	Revise misspelled word (M5)
st	Improve sentence structure (U4)
t	Change tense of verb (U1b)
trans	Provide better transition (C2d)
w	Reduce wordiness (U4)

Chapter 4

Usage
Using Standard English

U1 Standard English: Basics
    a Plurals of Nouns
    b Verbs and Time
    c Verbs and Number
    d Auxiliaries

U2 Standard English: Finer Points
    a Standard Pronouns
    b Adjectives and Adverbs
    c Other Nonstandard Expressions

U3 Formal and Informal
    a Informal Words
    b Pronoun Case
    c Adverb Forms
    d A Guide to Formal English

U4 Revising Written Sentences
    a Agreement
    b Pronoun Reference
    c Position of Modifiers
    d Shifts
    e Parallel Structure

For Further Study: Folk Speech and Slang

Chapter Preview 4

IN THIS CHAPTER:

- How to use the right kind of language at the right time.
- How to use standard forms of nouns, verbs, pronouns, adjectives, and adverbs.
- How to avoid double negatives and other nonstandard expressions.
- How to use formal and informal English.
- How to revise sentences to meet the requirements of written English.
- How to understand and appreciate the regional varieties of English.

Use language that your audience will understand and respect.

We want our audience to receive our message. We want them to understand what we are saying. But we are also concerned with the attitude the audience has toward us as people. This attitude is shaped in part by what kind of language we use. What kind of language will people expect of you in your own speaking and writing? The answer will depend on two things: (1) What *group* are you going to be with? (2) What is the *occasion?* An effective speaker and writer uses language that is approved by the group and appropriate to the occasion.

Using Standard English

STANDARD ENGLISH
A Bird's-Eye View

NOUNS

Plural Forms:	men, women, children, teeth, wives, leaves, shelves; ten years, two months

VERBS

Irregular Verbs:	go	went	have gone
	know	knew	have known
	bring	brought	have brought
Regular Verbs:	ask	asked	have asked
	solve	solved	have solved

Forms of *Be*:	(Present)	I am, you are, he is, she is we are, you are, they are
	(Past)	I was, you were, he was, she was we were, you were, they were

Third Person Present:	the wind *blows;* the grass *grows;* he *lies;* she *sings;* it *works;* he *does* his work; she *doesn't* like him
Auxiliaries:	she *is* waiting; we *were* sitting there; I *have* done it; where *have* you been; what *do* you know

PRONOUNS

Pointing Pronouns: (demonstrative)	*this* door, *these* doors *that* trip, *those* trips
Possessive Pronouns:	*my* work and *yours* *his* glass and *hers*
–*self* Pronouns: (reflexive)	he did it *himself;* they did it *themselves*

OTHER FORMS

Comparisons:	he is *taller;* she is *tallest*
Avoiding Double Negatives:	he *never* said *anything;* she *could hardly* talk
An before Vowels:	*an* apple, *an* hour, *an* A, *an* unforgettable evening

Usage

DIAGNOSTIC TEST

How well do you know standard English word forms and sentence structure? Study the three choices for the blank space in each of the following sentences. After the number of the sentence, write the letter for the choice that is best for standard written English.

EXAMPLE: Her cousin Edith _____ in New Jersey.
  a. live   b. lives   c. living

(Answer) *b*

1. Marcia and Sylvia had _____ ahead.
   a. went   b. gone   c. going
2. Interest in sports and leisure-time activities _____ growing.
   a. is   b. are   c. be
3. The mail truck brought a parcel for you and _____.
   a. me   b. I   c. my
4. Early in the year, everyone took _____ test.
   a. eye   b. a eye   c. an eye
5. Last year, he _____ out of all his clothes.
   a. growed   b. grown   c. grew
6. The new clerk couldn't do _____ right.
   a. anything   b. nothing   c. hardly anything
7. When the siren went off, the horse _____.
   a. panics   b. panicked   c. panicking
8. Your lack of money in no way _____ the situation.
   a. helps   b. help   c. helping
9. Customers should think twice before spending _____ money.
   a. your   b. his or her   c. their
10. _____ newcomers have to support each other.
    a. We   b. Us   c. Ourselves
11. You should have _____ them a letter to complain.
    a. writing   b. wrote   c. written
12. The warranty _____ cover ordinary wear and tear.
    a. don't   b. do not   c. doesn't
13. Your cousins got _____ arrested.
    a. themself   b. themselves   c. theirself
14. The hostages _____ released unharmed.
    a. were   b. was   c. been
15. They had learned their parts _____.
    a. real good   b. real well   c. really well
16. A player learns to be polite, accept the umpire's decisions, and _____ hands after a game.
    a. shake   b. shaking   c. shook
17. We _____ some of the gymnasts at last year's meet.
    a. saw   b. seen   c. seeing
18. The team's schedule had changed _____.
    a. considerable b. considabl   c. considerably

Standard English: Basics

19. The train ride was _____ than we had thought.
    a. worse b. more worse c. worser
20. _____ , the rodeo seemed boring.
    a. Being tired b. Because we were tired c. Being as we were tired

Do not let nonstandard English hold you back.

U1
STANDARD ENGLISH: BASICS

Standard English is the language of school and business. It is the language of government. It is used in the mass media by announcers, reporters, and interviewers. It is the kind of English we see in print in newspapers, magazines, and books. You might say that standard English is the official English of the country.

Nonstandard English is the "unofficial" English spoken by many Americans at home and on the job. It is typically spoken by people who do not write or read much and who do not become involved in public life. Here are some examples of nonstandard English from a rural setting. For each sentence, how would you say the same thing in standard English?

I *never* said *nothin'* to you.
My father *knowed* their whole history.
There *wasn't* many left.
Is they like gypsies?
How can they learn if someone *don't learn* them?

Here are some examples of nonstandard English from the streets of a big city. For each sentence, how would you say the same thing in standard English?

Time for school again but we don't go—*it too nice a day.*
When *you the leader you a big man.*
He always *say* that.
Everybody *laugh* when she *say* that.
He *make* it *hisself.*

When the people around you talk nonstandard English, they will expect you to talk nonstandard English. You talk like them if you want to be one of them. But when everyone talks *standard* English, it is the other way around. In places where everyone expects standard English, nonstandard English will hold you back. It will hold you back when you look for a job. It will hold you back when you complete your education.

243

Usage

U1a
Plurals of Nouns

Learn to use the standard plural forms of nouns.

Most English nouns have different forms for **singular** and **plural.** We use the plural to point to "more than one." Usually we simply add –s or –es to a noun to make it plural: one *boy*, two *boys;* one *girl*, two *girls;* one *church*, two *churches.*

But remember:

(1) Some English nouns do not form their plural by adding –s or –es to the singular. We call plurals not formed with –s or –es *irregular* plurals. The plural of *child* is not *childs* but *children*. The standard plural of *man* is not *mens* but *men*. Since *men* is already a plural, the –s is unnecessary.

Learn the standard plurals of the following nouns:

SINGULAR:	man	I saw a *man*.
PLURAL:	men	I saw two *men*.
SINGULAR:	woman	The *woman* did the work.
PLURAL:	women	Two *women* did the work.
SINGULAR:	child	A *child* brought the gift.
PLURAL:	children	Three *children* brought the gift.
SINGULAR:	tooth	The child had one *tooth*.
PLURAL:	teeth	The monster had many *teeth*.
SINGULAR:	foot	The board was a *foot* long.
PLURAL:	feet	The board was five *feet* long.
SINGULAR:	mouse	The *mouse* ate all the grain.
PLURAL:	mice	The *mice* ate all the grain.
SINGULAR:	ox	One *ox* pulled the cart.
PLURAL:	oxen	Two *oxen* pulled the cart.
SINGULAR:	goose	We killed a *goose* for dinner.
PLURAL:	geese	We killed several *geese* for dinner.

Note: When *man* and *woman* are used in combinations like the following, the plurals are still *men* and *women:*

several fire*men*
all the fresh*men*
three police*men*
several police*women*

too many club*women*
six post*men*
all the chair*women*
several sports*men*

Standard English: Basics

(2) *Many nouns that end in –f or –fe form their plural by changing the –f to –v and adding –s or –es.* The standard plural of *leaf* is not *leafs* but *leaves*. The standard plural of *life* is not *lifes* but *lives*.

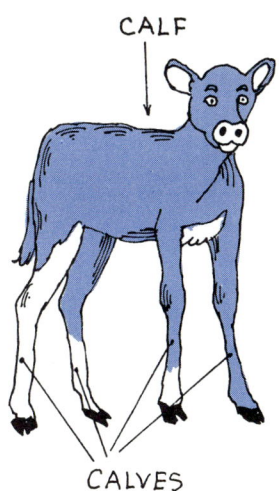

CALF

CALVES

Learn the standard plurals of the following nouns:

SINGULAR:	calf	The farmer bought a *calf*.
PLURAL:	calves	The farmer buys *calves*.
SINGULAR:	half	The score was 7 to 7 at the *half*.
PLURAL:	halves	A football game has two *halves*.
SINGULAR:	knife	The men saw the *knife*.
PLURAL:	knives	That man sharpens *knives*.
SINGULAR:	life	Men and women have only one *life*.
PLURAL:	lives	A cat has nine *lives*.
SINGULAR:	wife	His *wife* had gone out.
PLURAL:	wives	Many *wives* went to the party.
SINGULAR:	leaf	Jack took a *leaf* from his notebook.
PLURAL:	leaves	Many *leaves* covered the ground.
SINGULAR:	loaf	The baker broke the *loaf* in half.
PLURAL:	loaves	The baker broke the *loaves* into halves.
SINGULAR:	shelf	The knives were on the *shelf*.
PLURAL:	shelves	We needed more *shelves* in the kitchen.

(3) *Use plural forms after numbers higher than one.* When you use a number higher than one, you are referring to more than one thing. Use plural nouns after such numbers. Be especially careful with nouns that refer to time *(day, month, year)*; distance *(foot, yard, mile)*; and money *(cent, dollar)*:

It costs *fifty cents*.
She earns *eighty-five dollars* a week.
They walked *three miles*.

Note: The plural *–s* is left out in standard English only when the noun is part of a combination that comes before another noun: a *five-dollar* bill, a *five-minute* break.

For more about nouns, see S1a.

Usage

EXERCISE 1

All the italicized words in the following sentences are *standard* plural forms of nouns. Read the sentences over several times. Give the right form a chance to sink in.

1. The hall was filled with *men*, *women*, and *children*.
2. The monster had two *teeth* and three *feet*.
3. Several *women* were helping the two *policemen*.
4. Many *children* lose their *baby teeth* late.
5. In most factories, *men* and *women* work together.
6. The *firemen* saved two of the *children*.
7. All the *men* in our family have big *teeth*.
8. The *men* defended their *lives* with *knives*.
9. They gave the two *halves* to their *wives*.
10. We cut the *loaves* into *halves* with *knives*.
11. The *wives* gathered *leaves* for the *shelves*.
12. Some *men* spend their *lives* caring for *calves*.
13. The baker put the *loaves* on the *shelves*.
14. The *freshmen* played against the sophomores.
15. She had lived there for two *years* and eight *months*.

EXERCISE 2

Here are additional sentences showing standard plurals of nouns. Read each passage over several times. Give the right form a chance to sink in.

1. The child has only two *teeth*. He also has only two *feet*. His older sisters are *women*. His older brothers are *men*. His oldest brother has four *children* of his own.
2. I saw the brother's four *children*. They are all over three *feet* tall. The boys are not *men*. The girls are not *women*. All of them have good *teeth*.
3. They brush their *teeth* every day. The girls will be over five *feet* tall when they are *women*. The boys may be over six *feet* tall when they are *men*.
4. The *men* spread *leaves* all over the *shelves*. The bakers used their *knives* to cut the *loaves* into *halves*. We devoted our *lives* to the care of our *calves*.
5. The *wives* sliced the *loaves* with their sharp *knives*, risking their *lives*. The food for the *calves* was kept in the barn on *shelves*. The *loaves* were cut into *halves*.

EXERCISE 3

What form of the noun in parentheses would fit the blank space in the sentence? Write the *standard* form after the number of the sentence.

Standard English: Basics

1. (fireman) Several _____ were carrying an elderly person from the burning hotel.
2. (shelf) Many new _____ had been put in the library.
3. (man) Only one _____ was left of the whole platoon.
4. (half) The quarterback played through both _____ of the game.
5. (leaf) The many _____ from our trees were clogging the drains.
6. (child) People in my family have always had many _____.
7. (foot) The board was at least four _____ long.
8. (loaf) Two _____ of bread won't last till Monday.
9. (life) A cat has nine _____.
10. (mile) The next gas station is seven _____ from here.
11. (woman) Many _____ would rather work than stay home.
12. (calf) In the spring, Jeremy traded a _____ for seed potatoes.
13. (woman) In most jobs, a _____ must fight for promotion.
14. (policeman) The patrol car had two _____ in it.
15. (foot) Before the hike was half over, I had blisters on both _____.
16. (dollar) Each worker was paid two _____ and ten cents an hour.
17. (hour) It took us seven _____ to drive to Chicago.
18. (policewoman) _____ are taught how to handle dogs.
19. (wife) Only three of the _____ came to the picnic.
20. (child) No one remembered seeing this _____ before.

Usage

U1b
Verbs and Time

Use standard verb forms to show differences in time.

Verbs are the only words that can show a change in time by a change in the word itself. In addition, auxiliaries like *have* and *had* help us show differences in time. The forms that show time are the different **tenses** of a verb:

PRESENT:	I drive	(now or regularly)
PAST:	I drove	(in the past)
PERFECT:	I have driven	(recently)

Look at the chart for standard forms of commonly used verbs. Three forms are listed for each verb: the form used alone for action *now* or *regularly* (present); the form used alone for action in the *past* (past); the form used with *have, has,* or *had* (perfect). Study one group at a time. Be sure you know the three standard forms of each irregular verb.

For more about verbs, see S1c.

Remember:

(1) Do not use the present in place of the past. The past shows action that has already been completed, as in the following examples:

STANDARD	NONSTANDARD
They *came* last week.	They *come* last week.
We *saw* him yesterday.	We *see* him yesterday.
He *said* he had finished.	He *say* he had finished.

(2) Do not use a perfect form in place of the present or past. The perfect form must be used with a helping verb, usually a form of *have*. Notice the differences between the standard and nonstandard sentences below:

NONSTANDARD:	I *seen* him yesterday.
STANDARD:	I *saw* him yesterday.
STANDARD:	I *had seen* him yesterday.
NONSTANDARD:	He *done* his work on time.
STANDARD:	He *did* his work on time.
STANDARD:	He *has done* his work on time.

(3) Do not omit –ed from the past of regular verbs. Most English verbs form their past by adding *–d* or *–ed* to the present forms. The sound represented by these letters is *d* or *t*,

Standard English: Basics

STANDARD FORMS
Irregular Verbs

	PRESENT	PAST	PERFECT
GROUP 1	begin	began	have begun
	bend	bent	have bent
	blow	blew	have blown
	break	broke	have broken
	bring	brought	have brought
	buy	bought	have bought
	catch	caught	have caught
	choose	chose	have chosen
	come	came	have come
GROUP 2	dig	dug	have dug
	do	did	have done
	draw	drew	have drawn
	drink	drank	have drunk
	drive	drove	have driven
	eat	ate	have eaten
	fall	fell	have fallen
	fly	flew	have flown
	freeze	froze	have frozen
GROUP 3	get	got	have gotten, got
	go	went	have gone
	grow	grew	have grown
	know	knew	have known
	ride	rode	have ridden
	run	ran	have run
	say	said	have said
	see	saw	have seen
	sing	sang	have sung
GROUP 4	speak	spoke	have spoken
	swim	swam	have swum
	swing	swung	have swung
	take	took	have taken
	tear	tore	have torn
	throw	threw	have thrown
	wear	wore	have worn
	write	wrote	have written

Usage

as in *solved* and *asked*. Pronounce the final sound clearly in all the italicized verbs in the standard sentences below:

NONSTANDARD:	He *ask* her yesterday.
STANDARD:	He *asked* her yesterday.
NONSTANDARD:	The clerk *add* up the grocery bill.
STANDARD:	The clerk *added* up the grocery bill.

(4) Do not form the past of irregular verbs by adding –ed to the present. Regular verbs form their past tense by adding *–ed*. **Irregular** verbs do not follow this pattern. They make up their past forms in their own way. Read the standard sentences aloud:

NONSTANDARD:	We *knowed* he could do it.
STANDARD:	We *knew* he could do it.
NONSTANDARD:	They *goed* to the dance together.
STANDARD:	They *went* to the dance together.

(5) Know the standard form of be. *Be* is different from all other verbs: it has three present forms and two past forms. Read over the following forms until they sound natural:

PRESENT

I *am* here now.   We *are* here now.
You *are* here now.   They *are* here now.
He *is* here now.

I'*m* here now.   We'*re* here now.
You'*re* here now.   They'*re* here now.
She'*s* here now.

PAST

I *was* there yesterday.   We *were* there yesterday.
You *were* there yesterday.   They *were* there yesterday.
He *was* there yesterday.

PERFECT

I *have been* here before.   We *have been* here before.
You *have been* here before.   They *have been* here before.
She *has been* here before.

I'*ve been* here before.   We'*ve been* here before.
You'*ve been* here before.   They'*ve been* here before.
He'*s been* here before.

Standard English: Basics

Below are sentence drills for ten of the most commonly used *irregular* verbs. Read them aloud several times. Come back to this exercise until the sentences sound natural.

EXERCISE 1

1. I usually *begin* at eight.
   I *began* at seven yesterday.
   I *have* already *begun* my homework.
2. He *comes* to church on Sundays.
   He *came* to church last week.
   He *has come* to church often.
3. She *does* her work on time.
   They *did* their work well.
   We'*ve done* our work already.
4. We *give* money to charities.
   We *gave* fifty dollars last year.
   We *have given* to the United Fund.
5. I *go* there often.
   I *went* there last May.
   I'*ve gone* away.
6. She *says* she knows you.
   She *said* she saw him yesterday.
   She *has said* all she's going to say.
7. He *sees* her every day.
   She *saw* him yesterday.
   They'*ve seen* each other.
8. He *takes* his time.
   The thief *took* the car.
   They'*ve taken* the cake away.
9. He *throws* a good curve ball.
   The catcher *threw* the ball to second base.
   He *has thrown* the runner out.
10. I *write* to her every week.
    She *wrote* to me just yesterday.
    We *have written* to them already.

In the sentences below, use the *standard past or perfect form* of the verb given in parentheses. Use the perfect form only if *have, has,* or *had* already appears in the sentence. Write the appropriate form after the number of the sentence.

EXERCISE 2

EXAMPLES: Mary ———— us home. (drive)
(Answer) *drove*
           Joe had ———— the truck. (drive)
(Answer) *driven*

251

Usage

1. Jimmy _____ his father for fifty cents. (ask)
2. The cat _____ itself in the mirror. (see)
3. That boy _____ last June. (graduate)
4. I have _____ mine away. (throw)
5. They _____ for three hours. (talk)
6. They _____ themselves some new clothes. (buy)
7. The ranchers _____ the calves. (catch)
8. She _____ him better than he ever knew. (love)
9. He _____ eight hours a day, five days a week. (work)
10. Those children have _____ all the way. (run)
11. I _____ the lesson very well. (learn)
12. The catcher _____ while trying to catch the ball. (fall)
13. The prisoners' wives have _____ their husbands. (write)
14. We _____ the house last weekend. (clean)
15. Fred and I _____ the mountain yesterday. (climb)
16. She _____ her lesson well. (know)
17. The grocer has _____ three cents to the bill for tax. (add)
18. We have _____ those vegetables in our own garden. (grow)
19. My uncle always _____ with the housework. (help)
20. Charlie _____ to the ball game by himself. (go)

EXERCISE 3 Read the questions below. Then answer them, supplying the missing verb. Use the same verb that is used in the question, but change its form where necessary to make it fit the answer. Write the standard form after the number and letter of the sentence.

SAMPLE ANSWER: *7a. slept*

1. (a) Did Charlie go out? Yes, he _____ out.
   (b) Has Lily gone out? Yes, she has _____ out.
2. (a) Did you blow out the candles? Yes, I _____ them out.
   (b) Has he blown them out? Yes, he has _____ them out.
3. (a) Does she buy old coins? Yes, she _____ them.
   (b) Did he buy the old coins? Yes, he _____ them.
4. (a) Who came to the party? Lily _____ to it.
   (b) Hasn't he come back yet? No, he hasn't _____ back.
5. (a) Are you ready? Yes, I _____ ready.
   (b) Was I at the picnic? Yes, you _____ there.
6. (a) Does she drive? Yes, she _____ .
   (b) Did he drive the car himself? Yes, he _____ it himself.
7. (a) When did the leaves fall? The leaves _____ yesterday.
   (b) Whose book fell on the floor? His book _____ on the floor.
8. (a) Did you get wet? Yes, we _____ wet.
   (b) Has he got the money? Yes, he has _____ it.

Standard English: Basics

9. (a) Did you know **James**? Yes, I _____ him.
   (b) Has he known her long? Yes, he has _____ her two years.
10. (a) Did you wear your new shoes? Yes, I _____ them.
    (b) When will you wear your hat? I have already _____ it.
11. (a) Did you speak to her? Yes, I _____ to her.
    (b) When will you speak to her? I have already _____ to her.
12. (a) Were you his friend? Yes, I _____ his friend.
    (b) When will it be due? It has _____ due since April.
13. (a) Did you see her there? Yes, I _____ her there.
    (b) When did you see the movie? I have not _____ it yet.
14. (a) Did Susan throw the ball? No, Marcia _____ it.
    (b) Will he throw it out? He has already _____ it out.
15. (a) Which train do we take? We _____ the first one.
    (b) Which train did they take? They _____ the last one.

Use standard verb forms to show the differences between singular and plural.

U1c
Verbs and Number

A subject and its verb agree when they change together from singular to plural. We call this change a change in **number.**

SINGULAR:	This *boy*	*is*	my brother.
PLURAL:	These *boys*	*are*	my brothers.
SINGULAR:	The *moon*	*circles*	the earth.
PLURAL:	Several *moons*	*circle*	Jupiter.

Do the following to make subject and verb agree in standard English:

(1) Use a final –s for the verb when you are talking about "one third party, action now." In other words, use the –s form for the present when you are talking about *one* person or thing—when *he, she,* or *it* could take the place of the subject. These are the **third person** pronouns. They do not point to the person speaking (*I* or *we:* "number one" or "first person"). They do not point to the "second party"—the one we are speaking to (*you:* "second person"). Instead, they refer to someone else, a "third party."

The sentences below discuss a third party, with "action now":

He *hits* the ball.
She *studies* every night.
It *takes* courage.

253

Usage

Use the pronoun test to help you check for standard forms:

John *needs* help. (*He* needs help.)
The girl *plans* to be a doctor. (*She* plans to be a doctor.)
A fence *encloses* the field. (*It* encloses the field.)

Observe the rule for "third person, singular" when using *do* or *don't*:

NONSTANDARD: The boy *don't* know the answer.
(*The boy* is the subject. *He* can take its place. The helping verb should add *s*.)
STANDARD: The boy *doesn't* know the answer.

(2) *Use the standard forms of* be *in the present and past.* Unlike other verbs, *be* has three present forms and two past forms. Study the chart that shows the standard forms of *be* for first, second, and third person.

THIRD PERSON, SINGULAR:
–s ending for one person or thing, with "action now"

ZARKOV THROWS A LEVER FEEDING FUEL CARTRIDGES TO THE FORE ROCKETS, BUT THE ROCKETS, FROZEN OVER, FLARE BACK INTO THE CABIN.

WITH GREAT SKILL, FLASH LANDS THE SHIP, NOSE UP. SHE BOUNDS THROUGH THE SNOW, GRADUALLY LOSING SPEED--BUT A GREAT GLACIER LOOMS AHEAD!

Standard English: Basics

<table>
<tr><td colspan="3">SINGULAR:</td><td rowspan="8" style="text-align:center;">PRESENT</td></tr>
<tr><td></td><td>First Person</td><td>I *am* a student.</td></tr>
<tr><td></td><td>Second Person</td><td>You *are* a good worker, Tom.</td></tr>
<tr><td></td><td>Third Person</td><td>John *is* a scout. He *is* my brother.
The girl *is* absent. She *is* ill.
The car *is* cheap. It *is* old.</td></tr>
<tr><td colspan="3">PLURAL:</td></tr>
<tr><td></td><td>First Person</td><td>We *are* satisfied.</td></tr>
<tr><td></td><td>Second Person</td><td>You two *are* fortunate.</td></tr>
<tr><td></td><td>Third Person</td><td>The Smiths *are* friendly.</td></tr>
</table>

<table>
<tr><td colspan="3">SINGULAR:</td><td rowspan="8" style="text-align:center;">PAST</td></tr>
<tr><td></td><td>First Person</td><td>I *was* a student.</td></tr>
<tr><td></td><td>Second Person</td><td>You *were* a good worker, Tom.</td></tr>
<tr><td></td><td>Third Person</td><td>John *was* my friend. He *was* tall.
The girl *was* absent. She *was* ill.
The car *was* new. It *was* shiny.</td></tr>
<tr><td colspan="3">PLURAL:</td></tr>
<tr><td></td><td>First Person</td><td>We *were* friends.</td></tr>
<tr><td></td><td>Second Person</td><td>You two *were* seen.</td></tr>
<tr><td></td><td>Third Person</td><td>The Browns *were* there. They *were* friendly.</td></tr>
</table>

Avoid nonstandard uses of *be:*

STANDARD: You *are* wrong. (not *is*)
STANDARD: We *were* ready in time. (not *was*)

Use the pronoun test when the subject is a noun. Use *is* or *was* if *he, she,* or *it* can substitute for a noun. Use *are* or *were* if *they* can substitute.

SINGULAR: The dance *is* in the gym. (*It* is in the gym.)
PLURAL: The boys *are* in the gym. (*They* are in the gym.)

SINGULAR: The girl *was* here a moment ago. (*She* was here.)
PLURAL: The papers *were* on her desk. (*They* were on her desk.)

EXERCISE 1

Do you have trouble with the standard forms for the third person? If you do, read the following passages *several times* for oral practice. Go back to them several times during the next few weeks.

Usage

1. The dog *doesn't* bark. The cat *doesn't* do tricks. The cat *does* only what it wants to do. It *does* many things we *don't* want it to do. These animals *don't* like each other. They *don't* seem to think alike.
2. Jim *says* he doesn't like friends. He *says* they talk too much. People *say* that Jim's friend is his car. They *say* he never talks about anything else. They *say* he spends all his money on his car.
3. When Carla goes to New York, she *sees* her relatives. She *sees* her uncle and aunt. She *sees* her cousins. Then they *see* some of the sights together. They *see* the skyscrapers and Broadway, and they always *see* Central Park.
4. Nina *has* relatives in San Francisco. She also *has* friends there. When she *has* the money, she likes to visit them. Few cities *have* as many attractions as San Francisco *has*. Nina's friends *have* homes near the city.
5. Sue *likes* apple pie. Doris *likes* raisin pie. Their brothers *like* cherry pie. Their mother *likes* pies. She knows what the children *like*.

EXERCISE 2

Do you have trouble with the standard forms of *be*? If you do, read the following passages several times for oral practice.

1. I *am* here. He *is* there. She *is* nowhere. I *am* tired. He *is* rested. She *is* gone.
2. We *are* undecided. You *are* wrong. They *are* right. We *were* late. You *were* on time. They *were* early.
3. I *was* happy. You *were* sad. I *was* angry. You *were* glad.
4. The price *is* right. The prices *are* right. The shop *is* closed. The shops *are* closed. Her brother *is* tall. Her brothers *are* tall.
5. The door *was* closed. The doors *were* closed. A bird *was* singing. Birds *were* singing. One ship *was* in the harbor. Several ships *were* in the harbor.

EXERCISE 3

In each of the following sentences, a blank space is left for the verb (or auxiliary). At the end of the sentence is the verb to be put in the blank. If you can substitute *he, she,* or *it* for the subject, use an –s on the verb. If you cannot, do not use an –s. Use the present in all sentences. (Write your answer next to the number of the sentence.)

1. My friend _____ she knows the man. (say)
2. The coats _____ fur collars. (have)
3. This coat _____ n't have a fur collar. (do)
4. Some books _____ many things. (teach)
5. Some students _____ many things. (learn)

Standard English: Basics

6. That student _____ quickly. (learn)
7. The man _____ n't want any. (do)
8. Those people _____ n't have any. (do)
9. Our minister _____ to visit us. (like)
10. Birds _____ to sing. (like)
11. Jim _____ to play football. (like)
12. This machine _____ questions. (ask)
13. Those machines _____ answers. (give)
14. The doctor _____ what is wrong. (know)
15. Teachers _____ he's smart but lazy. (say)
16. Her dress _____ new. (look)
17. This store _____ open till nine o'clock. (stay)
18. Every spring, Father _____ a new cap. (need)
19. On the way home from work, Cindy _____ a paper. (buy)
20. The children usually _____ candy after school. (buy)

EXERCISE 4

The subjects in the following sentences have been italicized. In the blank spaces, use a form of *be* that agrees with the subject. Use only *am, are,* or *is* in the first ten sentences; use only *was* or *were* in the second ten. Write your answers on a separate sheet. Use standard forms only.

A. Choose *am, are,* or *is:*

1. *I* _____ on duty today.
2. *You* _____ on duty tomorrow.
3. *He* _____ my brother.
4. *They* _____ her friends.
5. *The notebooks* _____ on the desk.
6. *The pie* _____ in the refrigerator.
7. *We* _____ going to the picnic.
8. *Lucy and I* _____ going to the picnic.
9. *You* _____ the best dancer in the class.
10. *Two men* _____ at the door.

B. Choose *was* or *were:*

11. *We* _____ ready on time.
12. *The girls* _____ n't ready.
13. *You* _____ on the phone for an hour last night.
14. *I* _____ finally forced to get off.
15. *Helen* _____ the best runner.
16. *The boys* _____ given medals.
17. *The Bible* _____ his favorite book.
18. *You* _____ sitting in the front row.
19. *The man* _____ there an hour ago.
20. *You* _____ there until late afternoon.

Usage

U1d
Auxiliaries

Use helping verbs (auxiliaries) when they are required in standard English.

The three most common auxiliaries are *be, have,* and *do.* These auxiliaries are often left out in nonstandard speech and writing. But in standard English the missing auxiliaries are always filled in:

(1) Use am, are, is, was, *or* were *with the* –ing *form of verbs.* The –ing form of verbs (the **present participle**) is not used as a complete verb in standard English. It has to follow some form of *be.* Compare the standard and nonstandard sentences below. Read the standard sentences aloud:

NONSTANDARD:	He coming with us.
STANDARD:	He *is* coming with us.
NONSTANDARD:	We getting ready.
STANDARD:	We *were* getting ready.
NONSTANDARD:	You following me?
STANDARD:	*Are* you following me?

(2) Use have, has, *or* had *with the perfect form of verbs.* This form of verbs often ends in *–n* or *–en* with irregular verbs: *have chosen, have drawn.* It ends with *–d* or *–ed* for regular verbs: *have loved, have talked.* In standard English, the auxiliary is not cut off:

NONSTANDARD:	I seen him.
STANDARD:	I *have* seen him.
NONSTANDARD:	Where you been?
STANDARD:	Where *have* you been?

(3) Use do, does, *or* did *in questions when you have no other auxiliary and when the main verb is not some form of* be. One of the most common ways of asking questions in English is to use a question word like *what, where, when,* plus the auxiliary *do.* In such questions, standard English does not omit the *do* auxiliary:

NONSTANDARD:	What you know about it?
STANDARD:	What *do* you know about it?
NONSTANDARD:	Where he go?
STANDARD:	Where *did* he go?

Standard English: Basics

EXERCISE 1

Read the questions below. Answer the questions, using the same verb and the right form of the auxiliary. Your teacher may ask you to use the auxiliaries both in their regular and their shortened forms.

EXAMPLE: Is he coming tonight?   *Yes, he is coming.*
Yes, he's coming.

Have you been there?   *Yes, I have been there.*
Yes, I've been there.

1. Has he seen her lately? Yes, _____ .
2. Are you going to the pool? Yes, _____ .
3. Have they eaten dinner yet? Yes, _____ .
4. Is she buying that car? Yes, _____ .
5. Have they done the dishes? Yes, _____ .
6. Were they looking for me? Yes, _____ .
7. Have they brought their friends? Yes, _____ .
8. Was he writing that letter to me? Yes, _____ .
9. Have you been to class today? Yes, _____ .
10. Am I hurting you? Yes, _____ .
11. Has she written to him? Yes, _____ .
12. Is she having many guests? Yes, _____ .
13. Have they come home yet? Yes, _____ .
14. Have the teams chosen sides? Yes, _____ .
15. Is it raining outside? Yes, _____ .
16. Has the lake frozen? Yes, _____ .
17. Have you known him long? Yes, _____ .
18. Has the pitcher thrown the ball? Yes, _____ .
19. Is she running in the track meet? Yes, _____ .
20. Was she wearing her new shoes? Yes, _____ .

EXERCISE 2

Each of the sentences below contains a blank space and is followed by an auxiliary in parentheses. After the number of each sentence, write a form of the auxiliary that fits the context. Read your completed sentences aloud. (In many instances, *more than one* choice is possible.)

1. We _____ been there many times. (have)
2. My father _____ taking his vacation in August. (be)
3. Where _____ you want me to put this box? (do)
4. What _____ he ask you to do? (do)
5. The coach _____ done a good job. (have)
6. Sam _____ working all day. (be)
7. He _____ worked all day yesterday. (have)
8. Whom _____ you tell about it? (do)
9. The girl scouts _____ been to the zoo before. (have)

Usage

10. Nobody _____ seen him leave. (have)
11. He _____ said nothing about it. (have)
12. I _____ reading the book. (be)
13. Charlie _____ looking for his. (be)
14. The girls _____ having a good time. (be)
15. What _____ you mean by that? (do)
16. Where _____ he put the money? (do)
17. Vic _____ taken the job. (have)
18. I _____ been laughing about it all day. (have)
19. He _____ been here twice already. (have)
20. What _____ you tell him? (do)

UNIT REVIEW EXERCISE

Which of the following sentences are standard English? Put *S* after the number of each sentence that is standard. Put *N* after the number of each sentence that is nonstandard.

1. My grandfather came to Wyoming in 1908.
2. The new sheriff don't tolerate vandalism.
3. The hunter seen a duck right away.
4. Where are you going now?
5. The farm is three mile from that silo.
6. How many feet are there in a yard?
7. What you have in your pocket?
8. Rattlesnakes was everywhere in those hills.
9. Those tomatoes cost twenty cents.
10. Sylvia knowed what the trouble was.
11. How many knives do we need?
12. George has done his duty.
13. Time is running out.
14. Why he always complain?
15. We took a trip across the United States.
16. Your friends have gone home.
17. The storm done much damage.
18. We told him that you was waiting for us.
19. They took many pictures on their trip.
20. All our friends brought a picnic lunch.

U2 STANDARD ENGLISH: FINER POINTS

Know the finer points that help make the difference between standard and nonstandard English.

Standard English and nonstandard English are not separate languages. They use thousands of the same words. They follow hundreds of the same rules for putting words together

Standard English: Finer Points

in a sentence. The difference is often in the "little things." The following sections will give you a chance to look at some of the finer points.

Learn to use standard pronouns.

U2a
Standard Pronouns

In each of the following pairs, the same idea is stated two different ways. How would you say it naturally, when talking at home or with your friends?

NONSTANDARD: We saw one of *them* new trains.
STANDARD: We saw one of *those* new trains.

NONSTANDARD: John had built the shed *hisself*.
STANDARD: John had built the shed *himself*.

NONSTANDARD: Carol put *yourn* over there.
STANDARD: Carol put *yours* over there.

These examples show differences in *pronoun* forms. Would you have trouble using the standard form? Study and practice the most important standard pronoun forms.

(1) Use the standard forms of demonstrative pronouns. These are the *"pointing"* pronouns: *this, that, these,* and *those.* The first two of these pointers are singular and are used with singular nouns: *this man, that man.* The second two are plural and are used with plural nouns: *these men, those men.*

Nonstandard English often uses the following substitutes for the pointing pronouns:

NONSTANDARD	STANDARD
this here knife	*this* knife
that there jug	*that* jug
them children	*these* children
them tools	*those* tools

Read aloud the following sentences in which pointing pronouns are used in their standard forms:

This bus goes only to 34th Street.
That bus goes to 42nd Street.
These buses used to be the fastest in the city.
Those buses are now the fastest.
This store has reasonable prices.
That store is too expensive.

Usage

(2) Use the standard forms of the reflexive or –self pronouns. Here are the standard forms:

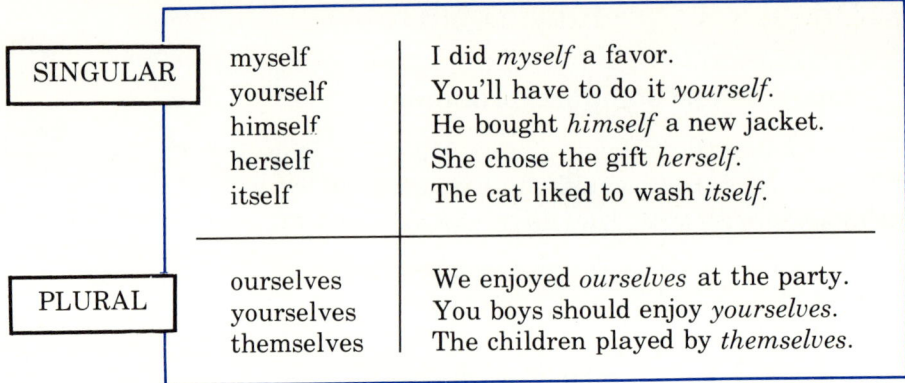

SINGULAR	myself	I did *myself* a favor.
	yourself	You'll have to do it *yourself*.
	himself	He bought *himself* a new jacket.
	herself	She chose the gift *herself*.
	itself	The cat liked to wash *itself*.
PLURAL	ourselves	We enjoyed *ourselves* at the party.
	yourselves	You boys should enjoy *yourselves*.
	themselves	The children played by *themselves*.

Avoid the nonstandard uses of these pronouns. Read the standard sentences aloud:

NONSTANDARD: He went to see it *hisself*.
STANDARD: He went to see it *himself*.

NONSTANDARD: You girls should see *yourself* in a mirror.
STANDARD: You girls should see *yourselves* in a mirror.

NONSTANDARD: They ate the pizza by *theirself*.
STANDARD: They ate the pizza by *themselves*.

(3) Use the standard forms of possessive pronouns. There are two sets of possessive pronouns in English. The words in the first set are used to mark nouns. The words in the second set are used *without* a following noun:

	SINGULAR		PLURAL
my	I did *my share*.	our	We have done *our share*.
your	*Your work* isn't done.	your	Did you do *your work*?
his	He didn't do *his work*.	their	*Their work* was done yesterday.
her	She knew *her job*.		
its	The cat knows *its name*.		
mine	I brought *mine*.	ours	We did *ours*.
yours	You brought *yours*.	yours	You did *yours*.
his	Did he bring *his*?	theirs	They did *theirs*.
hers	She has *hers*.		
its	Where is *its*?		

Standard English: Finer Points

Avoid nonstandard forms:

NONSTANDARD: Did you learn *you lesson?*
STANDARD: Did you learn *your lesson?*

NONSTANDARD: He says that *yourn* is on the shelf.
STANDARD: He says that *yours* is on the shelf.

Note: The standard spelling of *its* does not use an apostrophe. *It's* is a contraction of *it is.*

For subject form and object form, see U3b.

EXERCISE 1

Do you have trouble with standard pronoun forms? If so, read the following sentences over *several times.* Go back to them *several times.*

1. Please accept *this gift.* Please hand me *that towel.* Take a look at *these flowers.* Watch *those boys.* I just got *this letter.* It came in *that box. These candies* are spoiled. *Those men* come through here all the time. You should fix *this faucet.* Hand me *that wrench.* They don't make *these tools* anymore. *Those hats* are stylish.
2. I did it *myself.* He said it *himself.* We began it *ourselves.* They broke it *themselves.* Catch it *yourself.* Bring them *yourselves.* He drove *himself* crazy. We wore *ourselves* out. I sang *myself* hoarse. He saw *himself* in the mirror. They took *themselves* seriously. We had to protect *ourselves.* She *herself* knew the truth. The people organized *themselves.* He took care of *himself.* The problem took care of *itself.* He told *himself* not to worry. They locked *themselves* in the room. She punished *herself.*
3. I took *my* copy and she took *hers.* They went back to *their* car and we to *ours.* Jim fired *his* rifle and I fired *mine.* If you give me *mine* back, I'll give you *yours.* They claimed the land was *theirs.* This cat is *mine* and that one is *yours.* The towels were marked *his* and *hers.* Everything that is *mine* is also *yours.*

EXERCISE 2

For each of the following, write your answer after the number of the sentence.

A. For each sentence, write down a *–self* pronoun that would fit the blank space. Use only standard forms.

1. Jim was going to buy _____ a new coat.
2. My mother picked out this dress _____ .
3. Let them polish their car _____ .
4. I _____ never went to one of those dances.

Usage

5. You girls should clean your rooms _____ .
6. We wanted a quiet corner all to _____ .
7. The problem will take care of _____ .
8. She _____ refused to go.
9. The stranger smiled and introduced _____ .
10. People like to hear _____ praised.

B. Fill the blank spaces in the sentences below with possessive pronouns. Use only standard forms. Choose the possessive that fits the meaning of the sentence best.

11. I brought mine; did you bring _____ ?
12. He blamed us and said that the fault was _____ .
13. I did my homework; did he do _____ ?
14. We ate our lunch; did they eat _____ ?
15. I saw my coat and she saw _____ .
16. I found my phone number, but you lost _____ .
17. The dog has been given dinner; the cat is expecting _____ .
18. They are coming to get _____ themselves.
19. I did his chores for him, but did he ever do _____ ?
20. Everyone had a piece of cake, so I took _____ .

U2b
Adjectives and Adverbs

Use the standard forms of adjectives and adverbs.

In each of the following pairs, the same idea is stated two different ways. How would you usually say it when talking at home or with your friends?

NONSTANDARD: The weather has gotten *worser* each year.
STANDARD: The weather has gotten *worse* each year.

NONSTANDARD: They were *nowheres* to be found.
STANDARD: They were *nowhere* to be found.

These examples show differences in the use of adjectives and adverbs. Study and practice the standard forms:

(1) Use the standard English forms for adjectives and adverbs used in comparisons. In standard English, we compare adjectives and adverbs either by using *more* or *most* or by adding *–er* or *–est* to the word. Avoid the **double comparisons** illustrated in the following examples:

NONSTANDARD: Jim is *more taller* than Sally.
STANDARD: Jim is *taller* than Sally.

NONSTANDARD: Our class is the *most friendliest* of all.
STANDARD: Our class is the *most friendly* of all.

Standard English: Finer Points

(2) Use the standard forms of irregular adjectives and adverbs. Good, bad, well, and *ill* are not compared in standard English in the normal or regular ways. Below are the standard forms of these words:

PLAIN	COMPARATIVE	SUPERLATIVE
good	better	best
bad	worse	worst
well	better	best
ill	worse	worst
badly	worse	worst

Avoid nonstandard forms:

NONSTANDARD: She looks *worser* now.
STANDARD: She looks *worse* now.

NONSTANDARD: This year's play was the *baddest* yet.
STANDARD: This year's play was the *worst* yet.

(3) Learn the standard forms of anywhere, everywhere, nowhere, *and* somewhere. These words join *any, every, no,* and *some* to *where*. All four words are used without an *–s* in standard English.

The lamb followed her *everywhere*.
We couldn't find them *anywhere*.
Somewhere over the rainbow, I'll find love.
We're going *nowhere* today.

EXERCISE

In parentheses at the end of each sentence below is an adjective or adverb. To make it fit the sentence, change it to the standard form for comparative (higher degree) or superlative (highest degree). Write the changed form after the number of the sentence.

1. Nowhere is there a _____ girl than Carolyn. (smart)
2. This is the _____ book I have ever read. (great)
3. Your coat looks _____ than mine. (expensive)
4. I've never seen anyone _____ than she. (graceful)
5. It was the _____ grade in the class. (good)
6. Yesterday he looked bad but today he looks _____. (bad)
7. Vic brought his mother the _____ flowers available. (fresh)
8. It is _____ to play well than to win. (important)
9. You'll have to speak _____. (clearly)
10. We have never seen _____ milk. (creamy)

Usage

11. James is _____ than his brother. (thoughtful)
12. That cat is the _____ animal I've ever known. (independent)
13. I wrote a _____ essay than Tom. (good)
14. It was a _____ game than the one we played last week. (bad)
15. Martha is the _____ of all the girls. (friendly)
16. She drives _____ than he does. (slowly)
17. I've never seen her looking _____ . (happy)
18. The new gadget was _____ than the old one. (useful)
19. Who could have done a _____ job? (good)
20. He was ill when he left, but he is _____ now. (well)

U2c Other Nonstandard Expressions

Learn to shift from nonstandard to standard expressions.

Do you ever use words and expressions like *ain't, couldn't see nothing,* and *without you agree*? If so, learn how to shift to the standard ways of saying the same thing. Remember the following points:

(1) Avoid the double negative. The **double negative** is an expression that says no twice. Avoid using several negative words—such as *no, not (–n't), none, never,* and *nothing*—where it would be enough to say "No" once:

NONSTANDARD: He *never* said *nothing.*
STANDARD: He said *nothing.*

NONSTANDARD: She *doesn't* have *none.*
STANDARD: She *doesn't* have *any.*

NONSTANDARD: I do*n't* see *no* books.
STANDARD: I do*n't* see any books.

Similar to a double negative are expressions like *couldn't hardly* or *can't scarcely.* Standard English omits *–n't* from *could* and other auxiliaries when they are followed by such adverbs as *hardly, scarcely, barely*:

He *could* hardly see.
They *can* barely talk.
She *had* scarcely begun.

Note: A special case of the double negative is the nonstandard word *irregardless. Regardless* alone already means "without regard":

STANDARD: He went to the party, *regardless* of her wishes.

Standard English: Finer Points

> ### BY THE BACK FENCE WITH HUCK FINN
>
> One of the most famous characters in American literature, Huckleberry Finn, spoke nonstandard English. Below are some excerpts from the first chapter of *The Adventures of Huckleberry Finn*. See how many of the nonstandard expressions that you have studied are used by Huck. Write them on a piece of paper and write their standard English equivalents next to them.
>
> 1. You don't know about me without you have read a book by the name of *The Adventures of Tom Sawyer*.
> 2. But that ain't no matter.
> 3. I never seen anybody.
> 4. Judge Thatcher he took it.
> 5. The Widow Douglas she took me for her son.
> 6. She never meant no harm by it.
> 7. She put me in them new clothes.
> 8. I couldn't do nothing but sweat.
> 9. She learned me about Moses and the Bulrushers.
> 10. All I wanted was to go somewheres.

LANGUAGE IN ACTION

   (2) *Avoid nonstandard uses of* learn *and* leave.   In standard English, it is the teacher who *teaches* and the student who *learns*.

NONSTANDARD: She *learned* me how to count.
STANDARD: Those who wish to *teach* must first *learn*.

In standard English, *leave* means "to go away from," and *let* means "to permit or allow":

NONSTANDARD: Please *leave* me join the club.
STANDARD: Please *let* me join the club.

   (3) *Avoid nonstandard connectives.*   The expressions *being as, being that, seeing as how,* and *on account of* are all nonstandard when they start a clause instead of the standard connective *because:*

NONSTANDARD: *Being as* he was our friend, we lent him the money.
STANDARD: *Because* he was our friend, we lent him the money.
NONSTANDARD: *Seeing as how* the price wasn't listed, we asked the owner.
STANDARD: *Because* the price wasn't listed, we asked the owner.

Usage

Without and *on account of* are used as prepositions in standard English, not as connectives. They introduce nouns rather than clauses. To introduce clauses, standard English uses *unless* rather than *without* and *because* rather than *on account of*:

NONSTANDARD:	Martha couldn't see the road *without* she had her glasses.
STANDARD:	Martha couldn't see the road *unless* she had her glasses.
STANDARD:	Martha couldn't see the road *without* her glasses.
NONSTANDARD:	We file the report *on account of* the law requires it.
STANDARD:	We file the report *because* the law requires it.
STANDARD:	We file the report *on account of* the law.

The use of the word *as* is nonstandard as a substitute for *that* or *who*:

NONSTANDARD:	He wasn't sure *as* he could see her.
STANDARD:	He wasn't sure *that* he could see her.
NONSTANDARD:	Someone *as* knew the answer spoke up.
STANDARD:	Someone *who* knew the answer spoke up.

(4) Know the standard uses of a *and* an. Standard English uses *an* before words beginning with a vowel sound, *a* before other words:

STANDARD AN:	*an elephant, an astronomer, an implication, an hour, an F, an usher*
STANDARD A:	*a duty, a game, a horse, a C, a useful idea*

(5) Avoid miscellaneous nonstandard expressions. Avoid all uses of *ain't*. Standard English uses *off* or *from* rather than *off of*:

They took the dishes *off* the table.
I bought them *from* my friend.

Standard English does not use a pronoun directly after a noun in sentences such as, "The man, he fought the tiger" or "The children, they did the dishes." For correct usage, you may either omit the pronoun altogether or use a *–self* pronoun for emphasis:

NONSTANDARD:	The man, he fought the tiger.
STANDARD:	The *man* fought the tiger.
STANDARD:	The *man himself* fought the tiger.

Standard English: Finer Points

EXERCISE 1

All of the following sentences show the *right* form that will help you avoid familiar nonstandard expressions. Read each set of sentences over several times.

1. You are *an* hour late.
   Jim is *an* old friend.
   They placed *an* ad in the paper.
   It was *an* important meeting.
   My grades were *an* A and *a* C.
2. I *can scarcely* see you.
   The boy who had nearly drowned *could hardly* talk.
   They *had barely* been introduced.
3. He had *never* eaten *any* prawns.
   The hunters did*n't* see *any* deer.
   She *hasn't* said *anything* new.
   Pete has *never* done *anything* illegal.
   He *doesn't* have *any* answer.
   Don't say *anything*.
4. *Regardless* of what the dentist says, I don't like it.
   They're coming to visit, *regardless* of the weather.
5. The teacher *taught* me the first steps.
   Yesterday in school I *learned* something new.
   She was *teaching* students who *learned* fast.
6. You must *let* the dog run.
   Please *leave* me alone.
   Let them *leave*.
7. Mother took our names *off* the list.
   Chris borrowed some money *from* Judy.
   I got this book *from* a friend.
8. I won't go *unless* you go.
   I wouldn't go *without* my friend.
   We didn't go on the picnic *because* the weather was poor.
   Some of us didn't go *on account of* the rain.

EXERCISE 2

Each of the following sentences contains one word or expression that makes it nonstandard English. After the number of the sentence, write the standard form that should replace it.

EXAMPLE: We couldn't do nothing about it.
(Answer) *anything*

1. The driver couldn't hardly see through the windshield.
2. Those as have tickets may go in now.
3. He never does nothing right.
4. You won't get it without you pay for it.
5. She was learning my little brother how to ride a bike.

Usage

6. She worked as a usher at the theater.
7. The inspector ain't been around lately.
8. The sign said "Danger," but we went in irregardless.
9. Usually we couldn't find no parking space.
10. Her little sister can't barely walk.
11. Just leave the boxes sit there.
12. We looked for tracks but couldn't find none.
13. She borrowed the money for the trip off of her uncle.
14. There can't be no exceptions to the rule.
15. There was no film on account of the projector broke.
16. He never showed respect for a older person.
17. The money wouldn't hardly pay for food.
18. We don't allow no dogs on the beach.
19. Julie paid us a unexpected visit.
20. He never asked for help from nobody.

UNIT REVIEW EXERCISE

In each of the pairs below, which is *standard?* Write the letter of the standard sentence after the number of the pair.

1. (a) Give me some of them apples.
   (b) Give me some of those apples.
2. (a) I've never seen a worse case.
   (b) I've never seen a worser case.
3. (a) He shot the bird himself.
   (b) He shot the bird hisself.
4. (a) The story didn't leave nothing to the imagination.
   (b) The story didn't leave anything to the imagination.
5. (a) She brought her friend everywhere she went.
   (b) She brought her friend everywheres she went.
6. (a) He stole this here pen from the store.
   (b) He stole this pen from the store.
7. (a) That's a old story.
   (b) That's an old story.
8. (a) Teach me how to do it.
   (b) Learn me how to do it.
9. (a) I was able to borrow a book off of Mr. Jones.
   (b) I was able to borrow a book from Mr. Jones.
10. (a) The children caught it themselves.
    (b) The children caught it themself.
11. (a) Pearl gave her a apple.
    (b) Pearl gave her an apple.
12. (a) Dave is the most friendliest boy I know.
    (b) Dave is the friendliest boy I know.
13. (a) You won't have no trouble finding it.
    (b) You will have no trouble finding it.

Formal and Informal

14. (a) The movie was about a astronaut headed for Venus.
    (b) The movie was about an astronaut headed for Venus.
15. (a) Them directions are not very clear.
    (b) These directions are not very clear.
16. (a) My sister she loves to travel.
    (b) My sister loves to travel.
17. (a) You boys should be ashamed of yourself.
    (b) You boys should be ashamed of yourselves.
18. (a) Tommy could hardly hold his head up.
    (b) Tommy couldn't hardly hold his head up.
19. (a) Seeing as how everyone else had gone, I left too.
    (b) Because everyone else had gone, I left too.
20. (a) Selma couldn't go on account of her illness.
    (b) Selma couldn't go on account of she was ill.

Know how to change from informal to formal standard English.

U3 FORMAL AND INFORMAL

People who use standard English do not use exactly the same kind of language all the time. At school, people talk more informally during recess and in the cafeteria than they do in the classroom or in the office. Writing is generally more formal than speech: what we write down is often more important and more serious than what we just casually mention. There are two main varieties of standard English: **Informal** English is the English of conversation and the personal letter. **Formal** English is the English of a public speech, the business letter, and most books and magazines.

Here are several situations where you are expected to use formal English:

- a letter to a public agency;
- a letter to a newspaper;
- a report of an accident;
- a letter of application for a job;
- a business memo;
- papers or oral reports in school.

The differences between informal and formal English are like the differences between the clothes you wear to the beach and those you wear to school. One set of clothes is right for one occasion. The other set is right for the other. Learn to vary your language and discover which words and phrases are appropriate for formal occasions.

Usage

PREVIEW EXERCISE

The following samples of dialogue are from Paddy Chayefsky's play, *The Mother*. Would you agree that the italicized words and phrases are informal English? In each case, what would be a more formal word or phrase?

I *figured* you'd be up by now.
I was never so scared in my life when the *cop* called yesterday.
She worked in my *old man's* grocery store till twelve o'clock at night.
You've got a husband and two *kids* to take care of.
I'm *pretty sure* I could have *held onto* this job.
I've seen *plenty* of old people . . . sitting at those machines.
Why don't you *take it easy*?
Me and Frank will see that Mom's all right.

U3a Informal Words

Learn to recognize formal and informal words.

Words sound informal if people usually use them in a relaxed or friendly mood. We often use informal words when we are not very serious about something. We sometimes use them when we are not being very respectful. In each of the following pairs, the second word is more serious or respectful.

INFORMAL	FORMAL	INFORMAL	FORMAL
folks	family	pest	annoyance
flunk	fail	kids	children
clobber	defeat	goof	mistake
buddy	friend	bug	germ
mad	angry	stump	baffle

Remember:

(1) Informal English often uses simpler words than formal English. In formal English, you are likely to find many words that sound more technical than everyday talk. Many such words come to us from Latin and Greek:

INFORMAL	FORMAL	INFORMAL	FORMAL
boss	superior	faze	discourage
blow up	explode	smart	intelligent
cut down	reduce	quit	resign
fire	dismiss	job	position
live it up	celebrate	gripe	complain

Formal and Informal

U3a

LANGUAGE IN ACTION

SPEAKING INFORMALLY

Pretend you have just been hired as a contributor to a *New American Dictionary of Informal English*. How much help could you give the editors? Write a brief explanation for each of the following informal expressions.

1. They *cut us dead*.
2. She was *a cut above* your ordinary worker.
3. He *cut in* on them during the first dance.
4. *Cut it out!*
5. He just wasn't *cut out for* steady hard work.
6. The students in study hall were always *cutting up*.
7. The boss hadn't been getting his *cut*.
8. After the intermission, the band really *cut loose*.
9. Let's *cut* the noise.
10. The sergeant really *cut him down to size*.
11. He *cut quite a figure* in his new suit.
12. These excuses *cut absolutely no ice* with her.
13. Everything in the class was completely *cut-and-dried*.
14. The reviewer really *cut the play to pieces*.
15. They were always *taking shortcuts*.

But formal English does not mean stuffy English. It is simply serious, businesslike English. Formal English does not use big words merely to impress the audience. Often the simple and familiar word works just fine. "We *left*" is all right in formal standard English. There is no need to say "We *departed*."

(2) *Informal English makes use of clipped words and contractions.* We tend to shorten words used in everyday conversation. We use clipped words, such as *ad* for *advertisement*, and **contractions,** such as *they're* for *they are*.

INFORMAL	FORMAL	INFORMAL	FORMAL
phone	telephone	can't	cannot
photo	photograph	won't	will not
TV	television	there's	there is
sub	substitute	don't	do not
lab	laboratory	it's	it is
paper	newspaper	I've	I have
rep	representative	they've	they have

273

Usage

 (3) Informal English often uses groups of words where formal English would use a single, less-familiar word. Look at each of the following pairs:

INFORMAL: The criminals finally *turned themselves in.*
FORMAL: The criminals finally *surrendered.*

INFORMAL: Ken *read up on* Roosevelt's life.
FORMAL: Ken *studied* Roosevelt's life.

INFORMAL: The gas *spread all over the place.*
FORMAL: The gas *expanded.*

Note: When English becomes *extremely* informal, it turns into **slang.** *Butter up* for *flatter, kicks* for *excitement,* and *bread* for *money* are all *extremely* informal.

EXERCISE 1

Find a more formal word or expression for each of the following:

1. Sloppy, skinny, snappy, ornery, uppity.
2. Fib, gyp, scram, snooze, snoop.
3. Scuttlebutt, fiddle-faddling, wishy-washy, topsy-turvy.
4. Put something over on somebody, hand someone a line, give oneself airs, toe the line, give a fair shake.
5. Act up, come-on, getup, crackdown.

EXERCISE 2

Read each of the following sentences. Find a more formal word or expression in place of the one printed in italics. Write your replacement after the number of the sentence.

1. Don's room was *all messed up.*
2. The supervisor asked the boys to *cut down* the noise.
3. He was a *crabby* old man.
4. *A bunch of guys* were standing at the corner.
5. Martin rented a *tux* for the formal dance.
6. There were *lots of* guests there.
7. The boys *figured out* a plan.
8. The accused gangster *skipped* the country.
9. We wanted to visit the *old folks.*
10. The criminal tried to *throw them off* with his story.
11. I have been trying to *phone* her all day.
12. You should be able to *figure out* that problem.
13. The boss seemed *down on* everyone.
14. The police *frisked* the suspect.
15. You'll *flunk* that course if you do not study harder.

Formal and Informal

16. Nothing seemed to *faze* him.
17. Let's *get up* a game of football.
18. She *won't* say where she found it.
19. The Joneses have five *kids*.
20. Have you seen the *ad* in yesterday's newspaper?

U3b
Pronoun Case

Learn the formal uses of pronouns.

Half a dozen English pronouns have one form for use as a subject. They have another form for use as the object of a verb or a preposition. This difference is often called a difference in **case**. Here are the two forms in formal standard English:

SUBJECT FORM	OBJECT FORM	SUBJECT FORM	OBJECT FORM
I	me	we	us
he	him	they	them
she	her	who	whom

The **subject forms** are "before" pronouns. They are used *before* the verb in most sentences. The **object forms** are "after" pronouns. They are normally used *after* the verb and *after* prepositions:

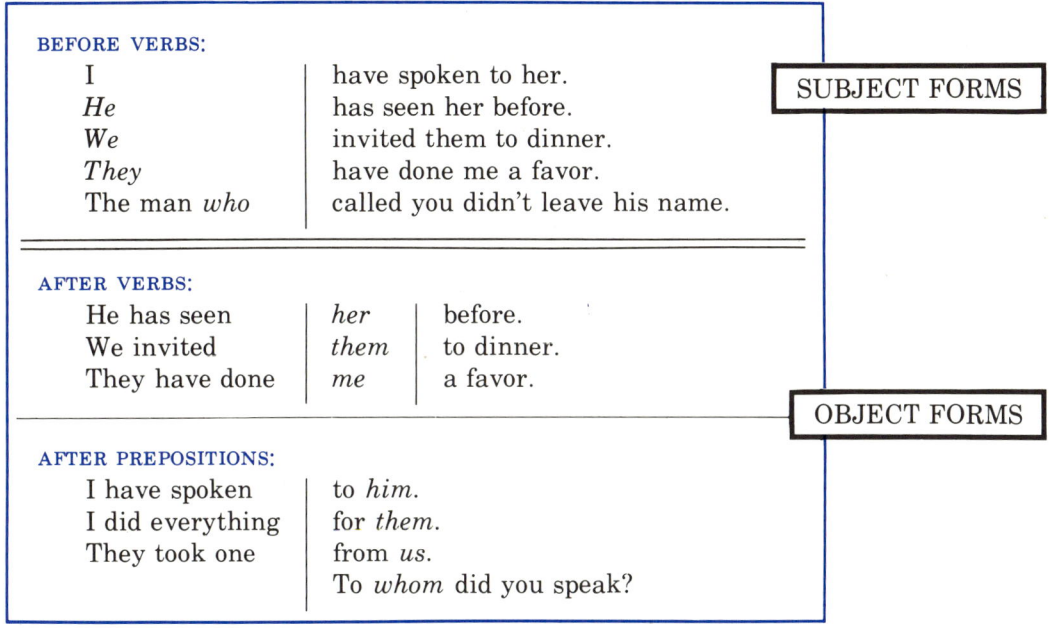

Usage

Do the following when shifting gears from informal to formal English:

(1) When you have two subjects or two objects, try them separately to make sure you have the right forms:

FORMAL: The scoutmaster and *I* put up the tent.
(*I* put up the tent.)
FORMAL: The principal questioned Jill and *me*.
(The principal questioned *me*.)
FORMAL: It's a secret between you and *them*.
(It's a secret between *them*.)

Here are *informal* pronoun uses that you should avoid in writing a paper or giving a serious talk:

INFORMAL: *Me* and Bob went shopping. (*Me* went shopping?)
FORMAL: Bob and *I* went shopping.
INFORMAL: Frank saw Mary and *I* in the store. (Frank saw *I*?)
FORMAL: Frank saw Mary and *me* in the store.
INFORMAL: Just between you and *I,* he's wrong. (Between *I* and somebody else?)
FORMAL: Just between you and *me,* he's wrong.

(2) After than *or* as, *use the pronoun forms you would use if the sentences were complete.* Study the following formal English sentences. Notice that a verb form is always required to complete the sentence.

FORMAL: Adam is as tall as *I*.
(Adam is as tall as *I* am.)
FORMAL: The music sounded better to her than *me*.
(The music sounded better to her than it did to *me*.)
FORMAL: Elsie liked Ted more than *I*.
(Elsie liked Ted more than *I* did.)

(3) When a pronoun combines with a noun, try the pronoun separately to make sure you have the right form:

FORMAL: *We* Americans like apple pie and milk. (*we* like pie)
FORMAL: The party was given for *us* girls. (given for *us*)

(4) In strictly formal English, use who *as a subject and* whom *as an object.* (In spoken English, *who* is more and more replacing *whom* and becoming an all-purpose form.) The form of these pronouns in formal English depends upon their use *in their own clauses.* Break a sen-

Formal and Informal

tence into two parts and see whether *he* or *him* would fit in. If *he* (or *they*) would fit, use the subject form: *who*. If *him* (or *them*) would fit, use the object form: *whom*.

> John is the student ―――― won first prize.
> (John is the student. *He* won first prize.)
> John is the student *who* won first prize.

> They questioned the man ―――― we pointed out.
> (They questioned the man. We pointed *him* out.)
> They questioned the man *whom* we pointed out.

If *who* or *whom* is used in questions, there may be only one sentence. Again, the *he*-or-*him* test will work:

> Who ordered pork chops?
> (*He* did.)

> *Whom* was she interviewing?
> (She was interviewing *him*.)

EXERCISE 1

All of the following examples show the *right* uses of pronoun forms in formal English. Read the sentences in each set over several times.

1. Lenny *and I* went in. Sue *and I* went out. My uncle *and I* drove home. *She and* her mother get along well. *He and* his friends are a menace. His sister *and he* grew up with their grandparents. *They and* their friends were waiting for us.

2. The sheriff questioned Marion *and me*. Gloria invited my sister *and me*. We asked both her mother *and her*. The club elected *him and* his running mate. The letter never reached his mother *and him*. We invited *them and* their families.

3. The letter was for Paolo *and me*. The parcel was addressed to my sister *and me*. This is strictly between you *and me*. Here are free tickets for you *and him*. We played against *him and* his brother. The invitation was for you *and her*. Everyone talked about *them and* their invention.

4. *We scouts* did the hard work. *We girls* must band together. *We Italians* have always been proud. They distrusted *us newcomers*. They invited *us boys* to their dance. Those were hard times for *us working people*. It was seven of them against *us two*.

5. I am faster *than she*. He is taller *than I* but shorter *than she*. I am as old *as he*. I see you more often *than them*. We are both his students, but he taught me more *than her*.

Usage

6. *Who* called you? *Who* invited them? *Whom* did you call? *Whom* did you invite? *To whom* did you talk? *With whom* did they want to work?

7. We need people *who* trust us. We need people *whom* we can trust. He remembered the coach *who* had taught him. She remembered the teammates with *whom* she had trained. Remember *who* helped you. She told us *whom* she had invited.

EXERCISE 2

For each sentence, choose the pronoun form that would be appropriate in formal standard English. Write the pronoun after the number of the sentence.

1. Mary and *(I/me)* will go to the party together.
2. Please send one to my mother and *(I/me)*.
3. I have seen Tom and *(he/him)* before.
4. Harold tried to hide from her and *(I/me)*.
5. She and *(he/him)* grew up together.
6. I wanted one for me and one for *(they/them)*.
7. She stood between him and *(I/me)*.
8. There are no secrets between Susan and *(he/him)*.
9. She had saved seats for my brother and *(I/me)*.
10. The younger boy was as tall as *(she/her)*.
11. We have been more generous than *(they/them)*.
12. They know much more than *(we/us)*.
13. I know you want to see her rather than *(I/me)*.
14. Irene weighs almost as much as *(he/him)*.
15. The coach praised *(we/us)* boys very highly.
16. The boys were going to join *(we/us)* girls later.
17. All *(we/us)* loyal party members support the President.
18. *(We/Us)* marines know how to fight.
19. The store gave free gifts to anyone *(who/whom)* stopped there.
20. The reporter told us *(who/whom)* she disliked most.

U3c
Adverb Forms

Use adverbs that are appropriate in formal standard English.

Informal English uses many unmarked adverbs that look like adjectives. "He had grown *considerable*." "Drive *slow*." Formal English uses separate adverb forms:

(1) In formal English, use the adverb with the –ly ending whenever you have a choice. Use the form with *–ly* to answer the question: "How does it work?" or "How is it done?" Look at the adverb in sentences like the following:

Formal and Informal

S	V	ADVERB
The engine	ran	smooth*ly*.
The girl	worked	steadi*ly*.
Some birds	sing	beautiful*ly*.

S	V	O	ADVERB
They	planned	their campaign	intelligent*ly*.
It	helped	him	considerab*ly*.
They	did	the cleaning	sloppi*ly*.

Remember that after a linking verb we usually find an adjective that is part of the S–LV–Adj pattern. There is usually no adverb at all:

S	LV	ADJECTIVE
The windows	were	*tight*.
The horse	looked	*slow*.
The music	sounded	*loud*.

(2) *Avoid the use of* real, awful, mighty, terrible, *and* pretty *as adverbs.* Use *really, very,* or *rather* instead:

INFORMAL: He gave a *real* good speech.
FORMAL: He gave a *very* good speech.

INFORMAL: She looked *pretty* grown-up in her new clothes.
FORMAL: She looked *rather* grown-up in her new clothes.

(3) *Use* badly *and* well *as adverbs to answer the question: "How was it done?"* After linking verbs, we use *bad* and *good* to show what something was like. After action verbs, use *badly* and *well* to show how something was done:

LINKING VERB + ADJECTIVE	ACTION VERB + ADVERB
The connection was bad.	He cooked badly.
The injuries looked bad.	She sliced the bread badly.
The water smelled bad.	You repaired it badly.
Fresh air is good for you.	The choir sang well.
The kick was good.	He kicks well.
It feels good.	He insulated it well.

Remember: Some adverbs don't have the *–ly* ending: "He talked *fast*." "They do not run *much* anymore."

For more on adverbs, see S1e.

Usage

EXERCISE 1 Read the following sentences over several times. All the forms used are formal standard English.

1. We left *quickly*. It worked *perfectly*. She dances *beautifully*. The hall emptied *rapidly*. The fire burned *fiercely*. He had changed *considerably*. We met *accidentally*. It happened *suddenly*. The prices rose *unexpectedly*.

2. He was *really* considerate. She was *really* helpful. We were *terribly* sorry. It was *very* short notice.

3. The food was *good*. Morale had been *good*. The play might be *good*. She handled the situation *well*. He skates *well*. Our team did *well*. She runs *well*. They speak Spanish *well*. They did not get along *well*.

4. Her eyesight was *bad*. The situation looked *bad*. The weather will be *bad*. He drives *badly*. His departure hurt us *badly*. Her broken arm had been set *badly*.

5. Sometimes the food tastes *good*, and sometimes it tastes *bad*. Sometimes he cooks *well*, and sometimes he cooks *badly*. Sometimes the thing works *well*, and sometimes it works *badly*.

EXERCISE 2 Choose the formal English form of the word given in parentheses. Write it after the number of the sentence.

1. The clouds were moving very _____. (swift)
2. The car was traveling _____. (slow)
3. They go to the ball games _____. (regular)
4. The music sounded _____. (terrible)
5. The movie frightened them _____. (terrible)
6. He was _____ excited about it. (real)
7. Vera insisted that the ghost was _____. (real)
8. She had grown _____. (considerable)
9. The screams were _____. (loud)
10. The students protested _____. (loud)
11. The surface was _____. (smooth)
12. It rained _____. (steady)
13. She played her role _____. (perfect)
14. We met them _____. (accidental)
15. The applause had been _____. (weak)
16. Their friends were driving _____. (reckless)
17. The animal looked quite _____. (harmless)
18. The driver stopped the car _____. (sudden)
19. The soup tasted _____. (salty)
20. The passenger waved his arms _____. (angry)

Formal and Informal

U3d

EXERCISE 3

For each sentence, choose the word that would be right in formal English. Write the formal form after the number of the sentence.

A. Use *bad* or *badly*.

1. Ralph played the game _____ .
2. She writes _____ .
3. The news sounded _____ .
4. He also hurt his hand _____ .
5. The band performed _____ .
6. The accident was _____ .
7. The car was damaged _____ .
8. Several persons were injured _____ .
9. The driver's injury was especially _____ .
10. He did everything _____ .

B. Use *good* or *well*.

11. The student did _____ on the test.
12. His grades had been _____ .
13. The new fullback ran _____ .
14. She would do _____ in the future.
15. The motor runs _____ .
16. The food tasted _____ .
17. It had been prepared very _____ .
18. The flowers smelled _____ .
19. The speech sounded _____ .
20. The boys spoke French very _____ .

Learn to recognize expressions that set apart formal and informal English.

U3d
A Guide to Formal English

For each of the following, the more formal choice is the safe form to use in serious speech and writing:

(1) Avoid these kind *and* those kind. In formal English, *this kind* and *these kinds* are all right but not *these kind*. *This* and *that* are singular and therefore pair off with *kind* and *sort*. *These* and *those* are plural and therefore pair off with *kinds* and *sorts:*

INFORMAL: I bought *those kind* of shoes last spring.
FORMAL: I bought *that kind* of shoes last spring.

INFORMAL: She was not interested in *these kind* of cars.
FORMAL: She was not interested in *these kinds* of cars.

Usage

(2) Know the formal uses of lie *and* lay, sit *and* set. In formal English, the verbs in the following pairs have *different* forms:

PRESENT:	lie	lay	sit	set
PAST:	lay	laid	sat	set
PERFECT:	lain	laid	sat	set
–ING FORM:	lying	laying	sitting	setting

Lie and *sit* are used in the pattern S–V, without an object. *Lay* and *set* are used in the pattern S–V–O, with an object. We can just *lie* or *sit*. But we *lay* (or place) *something* somewhere. We *set something* up or down.

(S–V) lie	He	*lies*	down at noon every day.
	He	*lay*	in his bed yesterday.
	He	*has lain*	in his bed all day.
	He	*is lying*	down now.
(S–V–O) lay	We	*lay*	*the mail* on the desk every day.
	We	*laid*	*the mail* on the desk yesterday.
	We	*have laid*	*the mail* on the desk already.
	We	*are laying*	*the mail* on the desk now.
(S–V) sit	I	*sit*	here often.
	I	*sat*	here this morning.
	I	*have sat*	here before.
	I	*am sitting*	here now.
(S–V–O) set	They	*set*	*the table* on weekends.
	They	*set*	*the table* last Saturday.
	They	*have set*	*the table* many times.
	They	*are setting*	*the table* right now.

Note: Sometimes these words are used with special meanings. They then do not follow the rule: Hens *lay;* the sun *sets.*

(3) Avoid the informal uses of like *and* most. Formal English uses *as* or *as if* instead of *like* as a connective introducing a clause: "Do *as* I say" (not "*like* I say"). *Like* is all right as a preposition—but only when it does *not* introduce a subject and its verb:

PREPOSITION:	She looks very much *like* me.
CONNECTIVE:	She acts *as if* she knew us.

Formal and Informal

CONNECTIVE: He tries to play *as* the professional players do.
CONNECTIVE: He did *as* he was told.

In formal English, do not substitute *most* for *almost* or *nearly*.

INFORMAL: *Most* everybody speaks like this.
FORMAL: *Nearly* everybody speaks like this.

INFORMAL: *Most* all of them were singing.
FORMAL: *Almost* all of them were singing.

(4) *Avoid informal reference to indefinite pronouns.* In formal English, use singular pronouns to point back to **indefinite** pronouns: *everybody (everyone), somebody (someone), nobody (no one),* and *anybody (anyone).* These pronouns do not refer to any one person. In formal English, they are treated as singulars:

INFORMAL: Does everyone have *their* ticket?
FORMAL: Does everyone have *his* ticket?

INFORMAL: Someone forgot *their* homework.
FORMAL: Someone forgot *her* homework.

INFORMAL: I never tell anyone what *they* should do.
FORMAL: I never tell anyone what *he or she* should do.

Note: Many people complain that the singular *he* is inaccurate when *everybody* or *somebody* might stand for people of either sex. Other people complain that *he or she* is awkward. You may want to use a simple plural instead:

SAFE: *All the people* in our class had *their* tickets.
SAFE: *Some guests* had parked *their cars* in the driveway.

EXERCISE 1

Read the following groups of sentences over several times. All these sentences contain expressions that are typical of formal English.

1. *This kind* of pill always disagrees with me.
   I have seen *that kind* of commercial too many times.
   They look *as if* they had seen a ghost.
   Do *as* I tell you.
   It looks *as if* it will rain.
   We thought the baby looked *like* his father.
   He moves *like* a turtle.
   Nearly all the students had left.
   This book should please *almost* everyone.

Usage

2. *Set* the table right away.
   Sit here.
   She was *setting* glasses on the table.
   She was *sitting* on the porch.
   The mail clerk *set* the package down.
   The mail clerk *sat* down.
   Someone has *set* the load down.
   Someone has *sat* here.
   They *set* a price.
   They just *sat* there.

3. Last summer we *lay* on the beach all day.
   The dog *lies* in the shade.
   The workers have *laid* the bricks.
   You must have been *lying* in the sun.
   The hen has been *laying* eggs.
   The town *lies* deserted.
   She *laid* her tools down.
   The letter was *lying* on his desk.
   He has *laid* the envelope on your desk.

4. Someone has written *her* initials here.
   Everyone knows *his or her* own address.
   Nobody likes to pay *his* bills.
   No one was allowed to park *his* bike.
   Has everyone done *his or her* best?
   Everybody liked *his* own ideas best.
   Did anyone forget *her* lines?
   Each child wore *his or her* new coat.

EXERCISE 2 Write down the right choice after the number of each sentence.

A. Choose *this* or *these:*

1. They had never seen _____ kind of apples.
2. The office constantly received _____ kind of complaints.
3. _____ kind of drug should be banned.
4. Every drugstore has all _____ kinds of toothpaste.
5. The librarian sorts out _____ kinds of books.

B. Choose *that* or *those:*

6. My aunt loved _____ kind of vacation.
7. No one in town sold _____ kind of motorcycles.
8. Everyone collected _____ kind of coupons.
9. His store stocked all _____ kinds of uniforms.
10. Her pet store did not sell _____ kinds of birds.

Formal and Informal

C. Choose *as* or *as if:*

11. The mule looked _____ it had been clawed by a bear.
12. We did everything _____ the instructions said.
13. You should have done _____ I told you.
14. Jim looked _____ he could not walk another step.
15. It seems _____ he visits us every holiday.

D. Choose *sit* or *set:*

16. The old-timers _____ in the sun and talk.
17. Small children find it hard to _____ still.
18. Game commissions _____ limits on people's hunting.
19. Wilma tried to _____ a new record.
20. We _____ on the beach and watch the sunset.

E. Choose *lie* or *lay:*

21. Books and papers should not _____ on the floor.
22. We were very tired and ready to _____ down.
23. During the summer, we _____ on the beach and relax.
24. Parents always try to _____ down the law.
25. Bricklayers _____ bricks.

EXERCISE 3

Each of the following sentences gives you two choices. Choose the one that would be right in formal English. Write the formal choice after the number of the sentence.

1. Everyone loves *(that/those)* kind of story.
2. The students told *(his/their)* story to the vice-principal.
3. Everybody should take care of *(his or her / their)* possessions.
4. Everyone will do *(his or her/their)* own work.
5. Some people left *(his or her/their)* car lights on.
6. The doctor had been *(sitting/setting)* up with a sick friend.
7. The books had *(lain/laid)* on the shelves for days.
8. The dogs have been *(lying/laying)* in the yard all day.
9. *(Sit/Set)* your parcels down and rest for a while.
10. We *(lie/lay)* on the beach all day and relax.
11. It has been *(lying/laying)* there all this time.
12. The cowboy has *(lain/laid)* down his six-shooter forever.
13. When will they be *(lying/laying)* the cornerstone?
14. They have *(sat/set)* there often.
15. We just *(sat/set)* in the living room and talked.
16. Herman *(sat/set)* up the pieces for a game of chess.
17. The painting didn't look *(as/like)* art to me.
18. She was sitting there *(as if/like)* she were a Buddha.
19. It seemed *(as if/like)* he had forgotten the answer.
20. The students filled out the forms *(as/like)* the teacher had shown.

Usage

UNIT REVIEW EXERCISE

After the number of each pair, write the letter of the sentence that would be right in formal English. (Be prepared to explain in class why you made the choice you did in each case.)

1. (a) It seemed like nothing could upset him.
   (b) It seemed as if nothing could upset him.
2. (a) We stopped when the officer blew the whistle.
   (b) We stopped when the cop blew the whistle.
3. (a) They sent notices to Jill and me.
   (b) They sent notices to Jill and I.
4. (a) Him and his friends got up and left.
   (b) He and his friends got up and left.
5. (a) The guests had a real good time.
   (b) The guests had a very good time.
6. (a) No one played the piano as good as Henry.
   (b) No one played the piano as well as Henry.
7. (a) My sisters act as if they were my teachers.
   (b) My sisters act like they were my teachers.
8. (a) A real surprise is waiting for you and her.
   (b) A real surprise is waiting for you and she.
9. (a) Everyone wants to see their talent recognized.
   (b) Everyone wants to see his or her talent recognized.
10. (a) The panel members were setting around the table.
    (b) The panel members were sitting around the table.
11. (a) Everyone in the group asked their questions.
    (b) All members of the group asked their questions.
12. (a) It has been raining steady for two hours.
    (b) It has been raining steadily for two hours.
13. (a) Like I said, I forgot the answer.
    (b) As I said, I forgot the answer.
14. (a) Some people refused to chip in.
    (b) Some people refused to contribute.
15. (a) They should lie down for a while.
    (b) They should lay down for a while.
16. (a) He had lain the books somewhere.
    (b) He had laid the books somewhere.
17. (a) They honored we winners at the assembly.
    (b) They honored us winners at the assembly.
18. (a) There was no love between Manny and I.
    (b) There was no love between Manny and me.
19. (a) No boy was as tall as her.
    (b) No boy was as tall as she.
20. (a) To whom should the letter be addressed?
    (b) To who should the letter be addressed?

Revising Written Sentences

U4a

U4 REVISING WRITTEN SENTENCES

Write sentences in which basic relationships are clearly worked out.

Many of the sentences we use in conversation are half finished. We change from one pattern to another as we change our minds about what we are going to say. Good *written* sentences, by contrast, are built to last. We put them together carefully. We have a chance to reread and revise them once they are down on paper.

U4a Agreement

Check your sentences for agreement of subject and verb.

We use the **singular** form of the verb if the subject points to one person or thing or to a quantity considered as one whole. We use the **plural** form of the verb if the subject points to several things that we can count separately. Look at the way the verb, or the first auxiliary, changes in each of the following pairs of sentences:

SINGULAR: One of them *was* telling the truth.
PLURAL: Both of them *were* telling the truth.

SINGULAR: A dolphin *communicates* with high-pitched sounds.
PLURAL: Dolphins *communicate* with high-pitched sounds.

Check your sentences for agreement when the subject of the sentence does not clearly stand out. You may have to ask: "Am I really talking about *one*—or about *several?*"

(1) Look for word groups that might come between the subject and its verb. Such word groups are like a wedge between the subject and the verb. Ignore the wedged-in group of words when choosing the right form:

SUBJECT		VERB	
The woman	*with the briefcase*	was	in a hurry.
Those boys	*at the corner*	are	my friends.
The girls	*walking the dog*	know	me.
Those bricks	*holding up the shelf*	are	unsteady.
The parts	*that she got from the store*	were	defective.
A person	*who wants friends*	has	to be a friend.

287

Usage

(2) *Check for agreement when there are two or more subjects for a single verb.* Such **compound subjects** are usually plural. Treat them as plurals when two or more subjects are joined by *and:*

PLURAL: The projector and the film *are* in the office.
PLURAL: Mike, Ted, and Joe *have* already been here.
PLURAL: Usually both our team and their team *win.*
PLURAL: Tomatoes and carrots *cost* very little this week.
PLURAL: Both George and Jane *have* to do the dishes.

But when subjects joined by *and* stand for *a single thing or person,* the verb is singular:

SINGULAR: Apple pie and ice cream *is* a good dessert.
SINGULAR: His classmate and friend *advises* him.

When *or* (or sometimes *nor*) gives *a choice between two singular subjects,* the verb is singular:

SINGULAR: Joan or her assistant *is* supposed to do the experiment.
SINGULAR: The station wagon or the convertible *was* to be inspected next.
SINGULAR: Neither the book nor the movie *was* very good.
SINGULAR: His or mine *is* going to win the award.

Note: *Together with, in addition to,* and *as well as* leave a singular subject singular:

Joan / together with her parents / *is* going to Paris.
His regular *salary* / in addition to the forty dollars / *was* in the envelope.
The main *road* / as well as the side roads / *is* being repaved.

(3) *Look out for subjects that do not include a clear signal for a singular or plural:*

• *A number of* looks singular, but it means "several." We treat it as a plural:

PLURAL: A number of men *were* waiting.

• **Collective nouns**, such as *team, club, committee, group, audience,* and *class,* may be followed by either a singular or a plural verb:

SINGULAR: The team *is* having its annual dinner on Friday.
            (Here, "the team" is a group as a *whole.*)
PLURAL: The team *are* dressing for the game.
            (Here, "the team" refers to the *individual* members.)

Revising Written Sentences

• A plural noun may be treated as singular when it stands for *the whole amount:*

SINGULAR: Two ounces *was* added to the solution.
SINGULAR: Fifty cents *is* enough to pay for that show.

Note: Make the verb agree with the subject even if the subject follows the verb: There *are* several books on the shelf. There *were* a jeep and a truck in the driveway.

EXERCISE 1

Study agreement in the following sentences. All of them are standard formal English. Be prepared to explain in class why the verb in the second sentence of each pair is different from the verb in the first sentence.

1. The boy in the car *is* my brother.
   The boys in the car *are* my brothers.
2. A cat with kittens *needs* little help.
   Kittens without their mother *need* care.
3. The acting and the directing *were* both poor.
   The acting as well as the directing *was* poor.
4. Jim or his sister *is* learning to play the piano.
   Jim and his sister *are* learning to play the piano.
5. Either pen or pencil *is* to be used.
   Both pen and pencil *are* to be used.
6. Our captain and best player *is* Jim Painter.
   Our captain and our best player *are* speaking for the team.
7. Some of my freedom *has* been taken away.
   Some of our freedoms *have* been threatened.
8. Three pennies *were* lying on the table.
   Ten cents *was* the price of most candy bars.
9. His fear *seems* irrational.
   The causes of his fear *seem* irrational.
10. Her height together with her speed *makes* her a top athlete.
    Her height and her speed *make* her an excellent athlete.

EXERCISE 2

Write your choice after the number of the sentence. Watch out for material that comes between the subject and its verb.

1. The papers on top of the piano *(is / are)* a day old.
2. The trainer of the dancing bears *(has / have)* changed the act.
3. One of the boards *(seems / seem)* to be loose.
4. Ten boys who waited for the bus *(was / were)* left behind.
5. Two members of the team *(was / were)* thrown out of the game.
6. The runner-up as well as the winner *(is / are)* going to attend.

Usage

7. The prince as well as his attendants *(has/have)* left the ball before midnight.
8. The coach in addition to the four girls who won the race *(has/have)* spoken to our students.
9. Charlie and I *(intends/intend)* to be there.
10. Scouts from all over the world *(has/have)* been camping at the fairgrounds.

EXERCISE 3

In each of the following sentences, make the verb agree with its subject. Write your choice after the number of the sentence.

1. The Bowie knife and the Colt *(was/were)* named after their inventors.
2. People using appliances *(knows/know)* about voltage.
3. Both volt and watt *(is/are)* named after scientists.
4. The inventor of diesel engines *(was/were)* named Diesel.
5. Prospectors who are looking for uranium *(uses/use)* the Geiger counter.
6. The Ferris wheel or the Mason jar also *(reminds/remind)* us of a person's name.
7. Lunch meat between slices of bread *(is/are)* called a sandwich.
8. These snacks that are now eaten by millions *(was/were)* first eaten by the Earl of Sandwich.
9. Our national capital as well as several states *(carries/carry)* the name of a person.
10. A king or a queen *(has/have)* often given a place its name.
11. Georgia and Maryland among our states *(is/are)* examples.
12. Another name used by British kings *(explains/explain)* the name Carolina.
13. Sometimes a name for old legends *(survives/survive)* today.
14. The cereals that we eat for breakfast *(is/are)* named after the goddess of the harvest.
15. A number of other familiar words *(reminds/remind)* us of legendary beings.
16. A lunar landing or a lunar vehicle *(reminds/remind)* us of the ancient goddess of the moon.
17. Often the people whose names we still use *(is/are)* almost forgotten.
18. The saxophone as well as the sousaphone *(was/were)* named after a musician.
19. Names like Santa Barbara *(calls/call)* to mind a city, not the saint.
20. Few people in this country *(remembers/remember)* the person after whom it was named.

Ferris wheel

Revising Written Sentences

U4b Pronoun Reference

Make your pronouns point clearly to what they stand for.

Pronouns like *he* or *they* usually do not make sense alone. They refer, or point back, to someone or something that was mentioned earlier. They point back to an **antecedent**—something that has "come before":

Joan said that *she* would help us.
The tribe had built *its* dwelling close to the cliff.
Candidates smile when *they* look into the cameras.

Sometimes a pronoun does not point clearly to its antecedent. We then have to shift or rewrite parts of the sentence:

CONFUSING: *Jim* told *Tom* that *he* would have to leave immediately.
(Who would have to leave immediately—Jim or Tom?)
CLEAR: *Jim* told *Tom* to leave immediately.

CONFUSING: *Sue* spoke to *her sister* before *she* went out.
(Who went out—Sue or her sister?)
CLEAR: Before *Sue* went out, *she* spoke to her *sister*.

THAT'S NOT REALLY WHAT I MEANT

Sometimes a sentence makes perfect sense to us when we first write it down. But when we reread it later, we may say: "That's not really what I meant!" Can you rewrite each of the following sentences so that it says more clearly what the writer originally meant?

1. When the police officers saw the criminals, they panicked and ran away.
2. Take the kitten out of the box and throw it out.
3. As the airplane touched down on the runway, it buckled.
4. The accused was chained after he threatened to kill the judge, which I think is a good idea.
5. The doctor gave Dave first aid after he passed out.
6. When Max pulled on the dog's leash, it snapped.
7. In this country, they go shopping with their hair up in curlers.
8. In ancient Rome, you were thrown to the lions for being a Christian.
9. The doctors operated on my nose twice, but it was a failure.
10. He rushed her to the hospital at eighty miles an hour so she could have her baby. This is punishable by a heavy fine in Massachusetts.

FOR REVISION PRACTICE

Usage

Remember the following points about pronoun reference in formal English:

(1) In formal English, avoid vague use of you *and* they. In formal English, *you* means "you, the listener" or "you, the reader." *They* points back to a specific group of people. Observe the differences between the following pairs:

INFORMAL: On our team, if *you* strike out, *you* pay a fine.
FORMAL: On our team, if *we* strike out, *we* pay a fine.

INFORMAL: *They* say that the polar ice cap is slowly melting.
FORMAL: *Scientists* (or *Arctic explorers*) say that the polar ice cap is slowly melting.

(2) In formal English, avoid vague this *and* which. Informally, we sometimes use *this* and *which* to point back to the whole idea expressed in a sentence. As a result, we sometimes have to ask: "What exactly does this *this* or *which* point to?"

INFORMAL: Elizabeth had bought a ticket for the opening performance on Tuesday, a holiday. Evidently she had forgotten *this*. (Had she forgotten about the *ticket*—or about the *holiday?*)
CLEAR: Elizabeth had bought a ticket for the opening performance on Tuesday. She had forgotten it was a holiday.

INFORMAL: The business manager suggested an idea, *which* surprised everyone.
CLEAR: The fact that the business manager suggested an idea surprised everyone.
CLEAR: The idea suggested by the business manager surprised everyone.

(3) In formal English, avoid the orphaned it. Because the *it* has lost its antecedent in the following sentences, the meaning is not clear:

He wanted to be an actor, but it wouldn't give him financial security.
I like to play games because *it* relaxes me.

In the first sentence, *it* cannot refer to *actor;* in the second, *it* cannot refer to *games*. Rewrite such sentences:

CLEAR: He wanted to be an actor, but *acting* wouldn't give him financial security.
CLEAR: I like to play games because *they* relax me.

Revising Written Sentences

EXERCISE 1

Check pronoun reference in the following pairs. Which sentence might confuse a reader because of vague pronoun reference? Which sentence is clear? Write the letter of the *clear* sentence after the number of the pair. (Be prepared to explain the difference between the two paired sentences.)

1. (a) He spent all his money on accessories for his motorcycle, which seemed unnecessary to me.
   (b) He had a motorcycle, and he spent all his money on accessories that seemed unnecessary to me.
2. (a) We sent the news in code, but it was known to the enemy.
   (b) The news that we sent in code was known to the enemy.
3. (a) The weather in many parts of Mexico is pleasant all summer.
   (b) In many parts of Mexico, they have pleasant weather all summer.
4. (a) His divorced wife came to the wedding in her limousine, which we considered bad taste.
   (b) His divorced wife came to the wedding in her limousine. We thought her presence at the wedding was in bad taste.
5. (a) In ancient Greece, students learned how to argue.
   (b) In ancient Greece, you learned how to argue.
6. (a) I understand that many Canadians speak French.
   (b) I understand that they speak French in Canada.
7. (a) When the animal wagged its tail, it was happy.
   (b) When the animal was happy, it wagged its tail.
8. (a) Agnes met Susan at Susan's house.
   (b) Agnes met Susan at her house.
9. (a) You need courage when you marry a man you hardly know.
   (b) A woman who marries a man she hardly knows needs courage.
10. (a) In Greek tragedies, the actors wore masks.
    (b) In Greek tragedies, they wore masks.

EXERCISE 2

Rewrite the italicized part of each passage to make it clearer or less confusing.

EXAMPLE: My mother asked Sue *to move her car.*
(Answer) to move my mother's car

1. The magician wanted to hypnotize Ed, *but he passed out.*
2. In ancient Rome, *you had slaves to do the work for you.*
3. Everyone wanted to hear the singers, *but it was sold out.*
4. Germany attacked in June, 1941. *This was a mistake.*
5. Rita looked for work everywhere, *but they were not hiring anybody.*
6. His mother became a lawyer, *although it was overcrowded.*

Usage

7. Elma Bugbee was assigned to Eleanor Roosevelt *after her husband became President.*
8. Politicians and movie stars often have reporters *digging into your personal lives.*
9. Every day Joan and her husband came over to our house on their new motorcycle—*which annoyed my father.*
10. The prisoners had been chained, *but they were struck off.*

U4c Position of Modifiers

Make sure that modifiers fit clearly into the sentence.

Modifiers are like attachments that we use to build up a sentence:

BARE: The rider waved.
MODIFIED: *Smiling broadly,* the rider *on the shiny big motorcycle* waved *at the crowd.*

Sometimes a modifier has become attached to the wrong part of the sentence. Or it does not fit into the sentence in the right way. Look at the modifier *washing his face* in the following sentence. It should be attached to *somebody* who was washing his face. But that person was left out of the sentence, and the modifier was left up in the air:

DANGLING: *Washing his face,* the water ran out of the bowl.
CLEAR: *Washing his face, Gil* saw the water drain from the bowl.

Like a man who has had a ladder removed from under him and is hanging from the roof of a building, such modifiers are dangling. **Dangling modifiers** need support—they need a specific word to modify.

Even when what is modified appears in the sentence, the modifier may be too far from it to point to it clearly. We call such a modifier **misplaced.** Here are the most common kinds of dangling and misplaced modifiers:

(1) Adverbs. Adverbs like *only, nearly, hardly, just,* and *almost* may confuse us if they are not placed close to what they modify:

MISPLACED: Jerry *nearly* lost all his money.
(Did he *nearly lose* the money? Or did he lose *nearly all* of it?)
CLEAR: Jerry lost *nearly* all his money.

MISPLACED: The women *only work* three days a week.
CLEAR: The women work *only three days* a week.

Revising Written Sentences

(2) Prepositional phrases. A prepositional phrase may be too far from the noun or verb it modifies:

MISPLACED: He gave a gift to the girl *in a red package.*
CLEAR: He gave the girl *a gift in a red package.*

MISPLACED: Roger and I met her on the day she was elected *by accident.*
(Was she *elected* by accident?)
CLEAR: Roger and I *met her by accident* on the day she was elected.

(3) Verbals. We can put forms like *called* and *calling* into a sentence without using them as the verb or as part of the verb. We often use them as modifiers. We then call such forms verbals, to distinguish them from real verbs. When these forms carry other material along with them, we get a verbal phrase:

VERB: The hiker *was shouting.*
VERBAL: *Shouting,* the hiker ran down the path.
VERBAL PHRASE: *Shouting for help,* the hiker ran from the bear.

If the person shouting were not named, the verbal would be left dangling: "*Shouting for help,* the bear was frightened off." A verbal can be confusing when it could point in two different directions:

CONFUSING: Bruce saw the messenger looking for the mailbox.
(Who was looking for the mailbox—Bruce or the messenger?)
CLEAR: Looking for the mailbox, *Bruce* saw the messenger.
CLEAR: The messenger *was looking* for the mailbox when Bruce saw him.

(4) Relative clauses. The *who, which, that,* or *whose* at the beginning of a relative clause is a pronoun. Whenever possible, it should directly follow its antecedent:

CONFUSING: Mr. Martin gave a message *to the boy that was marked "urgent."*
(Was *the boy* marked "urgent"?)
CLEAR: Mr. Martin gave the boy *a message that was marked "urgent."*

Remember that there is almost always more than one way to state an idea. If you find that you have not stated an idea clearly, try another way of saying the same thing.

Usage

EXERCISE 1 In each of the following pairs, which sentence is clear? Which is confusing? Write the letter of the *clear* sentence after the number of the pair. (Be prepared to explain the difference between the two sentences in each pair.)

1. (a) We almost stopped there on every trip.
   (b) We stopped there on almost every trip.
2. (a) While sitting on the pier, we saw many seagulls.
   (b) We saw many seagulls, sitting on the pier.
3. (a) Ben hit the ball that the pitcher threw on the handle of his bat.
   (b) The pitcher threw the ball, and Ben hit it on the handle of his bat.
4. (a) Don was in a good mood when he left the class.
   (b) Don left the class in a good mood.
5. (a) Looking out the window, we saw flowers everywhere.
   (b) Looking out the window, flowers were everywhere.
6. (a) The speaker almost said nothing before we got up and left.
   (b) The speaker said almost nothing before we got up and left.
7. (a) The cowboy tried to capture the steer with the lasso.
   (b) With his lasso, the cowboy tried to capture the steer.
8. (a) We found a purse made of black leather on the sidewalk.
   (b) We found a purse on the sidewalk that was made of black leather.
9. (a) Walking down the road, we heard the birds singing merrily.
   (b) Walking down the road, the birds were singing merrily.
10. (a) The soldiers just came to attention as the band started playing.
    (b) The soldiers came to attention just as the band started playing.

EXERCISE 2 Rewrite the italicized part to make each sentence less confusing.

EXAMPLE: The mailbox was damaged *backing out of the driveway.*
(Answer) *when we backed out of the driveway*

1. The school bought new desks *for its students with plastic tops.*
2. *Being a new student,* the coach did not know me.
3. The class sent flowers *to the girl who had been injured in the hospital.*
4. *Sleeping on the sofa,* the cat jumped on my shoulder.
5. We borrowed *a book from the library on tropical fish.*
6. *Digging in the yard, a skeleton came to the surface.*
7. *Parked at the top of the hill,* the lights of the city filled the whole valley.

8. We discovered *the name of the cheese we ate by accident.*
9. Jimmy kept talking *about the gopher that died in a frenzy of excitement.*
10. *Having a good appetite,* the salmon tasted delicious.
11. Last year, a young man *wanted to marry my sister, whose name I have forgotten.*
12. Janice saw two boys *standing in the corridor that she knew.*
13. *Running to catch the bus,* his hat fell off.
14. We *went fishing for trout with new equipment.*
15. I bought a book of *poems for my aunt that cost two dollars.*

Avoid shifts in perspective when referring to people and events.

U4d

Shifts

When things are done consistently, we can easily find our way. We consistently drive on the right side of the street. We consistently read from left to right. To write a well laid-out sentence, we have to be consistent in how we look at people and events. Are we talking *to* a person, or *about* that person? Are we describing things as happening now or in the past?

There are three major kinds of unnecessary shifts:

(1) Shifts in person. When you refer to yourself, you use such pronouns as *I, we, us, our* — "first person" pronouns. When you refer to the reader, you use such pronouns as *you* and *your* — "second person" pronouns. When you refer to people in general, you use such pronouns as *he, she, it, they, him, her, them* — "third person" pronouns. Do not needlessly shift from one of these to another:

SHIFT: *We* learned how to discuss things with *your* parents.
CONSISTENT: *We* learned how to discuss things with *our* parents.

SHIFT: It is one thing for *a person* to get admitted to college, but *you* also have to stay there.
CONSISTENT: It is one thing for *me* to get admitted to college, but *I* also have to stay there.

(2) Shifts in time. Present verb forms often refer to action currently going on. Past verb forms refer to action that has ended. Do not shift from the past to the present or future:

SHIFT: As I *was doing* my homework, a big bird suddenly *flies* into the room. (Shift from past to present.)
CONSISTENT: As I *was doing* my homework, a big bird suddenly *flew* into the room.

Usage

If something has happened before the present but still matters, we use the **perfect** forms. These forms use the auxiliary verb *have* or *has:* "Phil *has finished* his breakfast" (and now he is ready to go to work). If something had already happened before *other* events in the past, we use the **past perfect** forms. These forms use the auxiliary verb *had:* "The Japanese *had bombed* Pearl Harbor" (this was before this country declared war):

CONSISTENT: Historians *learn* from what *has happened* in the past.
CONSISTENT: We *are investigating* new drugs that *have come* on the market.
CONSISTENT: He *was speaking* about what he *had seen.*
He *spoke* about what he *had seen.*

(3) Shifts to the passive. Most sentences we use are *active* sentences. The *doer* of the action, the "agent," comes first and serves as the subject of the sentence. In a *passive* sentence, the "doer" is either unnamed or is placed at the end of the sentence, usually after the word *by:*

	"DOERS"	ACTIVE VERB	
ACTIVE	The hunchback	rang	the bell.
	Our pitcher	hit	a home run.
	A mechanic	could solve	that problem.
		PASSIVE VERB	"DOERS"
PASSIVE	The bell	was rung.	
	A home run	was hit	*by* our pitcher.
	That problem	could be solved	*by* a mechanic.

Do not shift from the active to the passive in the same sentence when the *same* person or thing is the doer in both parts:

SHIFT: After you *have finished* painting, the brushes *should be put* in water.
CONSISTENT: After you *have finished* painting, you *should put* the brushes in water.

SHIFT: If you *want* that job, a good education *is required.*
CONSISTENT: If you *want* that job, you *must get* a good education.

For more on the passive, see S3b.

Revising Written Sentences

EXERCISE 1 Check the following sentences for unnecessary or confusing shifts in time, in person, or to the passive. Mark sentences *S* for satisfactory or *U* for unsatisfactory. Put the right letter after the number of the sentence.

1. We today enjoy parks that earlier generations have provided for us.
2. Appliances took over much of the work that human hands had done before.
3. We were spreading our things for the picnic, when suddenly a a big dark cloud hides the sun.
4. The shoemaker would repair people's shoes while you wait.
5. When the umpire made the ruling, our coach turned red in the face.
6. When a person applies for a job, you have to make a good first impression.
7. Many people forget the hardships that their parents or grandparents have suffered.
8. The director reported that two valuable paintings had been stolen.
9. Consumer reports warn consumers of possible defects in the things you buy.
10. As the truck approached the crossing, we hear a train whistle.
11. A driver can solve many problems if you carry some simple tools in your glove compartment.
12. The warriors hunted with bows and arrows because firearms are unknown.
13. Stilts reached up, and another perfect throw had been made.
14. Students need a chance to apply what they have learned.
15. When we reached the cabin, the electricity had been turned off.

EXERCISE 2 Rewrite the italicized part of each of the following sentences. Revise shifts in person, in time, or to the passive.

1. While we were discussing the problem, *I am thinking of something else.*
2. People can be ambitious, *but you should not be dishonest.*
3. I realized *that I have learned a great deal through sports.*
4. The construction company designed the building, *and it was built by them, too.*
5. Even when you know you are wrong, *a person may find it hard to admit it.*
6. While the orchestra was playing, *a huge wave suddenly strikes the ship.*
7. When someone accepts a responsibility, *you should follow through.*

Usage

8. After I finished my breakfast, *my keys were picked up and I rush off to the car.*
9. She had wanted to speak to him *before he leaves.*
10. Before you leave the kitchen, *your plate should be cleaned.*
11. Parents can never know for sure *how your children will turn out.*
12. Every time I see her, *she was smiling.*
13. I think he was spying on us, but I'm sure *that he sees nothing.*
14. If travelers plan ahead, *your vacation will be more enjoyable.*
15. If you swallow poison, *an antidote should be taken as quickly as possible.*

U4e
Parallel Structure

Make sentences run parallel by coordinating only sentence parts of the same kind.

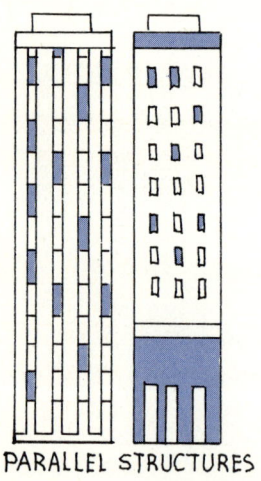

PARALLEL STRUCTURES

Your sentences will show parallel structure when you use the same kind of word (or phrase) to do the same kind of job. The rails of a railroad are parallel, and they must remain parallel or the train will run off the track. The sentences you write may also run off the track if parts within them are not parallel.

Problems with parallel structure arise when you want to join two or more parts of a sentence. For instance, you might want to have two subjects in the same sentence. Or you might want two objects or two prepositional phrases. Such parts are usually joined by *and, or,* or *but.* Make sure a word like *and* coordinates, or ties together, sentence parts of the same kind:

FAULTY: Frank was handsome, mature, and a very intelligent boy.
REVISED: Frank was *handsome, mature,* and *intelligent.*

FAULTY: To hike, swim, and *basking* in the sun make a perfect vacation.
REVISED: *Hiking, swimming,* and *basking* in the sun make a perfect vacation.

FAULTY: Helen rushed up the steps and entering her room.
REVISED: Helen rushed *up the steps* and *into her room.*

We can usually make such a sentence run parallel by changing all the coordinated parts to the *same kind* of item. We tie together two or three adjectives, or two or three nouns. But sometimes we rewrite the sentence altogether, taking out the *and:*

FAULTY: Sally was a cheerful girl and who had many friends.
REVISED: Sally was a cheerful girl with many friends.
REVISED: Sally was a cheerful girl who had many friends.

Revising Written Sentences

U4e

EXERCISE 1

Which sentence in each pair is satisfactory? Which shows faulty parallelism? Write the letter of the satisfactory sentence next to the number of the pair.

1. (a) Drugstores sell newspapers, magazines, and have comic books.
   (b) Drugstores sell newspapers, magazines, and comic books.
2. (a) To reach Denver by six and to sleep there were the only thoughts on our mind.
   (b) To reach Denver by six and sleeping there were the only thoughts on our mind.
3. (a) The man was old, sick, and had no teeth.
   (b) The man was old, sick, and toothless.
4. (a) My duties are to repair cars and driving the tow truck.
   (b) My duties are to repair cars and drive the tow truck.
5. (a) An auto mechanic learns to change oil, tires, and plugs.
   (b) An auto mechanic learns to change oil, tires, and how to replace plugs.
6. (a) I thought about going into the service and learn a trade.
   (b) I thought about going into the service and learning a trade.
7. (a) Plumbers are always asked to change faucet washers and can they repair a leaking sink.
   (b) Plumbers are always asked to change faucet washers and repair leaking sinks.
8. (a) Last winter in Florida, we spent our time swimming, fishing, and getting a tan.
   (b) Last winter in Florida, we spent our time swimming, fishing, and in getting a tan.
9. (a) The coach explained that we would try no trick plays but winning anyway.
   (b) The coach explained that we would try no trick plays but win anyway.
10. (a) We saw a movie star and who was wearing sunglasses.
    (b) We saw a movie star who was wearing sunglasses.

EXERCISE 2

Rewrite the italicized part of each of the following sentences to correct a lack of parallel structure. Do not change the meaning of the sentence.

1. You should think about your education, your future, *and are you going to find a job.*
2. James was tall, fast, *and had good coordination.*
3. In English we learned not only how to write *but also reading.*
4. The goal of a wrestling match is to press your opponent's shoulders to the mat *and holding them till the count of three.*
5. Lloyd was *a tireless tennis player and relaxed.*

Usage

6. The students asked the principal *if they could get the funds from student council and for his approval.*
7. I enjoy the mountains, the seashore, *and to walk on the beach.*
8. We woke up late *and feeling hungry.*
9. The doctor's advice was eating better, sleeping more, *and to study less hard.*
10. I was absent *for being sick or had important things to do.*

UNIT REVIEW EXERCISE

If a sentence is satisfactory, write *S* after the number of the sentence. If the sentence should be revised, put the right abbreviation after the number of the sentence:

Agr if there is an agreement problem;
Pr   if there is a problem with pronoun reference;
Mod if there is a dangling or misplaced modifier;
Sh   if there is a shift in time, in person, or to the passive;
Par if there is a lack of parallel structure.

1. All the people in the neighborhood come to these parties.
2. Standing on the corner, the airplanes flew by in groups of two and three.
3. Ben decided to marry because it would bring him happiness.
4. A traveler in a foreign country should follow its customs, not your own.
5. The people in the village followed the same customs that their ancestors had observed.
6. Many people get angry when a referee's decision goes against their team.
7. Few people can be star athletes, good students, and remaining popular at the same time.
8. He got up, ran to the door, and welcoming his guests.
9. Neither the crime nor the motive was easy to explain.
10. They are dropping the summer session at the high school, which I think is a good idea.
11. The comedy in the old silent movies were often hilarious.
12. The trainer was turning away from the bear to pick up his whip when it hit him.
13. I sent the flowers to the man in the same ward by mistake.
14. We were looking the other way when he walks in.
15. Three yards of material is not enough for the job.
16. Communication with people from other cultures are not always easy.
17. Either a doctor or a nurse are always on duty.
18. The girl tried to grab the snake by the tail but it bit her.
19. If you travel across the country, a good car will be needed.
20. Ray told his friends that they were late and to dress quickly.

Using Standard English

FOR FURTHER STUDY

FOLK SPEECH AND SLANG

The language we hear and read in school is typically language that is on its best behavior. Just as we expect children to be neat and well scrubbed when they head for school in the morning, so we expect them to use language there that is respectful and polite. We expect them to use the kind of language that educated people are supposed to use. But we also know that at home and with their friends they will continue to use a more informal kind of language: language with a homey, folksy touch; or slang—the kind of colorful, clever, disrespectful talk in which young people delight. What are some features of the language of the home, of the clique, of friends?

ACTIVITY 1

Talking about his childhood in Illinois in the 1880s, the American poet Carl Sandburg reported learning the following figurative expressions as part of everyday speech. Which of these do you still hear in informal, everyday talk? Make your own list of ten figurative expressions that you frequently hear among relatives or friends. Compare your list with those compiled by your classmates.

   bats in the belfry
   slow as molasses in January
   making money hand over fist
   as old as the hills
   busy as a cranberry merchant
   getting hitched
   doesn't know whether he's coming or going
   his ears must be burning
   chewing the rag

ACTIVITY 2

Pretend you could go fifty years back in time to an old-fashioned country store and listen to the old-timers talk. Do you think they would sound something like the speaker in the following passage? What expressions can you point out that have a "country" sound to you? Can you *rewrite* this passage so that it sounds more like educated city talk? (Your teacher may ask you and your classmates to work together.)

Usage

Here is how the old-timer talked:

> Yep, sonny, this is sure enough Indian Summer.
>
> Don't know what this is, I reckon, do you?
>
> Well, that's when all the homesick Indians come back to play. You know, a long time ago, long afore yer granddaddy was born even, there used to be heaps of Indians around here—thousands—millions, I reckon, far as that's concerned. Reg'lar sure 'nough Indians—none o' yer cigar store Indians, not much. They wuz all around here—right here where you're standin'.
>
> Don't be skeered—haint none around here now, leastways no live ones. They been gone many a year.
>
> They all went away and died, so they ain't no more left.
>
> But every year, 'long about now, they all come back, leastways their sperrits do. They're here now. You can see 'em off across the field. Look real hard. See that kind o' hazy, misty look out yonder? Well, them's Indians—Indian sperrits marchin' along and dancin' in the sunlight. That's what makes that kind o' haze that's everywhere—it's jest the sperrits of the Indians all come back. They're all around us now.—John T. McCutcheon in the *Chicago Tribune*

ACTIVITY 3

When English traders, explorers, and adventurers took the English language with them across the seas, colorful local varieties of English developed in the overseas territories. Have you ever listened to someone who learned to speak English in Jamaica? (Where is Jamaica? How did English get to be its language?)

Study the following Jamaican proverbs. Write a standard English version for each. Identify several major features that make "down home" Jamaican English different from standard English.

1. Sun set but danger never set.
2. When dog foot broke, him know master's door.
3. You follow fool, you fool yourself.
4. Slice off cut loaf never missed.
5. You catch cow by him horn, but man by him word.
6. Cheap bargain take money.
7. Man belly full, him say anything.
8. Handsome face woman not be best kind of woman.
9. Big word no tear man's jawbone.
10. Bottle no have stopper belong to cockroach.

Bonus: Could you make up some *imitation* Jamaican proverbs that sound almost like the real thing? (If you went to the Caribbean, how long would it take you to talk English "like a native"?)

ACTIVITY 4

Slang is often weird and colorful. Scholars who study it do not always agree on what sets it apart. But the following traits are often mentioned. For each trait, can you give several additional examples? Can you give examples for *other* traits not mentioned here?

PLAYING WITH SOUNDS (rhyme, repetition):	*yuk-yuk, heebie-jeebies, booboo*
ABBREVIATIONS:	*teach* (for *teacher*), *beaut*
WILD EXAGGERATION:	that *kills* me
DISRESPECTFUL ATTITUDE:	*kook, cracked, hillbilly*
RIDICULOUS COMPARISONS:	*fly off the handle, bonehead*

ACTIVITY 5

Slang develops fast, but it also goes out of style fast. What do the following expressions mean? Which of them do you recognize? You may want to ask older people which of these they remember.

moonshine, panhandle, hornswoggle, hick, glad rags, flat-foot, honky-tonk, tommyrot, rubberneck, hoosegow, flim-flam, palooka, the cat's pajamas, duds, spunk

Chapter 5

Mechanics
The Written Page

M1 End Punctuation
    a Sentences and Fragments
    b Questions and Exclamations

M2 Linking Punctuation
    a Commas with Coordinators
    b Semicolons with or without Connectives
    c Commas and Dependent Clauses

M3 Inside Punctuation
    a Commas for Modifiers
    b Commas for Minor Breaks
    c Colons, Dashes, and Parentheses

M4 Capitals and Special Marks
    a Using Capitals
    b Using Apostrophes
    c Using Quotation Marks
    d Using Hyphens
    e Using Italics (Underlining)

M5 Spelling
    a Commonly Misspelled Words
    b Spelling Rules
    c Confusing Pairs

M6 Manuscript Form
    a Dividing Words
    b Abbreviations
    c Numbers

Chapter Preview 5

IN THIS CHAPTER:

- How to use end punctuation and linking punctuation with complete sentences.
- How to use inside punctuation to show relationships within a sentence.
- How to use capitals, hyphens, apostrophes, and other special marks.
- How to handle direct and indirect quotations.
- How to spell commonly misspelled words and confusing pairs.
- How to improve your spelling by applying basic spelling rules.

Make things look right on the page.

Writing is a system for *recording* what would have been said face to face. For instance, we can call a person's name in two different ways. We can call "Henry" to make it sound like "Henry, come *here*." But we can also call the name in a questioning way, making it sound like "Henry, are you in there?" or "Is your name Henry?" In writing, we show the first meaning by the exclamation mark ("Henry!"). We show the second meaning by the question mark ("Henry?").

The mechanics of writing give us standard procedures for making such meanings clear when we write. The appearance of your writing on the page is the first thing to strike your reader. Make sure the mechanics of your written page make a good first impression.

PUNCTUATION MARKS: A Bird's-Eye View

COMMA

With coordinating connectives:
  The guard jumped forward, *and* the gun went off.

With nonrestrictive dependent clauses:
  Mr. Greene, *who lives upstairs,* has few friends.

With nonrestrictive modifiers:
  Shakespeare, *the world's greatest playwright,* wrote over thirty plays.

With sentence modifiers:
  To tell you the truth, I have never talked to him.

With elements in series:
  Vultures, bears, and *tigers* lived in the hills.

To replace *and* between two adjectives:
  He was a *handsome, active* boy.

With dates, addresses, and measurements:
  We lived at *130 High Street, Minneapolis, Minnesota.*

With elements interrupting the sentence:
  The bus driver, *I think,* was to blame.

SEMICOLON

With adverbial connectives:
  We rushed to the airport; *however,* the plane had left.

Between two independent clauses:
  The women came first; the men walked behind.

DASH

For heavy breaks:
  My uncle —*he used to live with us*— roared with laughter.

COLON

To introduce what follows:
  Bring your tools: *a saw, a hammer, and nails.*

PARENTHESES

For less important material:
  My aunt *(you met her once)* will also be there.

APOSTROPHE

For contractions:
  He *doesn't* live here anymore.

For possessive of nouns:
  We met at *Don's* house.

Mechanics

DIAGNOSTIC TEST

How well do you know basic requirements for satisfactory spelling and punctuation? Study the three possible choices for the blank space in each of the following passages. Put the letter of the best choice after the number of the passage.

1. The weather report said it would _____ rain.
   a. probaly   b. probably   c. probly
2. My cousins always had _____ rabbits, and guinea pigs.
   a. cats,   b. cats   c. cats;
3. Without a name tag, it's hard to tell _____ who.
   a. who's   b. whose   c. whos
4. Our old principal never forgot a _____ name.
   a. students   b. students'   c. student's
5. You will soon re____ve a printed invitation.
   a. cei   b. cea   c. cie
6. I do not want the brown _____ want the black ones.
   a. shoes I   b. shoes, I   c. shoes; I
7. People should not bring _____ bicycles into the hallway.
   a. there   b. their   c. they're
8. Uncle Ed returned from _____ completely new clothes.
   a. town with   b. town. With   c. town; with
9. Lee does not work in study _____ uses it to talk.
   a. hall she   b. hall; she   c. hall, she
10. The speedometer _____ work anymore.
    a. doesn't   b. dosent   c. doesnt
11. A disaster had _____ dam broke.
    a. happened the   b. happened, the   c. happened. The
12. We no longer bel____ved any of his stories.
    a. ie   b. ea   c. ei
13. We ate pork and _____ favorite meal.
    a. beans my   b. beans, my   c. beans. My
14. The most expensive shops were on _____.
    a. park avenue   b. Park avenue   c. Park Avenue
15. Her grandparents live in _____.
    a. Toledo Ohio   b. Toledo, Ohio   c. Toledo, ohio
16. Someone _____ called the police.
    a. should of   b. should have   c. shouldve
17. My favorite holiday was the _____.
    a. fourth of july b. Fourth Of July   c. Fourth of July
18. A train _____ bring commuters downtown.
    a. use to   b. used to   c. useto
19. The rescue operation required careful _____.
    a. planning   b. planing   c. plannyng
20. Her younger sister had been born in _____.
    a. febuary   b. Febuary   c. February

M1 END PUNCTUATION

End Punctuation

Mark the end of a sentence by a period, a question mark, or an exclamation mark.

In speech, the end of something we say is signaled by definite breaks, accompanied by a rising or falling tone of voice. The written symbols of these breaks are the period, the question mark, and the exclamation mark.

M1a Sentences and Fragments

Use the period at the end of a complete sentence.

The period is the basic stop-and-go signal that we use on the written page. We use it to set off one complete sentence from another. A complete sentence has its own subject and its own verb. (In request sentences, the subject has often been left out, but *you* is understood as the subject.)

SUBJECT	VERB	
Flies	*buzz.*	STATEMENTS
Joan	*loved* the blues.	
The tide	*will turn* soon.	
Our plane	*had been delayed.*	
	Make room.	REQUESTS
	Open the windows.	
	Organize your thoughts.	

Do *not* use a period to set off a group of words that is not a complete sentence. If you do, the result will be a **sentence fragment.** The most familiar kind of fragment is a phrase—a group of words that does not have a subject and a verb of its own. A phrase is not a complete sentence; it should be a *part* of a larger sentence.

Avoid four kinds of sentence fragments:

(1) Do not separate prepositional phrases from the rest of the sentence. Prepositional phrases start with a preposition like *in, at, with, for, on,* or *without.* Do not separate them from the sentence to which they belong:

FRAGMENT: My friends love to fish. *In the summertime.*
COMPLETE: My friends love to fish *in the summertime.*

FRAGMENT: Dad drove to the fair grounds. *With a load of children.*
COMPLETE: Dad drove to the fair grounds *with a load of children.*

Mechanics

(2) Do not separate appositives from the rest of the sentence. An appositive is a second noun that is put after the first noun to give more information about it. Often the second noun carries with it other material to make up an appositive phrase. There is no verb to make a second complete sentence:

FRAGMENT: The men asked for Pablo. *My older brother.*
COMPLETE: The men asked for Pablo, *my older brother.*

FRAGMENT: We wrote to Mr. Lee. *The man in charge of complaints.*
COMPLETE: We wrote to Mr. Lee, *the man in charge of complaints.*

(3) Do not separate verbals from the rest of the sentence. Many verbal phrases start with an *–ing* form (participle) or a *to* form (infinitive). To become part of a complete verb, such forms have to follow an auxiliary like *am, was, has, had, will, can, may,* or *should.* Do not separate verbals from the sentence if there is no auxiliary:

FRAGMENT: We were sitting in the dugout. *Waiting for the rain to stop.*
COMPLETE: We were sitting in the dugout, *waiting for the rain to stop.*

FRAGMENT: She drove downtown. *To buy a heater.*
COMPLETE: She drove downtown *to buy a heater.*

Prepositional phrases and infinitives usually blend into the rest of the sentence *without* any punctuation. Verbal phrases using the *–ing* form (participial phrases) and appositives are often set off by commas.

See M3a.

(4) Do not separate dependent clauses from their main clauses. A clause that starts with a subordinator—*if, because, although, whereas, when, while*—cannot stand by itself. It turns into a fragment when separated from the main clause by a period. A clause that starts with a relative pronoun—*who, which, that*—also turns into a fragment when set off.

FRAGMENT: We will buy the truck. *If we can raise the money.*
COMPLETE: We will buy the truck *if we can raise the money.*

FRAGMENT: She moved the truck. *Which was blocking the driveway.*
COMPLETE: She moved the truck, *which was blocking the driveway.*

For punctuation of dependent clauses, see M2c.

End Punctuation

M1a

EXERCISE 1

Many of the following pairs are two complete sentences, separated by a period. Put *S* for satisfactory after the number of each such pair. In some of the pairs, a complete sentence is followed by a sentence fragment. Write *Frag* after the number of each such pair. (Be prepared to explain how you recognized each sentence fragment.)

1. The rain was coming down in sheets. People were leaving the stadium.
2. Tarzan came to the rescue. Swinging from tree to tree.
3. She borrowed five books from the library. Including one dictionary.
4. You should take water with you. You will need it in the canyon.
5. Jean Daniel won the election. With a promise of lower taxes.
6. We finally found Pedro. He was hiding under the bed.
7. The bill was named after George Duchamps. A member of Congress from Maine.
8. The police had traced him from New York to Chicago. With the aid of his ex-fiancée.
9. We looked all over the basement for the hammer. It was in the kitchen drawer.
10. The little boy stood in the street. Crying for his mother.
11. The zoo had acquired a rare okapi. As a gift from China.
12. The car started instantly. The mechanic had done a good job.
13. Eagles are almost extinct. Except in a few wilderness areas.
14. She had written a book about Lindbergh. The American flier.
15. Burglars had ransacked the house. The strongbox had disappeared.

EXERCISE 2

Some of the following groups of words are just one complete sentence, with its subject and its verb. Write *S* for "sentence" after the number of each such group. Some of these groups of words are really *two* sentences, each with its own subject and its own verb. After the number of each such pair, write the last word of the first sentence. Then put a period. Then write the first word of the second sentence. (Capitalize the word.)

EXAMPLE: Hoboes used to ride the trains they called them the cinder trail.
(Answer) *trains. They*

1. Hoboes are wanderers they travel across the country.
2. For many years now the true hoboes have been a dying breed.
3. Modern freight trains are often carefully guarded.
4. Hoboes followed the good weather the cold sent them south.

Mechanics

5. In the spring the hoboes headed for beautiful scenery the Northwest was a favorite part of the country.
6. The penniless hobo usually carried only his bindle.
7. A bindle is a sleeping roll it also holds extra clothes.
8. The hobo slept in an empty boxcar he often slept outdoors.
9. Night watchmen sometimes gave him a corner in an office.
10. The Red Cross might give a free meal the Salvation Army might furnish a free bed.
11. Hoboes came to the back door to ask for bread.
12. A very dirty hobo did poorly a prosperous-looking hobo did poorly too.
13. Even a beggar must look just right for the job.
14. The hobo would buy a ring of red it was a hunk of baloney.
15. Hoboes cooked beans on a campfire they ate them out of the can.

EXERCISE 3

If the two groups of words should be punctuated as two complete sentences, write *2* (two sentences) after that number. If they should be combined into a single sentence, without punctuation or with a comma, write *1*.

1. The Grand Canyon is a gorge / cutting through mountains.
2. It is located in Arizona / near the border of Utah.
3. The Canyon was carved by the Colorado / winding along its floor.
4. The Colorado did not work alone / rains and frost helped.
5. Rain and frost loosened rocks / the rocks were carried through the gorge by the river.
6. The Canyon's walls are colored / from brown and red to yellow and green.
7. Grand Canyon National Park has two sections / the North Rim and the South Rim.
8. The distance between the rims is 12 miles by airplane / it is 21 miles by trail.
9. Visitors meet people / calling themselves the Havasupai.
10. *Havasupai* means people of "the blue-green water" / the name of Havasu Creek.
11. About two hundred Havasupai live here / they provide services to visitors.
12. Other tribes live in the region / the Navajo and the Hopi.
13. The reservation of the Navajos is the largest in the United States / covering 25,000 square miles.
14. The Hopi reservation is smaller / it is surrounded by the Navajo reservation.
15. The Grand Canyon National Park was established / during the Presidency of Woodrow Wilson.

End Punctuation

Remember to use question marks and exclamation marks where necessary.

M1b
Questions and Exclamations

Use marks to show that something is not a simple ordinary statement:

(1) Use the question mark to end sentences that ask for a reply. Many questions are signaled by question words like *who, whom, whose, which, when, where, what, why,* and *how:*

Whose hat is this? *Why* should I love you?
Which is the right key? *How* do you like it now?
Where are the posters? *When* did you leave?

Many questions are signaled by a reversal of the subject and its verb (or auxiliary):

Was the water warm?
Did the meter work?
Should we ask them to go to the play with us?
Has the gas company been notified?

Remember to put the question mark at the end of a *long* question:

Why do people blame their own problems on someone else?

(2) Use the exclamation mark for special emphasis. It shows that something is urgent, or that it is unusual, or that it is a surprise. It marks orders, shouts, or urgent requests. Use it as needed with single words, groups of words, or complete sentences:

Help! Stand firm!
The food is ready! Never again!
All the doors are locked! What a nice surprise!

EXERCISE

After the number of each item, write the abbreviation for the correct punctuation: *P* for period, *Q* for question mark, *E* for exclamation mark. Be prepared to justify your choice.

1. The score was three to two ____
2. Hit a homer ____
3. Should he bunt ____
4. Are you serious ____
5. Is it true that Sam is our weakest hitter ____
6. Play ball ____
7. Can you hit one over the fence ____
8. The next pitch was a slow ball ____

Mechanics

9. Stop right there _____
10. The coach had already used everyone on the team _____
11. The plane is on fire _____
12. Lock the gates _____
13. The pitcher threw two low fastballs _____
14. We just won first prize _____
15. The home team called for time _____
16. Who is coming to bat _____
17. What is the use of trying _____
18. The lion has got loose _____
19. There were two outs in the bottom of the ninth inning _____
20. Stop that car _____

UNIT REVIEW EXERCISE

Look at the blank spaces in each of the following passages. Should there be a punctuation mark? What kind? After the number of each blank space, put *P* for period; put *Q* for question mark. Put *No* for no punctuation. Use no other marks.

If you choose *P* or *Q* for the first blank of a pair, write down the first word that follows either mark. Start it with a *capital* letter to show the beginning of a new sentence.

EXAMPLE: What did we achieve _____ (1) the rule remains unchanged _____ (2)

(Answer) 1. Q The
          2. P

A. Black bears are often harmless _____(1) grizzlies are usually dangerous _____(2)
B. Campers protect their food _____(3) by hanging it from branches _____(4)
C. Who would camp in the middle of a swamp _____(5) with a million mosquitoes _____(6)
D. Visitors to the sierras can take mules _____(7) on backcountry trails _____(8)
E. We saw giant redwoods _____(9) they are the world's largest trees _____(10)
F. How do campers get hurt _____(11) rangers give many reasons _____(12)
G. What did I do _____(13) why am I always blamed _____(14)
H. Her aunt had left Baltimore _____(15) to start a new life in Alaska _____(16)
I. The gold rush started a few years later _____(17) in logging country in the hills _____(18)
J. Rita tried out for the finals _____(19) her cousin had won the last contest _____(20)

M2 LINKING PUNCTUATION

Use linking punctuation to help join two statements in a larger combined sentence.

When two statements are closely related in meaning, they may combine in a single sentence. They then become "subsentences" of a larger combined sentence. Such subunits are called **clauses:**

SEPARATE: We rushed to the office. The door was locked.

COMBINED: We rushed to the office; the door was locked.
We rushed to the office, but the door was locked.
When we rushed to the office, the door was locked.

When you punctuate the combined sentences, you have to recognize different *kinds* of clauses. There are basically two types. **Independent** clauses are not joined permanently. By simply putting a period between them, we can "unhook" them. We call them independent because they can easily go their own way. **Dependent** clauses are not so easily unhooked. When we separate them from their "partner sentence," they cannot easily stand alone. Dependent clauses start with a subordinator *(if, when, because)* or a relative pronoun *(who, which, that)*. When we "unhook" such a clause, it seems incomplete:

When we called the doctor ———— (then *what?*)
If you really love me ———— (then *what?*)

Linking punctuation is the kind of punctuation we use to help join these two different kinds of clauses.

See S4 for an overview of different kinds of clauses.

M2a Commas with Coordinators

Use a comma between two clauses joined by a coordinating connective.

Use a comma before *and, but, for, or, yet, nor,* or *so* when the word serves as a link between two independent clauses. These words are **coordinators.** They make two statements "work together":

The speaker raised his arms, *and* the crowd roared.
The spectators gasped, *but* the cable held.
They met at the corner, *for* they had no place else to go.
We must act now, *or* it will be too late.
The door was always open, *yet* no one ever came.
He insulted me, *so* I left.

Mechanics

You will encounter three variations from the basic rule:

(1) Some writers omit the *comma* when the clauses being joined are *very short:*

The team scored *and* the crowd roared.
Love me *or* leave me.

(2) Some writers use a *semicolon* instead of the comma between clauses that are *very long.* This semicolon is especially helpful when each clause already contains one or more commas. The semicolon then helps us see where the major break is:

We had our tickets, our suitcases, and our equipment; *but* the bus was nowhere to be seen.

(3) Some writers use a *period* instead of the comma to show a *very definite break:*

All this was upsetting. *For* at that time I had already decided to leave home.
I had never been so aware of the police. *Nor* had I ever been so aware of small knots of people.

EXERCISE 1

Decide whether there should be a comma at the break in each sentence. After the number of the sentence, write *C* for comma or *No* for no punctuation. Use the comma *only* if there is a coordinating connective between two *complete clauses.* Each must have a subject and a verb of its own.

1. People often consider all cats alike _____ but cats vary as much as human beings.
2. Some cats are independent _____ yet others are quite dependent.
3. Boots loved people _____ and went to bed with us every night.
4. Tiger was once badly frightened _____ so he runs at the slightest noise.
5. Even as a kitten, Puddy was not really cute _____ or playful.
6. You have to feed some cats frequently _____ or they will bite you.
7. Some cats hate other cats _____ and some cats hate people.
8. A good friend hates to visit us _____ for a cat once leaped from the floor to his shoulder.
9. We love cats _____ and they love us.
10. Our house is the wrong place _____ for people allergic to cats.

Linking Punctuation

M2b

EXERCISE 2

Join the two statements in each of the following pairs. Each time, use a coordinator to link the two, and use a comma for linking punctuation. Use as many *different* coordinators as you can.

1. The swinging doors of the Gold Dust Saloon opened. The sheriff walked in.
2. The stranger rode off into the sunset. His job in Long Branch was finished.
3. A rider galloped into the next town for help. The posse arrived too late.
4. The cowhands took good care of their horses. A good horse could save their lives some day.
5. The town marshall was feared by all outlaws. The outlaws seldom came to town.
6. The townspeople were suspicious of the stranger. He had phenomenal luck.
7. Life in the hills was rough. Hordes of men were out there looking for gold.
8. Robbers held up banks in broad daylight. Bankers employed heavily armed guards.
9. The government was too far away. Outlaws terrorized the townspeople.
10. In Western movies life is always dangerous. Audiences love excitement.

Use a semicolon between two clauses if there is an adverbial connective or no connective at all.

M2b

Semicolons with or without Connectives

Coordinators are not the only possible link between two independent clauses. Other kinds of "linking up" are possible. **Adverbial connectives** are similar to coordinators in meaning, but they work differently and require different punctuation:

COORDINATING: The adults enjoyed fishing, *but* the boys hated it.
ADVERBIAL: The adults enjoyed fishing; *however,* the boys hated it.

COORDINATING: He had lost his book, *so* he could not study.
ADVERBIAL: He had lost his book; *therefore,* he could not study.

COORDINATING: We did not know the address, *but* we had their telephone number.
ADVERBIAL: We did not know the address; *however,* we had their telephone number.

Mechanics

Make sure you can tell the two types of connectives apart. Unlike a coordinator, an adverbial connective can *shift* to a different place in the second clause:

Most of the class went on the trip; *however,* Don stayed at school.
Most of the class went on the trip; Don, *however,* stayed at school.
Most of the class went on the trip; Don stayed at school, *however.*

Coordinators, however, cannot be moved. Such combinations as "the boys *but* hated it" are not possible. Remember:

(1) Use a semicolon when the link between two clauses is however, therefore, then, besides, nevertheless, furthermore, accordingly, *or* in fact. These adverbial connectives cause a *stronger break* in a sentence than coordinators do. They therefore require a semicolon instead of a comma:

We tried to cash a check; *however,* the bank was closed.
Martha is ill; *therefore,* the meeting will have to be postponed.

(2) Use a semicolon when there is no connective *at all between two independent clauses.* The semicolon then shows that the two statements go together:

The post office closes at five; the stores close at six.
I play the piano; my sister plays the flute.

(3) Do not use a comma or omit punctuation where a semicolon is required. When you leave out the semicolon, the result is a **fused sentence.** When you use a comma instead, the result is a **comma splice:**

FUSED SENTENCE		
	FUSED:	I hate movies besides I have no money.
	IMPROVED:	I hate movies; besides I have no money.
	FUSED:	John Steinbeck wrote *The Grapes of Wrath* it was published in 1939.
	IMPROVED:	John Steinbeck wrote *The Grapes of Wrath;* it was published in 1939.

COMMA SPLICE		
	COMMA SPLICE:	The game had been canceled, therefore we left.
	IMPROVED:	The game had been canceled; therefore we left.
	COMMA SPLICE:	The subway was crowded, each car was packed.
	IMPROVED:	The subway was crowded; each car was packed.

M2b
Linking Punctuation

Note: Adverbial connectives are often set off *from the rest of the second clause*. If the connective appears at the beginning or the end of the second clause, only one comma is needed. If the connective *interrupts* the second clause, two commas are needed. But many writers do not feel the need for this additional punctuation. In each of the following pairs, both versions are acceptable:

RIGHT: The bell rang; *however,* the lecture went on.
ALSO RIGHT: The bell rang; *however* the lecture went on.

RIGHT: His reputation was shady; his credit, *nevertheless,* was good.
ALSO RIGHT: His reputation was shady; his credit *nevertheless* was good.

EXERCISE 1

Most of the following sentences are satisfactory. A few, however, illustrate the comma splice or the fused sentence. After the number, write *S* for each satisfactory sentence. Write *CS* for each comma splice and *F* for any fused sentence. (Your teacher may ask you to revise the unsatisfactory sentences.)

1. The show was over; the audience filed out of the theater.
2. The birds were singing, signs of spring were in the air.
3. The umpire had given the signal; the first batter stepped into the batter's box.
4. Jim was supposed to meet his sister at nine o'clock as usual he was late.
5. The first shall be last; the last shall be first.
6. Sue had been with the firm for five years; she was, accordingly, promoted first.
7. I have seen the movie three times, yet I still don't understand the story.
8. The event was widely advertised; the audience, nevertheless, was smaller than in previous years.
9. My alarm didn't go off on time, consequently, I missed the school bus again.
10. A girl was at the door; she was collecting for the paper.
11. Jack knew the answer to their problem, but he couldn't tell them.
12. The morning clouds had disappeared, in fact, it had become a perfect day.
13. The boy wrote a poem for his girl friend; he was too shy, however, to send it.
14. Ken liked the song, so he called the record store for a copy.
15. We have chosen our path we shall follow it.

Mechanics

EXERCISE 2

What would be the right punctuation at the break indicated in the following sentences? Put one of the following abbreviations after the number of each sentence:

SC (for semicolon) if there are two clauses related by an adverbial connective or no connective at all;

C (for comma) if two clauses are joined by a coordinator;

No (for no punctuation) if the second part of the sentence is not a complete clause.

(Do not use any periods not already printed in the text.)

1. I mailed the letter on Friday _____ it arrived Tuesday.
2. The cheerleaders did their best _____ the team, however, was losing 28 to 0.
3. You have to use the secret knock _____ or you won't be admitted to the clubhouse.
4. We visited relatives _____ on our trip to Georgia.
5. Jenny loved to read _____ consequently, she majored in English.
6. Paintings are like people _____ we gradually come to know them better.
7. George sang like a nightingale _____ yet he looked like a turtle.
8. I want to see you in my office _____ after the session.
9. Smoking cigarettes is bad for one's health _____ many people, nevertheless, cannot break the habit.
10. The best solution is not to smoke in the first place _____ then there will be no habit to break.
11. You should begin studying French early _____ young people learn languages easily.
12. I wanted the party at my house _____ Sue wanted it at hers.
13. You should go to the dentist regularly _____ in fact, you should see one every six months.
14. The coach wanted a championship team _____ so he started practice a month earlier than usual.
15. Both Dad and Mother liked pets _____ our house, therefore, was always filled with lazy dogs and spoiled cats.
16. The survivors had given up hope _____ but then a sail appeared on the horizon.
17. Mother sent me to the store _____ she needed more paint.
18. No one knew the answer _____ consequently, we sought the advice of an expert.
19. We called off the picnic because of bad weather _____ besides, there was a good movie in town that afternoon.
20. The mural showed slaves _____ the student council, therefore, wanted it removed.

Linking Punctuation

M2c
Commas and Dependent Clauses

Use a comma when necessary to set off a dependent clause.

Dependent clauses are introduced by their own kinds of connectives. A dependent clause may be signaled by a **subordinator:** *although, after, as, because, before, when, where, while, whenever, wherever, since, if, than, unless, until.* Or the dependent clause may be signaled by one of the **relative pronouns:** *who, whom, which,* and *that:*

> The pilot turned pale *when the engine failed.*
> *Before he died,* Langston Hughes had become America's best-known black poet.
> The courthouse, *which was built many years ago,* is being remodeled.

Remember:

(1) *Use no punctuation for essential dependent clauses.* Many dependent clauses state an essential condition. They narrow things down for us—they restrict the possibilities. We call them **restrictive** clauses. Restrictive clauses blend into the sentence *without a break*—no commas.

• Most of the subordinators—*when, if, unless, after, before, whenever, until*—start restrictive clauses. They add essential conditions:

RESTRICTIVE: She will speak to you *if you apologize.* (only then)
             You can talk *after I am through.* (but not before)
             The light will be turned off *unless you pay the bill.*

COMMA AFTER AN INTRODUCTORY CLAUSE:

If you can read this sign, you are following too close.

If you don't register, you can't vote

When the cat is away, the mice will play.

If you don't vote, don't holler

When women are honored, the gods are pleased.

If you save one person from hunger, you have worked a miracle.

Mechanics

• Relative clauses give us essential clues when we ask "which one?"

RESTRICTIVE: The person *who sold us the carpet* was a crook.
(That particular person—not anyone else)
RESTRICTIVE: Don't take the medicine *that was prescribed for Lee.*
(That particular kind of medicine)

(2) Use a comma when a dependent clause merely gives added information. We call such a clause **nonrestrictive:**

• Use a comma when the subordinating connective is *although, though, whereas,* and, sometimes, *because.* When we use *though,* what the main clause says is true *regardless:*

NONRESTRICTIVE: He loved checkers, *though he usually lost.*
Charlotte likes a challenge, *whereas her brother prefers to coast.*

Because is essential when it answers the question *why.* It is nonessential when it is added after the main point:

Why were you absent? I was absent *because I was sick.*
What did you do? I shut the door, *because it was raining.*

• Use a comma (or two commas) with a relative clause if the main clause has already told us "Who?" or "Which one?" Study the restrictive and nonrestrictive pairs below.

NO COMMA: The teacher *who taught history* came from Utah.
COMMAS: Janet Rigley, *who taught history,* won the award.

NO COMMA: We are looking for someone *who can help us.*
COMMA: We are looking for Mr. Short, *who can help us.*

(3) Use a comma if a dependent clause comes first. When the dependent clause comes first, use the comma to show where the main clause starts:

When you get to the corner, look for a white picket fence.
After the girls passed by, the dog growled.

EXERCISE 1

Each of the following sentences shows the *right* punctuation for restrictive and nonrestrictive clauses. Read these sentences out loud, or listen to them read out loud. Make sure you can hear a break where the comma appears in writing.

1. Al Jervis, who works in the shoe department, is the fastest talker in the store.
2. The building that used to stand here was torn down after the fire.

Linking Punctuation

3. The aunt asked for my father, whom she had not seen in years.
4. I enjoy walking, although no one else in my family does.
5. The girl whose car had broken down asked us for a ride.
6. The letter will be returned if you forget the postage stamp.
7. When you get your check, taxes have already been deducted.
8. Golden eagles, which were protected by law, were becoming more numerous.
9. The movie starred Fred Astaire, who danced his way through dozens of Hollywood musicals.
10. If you assemble the set yourself, you save half the money.
11. The students whose names had been left out were upset.
12. After the warranty expires, the owner pays for repairs.
13. The messenger that brought the news feared for his life.
14. Basketball is a high-scoring game, whereas a soccer game may end without a single goal.
15. The people in the theater panicked when the lights went out.

EXERCISE 2

What should be the punctuation at the breaks in the following sentences? Put one of the following abbreviations after the number of each sentence: *SC* (for semicolon), *C* (for comma or commas), or *No* (for no punctuation).

1. Students ———— who want to learn an African language ———— often study Swahili.
2. When Pizarro came to Peru ———— he destroyed the empire of the Incas.
3. He was running for the bus ———— when his shoe came off.
4. After Fred told his parents ———— he felt much better.
5. Polly became a surgeon ———— though her mother would have preferred another profession.
6. Look twice ———— before you cross the street.
7. Before he wrote his book report ———— he reread the last chapter of the novel.
8. The primaries in New Hampshire ———— which are the first in the nation ———— can hurt a candidate.
9. You can always trust a man ———— who smokes a pipe.
10. Although the movie was sad ———— we laughed all the way through it.
11. Wilma suggested the plan ———— that was adopted by the committee.
12. Bill was unhappy ———— when the final vote was announced.
13. Sigrid liked animals ———— that her friends hated.
14. The boys visited their grandmother ———— whenever they had a free weekend.
15. San Francisco ———— which was shaken by the earthquake ———— was almost destroyed by the fire.

Mechanics

UNIT REVIEW EXERCISE

The following sentences retell an Ibo legend from Nigeria in Africa. What should be the punctuation between the two clauses in each sentence? After the number of the sentence, write *SC* (for semicolon), *C* (for comma), or *No* (for no punctuation). Do not use any periods not already provided.

1. When the Creator created life _____ he made the parts of the body.
2. They were happy _____ for they lived in peace in a beautiful garden.
3. They obeyed all the laws _____ that the Creator had set down for them.
4. The Creator commanded hospitality _____ when a stranger asked for assistance.
5. The Creator loved his creatures _____ nevertheless, he tested their loyalty.
6. After he disguised himself _____ he appeared to them as a leper.
7. He asked the eyes for assistance _____ but they drove him away.
8. Then the leper turned to the head _____ however, he asked for help in vain.
9. He was turned away by the hands _____ that should have prepared food for the stranger.
10. The feet walked quickly away _____ after they heard his plea for help.
11. The stomach finally helped _____ although he too was disgusted by the sick visitor.
12. The Creator was angry _____ so he sent punishments to the offenders.
13. He sent blindness for the eyes _____ he sent headaches for the head.
14. The feet suffered from rheumatism _____ and the hands shook.
15. Then the Creator decreed a further punishment for the creatures _____ who had violated the law of hospitality.
16. They had chased the stranger away _____ or they had ignored his pleas for help.
17. They now became servants to the stomach _____ for the stomach had treated the stranger kindly.
18. The eyes would watch for his food _____ and the hands would pick it up.
19. The feet would carry him _____ wherever he wished to go.
20. A traveler in a strange country needs help _____ hospitality therefore was an ancient custom among many tribes.

M3 INSIDE PUNCTUATION

Use punctuation marks to clarify relationships inside a sentence.

A sentence is like a shelf. If we have just a few items stored there, we can take them in at a glance. We do not need signs and labels to help us find what we are looking for. But the more things we put on the shelf, the harder it becomes to see what we have stored there. Likewise, the more information we put into a single sentence, the harder it becomes for the reader to take in what the sentence contains. Punctuation marks *within the sentence* can help us find our way. They help us see how things are arranged in the sentence.

M3a Commas for Modifiers

Use commas where necessary to set off modifiers.

As long as a sentence contains little more than the basic sentence pattern, we need no commas or other marks to help us find our way. No punctuation is needed within any of the following sentences:

My friends had changed jobs.
The family moved to a new city.
The President had declared a national emergency.

We can add attachments to each of the basic parts of such a sentence. We call such attachments **modifiers.** Some modifiers blend into a sentence without a break. Others are set off by commas:

(1) Use commas to set off nonrestrictive modifiers. Modifiers are **restrictive** when we need them to tell us "which one?" or "what kind?" They narrow down, or restrict, the possibilities:

RESTRICTIVE: Look at the girl *in the blue dress.*
               (tells us which one)
               She wanted a car *needing little upkeep.*
               (tells us what kind)

Modifiers are **nonrestrictive** when we already know which one or what kind. They merely add something that we might *also* want to know. Use commas to set off such added information:

NONRESTRICTIVE: We ate refried beans, *my favorite meal.*
                  My sister, *wearing her blue dress,* joined the crowd.

327

Mechanics

Watch for the following kinds of modifiers:

• **Prepositional phrases** are usually restrictive. They are usually not set off by commas:

> The man *in the stovepipe hat* thinks he is Abe Lincoln.
> I like that new boy *from New York*.

• **Appositive phrases and adjectives following nouns** are usually nonrestrictive. They are then set off by commas:

> Our new car, *a six-cylinder Mustang,* is a convertible.
> The Queen's gown, *expensive but gaudy,* was the talk of the court.

• **Verbals that modify nouns** are sometimes restrictive and sometimes not. Ask, "Is this modifier necessary to tell me *which one?* Or do I already know?" Study the differences between the two sentences in each of the following pairs:

> My old tennis racket, *hanging on the wall,* needs restringing.
> The old tennis racket *hanging on the wall* needs restringing.

> Mini and Mollie, *dressed in dungarees,* were washing cars.
> The girls *dressed in dungarees* were washing cars.

Note: A modifier set off at the beginning or at the end of a sentence requires only *one* comma. But a modifier set off in the middle of a sentence requires *two*.

(2) Set off introductory modifiers. When you use a verbal to introduce a sentence, use the comma to show where the main part of the sentence starts. Use the comma also with long prepositional phrases—four words or more:

> *Singing,* they danced around the fire.
> *To save energy,* lower your thermostat.

> *On a hot summer afternoon,* we would sit on the porch.
> *By a strange coincidence,* my brother was also in town.

(3) Set off modifiers that go with the sentence as a whole. When a word or a group of words modifies a sentence as a whole, is it called a **sentence modifier.** Sentence modifiers typically appear at the beginning or end of sentences. But they also appear in the middle of sentences. The most common sentence modifiers are verbal phrases, using either the *–ing* form (participle) or the *to* form (infinitive):

> *Considering the weather,* we made good time.
> I didn't like her, *to be quite truthful.*

Inside Punctuation

Expressions like *as a rule, generally, obviously, in the first place,* and *unfortunately* also often apply to the sentence as a whole. With them, the comma is *optional*. Use the comma (or commas) if *in speaking* you would set such a word or phrase off by an audible break. Can you hear a difference in the following?

> She *obviously* doesn't like you.
> *As a rule,* we go to the mountains every summer.
> *Generally* we go to church on Sundays.

EXERCISE 1

Each of the following sentences shows the *right* punctuation of modifiers. Read these sentences out loud, or listen to them read out loud. Be sure you can hear the break where a comma appears in writing. (Can you explain why each of the italicized modifiers was punctuated the way it was?)

1. *Riding her bicycle,* Diana soon left the hikers behind.
2. My father, *holding his bundle over his head,* crossed the river safely.
3. The cheerleader *standing in front of the others* is only a junior.
4. Prisoners *loitering in the corridors* were told to move on.
5. The car *with the daisies painted on the trunk* is mine.
6. The play was about Helen Keller, *famous for her fight against handicaps.*
7. My prize possession was a pocket watch, *a gift from my aunt.*
8. *Huddled in our ponchos,* we waited for the end of the rain.
9. Students *confused by the directions* did badly; the others did well.
10. *Considering their age,* they had done very well.

EXERCISE 2

Look at the blank space in each of the following sentences. Which should be filled by a comma? Put *C* after the number of the sentence if there should be a comma in the blank space. Put *No* if there should be no punctuation.

1. The story was about a sea monster _____ living on the Scottish coast.
2. I have always been interested in carpentry _____ an outdoor job.
3. To tell you the truth _____ baseball has always bored me.
4. They called the ambulance a bone box _____ a trucker's term.
5. A driver has to watch out for people _____ crossing the road.
6. A truck with a new bright red paint job _____ pulled into the driveway.

Mechanics

7. We always looked forward to the fireworks _____ on the Fourth of July.
8. The Mormons moved on to Utah _____ their new home.
9. The boys sleeping outside _____ were awakened by raccoons.
10. Walking up the driveway _____ I saw a note pinned to the door.
11. He loved the smell of the pine needles _____ carpeting the forest floor.
12. On the screen was the President _____ talking about energy.
13. Big Ben, a clock at the top of a tower _____ is famous for its chime.
14. Our first-aid kit _____ stowed in the trunk, contained bandages and aspirin.
15. A surgeon operates with a scalpel _____ a small razor-sharp knife.
16. George Washington _____ our first President, had been a general.
17. Considering her handicap _____ her achievement has been outstanding.
18. Animals hunting at night _____ often see well in the dark.
19. Pat and Gina _____ dressed in overalls, were working in the garden.
20. The trip had been tiring _____ to say the least.

M3b Commas for Minor Breaks

Use commas where necessary to signal minor breaks in a sentence.

Several kinds of repetition or interruption cause minor breaks in a sentence. Look for the following:

(1) When several elements of the same kind appear in a sentence, separate them by commas. A sentence may have more than one subject, or verb, or object, or modifier. Three or more elements of the same kind are called a **series.** Use commas between the elements in a series:

SERIES: *Saturn, Mars, and Venus* are planets of our solar system.
SERIES: The ball *wobbled, bounced, and rolled* dead.
SERIES: The tools of the dog-grooming trade include *clippers, blades, and drivers.*
SERIES: She supported herself by *working in a restaurant, cutting firewood, and painting houses.*

Remember the following variations:

• A series may have *four* parts or more:

We brought along *bread, mayonnaise, lunch meat, and lettuce.*

COMMAS FOR MINOR BREAKS:

Cheyenne, Wyoming

Hello, Sylvia, what's new?

I helped him, didn't I?

Phoenix, Arizona

• The parts of a series may already include commas. We then use *semicolons* to separate the parts:

We talked about *Frances, my sister; Dolly, her friend; and Nip, her dog.*

• When there is more than one adjective, a comma can replace an *and* between *two* adjectives.

The *short and heavy* bear couldn't reach the limb.
The *short, heavy* bear couldn't reach the limb.

A *tall and bearded* stranger stood at the door.
A *tall, bearded* stranger stood at the door.

Note: The last comma in a series is *optional*. It is often left out in newspaper and magazine writing. Many teachers and editors, however, ask for it because it helps us see clearly the three or four parts that go together.

(2) Use commas in dates, addresses, page references, and measurements with two or more parts:

DATES:	February 7, 1980
ADDRESSES:	3030 Liberty Avenue, Pittsburgh, Pa.
	Apartment 3A, Alden Manor, Chicago, Illinois
REFERENCES:	Chapter 8, Book II
	Volume 6, page 63, line 2
MEASUREMENTS:	6 feet, 2 inches

• When items such as these are used in sentences, a comma is generally used at the end of the date, address, or reference:

On the third of June, 1950, the first light of dawn found us still clinging to the tent poles at Camp V. (Maurice Herzog)

Mechanics

● With measurements in two or more parts, no additional comma is used after the last item:

Jack weighed 170 pounds, 12 ounces on the doctor's scale.
He measured 5 feet, 4 inches in his bare feet.

(3) Use commas to set off elements that are not part of the structure of the sentence. Such **interrupters** are set off from the main sentence with a comma or commas. In speaking to someone, we often hold up the rest of what we are saying to call the person by name:

Philip, come here!
That building, *Linda,* is the new gymnasium.
The doctor will see you now, *Mr. Starkman.*

Here are some other common types of interrupters:

Well, what should we do next?
Yes, I know.

The picnic, *it seems,* will be held on Friday.
The day, *they agreed,* had been wasted.

You can overrun first base, *not second.*

He is ill, *is he?*
The train left, *didn't it?*

EXERCISE 1

Why are commas used in the following sentences? After the number of each sentence, put down the right abbreviation:

S   for series punctuation (or as part of it);
M   for dates, measurements, and similar information in two or more parts;
I   for interrupters.

(Read each sentence out loud, or listen to it read aloud. Make sure you can hear the break where a comma appears in a sentence.)

1. A hometown newspaper prints local news, recipes for pork chops, and articles about termites.
2. The Sunday *Times* weighed four pounds, two ounces.
3. The *New York Daily News,* believe it or not, sold two million copies a day.
4. The *New York Times,* the *Chicago Tribune,* and the *Washington Post* are the nation's best-known newspapers.

Inside Punctuation

5. Regular contributors interview celebrities, write shopping tips, and do restaurant reviews.
6. Reporters, we all know, do more than cover the news and write articles.
7. The *New York Times* is read by readers in Jacksonville, Florida, and Albuquerque, New Mexico.
8. The three sisters who owned the paper were Ruth, a publisher; Judith, a physician; and Marian, a publisher's wife.
9. The *New York Daily News,* not the *New York Times,* is our largest newspaper.
10. You will find the article on canning vegetables at home in section C, page 18.
11. The new editorial offices are located at 1229 Oak Street, Rocksville, Missouri.
12. The *Saturday Evening Post* was a very widely read magazine, wasn't it?
13. The first issue appeared on March 18, 1979.
14. Many favorite magazines and newspapers, dear reader, have disappeared.
15. Advertisers, not readers, provide most of the income.
16. Successful specialized magazines print articles about crafts, hobbies, and sports.
17. Editors select material, give assignments, rewrite articles, and write headlines.
18. The new printing machine was eight feet, twelve inches high.
19. New York, New York, has always been a favorite address of publishing companies.
20. Yes, journalism is an interesting profession.

The Washington Post

Chicago Tribune

The New York Times

Mechanics

EXERCISE 2

Which of the following sentences need punctuation in the spaces indicated? Put *C* after the number of the sentence if a comma (or commas) is required, *SC* if a semicolon (or semicolons) is required, and *No* if no punctuation is required. (Be prepared to explain in class why you punctuated each sentence as you did.)

1. The team's colors are red ___ blue ___ and gold.
2. They had a record of three victories ___ three defeats ___ and one tie.
3. We have a young ___ aggressive team this year.
4. In the last game, we scored a field goal ___ a touchdown ___ and a safety.
5. In the morning, we played tennis, my favorite sport ___ baseball, which I can't stand ___ and basketball.
6. Our cats include Martha, a Persian ___ Lulu, a Siamese ___ and Sam, an alley cat.
7. The horse jumped over the fence ___ landed with a thud on this side ___ and vainly struggled to get to its feet.
8. Some people invest in the stock market ___ and lose money.
9. May 18 ___ 1979 ___ was an unlucky day for my family.
10. I have been living in Baltimore ___ Maryland, for two years.
11. We visit Bar Harbor, Maine ___ every summer.
12. The package weighed three pounds ___ four ounces.
13. She bought two yards, two feet ___ of material.
14. The famous speech occurs in Act I, Scene 2 ___ lines 38 to 44.
15. No ___ I didn't see you at the party last night.
16. Five feet, ten inches ___ is very tall for a ten-year-old.
17. The answer, it appears ___ was wrong.
18. Jack ___ please bring me your geometry book.
19. Give me five pounds of potatoes ___ not six.
20. Linda took off her wet ___ muddy shoes.

M3c
Colons, Dashes, and Parentheses

Know when to use inside punctuation other than commas.

Follow these guidelines for the use of colons, dashes, and parentheses:

(1) Use the colon to introduce lists and explanations. Use the colon when it takes the place of an expression like *namely* or *as follows:*

> He had lived in the three largest states: *Alaska, Texas, and California.*
> One thing was sure: *Mokabu was dead.*

Inside Punctuation M3c

(2) Use dashes to signal strong breaks. Dashes make things stand out:

> The officer pointed at the suspect—*a five-year-old child.*
> The eagle has many dangerous enemies—*all of them human.* (Donald Culross Peattie)

• Use dashes when *a whole sentence* interrupts and breaks up another sentence:

> These five passages—*I could have quoted far worse*—illustrated various mental vices.
> The soldiers—*I couldn't begin to count them*—had surrounded us on all sides.

• Use dashes to set off modifiers that *already contain commas:*

> Smoking anything—*cigarettes, cigars, or pipes*—is bad for your health.
> I usually have breakfast—*bacon, eggs, toast, and coffee*—at noon on Sunday.

(3) Use parentheses to enclose added comments or explanations. Parentheses may show that an explanation or comment is of relatively little importance:

> It is a beautiful creature and rather young *(about eight feet long).*
> He asked for coffee *(with sugar, but without cream).*

• But parentheses also give us a chance to add exact details for readers who may want them:

> It was a huge book *(897 pages).*
> She wrote a check for the exact amount *($23.25).*

• Sometimes material in parentheses is a *complete, separate sentence:*

> The high school honor roll was published in the *Franklin News-Herald.* (The *Herald* had been taken over by the *News.*)

Study the *right* use of colons, dashes, and parentheses in the following examples. Be prepared to explain why these marks were used the way they were.

EXERCISE 1

1. Bears are a problem in national parks: Glacier, Great Smoky, and Yosemite.
2. Hikers often do not know a bear's strength and speed (up to 35 miles an hour).

335

Mechanics

3. Bears have been known to break into cars to find food—even in the trunk.
4. Many bears have abandoned their natural diet—grasses, roots, and berries—and prefer human food.
5. Some bears in national parks have learned to beg for food—like zoo bears.
6. Park rangers now recommend hard-sided shelters (no tents).
7. They tell visitors a basic park rule: Never feed a bear.
8. Unruly bears are captured and moved to distant areas. (Very dangerous bears are sometimes killed.)
9. Researchers are testing ways to drive bears away: electric fences, flares, and recordings of growling dogs.
10. Grizzlies still live in two popular parks: Glacier in Montana and Yellowstone in Wyoming.

EXERCISE 2

How would you use colons, dashes, and parentheses in the following sentences? After the number of the sentence, write *C* for colon, *D* for dash (or dashes), *P* for parentheses. (In these sentences you often have a *choice between two* of these punctuation marks. Be prepared to explain why you picked the one you preferred.)

1. The family had three boys ____ Paul, Edward, and Frank.
2. Ken ____ he is my brother ____ read fourteen books last summer.
3. There is only one way out ____ admit everything.
4. Carnaby ____ a street in London ____ suddenly became famous.
5. He could think of only one thing ____ water.
6. *The Souls of Black Folk* ____ published in 1903 ____ was written by W. E. B. DuBois.
7. None of the three sisters ____ Lucy, Trina, and Mary Ann ____ ever wrote.
8. The last quotation ____ page 345 ____ was from Charles Dickens.
9. The clock on the tower ____ my watch had been stolen ____ said six o'clock.
10. We've found the source of the trouble ____ we are out of gas.
11. Rita is a member of all three groups ____ the honor society, the student council, and the debating team.
12. The bagels ____ a kind of roll ____ were delicious.
13. The boss ____ you will meet him tomorrow ____ likes punctual people.
14. She was active in many sports ____ swimming, cross-country, track, and soccer.
15. He always talked about one thing ____ money.

Capitals and Special Marks

M4a

UNIT REVIEW EXERCISE

What punctuation should appear in each blank space in the following sentences? After the number of each blank, write one of the following abbreviations:

C	for comma;	*CL*	for colon;
SC	for semicolon;	*No*	for no punctuation.

A. We were making boxes ____(1) packing fruit ____(2) and loading refrigerator cars.
B. The people ____(3) working in the packing houses ____(4) were used to the pace.
C. We did three kinds of work in the orchards ____(5) irrigating ____(6) spraying for pests ____(7) and picking the crops.
D. We drove from Fresno ____(8) California ____(9) to Olympia ____(10) Washington.
E. We were looking for farms ____(11) offering temporary jobs.
F. My sister Margaret ____(12) dressed in overalls ____(13) was driving the truck.
G. They offered pineapples ____(14) mangoes ____(15) and papayas.
H. Their motive ____(16) gentlemen ____(17) is now clear.
I. We traveled with Ed, my cousin ____(18) Joel, a friend ____(19) and Charles, a total stranger.
J. To tell you the truth ____(20) your father never liked it here.
K. The owner ____(21) a friendly woman in her fifties ____(22) had moved there from Montgomery ____(23) Alabama.
L. You will find an article ____(24) describing these ships ____(25) in Volume 7 ____(26) page 84.
M. You locked the door ____(27) Maureen ____(28) didn't you?
N. The engine coughed ____(29) sputtered ____(30) and rumbled.

Learn to use capitals and special marks of punctuation.

Learn how to handle capital letters and special marks like apostrophes, hyphens, and quotation marks.

M4 CAPITALS AND SPECIAL MARKS

Use capital letters for proper names, for most of the words in a title, and for the first word of a sentence.

The most basic function of a capital letter is to start a **proper name.** A proper name sets an individual or a group off from other examples of the same kind. In a group of children, only one may be called *Tom.* In a softball league, only

M4a
Using Capitals

337

Mechanics

one team is likely to be called the *Falcons*. Look at the difference between the following general words and proper names:

GENERAL WORD: freshman, sophomore, athlete, swimmer
PROPER NAME: Tom, Marcia, Cynthia, Dennis

GENERAL WORD: car, vehicle, motorcycle, truck
PROPER NAME: Buick, Honda, Chevrolet, Volkswagen

Capitals also serve some special purposes. Remember:

(1) Capitalize the pronoun *I*.

(2) Capitalize the *first word in a sentence or a direct quotation*.

The coach said, "Let's celebrate our victory."

(3) Capitalize the first word in *titles of books, movies, poems, articles, songs, television shows,* and the like. Also capitalize all other words in such titles except articles, prepositions, and connectives of fewer than five letters. For example, use a lower-case letter for *at, with, into, and, but, when, if*. This rule also applies to the title of your own themes:

Gone with the Wind
The Invaders from Outer Space
Why People Stay Away from Dentists
Things to Do on a Rainy Day

See M4e for when to italicize titles.

(4) Capitalize the *names (and initials) of persons and any titles or ranks used with the name*. Note the contrast between a *general* and a *specific* use of a title or rank:

GENERAL WORD: Three governors attended the conference.
PROPER NAME: Governor Wilson, Governor Pierce, and Governor Hanson attended the conference.

GENERAL WORD: There was a father serving as the coach.
PROPER NAME: Yes, Father will coach this year.

Note: When words like *my* and *our* precede family names like *father* and *mother,* the family names are not capitalized:

My mother is a good sport.   Our grandfather is nearly ninety.

(5) Capitalize the names of *religions, nationalities, races,* and *political parties:*

Lutheran, Democrat, Republican, American, Jew

USING CAPITALS

Explain how capital letters are used in these examples of names, addresses, and titles.

The Guggenheim Museum

Norwegian
America
Line

Wishing on a Star

Old Things Made New

Hot Blues, Cool Jazz

**London Paris Tel Aviv
Jerusalem Athens Rome**

1187 Valley Road, Stirling, New Jersey

---

(6) Capitalize the names of countries, states, cities, towns, streets, rivers, mountains, and other *geographical features:*

> France, Georgia, San Francisco, Belden Street, Missouri River, Long's Peak, Moffat Tunnel

(7) Capitalize *specific documents, historical events, buildings, churches, schools,* and *clubs or other organizations:*

GENERAL WORD:	I will go to high school in the fall.
PROPER NAME:	I will go to Central High School in the fall.
GENERAL WORD:	He fought in two world wars.
PROPER NAME:	He fought in World War I and World War II.

(8) Capitalize the names of the *days of the week, months,* and *holidays*. But do *not* capitalize the names of the seasons:

> Monday, May, Thanksgiving Day, Christmas
> spring, summer, fall, autumn, winter

(9) Capitalize *compass points* — north, east, south, west, northeast, and so on — when they name a region. Do not capitalize them when they show a general direction:

GENERAL WORD:	Turn east at the intersection.
PROPER NAME:	My grandparents live in the East.
GENERAL WORD:	The ship was moving southeast at twenty knots.
PROPER NAME:	Have you ever visited the American Southwest?

Mechanics

(10) Capitalize the names of all *languages,* regardless of whether or not you think of them as school subjects. Do not capitalize the names of other school subjects, unless they are part of a specific course title:

> Jim speaks English, French, and Spanish.
> She is now taking a course in Russian.
> I intend to take Algebra I and Art II.
>
> I intend to take algebra and art.

(11) Capitalize the name of *the Deity.* Also capitalize all pronouns referring to Him. The names of sacred figures, the Bible, and parts of the Bible are also generally capitalized.

> The Lord gives and He may take away; blessed be His name.
> Virgin Mary, Holy Ghost, Genesis

(12) Capitalize *adjectives derived from proper nouns.* But do not capitalize the nouns following such adjectives unless they themselves are proper nouns:

> Danish pastry (first made in Denmark)
> French bread (first made in France)
> Italian pizza (first made in Italy)
> an African country (located in Africa)
> A Roman emperor (who reigned in Rome)

(13) When something has been *named after a person,* capitalize the person's name:

> Geiger counter, Ferris wheel, Franklin stove

Note: Sometimes the person who gave something its name has been forgotten, and a lower-case letter is used:

> diesel engine, a maverick senator

(14) Capitalize *trade names* of all kinds, but not the word following the trade name unless it is part of the name.

> Lipton tea, Pepsi-Cola, Wise potato chips

Note: Do not capitalize the following when they are part of a proper name: the articles *(the, a, an);* short prepositions and connectives—less than five letters *(of, by, with; and):*

> Institute for the Blind
> Fourth of July
> Speech and Drama Department

Capitals and Special Marks

M4a

SOME CAPITALIZED NAMES
A Reminder

PEOPLE:	Gerald Sims, Booker T. Washington, Florence Nightingale, Georgia O'Keeffe	PERSONAL NAMES
TITLES:	Governor Pearson, Senator Smith, Queen Elizabeth, Dr. Goodrow; the President	
IMAGINARY PEOPLE:	Cinderella, Robin Hood, the Lone Ranger, Zeus, Lady Macbeth	
CONTINENTS:	Asia, America, Europe, Australia, the Antarctic	GEOGRAPHIC NAMES
COUNTRIES:	United States of America, Canada, Great Britain, Mexico, Denmark, Japan	
REGIONS:	the Southwest, the East, the Near East, the Midwest	
STATES:	Iowa, North Dakota, New Hampshire, Rhode Island	
CITIES:	St. Louis, Dallas, Baltimore, Los Angeles; Washington, D.C.	
SIGHTS:	Lake Erie, Mount Hood, Death Valley, Pike's Peak	
ADDRESSES:	Park Lane, Fleet Avenue, Oak Street, Washington Square	
MONTHS:	January, March, July, October	CALENDAR NAMES
WEEKDAYS:	Monday, Wednesday, Saturday, Sunday	
HOLIDAYS:	Labor Day, Thanksgiving, Easter, the Sabbath, Mother's Day, the Fourth of July	
INSTITUTIONS:	the Supreme Court, the Department of Agriculture, the U.S. Senate	INSTITUTIONAL NAMES
BUSINESSES:	Ford Motor Company, Standard Oil	
SCHOOLS:	Grossmont High School, Las Vistas Junior College, University of Maine	
GROUPS:	the Republican Party, the American Legion, the Garment Workers' Union	
PROPER NAMES:	the Virgin Mary, St. Thomas, Luther	RELIGIOUS NAMES
FAITHS:	Christian, Muslim, Jewish, Hindu	
DENOMINATIONS:	Methodist, Baptist, Unitarian, Roman Catholic	

341

Mechanics

EXERCISE 1

Write down and capitalize the following:

1. The names of three of the least-known American states.
2. Three place names that you consider unusual or beautiful.
3. The names of three famous ships or planes.
4. The names of your three favorite holidays.
5. The three longest titles of books or movies that you can remember.
6. The names of three parks or landmarks that you know.
7. The names of three famous buildings.
8. Your complete actual address.
9. An imaginary address that you would like to have.
10. The names and any titles of the three people in history that you are most interested in or that you know best.

EXERCISE 2

Copy each of the following. Use capitals as needed *within* each group of words.

1. a small high school in florida
2. at sunnyvale high school in california
3. the empire state building
4. a tall building downtown
5. a ford thunderbird
6. a chevrolet station wagon
7. his swiss watch and her japanese camera
8. a democratic governor and his republican opponent
9. fair democratic elections
10. a trip through the south, going north from new orleans

EXERCISE 3

After the number of each sentence, write down (and capitalize) each word that should start with a capital letter. If there are no words in the sentence that should be capitalized, write *No* after the number of the sentence.

1. Margaret chase smith came to the united states senate from maine.
2. He goes to a high school in north philadelphia.
3. Two of my favorite books are *wind in the willows* and *the little prince*.
4. Turn right, then drive several blocks south until you reach north broad street.
5. I love maine lobsters and new jersey crabs.
6. In the korean conflict, the united nations fought on the south korean side.
7. The bill of rights safeguards every one of us.

Capitals and Special Marks

8. My sister sarah said she didn't know where mother was.
9. I will see you next spring, probably on a saturday or sunday in april or may.
10. Frost's "stopping by woods" is included in *great american poems*.
11. An ensign, a captain, and two admirals were arguing in the dining room.
12. The methodist church is holding a convention in st. louis, missouri.
13. Mount cadillac, which is in acadia national park, is the highest point on the east coast.
14. He has a roman nose but an irish accent.
15. We celebrated memorial day with a picnic on snake river.
16. His aunt still lives in wilson, north carolina.
17. Captain kirk traveled to distant planets on a spaceship called enterprise.
18. Many pioneering families from norway settled in the midwest.
19. Few schools offer courses in russian and chinese.
20. The fourth of july has always been my favorite holiday.

M4b Using Apostrophes

Use the apostrophe to show contractions and the possessive of nouns.

Like a capital letter, the apostrophe is strictly a *written* symbol. We cannot hear it when we read a sentence aloud. Learn to recognize the situations where an apostrophe is required:

(1) Use the apostrophe to show where letters have been left out. In speech we often shorten (contract) words by leaving out sounds. We say *I'd* for *I would*, *she'll* for *she will*, *don't* for *do not*. Look at the use of the apostrophe in the **contractions** shown in the brief chart.

CONTRACTIONS

I am → I'm	are not → aren't
I will → I'll	do not → don't
he will → he'll	does not → doesn't
she would → she'd	cannot → can't
he is → he's	will not → won't
we are → we're	would not → wouldn't
you are → you're	has not → hasn't
they are → they're	had not → hadn't
could have → could've	is not → isn't

USING APOSTROPHES

Look at these advertising slogans. Explain how and why the apostrophe is used in each case.

There's a Reason

America's Greatest

EVERYBODY'S NEWSPAPER

Don't Economize

30 days' Trial Offer

Some contractions sound exactly like other *un*contracted forms. Notice the difference between the following:

• *It's* always means *it is*. *Its* without the apostrophe means *of it*.

it's	*It's* (it is) time to go now. I know *it's* (it is) true.
its	The cat scratched *its* master. (the master of it) Honesty is *its* own reward. (the reward of it)

• *They're* always means *they are*. *Their* without the apostrophe means *of them*:

they're	*They're* (they are) coming at noon. She says *they're* (they are) lucky.
their	They are buying *their* house. (the house of them) *Their* loyalty was questioned. (the loyalty of them)

• *Who's* always means *who is*. *Whose* without the apostrophe means *of whom*.

who's	*Who's* (who is) at the door? I'm not sure *who's* (who is) coming.
whose	*Whose* house is this? (the house of whom) I want to know *whose* pen this is. (the pen of whom)

(2) *Use the apostrophe and* –s *to form the possessive of nouns.* The **possessive** shows where or to whom something *belongs*. There must be something it "goes with." Often that something directly follows the possessive noun. We then have the following pattern: "First Noun + 's + Second Noun."

Capitals and Special Marks

FIRST NOUN + 's + SECOND NOUN			POSSESSIVE
the teacher	's	books →	the *teacher's* books
my brother	's	friend →	my *brother's* friend
Vera	's	records →	*Vera's* records
the children	's	father →	the *children's* father
a moment	's	silence →	a *moment's* silence
a dollar	's	worth →	a *dollar's* worth
a week	's	wage →	a *week's* wage

POSSESSIVE OF NOUNS

• Sometimes, the first noun already ends in –s. In that case *only* the apostrophe is used. Do *not* use an additional –s.

    the girls → the *girls'* uniforms (several girls)
    the parents → the *parents'* duty (both parents)

    two *weeks* → two *weeks'* pay
    five *dollars* → five *dollars'* worth

(**Note:** When a proper name ends in –s, *either* of the following is acceptable: *Charles'* letter, or *Charles's* letter; *Keats'* poetry, or *Keats's* poetry.)

• Usually, you can change a possessive into an *of* phrase by changing the order of the nouns. Use this test to see if a word is used as a possessive:

    the teacher's books = the books of the teacher
    my brother's friend = the friend of my brother
    Vera's records = the records of Vera
    five dollars' worth = the worth of five dollars
    two weeks' salary = the salary of two weeks

• The –'s is added to *nouns*. The rule does *not* apply to possessive pronouns: *his, hers, its, ours, yours,* and *theirs*. Do not add an apostrophe or an apostrophe s to them:

    Give him *his* books.
    These are *hers*.
    This house must be *theirs*.
    Pay us *ours*.

(3) *Use –'s to form the plural of numbers, letters, and of words discussed as words:*

    There were four *3's* in the telephone number.
    How many *e's* are there in *Tennessee?*
    There are too many *and's* and *so's* in your essay.

Mechanics

LANGUAGE IN ACTION

HOW WE USE SPECIAL MARKS

Look at the following sample of language in action. Explain all uses of apostrophes and capital letters in these examples.

Gone with the Wind

Godzilla's Revenge

Uncle Tom's Cabin

Fiddler on the Roof

The Greatest Story Ever Told

Frankenstein's Bride

The Ten Commandments

Gulliver's Travels

The Wizard of Oz

Dr. Jekyll and Mr. Hyde

The Old Wives' Tale

Alice's Restaurant

Where's Poppa

EXERCISE 1

Rewrite each group of words, using a contraction. Put your rewritten version after the number of the group.

1. I would
2. he does not
3. they will
4. you cannot
5. she is not
6. it is
7. we are
8. they are
9. they are not
10. you do not
11. we will not
12. I am
13. we have not
14. it does not
15. they did not
16. who is
17. he will not
18. we were not
19. they do not
20. we could have

Capitals and Special Marks

EXERCISE 2

After the number of the sentence, write the form that fits the meaning of the sentence.

1. The bird has finished *(its/it's)* song.
2. The farmer said that *(its/it's)* five miles as the crow flies to the nearest town.
3. *(Its/It's)* the best idea I've heard in months.
4. Has the board made *(its/it's)* decision?
5. It looks as if *(their/they're)* fighting again.
6. The children took *(their/they're)* dog for a walk.
7. *(Their/They're)* being married in May.
8. *(Whose/Who's)* to blame?
9. Can you tell me *(whose/who's)* briefcase this is?
10. The person *(whose/who's)* car is parked by the hydrant is getting a ticket.

EXERCISE 3

Rewrite each of the following groups of words, using the possessive form. Write your version after the number of the group.

EXAMPLE: the farm of my aunt   (Answer) *my aunt's farm*

1. the victory of our team
2. the vacation of my family
3. the bicycles of the girls
4. a holiday of a week
5. the grandparents of Josefina
6. the speech of the President
7. a tomb of a queen
8. a cap of a boy
9. the programs of this week
10. the duty of a citizen
11. the wages of two weeks
12. salaries of teachers
13. the dreams of a child
14. the clock of my grandfather
15. the car of her parents
16. the decision of the umpire
17. the yard of our neighbor
18. the yards of our neighbors
19. the job of a carpenter
20. the cabins of the families

EXERCISE 4

After the number of the sentence, write the form that fits the meaning of the sentence.

1. George rescued the *(childs/child's)* balloon.
2. She asked for a *(week's/weeks')* pay in advance.
3. I served for three *(years/year's/years')* in the navy.
4. The emcee had forgotten the *(guests/guest's)* name.
5. The *(referees/referee's)* decision was questioned.
6. June's sister's hair is longer than *(hers/her's)*.
7. The teacher knew all his *(student's/students')* names.
8. Where are these *(girl's/girls')* books?
9. How many *(Cs/C's)* did you get on your report card?
10. There were several *(7s/7's)* in the answer.

347

M4c Using Quotation Marks

Use quotation marks to set off material quoted word for word.

Observe these guidelines in punctuating quotations:

(1) Use quotation marks to set off someone's exact words. Use quotation marks only if you are reporting the actual words. The result is called **direct quotation:**

DIRECT: He said to the locksmith, "Please try one more time."
The sign said: "Go back. No access to the sea."
The speaker kept saying, "They shall not pass."

(2) Use a comma to separate a short quotation from its **credit tag:**

The ranger said, "Watch out for bears."
"Don't leave me here," *he shouted.*

• When the credit tag *splits* a complete sentence, use commas on both sides of the tag. When the credit tag *separates* two complete sentences, put a comma before it, and a period after it:

ONE SENTENCE: "The map," *she said,* "is on the back of the envelope."
TWO SENTENCES: "I have a map," *she said.* "It is on the back of the envelope."

• Use the colon to introduce *long or formal* quotations:

The judge looked at him and said: "I shall give you one more chance."

Note: When a single quoted word or phrase appears in a sentence, you do not need a comma or a colon to set it off:

He shouted "All right!" every time the team scored.

(3) Put quotation marks and other marks in the right order. Commas and periods remain *within* the quotation marks. Question marks are placed *inside* the quotation if the quoted part asks a question. They go outside the quotation if you are asking a question *about the quotation:*

Sue asked, "Is Barbara coming to the dance?"
Was it Franny or Rae who said, "I don't like you"?

Exclamation marks are handled the same way as question marks. If the *quoted* part has strong stress, the exclamation mark goes inside the quotation marks. If you are making a strong point *about the quotation,* the mark goes outside:

> Everyone was yelling, "Let's go, Central!"
> Don't you tell me, "Shut up"!

Note: If a question mark or an exclamation mark appears at the end of a quotation, do *not* use an additional comma to separate the quotation from any remaining part of the sentence:

> "This is the last straw!" my uncle said.

(4) When you shorten a quotation, show where you have left something out. Use three spaced periods called an **ellipsis.** Use four periods if the omission follows the period at the end of a complete sentence.

> The rule said: "When the ball hits the net, the player . . . repeats the serve."

When you add a comment or a correction of your own to something you quote, put the added part between **brackets:**

> The diary continued: "The storm is getting worse. No chance to reach the base that we left May 15 [actually May 13]. Food is running low."

USING QUOTATION MARKS

Look at the quotations in these captions from a cartoon serial. Is this the way you would have punctuated the quotations? Explain why.

> "Where is the land of the cannibals?" Tarzan demanded. "Beyond the inland sea," Thorik replied.

> "I shall try!" Tarzan answered grimly.

> "They devour all who cross their boundaries," said the Viking. "No one can save Sigreda now."

Mechanics

(5) Do not use quotation marks when you repeat in your own words what someone else has said. An **indirect** quotation gives the meaning of what someone has said, but not the exact words. Many indirect quotations start with *that*. Many start with question words like *what, which, how,* or *where*.

INDIRECT: He announced *that applications would now be accepted.*
INDIRECT: The sick passenger kept asking *how long it would take.*
INDIRECT: The ranger said *that we should watch for bears.*

(6) Use quotation marks for these special purposes:

• Use quotation marks around the *title* of something that is part of a magazine, book, or larger collection. Use quotation marks this way around the titles of songs, short poems, articles in a newspaper or magazine, short stories, and the like. But *underline* the titles of complete books or collections. In print, such titles are italicized:

Poe wrote "The Raven" and "The Tell-Tale Heart."
The song "Little Bird, Little Bird" is from *Man of La Mancha.*
"Recalled to Life" is the first chapter of *A Tale of Two Cities.*

• Use quotation marks around *technical terms* and around words that you are discussing as words. (Such terms and words are often italicized.)

The astronaut called the crane a "cherry picker."
An "environmentalist" believes that nature needs more protection against people.
The Spanish word *chico* means boy.

(7) Use **single quotation marks** *for a quotation within a quotation.* Use them to show that someone you are quoting was in turn quoting someone else:

The coach kept telling us: "I don't ever want you to say, 'It can't be done.'"

EXERCISE 1

Most of the following examples show the *right* way of punctuating quotations. Put *S* after the number of each satisfactory example. Put *U* after the number of each unsatisfactory example. (Be prepared to explain what went wrong.)

1. He said quietly, "I don't believe what you say."
2. "You must never look back," the King of the Underworld said.
3. "The noisy people here," the teacher said, are being very selfish."
4. The sentence read: "Misery is stepping on a slug barefoot."

Capitals and Special Marks

5. She read the article on "Early Egyptian Treasures" in *Life*.
6. We asked the conductor "why our bus was always late."
7. The employer always asks, "Why do you want to work with us?
8. The instructions stated: "First assemble a pot, soil, charcoal, a broken piece of clay pottery, and scissors."
9. Who said to you, "No school today"?
10. "Traffic on the highway," the report said, "was backed up for miles in each direction."
11. There were "For Sale" signs on many homes in the neighborhood.
12. "Jacques is my artist's name," I said, "my real name is Jack."
13. He said, "Remember: 'The watched pot never boils.'"
14. She asked, "Why do we have to leave so early?"
15. They asked her if women still wore veils in Saudi Arabia.

EXERCISE 2

After the number of each passage, write the punctuation needed in the blank space. Often, quotation marks will be needed along with another mark. Write the needed marks in the right order. If no punctuation is needed, write *No*.

EXAMPLE: "Where were you all day _____ my mother asked.
(Answer) ?"

1. The usher said _____ No one comes in in bare feet."
2. "Halt or I'll shoot _____ the officer shouted.
3. Will said casually, "The clouds are going away _____
4. "Your bill," the clerk said, "is still unpaid _____
5. "That answer," Sybil whispered _____ can't be right."
6. Did he really say, "I know your kind _____
7. "When can you play again _____ he asked.
8. Verna asked, "Where are the keys to the car _____
9. "He was a great friend," Alan said _____ He always lent me money when I needed it."
10. "How can I find the author of the quotation _____ he asked.
11. Was it Josh Billings who said, "Remember the poor; it costs nothing _____
12. He said _____ Stop me if you've heard this one."
13. I said, "No, I didn't see the movie _____
14. Did Tom really say to Mary, "I'll marry you _____
15. He asked me _____ why he was never invited.
16. He whispered _____ Someone is breaking into the house."
17. A sign saying "Out to Lunch _____ dangled from the doorknob.
18. "You may have lost the game," he said _____ but your team has won our respect."
19. Who first said, "A stitch in time saves nine _____
20. "I know him well," she said _____ I've been married to him for twenty years."

Mechanics

EXERCISE 3

Quotation marks are needed in most of the following sentences. If they are needed, write the word or words that need them with the quotation marks around them. If no quotation marks are needed, write *No* after the number of the sentence.

1. Robert Frost's Stopping by Woods is one of my favorite poems.
2. In cabdrivers' jargon, the term wire refers to a call for a cab by telephone.
3. Benny asked why I didn't like him.
4. I just read the article, Don't Jog Too Hard, in the *Reader's Digest*.
5. Speaking of Books was a section of the *New York Times* on Sundays.
6. She said she wanted to be there.
7. Love, in tennis, has nothing to do with love in life.
8. He asked me whether I believed in God.
9. The last portion of the album was Revolution.
10. The most exciting story in the book was The Most Dangerous Game.

M4d
Using Hyphens

Use hyphens with compound words, compound numbers, and some prefixes.

Observe the following guidelines:

(1) Use the hyphen with *compound words* that are shown with hyphens in your dictionary:

bull's-eye	mother-in-law	court-martial
cave-in	in-laws	sit-in
hocus-pocus	great-aunt	six-pack

(2) Use hyphens in *compound numbers from twenty-one to ninety-nine* and with *fractions used as modifiers:*

She will be *twenty-one* next June.
There are *forty-five* seats in the room.
The room was only *one-third* occupied.
His gas tank was *three-quarters* full.

(3) Use hyphens with the *prefixes all–, self–, ex–* when it means "former," and sometimes between a *prefix ending in a vowel and a root beginning with the same vowel:*

God is *all-knowing* and *all-powerful.*
They liked the candidate's *self-possession.*
The *ex-champion* was dining with his *ex-wife.*
He entered the contest as the *anti-intellectual* candidate.

USING HYPHENS

Explain how hyphens are used in these headlines.

EX-HUSBAND TERRORIZES IN-LAWS

PANIC AT DRIVE-IN

COURT-MARTIAL CONTINUES

---

(4) Use hyphens *between a prefix and a capitalized noun or adjective:*

She is neither *un-American* nor *pro-German*.

(5) Use hyphens between the words of *a group of words taking the place of a single adjective before a noun:*

The student consulted an *up-to-date* dictionary.
I decided to make a *person-to-person* call.
It was a *well-documented* report.
He is a typical *cigar-smoking* banker.

Note: If the first part of the modifier is an adverb ending in *–ly*, no hyphen is used:

The badly damaged homes were repaired.
It was a hopelessly lost cause.

See M6a for hyphen used to divide words.

EXERCISE

In each of the following sentences, find the combination that needs one or more hyphens. Write the hyphenated word or expression after the number of the sentence.

1. Marcia had always liked her mother in law.
2. The implement was used by a pre Pueblo culture.
3. The President's middle of the road policies made him popular with great numbers of voters.
4. My glass is two thirds empty.
5. Peter has always been pro Republican.
6. She looked extremely self satisfied.
7. The Grand Canyon is an awe inspiring sight.
8. Jim has a devil may care attitude about most things.
9. Pro Arab sentiment seems to run high in Russia.
10. The Johnsons are a well to do family.
11. He was a self made man.

Mechanics

12. The teacher said that it was a first rate paper.
13. There was an all star cast at the benefit performance.
14. Let's go round on the merry go round.
15. College students who help to support themselves can be described as self reliant.
16. My great grandfather will be the guest of honor at the banquet.
17. Many books were written about the ex President.
18. We have many drive in movies in our neighborhood.
19. It was a well built house.
20. Everyone knows Debby is a good natured person.

M4e Using Italics (Underlining)

Use italics (underlining) to show titles and to call special attention to words.

Remember the following uses of italics:

(1) Use italics—underlining in typed and handwritten papers—to indicate *the titles of complete publications,* such as books, newspapers, and magazines:

> The students read *American Heritage* regularly.
> *The Yearling* was written by Marjorie Kinnan Rawlings.
> The *Times,* the *Post,* and the *Daily News* are three of New York's newspapers.

(2) Use italics for *single letters and for words referred to as words:*

> Dot your *i*'s and cross your *t*'s.
> *Muscle* originally meant "little mouse."
> Was the first word of the title *a* or *the?*

(3) Use italics for *words borrowed from foreign languages* and still considered foreign:

> The French word for beach is *plage.*
> The dragonfly *(Diplax elisa)* is actually harmless.

(4) Use italics to *emphasize a word or group of words:*

> It was only that I *had* hated him and I wanted to hold on to this hatred. (James Baldwin)

> I'm going to advise her to run away from home and live her own life. And *be* somebody! (Ring Lardner)

Note: Do not underline the titles of your own themes:

> Memoirs of an Overachiever
> A Summer to Forget

Capitals and Special Marks

EXERCISE

Be prepared to explain why and how italics are used in the following examples.

1. My family subscribes to *Time, Reader's Digest,* and *Scientific American.*
2. We need a doctor, and we need one *now.*
3. *The New Yorker* magazine comes out weekly.
4. We discussed the uses of the word *home.*
5. Alexander Haley, the author of *Roots,* wrote an article called "The Search for Roots."
6. Charles Dickens wrote *A Christmas Carol* and *A Tale of Two Cities.*
7. All guests must register at the office *with no exceptions.*
8. The name of the restaurant was taken from the Spanish word *rebozo.*
9. Few English words begin with *x, y,* or *z.*
10. He always used words like *hoi polloi* and *touché.*
11. The *St. Louis Post-Dispatch* is one of the best-known Midwestern newspapers.
12. The screech owl *(Otus asio)* is common in the eastern United States.
13. His name ends with a double *t.*
14. The only French words he knew were *amour* and *monsieur.*
15. *Roughing It* is a travel book by Mark Twain.

UNIT REVIEW EXERCISE

Look at the three choices for the blank space in each of the following passages. Put the letter for the right choice after the number of the passage.

EXAMPLE: My aunt _____ You always give me the same excuse."
       a. said, "   b. said. "   c. said:

(Answer) *a*

1. Sylvia was driving a _____ .
 a. chevrolet truck   b. Chevrolet truck   c. Chevrolet Truck
2. He had attended a small _____ in Vermont.
 a. high school   b. High school   c. High School
3. She listened politely to her _____ advice.
 a. fathers   b. fathers'   c. father's
4. The waiter said, "Sorry, we are _____
 a. closed"   b. closed".   c. closed."
5. The book was called _____ .
 a. *Now and Then*   b. "Now and Then"   c. *Now And Then*
6. We always ate in the _____ dining room.
 a. employees   b. employees'   c. employee's
7. The club was moving _____ headquarters.
 a. it's   b. its   c. it is

M4e

355

Mechanics

8. My friend was born in _____ .
   a. waco, texas   b. Waco, texas   c. Waco, Texas
9. Her special field was _____ diseases.
   a. childrens   b. children's   c. childrens'
10. Why did you say, "Tell me _____
    a. later."   b. later?"   c. later"?
11. He refuses to say why _____ angry.
    a. they're   b. their   c. there
12. They were married by a _____ minister.
    a. lutheran   b. Lutheran   c. "Lutheran"
13. Her father had admired _____ .
    a. Pope John   b. pope John   c. pope john
14. They loved _____ like Nevada.
    a. western states   b. Western states   c. Western States
15. He shouted _____ and rushed to the door.
    a. fire   b. Fire"   c. "Fire!"
16. Repeat: "We will never say, 'It's _____
    a. impossible.'"   b. impossible."   c. impossible.'
17. Father always worried about his _____ health.
    a. familys   b. family's   c. families'
18. The speaker was talking about _____ future.
    a. America's   b. Americas   c. america's
19. She _____ Some day you will be sorry."
    a. said: b. said, "   c. said "
20. That day, _____ and Muslims worshiped together.
    a. Christian's   b. christians   c. Christians

M5 SPELLING

Improve your spelling.

English is a difficult language to spell. We often have several different ways of showing the same sound:

ee: b*e*, b*ee*, l*ea*ve, gr*ie*f, k*ey*, c*ei*ling
a: b*a*le, b*ai*t, *ei*ght, gr*ey*, m*ay*
f: *f*ail, *ph*one, cou*gh*

We write many *silent* letters that were once pronounced but no longer are:

final *e*: hop*e*, lan*e*, drap*e*
gh: ni*gh*t, ri*gh*t, brou*gh*t, cau*gh*t
k: *k*night, *k*nave, *k*nife

Nevertheless, with a few exceptions, English spelling is an either-or matter. Like a telephone number you have dialed, the spelling you have written down is either right or wrong.

Spelling

Follow these guidelines in order to help you improve your spelling:

(1) Do not guess at the spelling of a word—look it up in a dictionary. Make this a habit. The more often you spell a word correctly, the better the chance that the correct spelling will stay with you.

(2) Look carefully at the word. Many people have a good *visual memory*. Give this ability a chance to work. If you merely glance at a word, you cannot expect to print it in your mind. If you pay close attention to the individual letters and then to the shape of the word as a whole, you may lock the proper spelling in your mind.

(3) Say the word distinctly. Then spell aloud each letter individually: R-E-C-E-I-V-E. Many people have a good *auditory memory*.

(4) Write the word clearly, in large letters. Many people have a good *muscle memory*. Give your memory a chance to learn what it *feels like* to write the word. Bring your nerves and muscles to bear on your spelling problems.

(5) Associate the word with something else. Does *attendance* have an *a* or an *e* in the final syllable? You will remember that it has an *a* if you think something like: "I want to ATTEND the DANCE." You will find many such memory aids in this section.

(6) Concentrate on the words that are likely to give you trouble again—and again. Make a list of the common words that give you the most difficulty and practice them periodically. A list of commonly misspelled words is included in this chapter. After you learn which of them are your special enemies, write them out in a notebook, and keep after them.

Use the look-say-write attack on commonly used words.

On the following pages is a list of "unforgivables." They are words commonly used but also commonly misspelled. Practice the look-say-write attack on each of these words. Take up one group of nine or ten words at a time. Continue until you have mastered all the groups.

M5a
Commonly Misspelled Words

Mechanics

GROUP A

accept Remember the *a* in this word. Carefully break the word into syllables: ac-cept. When you *accept* something, you *join in*. When you *except* something, you *take it out*. REMEMBER: Everyone *ac*cepted the *ac*count *ex*cept the *ex*perts.

all right These two words are also run together in speech, but they are always two distinct words. (*Alright* is *not* a correct spelling.) REMEMBER: *All right* means **all** is **right.**

a lot When you pronounce these words, you will tend to run them together, but they are always spelled as two words. Practice pronouncing them as two distinct words: a-lot. REMEMBER: I have *a little*, he has *a lot*.

beginning Practice the pronunciation: be-gin-ning. In normal speech, you will not hear the second *n*, but it must be there in writing. REMEMBER: There is an **inning** in beg*inning*.

believe Although the "i before e" rule applies here, the word is very commonly misspelled. REMEMBER: Use *i* before *e* in bel*ie*f and bel*ie*ve.

business The *i* in this word is silent. You will remember to put the *i* in if you keep in mind that the word is a combination of *busy* (with the *y* changed to *i*) and *–ness:* busy + ness = business. REMEMBER: *I* am in bus*i*ness.

choose The infinitive of this verb is *to choose* (rhyming with *ooze,* and spelled with two *o*'s). The double *o* is used for the present and the *–ing* verbal *(choosing).* The past form is *chose* (rhyming with *hose,* and spelled with one *o*). The fourth form is *chosen.* REMEMBER: I *choose* now, but I *chose* in the past.

coming Visualize the two syllables: com-ing. REMEMBER: Mr. Ming is co*ming*.

definite Pronounce this word distinctly: def-i-nite. REMEMBER: There are two *i*'s in def*i*nite.

Spelling

M5a

GROUP B	

friend — As with the word *believe,* the "i before e" rule applies here also. REMEMBER: A **fiend** is no *friend* of mine.

government — Pronounce the word distinctly and do not leave out any letters: gov-ern-ment. REMEMBER: **Vern** is studying go*vern*ment.

grammar — Remember that if you take the *g* out of the word *grammar,* it is spelled the same backward and forward: *rammar.* REMEMBER: **Mar**vin and **Mar**ilyn know their English gram*mar* extremely well. Do you?

hoping — *Hoping* is related to *hope. Hopping* is related to *hop.* REMEMBER: *Hoping* rhymes with m**oping;** *hopping* rhymes with st**opping.** When *hope* changes to *hoping,* do not double the *p.*

its — *Its* is a possessive pronoun and points to a following noun: "The animal bit *its* master in revenge." *It's* always means *it is.* REMEMBER: Never write *it's* unless you can substitute *it is.* "*It's* a good day for singing a song" = "*It is* a good day for singing a song."

library — This word contains an *r* on both sides of an *a.* Pronounce the word distinctly and do not leave out any letters: li-brary. REMEMBER: The li**br**arians **br**ought **br**icks for the **br**anch li**br**ary.

lose — If a team does not win, it *lo*ses. If something is not tight, it is *loo*se. There is a single *o* in lose, but a double *o* in loose. REMEMBER: If your ring is *loo*se, you may *lo*se it.

occurred — There is a single *r* in *occur* and *occurs,* but a double *r* in *occurred* and *occurring.* REMEMBER: Double the *r* when adding *–ed* and *–ing.* The occu*rr*ence occu*rr*ed yesterday.

perform — Pronounce the word carefully and distinctly: per-form. (*Preform* means something entirely different.) REMEMBER: *Per*cy will *per*form if you *per*mit him.

Mechanics

LANGUAGE IN ACTION

SPELLING REFORM

Noah Webster, whose *American Dictionary of the English Language* was published in 1828, proposed several spelling reforms. Some have been adopted. This list of words uses the English spelling of the time. Write the modern spelling of each word.

1. favour	6. honour	11. gaol	16. centre
2. traveller	7. waggon	12. mediaeval	17. plough
3. fibre	8. axe	13. frolick	18. musick
4. tyre	9. theatre	14. masque	19. metre
5. storey	10. harbour	15. colour	20. cheque

GROUP C

prejudice — The syllables are as follows: prej-u-dice. *Prejudice* adds a –*d* after a linking verb: He is prejudice*d*. REMEMBER: A *prej*udice is a *prej*udgment.

principle — Pronounce the word distinctly: prin-ci-ple. *Principle* means a basic rule or idea. *Principal* is the head of a school. Pronounce: prin-ci-pal. REMEMBER: The dis*c*iple of Jesus was a man of prin*c*iple. Our princi*pal* is a *pal*.

probably — Visualize each syllable: prob-a-bly. REMEMBER: There is an *ably* in *probably*.

quite — The word with *ite* means "entirely": "You are quite (entirely) right." The word with *iet* means "silent": "Keep quiet (silent)." REMEMBER: *Quite* rhymes with **kite**; *quiet* rhymes with d**iet.**

receive — This word follows the rule: "*i* before *e*, except after *c*." REMEMBER: R*ecei*ve a r*ecei*pt for the *cei*ling!

separate — Visualize this word by syllable: sep-a-rate. REMEMBER: There is **a rat** in sep*a*r*at*e.

similar — Visualize this word: sim-i-lar. Focus on the –*lar* ending. REMEMBER: The popu**lar** sky**lark** and meadow**lark** are simi*lar*.

studying — *Studying* is composed of *study* + *ing*. REMEMBER: The student is stud*y*ing in the **study.**

succeed — Visualize the two syllables in suc-ceed and suc-cess. REMEMBER: Double *c* and *s* in *success*, and double *c* and *e* in *succeed*.

360

Spelling

| GROUP D | |

surprise — We usually omit the *r* sound when pronouncing this word in rapid speech. REMEMBER: When the **sur**fer **sur**faced, we were *sur*prised.

than — This word is used in comparisons (taller *than*). Because it is normally unaccented, it often sounds like *then*. The latter is used in talking about time (now and *then*.) REMEMBER: The **an**ts were more **an**noying th*an* the **an**teater.

there — The *ere* spelling is used when pointing to a place (not here but *there*) and in the *there is/there are* combination (*there* is no one here). The *eir* spelling is used when the word is working with a following noun (they did *their* dance). *They're* is used only when you can substitute *they are* (they're my best friends). REMEMBER: *They're* going to park th*eir* car th*ere*.

to — *To* is a preposition, usually working with a following noun or pronoun (*to* the party, *to* her). It is also the word that signals an infinitive (they began *to* cry). *Too* is an intensifying adverb, followed by an adjective or adverb (*too* lazy, *too* late). *Too* is also a regular adverb, meaning "also" (we are going, *too*). *Too* and *to* are normally distinguished in speech: There is a long *o* sound (as in f*oo*d) in *too*, a shorter *o* sound (as in f*oo*t) in *to*. REMEMBER: *Too* late, he *too* came *to* school *to* learn.

together — Visualize this word: to-geth-er. REMEMBER: They suggested we **get** to*geth*er.

tries — A *y* is often used in this word instead of an *ie*. This is a misspelling. REMEMBER: If you take the *r* out of *tries*, you get **ties**.

whose — "Whose book?" means "belongs to whom?" *Who's* is used only when you can substitute *who is*. REMEMBER: Wh*o's* the boy wh*ose* book you have?

women — Just as we say "*one* m*a*n," "*two* m*e*n," so we say "*one* wom*a*n," "*two* wom*e*n." REMEMBER: There were several m*en* and wom*en* m*en*tioned.

writing — There is only one *t* in wri*t*e and wri*t*ing, two *t*'s in wri*tt*en. REMEMBER: Wri*t*ing rhymes with b*it*ing; wri*tt*en rhymes with b*itt*en.

Mechanics

EXERCISE 1 Have someone dictate the following sentences to you. Then check to see which words, if any, you have misspelled. Give them your special attention. Use the look-say-write attack on any misspelled words.

1. Their business was all right in the beginning.
2. I was hoping to surprise you in the library.
3. My friend does not believe in government.
4. They perform together but receive separate checks.
5. A similar thing occurred when I was writing.
6. The women there are probably studying.
7. Someone who tries may succeed in spite of prejudices.
8. Choose a definite time this coming week.
9. People with principles may lose a lot of friends.
10. The troop was quite ready to accept its reward.

EXERCISE 2 The following six groups of words list some additional common spelling problems. Have someone dictate one group at a time to you. Then check the words in the group to see which words, if any, you have misspelled. Give them your special attention.

GROUP 1	GROUP 2	GROUP 3
accidentally	captain	eliminate
acquainted	children	embarrass
acquire	clothes	enough
across	colonel	entrance
address	competition	equipment
already	completely	exaggerate
among	criticize	existence
apology		experience
argument	decision	explanation
athlete	describe	extremely
attitude	description	
	different	finally
basically	disappoint	foreign
beautiful	disastrous	forty
breath	disease	fourth
breathe	dropped	
		height

Spelling

GROUP 4	GROUP 5	GROUP 6
immediately	occasion	really
independent	omission	repetition
intelligent	operate	
interest	opinion	scene
	oppose	sense
knowledge		several
	perhaps	shining
license	persuade	sincerely
listener	possible	strict
	practical	suppose
marriage	practice	suspense
mathematics	preceding	swimming
meant	preferred	
medicine	prepare	thorough
minute	privilege	tragedy
	pursue	truly
necessary		
ninety		usually
ninth		

Know the most basic spelling rules.

The advantage of learning spelling rules is obvious: By learning *one* rule, you can learn to spell *many* words. The following rules should help you to gain a great deal of spelling power:

(1) When choosing between *ei* and *ie* for the long *ee* sound, write *i* before *e* — except after *c*. All of the following words have the long *ee* sound:

M5b
Spelling Rules

| I BEFORE E: | believe | achieve | piece | chief | grief |
| EXCEPT AFTER C: | receive | receipt | ceiling | conceited | deceit |

The following words are exceptions to this rule: *neither, either, financier, species, weird, leisure,* and *seize*. Keep the following sentence in mind in order to help you remember the exceptions:

Neither weird financier of either species seized leisure.

Mechanics

(2) *Double the final consonant* when adding endings to words—if the ending starts with a vowel. Make sure the final letter of such a word is a *single* consonant, preceded by a *single* vowel:

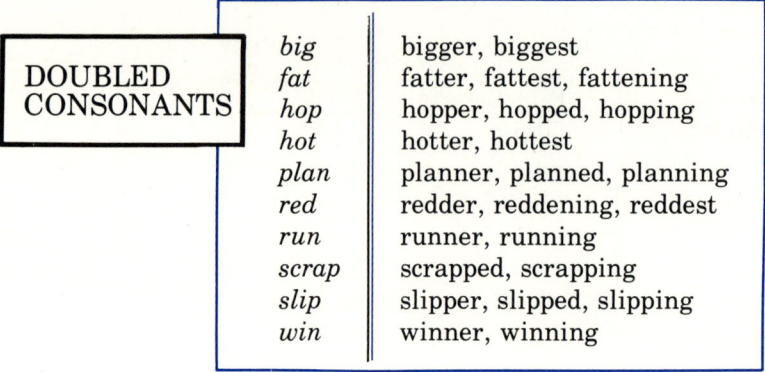

big	bigger, biggest
fat	fatter, fattest, fattening
hop	hopper, hopped, hopping
hot	hotter, hottest
plan	planner, planned, planning
red	redder, reddening, reddest
run	runner, running
scrap	scrapped, scrapping
slip	slipper, slipped, slipping
win	winner, winning

Do *not* double the consonant if the final syllable has a double vowel *(oo, oa, ea,* etc.*)* or a silent *e:*

NO DOUBLING

DOUBLE VOWEL	SILENT E
heat —heated, heating	hate —hated, hating
read —reading, reader	plane —planed, planing
neat —neater, neatest	love —lover, loving
sleep —sleeper, sleeping	hope —hoper, hoping
doom —dooming, doomed	dome —domed, doming

The syllable with the doubled consonant must be the one *stressed* when you pronounce the word. If the stress shifts *away* from the syllable, doubling does *not* take place:

DOUBLING	NO DOUBLING
adMIT, adMITTed	BENefit, BENefited
overLAP, overLAPPing	deVELop, deVELoping
reGRET, reGRETTed	exHIBit, exHIBited
beGIN, beGINNing	WEAKen, WEAKening
forGET, forGETTing	ORBit, ORBiting
reFER, reFERRed	REFerence
preFER, preFERRing	PREFerable

Spelling

(3) Drop a silent *e* before an ending that starts with a vowel. Keep the silent *e* if the ending starts with a consonant:

	VOWEL	CONSONANT
love	loving	lovely
bore	boring	boredom
fate	fatal	fateful
like	likable	likely
state	stating	statement

SILENT E

Exceptions: *argument, awful, duly, judgment, mileage, truly, wholly.*

Note: When the final *e* comes after *c* or *g*, keep the *e* before *a* or *o* to show that the *c* or *g* has the soft sound: *changeable, courageous, noticeable.*

(4) Change a final single *y* to *ie* before *–s*. Change it to *i* before most other endings. Keep the *y* before *–ing*.

ie:	try–tr*ies*, dry–dr*ies*, city–cit*ies*, carry–carr*ies*, hurry–hurr*ies*, sixty–sixt*ies*
i:	beauty–beaut*i*ful, copy–cop*i*ed, dry–dr*i*es, easy–eas*i*ly, happy–happ*i*ness, merry–merr*i*ment
y:	carr*y*ing, cop*y*ing, hurr*y*ing, stud*y*ing

FINAL Y

A final *y* preceded by a vowel usually does not change:

delays　　*employer*
enjoyed　　*joys*
grayness　　*valleys*

A few exceptions to this rule are the following:

day–daily　　*pay–paid*
gay–gaily　　*say–said*
lay–laid

Mechanics

(5) When you add –*ly* to a word ending in *l*, keep the double *l*. When you add –*ness* to a word ending in *n*, keep the double *n*. When you add –*ful* to a word, use only the single *l*.

actual   + ly = actually | mean + ness = meanness
careful   + ly = carefully | even + ness = evenness
eventual + ly = eventually | thin   + ness = thinness

mouth + ful = mouthful
cup   + ful = cupful
spoon + ful = spoonful

(6) When a *prefix* is added to a word, the spelling of the word remains the same. Be sure you know the spelling of these prefixes: *dis–, il–, im–, in–, mis–, re–, un–*. If a word to which you add one of these prefixes begins with the same letter as ends the prefix, you will get a *doubled* letter:

dis + appoint = disappoint | in + numerable = innumerable
dis + satisfy = dissatisfy | mis + manage   = mismanage
il + legal   = illegal | mis + spell   = misspell
il + legible = illegible | re + enter   = reenter
im + mortal = immortal | re + store   = restore
im + prove   = improve | un + aware   = unaware
in + crease = increase | un + natural   = unnatural

EXERCISE 1

Write the complete words called for in the instructions:

A. Fill in *ei* or *ie:*

1. rec____ve   6. l____sure
2. spec____s   7. rel____f
3. bel____ve   8. n____ther
4. ach____vement   9. rec____pt
5. s____ze   10. p____ce

B. Add –*ing* to the following words:

1. judge   3. state   5. hope   7. copy   9. heal
2. love   4. move   6. try   8. win   10. read

C. Add –*er* to the following words:

1. hit   3. float   5. hop   7. hat   9. run
2. plan   4. begin   6. red   8. hate   10. sad

D. Add –*able* to the following words:

1. prefer   3. forget   5. enjoy   7. change   9. control
2. envy   4. notice   6. regret   8. inhabit   10. break

Spelling

M5b

EXERCISE 2

Of the two possible words in each sentence, choose the one that fits the context.

1. Rabbits were *(hoping/hopping)* all over the lawn.
2. George was *(moping/mopping)* up the kitchen floor.
3. The animal *(bared/barred)* its teeth.
4. We *(planed/planned)* the picnic very carefully.
5. Two strangers *(robed/robbed)* us last night.
6. The man was *(fined/finned)* for disobeying traffic regulations.
7. We were always *(griping/gripping)* about the food in the army.
8. My father *(caned/canned)* my legs with a switch.
9. The doctor *(taped/tapped)* her ankle so that she could walk comfortably.
10. She was *(pining/pinning)* away for her lost dog.

EXERCISE 3

From the list below, add a prefix or suffix to the word before or after which a blank space occurs. Write the whole word after the number of the sentence. Be sure to pick a prefix or suffix that fits in with the meaning of the sentence.

PREFIXES: *dis–, il–, im–, in–, mis–, re–, un–*
SUFFIXES: *–ly, –ness, –ful*

1. There was a ____ understanding between them.
2. She asked for a cup ____ of rice.
3. Charles has ____ signed as treasurer.
4. How often have you ____ spelled that word?
5. It is ____ natural for parents to hate their children.
6. The scientist was ____ satisfied with the results of his experiments.
7. An umpire has to be ____ partial.
8. The pitcher studied the batter careful ____ .
9. His mean ____ of temper made him many enemies.
10. Joe's argument was ____ logical.
11. They got a ____ similar result.
12. He reached in his pocket and pulled out a hand ____ of coins.
13. The dog usual ____ stays by his master's side.
14. The senator was ____ elected a dozen times.
15. The Greeks thought their gods were ____ mortal.
16. I cannot find my pen; I must have ____ placed it.
17. Helen's grades were ____ satisfactory.
18. The teacher returned his essay because of the thin ____ of the paper.
19. The dinosaur was an ____ mense creature.
20. For the party we ____ luminated the garden with Chinese lanterns.

Mechanics

M5c Learn to distinguish between confusing pairs.

Confusing Pairs

The following are the major categories of confusing pairs of words in English:

(1) The same root word in different uses. Study the spelling changes in the following pairs. Note the differences in spelling of the noun and the verb or adjective.

court*eous*	but	court*e*sy	**CONFUSING PAIRS**
curi*ous*	but	curi*o*sity	
describ*e*	but	descri*p*tion	
f*o*ur, f*o*urteen	but	forty	
gener*ous*	but	gener*o*sity	
ni*n*e, ni*n*ety	but	n*i*nth	
num*b*er	but	num*e*ral, num*e*rate	
prono*u*nce	but	pron*u*nciation	
sp*ea*king	but	sp*ee*ch	
*th*rough	but	*th*orough	
ti*ll*	but	unti*l*	

Watch for the following shifts in spelling as a word shifts from one word class to another or from the present tense to the past tense:

VERB: I will advi*s*e him.
NOUN: I gave him advi*c*e.

VERB: We pa*ss*ed the Ford.
NOUN: The pa*st* was forgotten.

NOUN: She had one strong prejud*ic*e.
ADJECTIVE: He was prejudi*c*ed.

NOUN: He was wearing the latest fashi*on*.
ADJECTIVE: She is not old-fashi*on*ed.

PRESENT: We us*e* inexpensive paper.
PAST: We us*ed* to see her often.

PRESENT: We suppos*e* that he will come.
PARTICIPLE: We were suppos*ed* to be there.

(2) Words that sound similar or alike. Study the confusing pairs on the next page carefully. For each of these learn to ask: "Which twin is it?"

Spelling

capital	Washington, D.C., is our capital; a business must have capital; use capital letters.
capitol	The legislative branch of our government meets at the Capitol (a building).
coarse	The material was coarse; he has coarse features.
course	The course of true love never runs smooth; we visited the race course.
counsel	The counseling staff in schools and camps gives advice (its members are counselors). Mr. Smith will counsel you this year.
council	A governing board or committee is sometimes called a council, as in a student council. (Its members are councilors).
desert	I wouldn't want to live in a desert; please don't desert me; give him his just deserts.
dessert	Because we were watching our weight, we had no dessert (use two *s*'s only for what you eat).
lead	Lead is a heavy metal; the pencil had no lead.
led	The sergeant led his men into battle. (NOTE: When *lead* is pronounced like *led,* it is a noun. When *lead* rhymes with *need,* it is a verb: The sergeant will *lead* us into battle.)
meet	He will meet us at the track meet (*meet* is both verb and noun).
met	I met him at the track meet (*met* is the past of *meet*).
site	We visited the site of the new campsite (*site* tells where something is).
cite	John cited a verse from the Bible; the man was cited for contempt (*cite* means to quote or to call before a court).
stationary	He stood stationary for an hour; the desks were stationary (they could not be moved).
stationery	Stationery is sold in a stationery store by stationers.
weather	The weather is bad; they weathered the storm.
whether	I asked whether he was going or not.

Mechanics

(3) Words with suffixes that sound similar or alike.

-able -ible	accept*a*ble, cap*a*ble, port*a*ble poss*i*ble, terr*i*ble, vis*i*ble
-ance -ence	attend*a*nce, mainten*a*nce, perform*a*nce experi*e*nce, exist*e*nce, excell*e*nce
-ant -ent	attend*a*nt, brilli*a*nt, command*a*nt differ*e*nt, excell*e*nt, intellig*e*nt
-er -or	farm*e*r, lead*e*r, shoemak*e*r doct*o*r, sail*o*r, tail*o*r

Note: In rapid speech, the sound of the verb *have* is typically shortened when it comes after another auxiliary and before a main verb: *must have spoken, could have learned*. In order to reflect this shortening, the *have* is sometimes contracted in writing: *must've spoken, could've learned*. Such a contraction is best reserved only for writing dialogue. There is no such form as *must of spoken* or *could of learned*. Write:

RIGHT	WRONG
should *have* seen	(never *should of*)
might *have* bought	(never *might of*)
would *have* been	(never *would of*)
will *have* picked	(never *will of*)

EXERCISE 1

Which of the two words in each pair is the right choice? Write the word that should fill the blank after the number of the sentence.

1. *(cite/site)* We picked a good _____ for the picnic.
2. *(advice/advise)* The minister gave us excellent _____ .
3. *(capital/Capitol)* The _____ of Maine is Augusta.
4. *(counsel/council)* Our town _____ holds meetings every month.
5. *(lead/led)* The guide _____ the march.
6. *(weather/whether)* Does he forecast the _____ accurately?
7. *(desert/dessert)* The _____ today was French pastry.
8. *(coarse/course)* Anyone who leaves the _____ will be disqualified.
9. *(stationary/stationery)* Do you have enough _____ to finish all those letters?

M5c

Spelling

10. *(prejudice/prejudiced)* Yolanda is _____ in favor of Teddy because he is her brother.
11. *(use/used)* We _____ to swim every day when we were children.
12. *(passed/past)* The bus _____ us at sixty mph.
13. *(suppose/supposed)* "I _____ you know everything," she said.
14. *(counselor/councilor)* The _____ advised him to take the academic course.
15. *(meet/met)* I _____ him for the first time yesterday.
16. *(old-fashion/old-fashioned)* They played many _____ songs.
17. *(use/used)* The state legislature _____ to meet in the Capitol building.
18. *(desert/dessert)* There are frequent sandstorms in the _____.
19. *(weather/whether)* We wondered _____ it would rain.
20. *(lead/led)* You should have brought some spare _____ for your pencil.

EXERCISE 2

Write down the following. Add the missing letter or letters to each word.

1. attend____nt
2. exist____nce
3. f____rty
4. num____al
5. unti____
6. descri____tion
7. attend____nce
8. sp____ch
9. ni____ty
10. courte____s
11. pron____nciation
12. brilli____nt
13. differ____nt
14. tail____r
15. counsel____r
16. poss____ble
17. doct____r
18. command____nt
19. gener____sity
20. curi____sity

UNIT REVIEW EXERCISE

Which of the three possible choices is the right one for the blank space in each of the following sentences? Put the letter for the right choice after the number of the sentence.

EXAMPLE: 1. Teachers keep a record of attend_____.
   a. ence   b. ance   c. ents
(Answer)   *1b*

1. The leaves were beg_____ to grow.
   a. inning   b. ining   c. ing
2. We found the story hard to bel_____.
   a. eave   b. eive   c. ieve
3. The guard would not _____ our apology.
   a. accept   b. acept   c. except

Mechanics

4. Our neighbor had bought a very simi_____ car.
   a. ler b. lar c. liar
5. Justice must take _____ course.
   a. it's b. its c. its'
6. We had _____ a vacation in Florida.
   a. planned b. planed c. pland
7. Many older _____ have beautiful parks.
   a. citys b. cities c. city's
8. Both pro_____ciations were right.
   a. noun b. nou c. nun
9. Her grandmother was over _____ years old.
   a. ninty b. nienty c. ninety
10. The alarm was sup_____ to ring.
    a. pose b. poze c. posed
11. His letter came as a complete _____prise.
    a. su b. sur c. sup
12. I don't care _____ you believe me or not.
    a. weather b. wether c. whether
13. The hall was sold out for every _____.
    a. preformance b. performance c. performence
14. Someone should _____ notified the police.
    a. of b. have c. off
15. This pizza certainly tastes _____.
    a. diferent b. differant c. different
16. The girls will re_____ a reward.
    a. ceave b. cieve c. ceive
17. This time you are prob_____ right.
    a. ably b. ly c. ally
18. Joan and Donna were always stud_____ together.
    a. ing b. iing c. ying
19. We would have pref_____ to stay home.
    a. ered b. erred c. erd
20. Their happ_____ showed in their faces.
    a. yness b. iness c. ines

M6 MANUSCRIPT FORM

Write or type your manuscript legibly according to standard form.

When we write something for our own use, we may scribble and take shortcuts. But when we write something for somebody else's attention, we take more care. We want the reader to be able to say: "Someone considered this material important enough to lay it out clearly for my attention." Make sure your writing lives up to the following minimum standards:

Manuscript Form

- *If you handwrite your papers,* use paper of standard size (eight-and-a-half by eleven inches), ruled in wide lines. Use letters of standard size and proportion. Fancy flourishes and squiggles may please you, but they often annoy your reader.

- *If you type your papers,* type the original copy on non-transparent paper, unlined, of standard size. (Semitransparent paper—onionskin—is for carbon copies only.) When your type becomes dirty, it is time to clean the keys. When your type becomes light, it is time to change the ribbon. *Double-space* all material except block quotations and footnotes. Leave two spaces after colons and end punctuation. Leave one space after commas and semicolons. Dashes should be shown by two hyphens--with no space on either side.

- *Margins* in both handwritten and typed papers should be about an inch-and-a-half at the top and left-hand side. Leave about an inch at the bottom and right-hand side. *Indent* the first line of your paragraphs about an inch when writing longhand. Indent five spaces when typing.

- Capitalize all major words in the title you give your paper (see **M4a**). Do not underline your titles. Do not put them in quotation marks (unless they are quotations). Do not put a period after your titles, though you may use a question mark or exclamation point when appropriate.

- The following *corrections* are permissible on the final copy if they are neat and few in number:

(1) Draw a line through words or phrases that you want to omit. Do not use parentheses or brackets to make these corrections.

```
        for which he had already paid for.
```

(2) To correct a word, draw a line through it and write the corrected word in the space immediately above it.   Do not cross out or insert individual letters:

```
                    believe
        he could not beleive his eyes.
```

Mechanics

(3) To add a missing word or phrase, insert a caret (∧). Then write the word or phrase immediately above:

<pre>
                          the
       had talked to first victim
                    ∧
</pre>

(4) To change the paragraphing of a paper, insert the symbol ¶ to indicate an additional paragraph break. To indicate that an existing paragraph break should be ignored, insert no *¶ in the margin.*

M6a
Dividing Words

Divide words at the end of a line when necessary.

If you must divide a word at the end of a line, divide it between syllables. Consult a dictionary if you are unsure of where the word should be divided. In addition, the following simple rules may help:

(1) Words with prefixes and suffixes are usually divided between the prefix and the root, or between the root and the suffix:

non-essential   dis-agree
speak-ing   profit-able

(2) Words with double consonants should be divided between the consonants:

com-mit   ves-sel
neces-sary sur-render
shal-low   hap-py

When a double consonant is immediately followed by a suffix, the division is sometimes made at the suffix:

fill-ing   spell-ing

(3) Never divide a one-syllable word:

does (never *do-es*), street (never *str-eet*), stayed (never *stay-ed*), doubt (never *dou-bt*)

(4) Never divide a word so that a single letter stands alone. Also, avoid carrying only two letters over to the next line:

about (not *a-bout*), event (not *e-vent*)
pris-oner (not *prison-er*), even-tual (not *eventu-al*)

M6b Abbreviations

Use abbreviations only when they are generally acceptable.

Abbreviations are shortcuts. Obviously, you would not want to seem in a hurry in a paper that is supposed to be carefully worked out. Use only these acceptable abbreviations:

(1) *The following abbreviations are generally acceptable before names: Mr., Mrs., Ms., Dr., St.* (Saint), *Rev.; or after names: Jr., Sr., M.D., A.B., Ph.D.*

> Mr. and Mrs. Taylor have agreed to chaperon the dance.
> The sermon was given by the Rev. Charles Smith, Jr.

(2) *The following abbreviations are generally acceptable with numerals: No.,* A.D., B.C., A.M., P.M., *the symbol $.*

> The plane will arrive at 8:30 A.M.
> Nero was born in A.D. 37.

(3) *Initials standing for the name of an agency, business firm, technical process, or the like are generally acceptable, if they are in common use:*

> I am flying by TWA.
> The money was insured by the FDIC.
> They called in the FBI.

(4) *The following Latin abbreviations are generally acceptable:* e.g. (for example), i.e. (that is), and etc. (and so on).

> The possessive pronouns *(my, your, his, etc.)* are used before nouns.
> The major characters in Shakespeare's tragedies (e.g., Hamlet, Macbeth, and King Lear) die before the end of the play.

(5) *As a general rule, do* not *abbreviate—or shorten— the* names of countries, states, cities, streets, *and the like, except in business records or addresses:*

> Hawthorne lived for twelve years on Herbert Street, in Salem, Massachusetts.
> Dallas is one of the most interesting cities in the United States.

(6) *As a general rule, do* not *abbreviate* units of measurement, *such as lb. (pound), oz. (ounce), and yd. (yard), with the exception of mph (miles per hour) and rpm (revolutions per minute).*

> Helen needed 2 yards of material; she was short by 3 feet.

Mechanics

Note: Do not use the abbreviations in (1) and (2) above unless they are preceded or followed by a specific name or numeral, with the exception of college degrees.

WRONG: We called for a Dr.
RIGHT: We called for a doctor.

WRONG: I awoke in the p.m.
RIGHT: I awoke in the afternoon.

WRONG: Bill said he needed $.
RIGHT: Bill said he needed money.

RIGHT: Last year, he earned his Ph.D.

M6c Numbers

Know when numbers should be written as numerals and when they should be spelled out.

Like abbreviations, numerals save time and space. In some cases, however, such "savings" are not recommended in ordinary writing.

(1) *Spell out numbers in the following cases:* (a) at the beginning of a sentence; (b) when the number is from one to ten; and (c) when the number is a round number requiring no more than two words, e.g., *forty, two hundred*.

Thirty-three teachers came to the meeting.
I knew only seven of them.
There must have been three thousand people at the rally.
That man has four children.

(2) Use numerals for numbers in references to *dates* and *years, street numbers* and *page numbers, exact sums* and *technical measurements*, especially those referring to *percentages* or including *decimal points*.

She was born on June 3, 1948.
You will find the information on page 52 or 53.
There are 348 beds in the hospital.
The current rate of interest at our bank is 4.25 percent.

(3) Write out *fractions*. Do not use numbers with endings such as *st, nd, rd,* and *th*.

One-fourth of the population was Catholic.
The theater was four-fifths empty.
The first, third, and fifth boys were chosen.
She lives on Second Street.

Manuscript Form

M6c

UNIT REVIEW EXERCISE

About half of the sentences in the following exercise use abbreviations and numbers in a way that would be satisfactory in ordinary writing. Put *S* for satisfactory after the number of each such sentence. The remaining sentences need to be revised. Put *R* (for revise) after the numbers of these sentences. (Be prepared to explain why and how each of these should be revised. Your teacher may ask you to write down the revised versions.)

1. We decided to hold our meeting on June 19.
2. Mr. and Mrs. Young attended church at St. Timothy's.
3. My best friend lives on Dale St. in Swampscott, Mass.
4. The grocer's scale read five pounds, six ounces.
5. Polly will get her A.B. degree this June.
6. 22 has always been my lucky number.
7. She will be thirty-five on July 16, 1986.
8. The Dr. and the Rev. sat side by side.
9. There are about 40 students in our student council.
10. The lucky number was 55 906.
11. Our neighbor just bought a nineteen seventy-eight Chevrolet.
12. The 3rd and the 6th grades were the hardest for me.
13. Nearly one tenth of the population died in the earthquake.
14. Frank earned 6.5 percent interest on his savings.
15. Last summer we drove to California and visited L.A.
16. The speedometer reached 12 mph.
17. The article was signed by J. Wright, Jr., Ph.D.
18. Alexander was King of Macedon from 336 to 323 B.C.
19. UNESCO is one of the most important agencies of the U.N.
20. Joey is two ft., five in. tall.

Chapter 6

Oral Language
The Brief Talk

O1 The Speaker's Resources
    a   Using Your Voice
    b   Talking with Your Hands

O2 Preparing a Brief Talk
    a   The Informative Talk
    b   The Personal Viewpoint
    c   The Commentary

O3 The Interview

For Further Study: Acting Things Out

Chapter Preview 6

IN THIS CHAPTER:

- How to use the full resources of spoken English in talking to and with people.
- How to use voice and gesture confidently and effectively.
- How to use a brief informal talk to present background information, to express a personal point of view, or to comment on current events.
- How to practice effective two-way communication in an interview.

Learn how to speak up and how to listen to others.

We admire people who can get up in front of a group to explain something in a convincing manner. We are impressed by speakers who can hold our attention and clearly present their point of view. But speaking to a group is not just a one-way street. Effective speakers know how to listen as well as talk. They take in the feelings and reactions of others. They know how to join in the give-and-take by which people make up their minds.

PREVIEW EXERCISE

Do one or more of the following for practice in talking to a group:

1. Some stories have been told by word of mouth from generation to generation. Pretend you are the storyteller of a tribe living long before books were first printed. Tell a myth from a book such as Edith Hamilton's *Mythology* or some other collection of ancient myths.
2. Go to the library and find a fairy tale that is *not* widely known. Try the collections by the Brothers Grimm or Hans Christian Andersen, or try a collection of Russian, Scandinavian, or African tales. Tell the tale.
3. Parents (or sometimes grandparents or other older relatives) often feel that their children have an easier time than they did. Have you ever listened to someone's tale of hardships from earlier days? Pretend you are that person. Tell the story to the younger generation.

O1 THE SPEAKER'S RESOURCES

The Speaker's Resources

Learn to speak confidently and effectively to a group.

Speaking in front of a group is like learning to dance, or ski, or play the piano. The most basic requirement for success is *practice.* You have to do enough of whatever you are trying to learn so that you can say: "No need to get all tense—I've done this kind of thing many times before."

O1a Using Your Voice

Use the full range of your voice.

A steady, monotonous voice puts people to sleep. Watch how successful comedians vary their pace to keep the attention of their audience. They pause at the right point for suspense. They make sure everyone is paying attention when they deliver the punch line. Each joke is a little drama, acted out on the stage.

In music, a gradual "turning up" of the volume from soft to much louder is called a **crescendo.** The following student-written poem gives you a chance to practice a similar kind of crescendo in using your voice. Read the poem, making your voice change gradually from the "whisper" at the beginning to the "scream" at the end. You may split up the reading as a *choral reading:* one voice (or several voices) for the narrator, another voice (or several other voices) for "the man."

EXERCISE 1

The Man Who Shouted "I Am!"

Who is the one, who helped himself?
The man whispered, "I am."
Who is the one, who taught himself?
The man whispered, "I am."
Who is the one who made tools to lighten his load?
The man whispered, "I am."
Who is the one who controlled the beasts?
The man murmured, "I am."
Who is the one who recorded his thoughts and learning?
The man murmured, "I am."
Who is the one who organized and governed?
The man said, "I am."
Who is the one who built cities?
The man said, "I am."

Who is the one who made weapons?
The man said louder, "I am."
Who is the one who crosses oceans and continents?
The man said louder, "I am!"
Who is the one who fought and killed his own kind?
The man shouted, "I am!"
Who is the one who built the factories?
The man shouted, "I am! I am!"
Who is the one who pollutes the lakes, the air and the earth?
The man screamed, "I am! I am!"
Who is the one who witnesses starvation and terror?
The man screamed louder, "I am! I am!"
And who is condemned forever to hell?!
"I am! I am! I am! I am! I am!"

EXERCISE 2

How good are you at varying your voice to reflect different feelings? In the following poem, how would you read the three parts: the first speaker, the beautiful ghost, and the narrator? (You may want to split up the three voices for a choral reading.)

The Ghost

"Who knocks?" "I, who was beautiful,
   Beyond all dreams to restore,
I, from the roots of the dark thorn am hither,
   And knock on the door."

"Who speaks?" "I—once was my speech
   Sweet as the bird's on the air,
When an echo lurks by the waters to heed;
   'Tis I speak thee fair."

"Dark is the hour!" "Ay, and cold."
   "Lone is my house." "Ah, but mine?"
"Sight, touch, lips, eyes yearned in vain."
   "Long dead these to thine . . ."

Silence. Still faint on the porch
   Brake the flames of the stars.
In gloom groped a hope-wearied hand
   Over keys, bolts, and bars.

A face peered. All the grey night
   In chaos of vacancy shone;
Nought but vast sorrow was there—
   The sweet cheat gone.

—Walter de la Mare

The Speaker's Resources

EXERCISE 3

How good are you at using your voice to imitate different *sound effects?* When you read lines like the following, can you make your listeners *hear* the lion growl and *see* the lion bite?

Why Nobody Pets the Lion at the Zoo

The morning that the world began
The Lion growled a growl at Man.

And I suspect the Lion might
(If he'd been closer) have tried a bite.

I think that's as it ought to be
And not as it was taught to me.

I think the Lion has a right
to growl a growl and bite a bite.

—John Ciardi

EXERCISE 4

How good are you at *impersonating* the different speakers that appear in poems? Find a poem in one of the following categories. Read it several times until you feel you understand the person represented by the speaker (or speakers) in the poem. Then read the poem to the class. Have them discuss how close you came to sounding like the intended speaker.

1. Ballads of the English and Scottish border
2. Poems by Langston Hughes
3. Poems by Edgar Allan Poe or Emily Dickinson
4. American folk poetry: ballads, spirituals, blues
5. Poems by Carl Sandburg or Vachel Lindsay
6. Poems by Stephen Crane
7. Poems by e. e. cummings
8. Poems by Edna St. Vincent Millay or Elizabeth Barrett Browning

EXERCISE 5

Some poems make striking use of the *sound resources* of poetry—rhythm, rhyme, and the like. Select about thirty to forty lines of such a poem and read them to the class. Have your classmates discuss how fully you exploited the sound effects made possible by the poem. Here are examples of the kind of poem you might choose:

Edgar Allan Poe, "The Raven"
Lord Byron, "The Destruction of Sennacherib"
Sidney Lanier, "Song of the Chattahoochee"

Oral Language

> Vachel Lindsay, "General William Booth Enters into Heaven"
> Lord Tennyson, "The Charge of the Light Brigade"
> Robert Browning, "Childe Roland to the Dark Tower Came"

O1b
Talking with Your Hands

Let your face and hands do their share of the talking.

A good speaker does not just "stand there"—stiff, never batting an eyelash. A good speaker projects: The face and gestures help act out the main points. The eyes light up at the right moment. A smile or a frown helps steer the reactions of the audience. The hands underline something that is especially important.

Some people have very expressive *faces*—the looks they give us tell a whole story. Write a caption for each of the following pictures. In each case, what does the face say?

Some people have very expressive *hands*. Their gestures help us see what they think and feel. Write a caption for each of the following. In each case, what do the hands say?

The Speaker's Resources

O1b

Often, face and hands go together. The whole body, the whole person talks. Write a caption for each of the following six pictures. What is each person saying?

Oral Language

EXERCISE 1

Pretend you are traveling in the American Southwest. You don't know Spanish, but a friend has given you instructions on how to use gestures to communicate with *Spanish-speaking* people. Can you act out the following instructions?

1. **Tengo hambre:** (I'm hungry) Use right or left hand, or even both hands; place them over the abdominal area and either rub or pat very gently. We use a similar gesture in English to mean the same thing.

2. **Dinero:** (Money) Use either the right or left arm, bend it at the elbow and hold hand comfortably in front of you with palm up. Rub thumb back and forth several times across the tip of the index and middle fingers.

3. **Excelente; Magnífico:** (Wonderful! Great!) Use either hand. Bring the tips of the thumb and four fingers together, raise them to your lips, pucker your lips well and kiss them, gently throwing the kiss forward and upward by raising the hand and separating slightly the thumbs and fingers.

Preparing a Brief Talk

EXERCISE 2

Write instructions trying to explain how *English-speaking Americans* talk with their hands. Select three of the following. See if your classmates can act out your instructions and get across the right message.

1. "Finished: all gone, no more."
2. "That's crazy—stupid!"
3. "Silence!"
4. "OK—that's enough explanation; I understand."
5. "That's done with—I've finished the job."
6. "Just a teeny little bit."
7. "Keep talking—tell us more."
8. "No, thank you; not for me."
9. "Here—sign here."
10. "Beats me—I know nothing about it."

EXERCISE 3

From time immemorial, people have used signs and gestures to communicate with others speaking a language different from their own. When Spanish and Portuguese explorers first came to the New World, they used signs to communicate with the Indians who came to greet their ships. Here is an account of the landing of Cabrillo in San Diego Bay:

> And the following day, in the morning, there came to the ship three large Indians, and by signs they said that there were traveling in the interior, men like us, with beards and clothes and armed like those of the ships. And they made signs that they carried crossbows and swords, and made gestures with the right arm as if they were throwing lances, and went running in a posture as if riding on horseback, and made signs that they killed many of the native Indians, and that for this they were afraid.

Pretend you are one of the three Indians who came to the ship. Using sign language, tell the story about the people traveling in the interior.

O2 PREPARING A BRIEF TALK

Learn to prepare a brief talk for presentation to a group.

Have you ever been chosen as the resource person or expert who had to explain something to a group? How well do you do when your turn comes to "take the floor"? The following projects will give you a chance to experiment with different

Oral Language

kinds of presentations to a group. They will give you a chance to build up your confidence. They will give you a chance to learn something about audience response.

O2a
The Informative Talk

Mobilize your resources of information for a short background talk.

How good are you at working up background information for a brief talk? An effective speaker cannot always be just guessing. If you want to speak with confidence, there must be some things you *know*. Take time to look up dates and facts and figures.

Preparing a brief informative talk gives you practice in recording information for future reference. Remember the following advice:

(1) Learn how to *pick and choose*. Do not just copy big chunks of material from your sources. Pick out the facts or the details you need. Learn to condense and abbreviate the material you read.

(2) Experiment with different ways of taking notes. Try using *note cards* of different sizes. If you use cards instead of sheets of paper, you can shuffle and rearrange your material more easily.

(3) Learn to *speak freely* from notes. Remember to raise your eyes from your note cards to look at the audience. In a "live talk," you are not just reading a prepared text. You should seem to be *thinking* and putting things together as you talk.

The following projects will give you a chance to explore the resources that your school or public library has for *general interest* topics. Choose one of the topics. Gather enough material for a three-to-five minute informative talk.

EXERCISE 1

GENERAL CULTURAL HISTORY What kind of help does one get from encyclopedias and other reference books? Turn to sources like *World Book Encyclopedia* and *Compton's Encyclopedia* for information on one of the following:

1. The earliest tools used by human beings
2. What we know about comets

Preparing a Brief Talk

3. How bicycles were invented
4. A short history of the hat
5. The history of the dirigible
6. The aborigines of Australia
7. Horses and human civilization
8. The history of cooking
9. The history of household pests
10. Sports in ancient Greece

HISTORY AND BIOGRAPHY What books can you find that explain American history to the general reader? Have you ever looked at a biographical dictionary? Your teacher or school librarian may suggest other sources. Find information on one of the following:

EXERCISE 2

1. Washington's military career
2. What town meetings were like
3. The story of Sitting Bull
4. How Mexico became a nation
5. The story of Harriet Tubman
6. The Cherokee nation
7. The story of Ellis Island
8. The Dutch settlements in North America
9. The first black judge on the U.S. Supreme Court
10. Darwin as a young scientist

SCIENCE AND TECHNOLOGY What handbooks or encyclopedias can give you help with scientific or technical subjects? How well do they explain these subjects to readers who are not trained scientists or engineers? Ask your teacher or school librarian to recommend additional sources. Find information on one of the following:

EXERCISE 3

1. The discovery of electricity
2. How steam engines work
3. Producing a photographic image
4. The earliest ancestors of our plant life
5. The early history of glass
6. The chemistry of breathing
7. The flight into space
8. The splitting of the atom
9. The nature of radiation
10. Insect communities

Oral Language

O2b
The Personal Viewpoint

Learn to express your own personal point of view.

Sometimes we feel that every point of view has been heard—except our own. Have you ever wanted to express strongly what *you* thought—even though other people might not agree? Select a topic that would give you a chance to express strongly your own personal viewpoint. Choose one where you know your opinion might be different from what other people think. Choose a topic where your program for a brief talk might be something like the following:

- "I know that few young people today really respect politicians, and I want to see whether I can change this attitude."

- "I know that few high school freshmen have thought seriously about their future career, and I want to convince them that it is not too early."

- "I know that many parents object to 'frills' in a high school budget, and I want to show them that many so-called frills are really essential."

- "I know that many boys do not really take girls seriously, and I want them to see that this attitude is biased and unfair."

Remember the following advice when you want your own point of view to be recognized:

(1) Try to sum up your main point in a *single sentence*. Make sure your audience can tell where you take your stand. State your opinion directly and strongly early in your talk. Make sure people can say: "So this is the point!"

(2) Follow a *simple overall scheme*. Work out a rough outline with three (or at the most four) major stages. Present three or four major reasons for thinking the way you do. Make sure your audience does not get lost trying to follow you through too many minor miscellaneous points.

(3) Take time to give at least one or two detailed *real-life examples*. Show the audience what you learned from firsthand experience, or how things would work in everyday practice. Make sure that after your presentation the audience cannot say: "That's a beautiful theory—but it just doesn't work that way in real life."

Preparing a Brief Talk

EXERCISE 1

The following topics will give you a chance to go on record with your own personal point of view.

Show why you like (or dislike) the way representatives of one of the following groups are shown in current television programs:

1. doctors
2. nurses
3. teachers
4. politicians
5. criminals
6. police officers
7. working people
8. blacks
9. Italians (or other nationality)
10. Southerners

EXERCISE 2

Choose one of the following pairs. Show why you would rather be the one than the other.

1. A teacher or a student
2. A farm worker or a factory worker
3. A waiter (waitress) or a cook
4. A sailor or a flier
5. A player or a coach
6. A minor or an adult
7. Someone who gives or who follows orders
8. A salesclerk or a telephone operator
9. An athlete or an artist
10. A painter or a musician

O2c
The Commentary

Tell people what you have to say about current events.

Many news programs start with the straight news. But then they go on to a commentary by an experienced observer whose judgment people respect. We want someone to *evaluate* the news. We want someone to tell us what it all means. A commentator may explain to us how an event fits into the larger picture.

In India, people call a wise person who comments on the passing scene a pundit. Everyone has seen our own pundits on television, giving their opinions on current events. How well would you do if you could be "pundit for a day"?

Oral Language

EXERCISE 1

Read the following account of what happened to a speaker who gave a talk in a small town. Think about it. Then be the commentator. First, tell the story of what happened in your own words. Then explain to your listeners what the story shows. What *does* it show—about newspapers, about small towns, about race relations in this country? Your class may arrange to have *different* pundits give their commentary on what happened. (Your teacher may also want to select one or more more *recent* news stories for commentary by a panel of observers.)

The Biggest Event in Town

Booker T. Washington had gone to some little border state town to make a speech, and it seemed that everybody in the town had turned out to hear him, all the whites and all the blacks. The whites sat on one side of the auditorium and the blacks on the other, as was the local custom. Washington made the best speech that he was capable of, and the audience clapped their hands.

The editor of the local paper was there on a front seat, and he seemed to enjoy the speech more than anyone else. He clapped harder and laughed harder than the rest. Washington stayed in the little town until the next day because he wanted to see what the editor would say about his speech. His speech and meeting had undoubtedly been the biggest thing in town the day before. Washington naturally expected to find it reported on the first page. The little paper had only four pages. He found nothing on the first page, nothing on the second page, and nothing on the third page. He was just about to give up when he discovered his name in the last column of the last page, with about two inches of space under an advertisement.

On that same day and in that same paper another black man had all of the front page to himself. It seems that when Booker T. Washington entered that town to make a successful speech, another black man entered that town to make an unsuccessful attempt to snatch a white woman's purse. He got the whole front page with his picture, his biography, and his pedigree on it.
—Adapted from *The Book of Negro Folklore*

EXERCISE 2

Most of the commentary we read in newspapers and in current events magazines is concerned with the big dramatic events of the day. But sometimes a minor news item, buried

The Interview

somewhere on the back pages, also makes us think. What would you say if you had a minute or two to comment on one of the following:

1. In 1937, 66 percent of those polled said that they would *not* vote for a qualified woman for President. Thirty-five years later, the same percentage of those polled said that they *would* vote for a qualified woman for President. What do you think these figures mean? What happened in those thirty-five years?

2. In one twelve-month period, a Chicago woman received a grand total of 171 letters that her credit card company's computer churned out. Each threatened her with legal action if she didn't pay $0.00 immediately. What does this incident show about human beings and machines?

3. The Coast Guard, overseer of the Merchant Marine under the Treasury Department, at one time had on record the names of 250,000 sailors. At that time the Coast Guard said there were just over 600 vessels sailing under the U.S. flag. Modern ships require a crew of about 35. That left one opening for every 10 sailors. Shippers say the tramp steamer, the vessel that bounced from port to port in search of profitable cargo, has all but vanished from the ocean.

4. "The Eternal Monument" was an invention of Frank Wells of Cleveland. His tombstone device would feature organ music and movies of the deceased, powered by solar batteries and bullet-proof to guard against vandalism. "It adds a whole new dimension to going to the cemetery," Wells said of the $5000 device.

Learn how to listen and how to get others to talk.

O3
THE INTERVIEW

A good speaker knows how to listen as well as talk. Effective communication is a two-way street. One good way to study and practice effective two-way communication is to conduct interviews. Interviewers learn how to ask questions. They learn how to listen. They learn how to adjust and improvise in order to keep things going in the right direction.

What really makes people talk? What subjects are close to their hearts? What tends to make them suspicious, and what makes them "open up"?

Try one or more of the following questions to get people to talk. Take notes of what they say. (You may want to experi-

Oral Language

ment with recording some of your interviews, using a tape recorder.) Try to put your subjects at ease so that they will respond spontaneously to your questions.

(1) "What was the scariest moment of your life?" Here is a sample response from a tightrope artist talking about a stunt performance on high voltage wires:

> This last accident had nothing to do with the high wire. I was working on the high wire. My daughter's husband, who was very ambitious, wanted to help me; he wanted to climb up that pole. Unfortunately, he touched one of the high-tension clamps. There was only one wire clamp—about two feet away from the pole—that was not insulated and he touched it. I saw it with my own eyes. I was up there. My daughter saw her husband falling; she screamed to me, "Daddy." I thought that the whole thing was electric and we would all get killed. I didn't know how to get off. I was standing about 70 feet up in the air and everybody said, "Don't come to the pole, don't touch the pole. You'll be electrocuted." So we shut all the lights off and I had to go down that pole in the dark to save myself.

(2) "How did you get to be what you are now?" "What events in your early life influenced your choice of career?" These questions give people a chance to "tell their story." Here is part of an interview with Frank Gallo, an American sculptor. The interviewer had asked: "How did you decide to become a sculptor?"

> We lived between a factory and an art museum on Lincoln Avenue in Toledo. At one end of the block was a die-casting factory, and at the other end was the Toledo Museum. I used to play around the factory and on the Museum grounds. When we got hot and sweaty we used to go into the Museum, because it was so nice and cool in there. The first thing you saw when you came into the Museum was a sculpture of Paul Manship. Then there was the Egyptian Room with the great granite, Tutankhamen. It was so awesome that I never looked at the paintings. I'd just go in there and rub my hands over the big statue of Tutankhamen. Then I'd go home and model Egyptian sarcophagi out of dirt in the back yard. My mother still has sticks that I carved figures out of and painted. It seems like I always wanted to be a sculptor. I could have gone either to the factory or to the Museum. I went to the Museum, all my friends went to the factory, and some of them are still working there.—from *The American Artist*

The Interview

03

LANGUAGE IN ACTION

> ### PARDON ME, BUT WE'RE TAKING A SURVEY
>
> People working for public opinion polls are continually feeling the public pulse. They are constantly asking for our opinions on the serious issues of the day, from the performance of the President to what's happening to the dollar. But once in a while, pollsters will also sample public opinion on a more frivolous subject, like the length of skirts.
>
> Present the following not-so-serious questions to a cross section of adults in your community. Give them a chance to talk. Report your findings to the class.
>
> 1. Should high school students drive their own cars to school?
> 2. Do you prefer skirts or pants for girl students?
> 3. How long is *too* long for a boy's haircut?
> 4. Are chaperones out of date?
> 5. What is the one single thing that tends to annoy you most about today's younger generation?

(3) "What is it like to do what you do?" For instance, what is it like to be a used-car dealer, or the manager of a service station? Here is a report on a sample response to such a question:

> Jack does not often have much trouble with an automobile, and more likely it is a customer who will give him pain. He says that, as a rule, the only *kind* of people who get to him are members of what he calls the intelligentsia, and that this is because they stomp in, demand their rights, and all the time never know the difference between a warranty on a car and a guarantee. He says, however, that these are almost always people from outside Delhi. He also says that he tries to accommodate the professors and administrators from Delhi Tech, which is a two-year agricultural and technical college, even when they are not driving Chrysler products, but that once or twice he has had a problem there, too. There was a lady from Delhi Tech, he says, who drove an old heap not Chrysler's, and who was forever coming in and demanding that the mechanics stop whatever they were doing, and fix her car immediately. Jack says that he helped her a few times, but that she became so wearisome that he asked her to take her business someplace else. In fact, he says, he asked her to do this several times. Then, one busy afternoon, he says, she called, saying that she was on the way to Kansas, or some-

Oral Language

where, and that her car had broken down, and would he send someone to help? Jack said that he could not, and she said, The h— you can't, I have been a good and faithful customer, and Jack said, The h— I can, and I have tried to tell you that I do not want you for a customer at all. Well, the lady said, to h— with you, and to h— with Hertz, from whom I have rented this car. Hertz, for crying out loud! The lady was trying to get Jack to bail out Hertz.—John Corry, *"Son of the Catskills"*

(4) "If you could give other people one basic piece of advice, what would you say and why?" Here is a question of this kind, with the answer given by a well-known television actor:

Question: In the course of your relationship, have you developed any rules of behavior for yourself to keep things running smoothly?

Answer: Only one: I try to control my temper. I succeed now more than I did years ago. My advice to anybody is to try to get control early on. It's like a hole in a dike, that temper thing. If you don't patch it up when it happens, it gets bigger and bigger and all kinds of other troubles come flooding in. So you have to stifle yourself.

Write down two or three questions that *you* would like to ask people. Discuss with your classmates what kind of reactions your questions would be likely to trigger.

EXERCISE 1

How well do you know the people who do much of the *day-to-day work* in your community? Interview one of them. Ask the person to describe a typical task. Ask about a typical problem. You may want to ask how the person got into this type of work. For instance, you may want to interview one of the following people:

1. Someone working in a small independent store or other small local business.
2. Someone working in a nursery school, old-age club, day-care center, or the like.
3. A mechanic working in a local gas station or garage.
4. A police officer, firefighter, or guard.
5. Someone working in a restaurant or fast-food place.

Take notes. Be prepared to report on the results of your interview.

The Brief Talk

EXERCISE 2

Do you know anyone in your community whose background is different from that of most of the other people there? Find someone with a *different background,* or from a different part of the country, or from a different part of the world. Interview the person about memories of a different kind of place or different kind of life.

Be prepared to report the results of your interview to your classmates.

EXERCISE 3

Interview one of the *old-timers* in your community or in your family about life in earlier times. What kinds of things do they like to talk about? How much do they remember?

FOR FURTHER STUDY

ACTING THINGS OUT

Good speakers are often good mimics. They can imitate the way other people talk. They know how to play different roles. They know how to create different moods—serious or funny, solemn or angry. The following activities give you a chance to broaden your *range* as a speaker. They ask you to play different roles and to use different resources.

ACTIVITY 1

When a person just goes on and on without stopping to listen to other people, the result is a **monologue.** Read the following student-written monologue. A person who is exceptionally innocent or naïve is talking in the manner of Mark Twain's Huckleberry Finn. Huck encountered many things that were new or mysterious to him, but he wouldn't let on. Read the monologue so that it would sound like this kind of person. Can you improvise a similar monologue by some wide-eyed innocent witnessing things that are new or strange?

Huck Finn's Crazy Box

"Goodness sakes," I says, "Why in the world would a person want to watch a box with a glass front on it for?"

Of course the poor clerk didn't rightly want to answer me none. He jest says to me sort of unbelieving-like, "Son,

Oral Language

you've been asking a lot of questions. You mean to tell me you've never seen a TV before?"

Not want'n to say I hadn't, I thought me up an answer and I says, "Why shore, I've seen one before but I just didn't never bother to wind the thing up, that's all!"

He jest sorta looks at me, like he knows I'm a lie'n and then he says to me, "If you want you can watch one of our TV's on display, just pull up a chair and make yourself at home."

So I done as that man said and pretty soon I'm tired of watching the thing and ready to leave. About this time an ol' clerk comes around a laughing his head off and he say to me, "Let me do you a favor." And with that he goes over and pushes a knob and then there's these little people behind the glass. Then I hears this laugh'n and this talk'n so I turned around and all these people were gawk'n and talk'n about how I was so dumb.

Boy, I was embarrassed somethin' bad. Jest then a lady comes on behind the glass and starts telling me that what I need is this spray stuff called deodorant but that it was a secret. It would keep me from sweat'n she says. She said that one squirt under each arm keeps her good all day long. Boy, I wished I had some of the stuff so that the old widder could see me being good for once. I was about to ask the honest looking lady where I could get the secret stuff she was talking about when this man impolitely jumps in behind the glass and asks me how I spell relief. Well, I was about to tell him when this other man butts in and says, "I spell it R-O-L-A-I-D-S." Many other people also said that they spelled it the same way. If teacher would a been there, she would a died for anybody that's had any learning knows it's spelled R-E-L-E-A-F.

Nobody would never answer any of my questions when I asked them. They was mad and just pretended not to hear me. I finally figured out why. You see, watching TV is like watching a play; you have to be in your Sunday's best. So naturally they was hurt that I watched in my old fishin' clothes. Well, I didn't like none of their shows anyhow and I didn't like their trying to sell me stuff all the time.—from *Young Kansas Writers*

ACTIVITY 2

What do people say around the dinner table in an ordinary family? With some of your classmates, stage a dinner table conversation. Act out the following sample as a model and for practice:

The Brief Talk

Friday came at last. I put on my only suit, slicked my hair down with liquid vaseline, and doused myself with Dulce Nombre's perfume.

"Amado's going to serenade that pretty girl everyone calls La Americana," my sister Consuelo told my mother and uncle when I sat down to eat. "Then he's going to take her to the movies."

This made my uncle laugh and my mother scowl.

"Qué pantalones tiene (what nerve that boy's got)," my uncle said, "to serenade a twenty-year-old woman."

"La Americana," my mother said derisively. "That one's Mexican as pulque cured with celery."

They made me so nervous I forgot to take off my cap when I sat down to eat.

"Amado, take off your cap," my mother said. "You're not in La Lagunilla Market."

My uncle frowned. "All this boy thinks about is kissing girls," he said gruffly.

"But my boy's never kissed one," my mother said proudly.

My sister Consuelo laughed. "That's because they won't let him," she said.—Amado Muro, "Cecilia Rosas"

ACTIVITY 3

In the following poem, the poet has allowed her imagination to run wild. The lawn in front of the house has been turned into a battlefield. The yellow stars of the dandelions growing in the grass are the fiery bursts of exploding shells. The next day, the wisps blown by the wind from the old flowers are like smoke drifting across the battlefield. Can you use your voice to do the different sound effects in this poem? (You may want to distribute different parts in this poem for a choral reading.)

Dandelions

under cover of night and rain
the troops took over.
waking to total war in beleaguered houses
over breakfast we faced the batteries
marshalled by wall and stone, deployed
with a master strategy no one had suspected
and now all
firing

pow

Oral Language

all day, all yesterday
and all today
the barrage continued
deafening sight.
reeling now, eyes ringing from noise, from walking
gingerly over the mined lawns
exploded at every second
rocked back by the starshellfire
concussion of gold on green
bringing battle-fatigue
pow by lionface firefur pow by
goldburst shellshock pow by
whoosh   splat   splinteryellow   pow   by
pow   by   pow
tomorrow smoke drifts up
from the wrecked battalions,
all the ammunition, firegold fury, gone.
smoke
drifts
thistle-blown
over the war-zone, only

here and there, in the shade by the
peartree
pow   in the crack by the
curbstone   pow   and back of the
ashcan, lonely
guerrilla snipers, hoarding
their fire shrewdly
never

pow

surrender

—Deborah Austin

ACTIVITY 4

Some people are always stuck in one particular role —they always play the same part. How versatile are *you*?

Do a brief series in which you recreate in turn *three* different people talking about the same event. For instance, you might be, in turn, a player, a coach, and a spectator talking about a game. Or you might be, in turn, Columbus, a sailor, and an Indian at the first landing in the New World.

The Brief Talk

ACTIVITY 5

Do you ever find that "you don't quite know what to say"? Later, thinking about what happened, you may say to yourself: "This is what I *should* have said!" For each of the following, can you think of three or four different things you could say *in return?* (Have a friend "feed" you the original statement, so that you can act out some of your "brilliant answers.")

- "Sorry, you came on the wrong day. The party is not this Friday but *next* Friday."
- "Sorry, but this club is only for (boys) (students over sixteen) (Americans of European ancestry) (people with a record of athletic achievement) (members of our church)."
- "Sorry, but we cannot allow families with pets in this building."
- "Sorry, but our new delivery boy dropped the box with your priceless vase in it."
- "Sorry, your family will not get the check this month. Your mother filled in the last part of the form incorrectly."
- "Sorry, _____" (fill in a statement of your own choice).

Chapter 7

Resources
The Library, Study Skills, Taking Tests

R1 Using the Library
    a Finding Library Materials
    b Using the Card Catalogue
    c Finding Magazine Articles
    d Using Reference Materials

R2 Improving Study Skills

R3 Taking Tests
    a Vocabulary Tests
    b Tests of Written English

R1
USING THE LIBRARY

Learn how to use a library.

Libraries are storehouses of wisdom, of information, and of entertainment. In a well-stocked library, all the great ideas of the past are at your fingertips. There is also practically no question to which you cannot find an answer. You can sit down and read about last night's ball game or find out what is playing at the neighborhood movie house. You can entertain yourself by reading a good book.

R1a
Finding Library Materials

Learn the layout of your library.

Even very small school and public libraries have thousands of books. Obviously, these books have to be stored according to some system, or it would be impossible to find a book you wanted. You should know the system and the layout of your library. That way you will be able to use it effectively and efficiently.

Probably the first thing you will see as you enter your library is the **circulation desk.** This is where you sign out books and other materials and where you return them. It is also a good place to ask questions about the library, for behind the circulation desk, you will usually find a librarian or a library aide.

Also near the entrance, usually, is the **card catalogue.** It is a cabinet full of small drawers. In these drawers are cards that tell the location of the books. (See **R1b** for further information on the card catalogue.) In the same or in a separate place, you may find catalogues of the magazines, records, and other materials the library has.

The area of the library where the books are shelved is called the **stacks.** Here, it is especially important to learn the system of your library. Usually, the books and other materials are shelved in several main divisions:

(1) *Fiction* (book-length stories) is usually kept apart from other books. The fiction collection will be arranged alphabetically by the last name of the author. If there are more books than one by the same author, they will be arranged alphabetically by their titles.

Within the fiction category, there are often separate shelves for collections of short stories. These are arranged also by the author's last name. Often, however, we find a collection of short stories by a variety of authors. In such a case, the book will be alphabetized by the last name of the *editor. Everything That Rises Must Converge,* for example, is a book of short stories, all of which were written by Flannery O'Connor. You would find it under her last name. *Great Modern Short Stories,* however, contains twelve stories, each written by a different author. You would find this collection under the last name of its editor, Bennett A. Cerf.

(2) *Biographies of individuals* are usually separately shelved. They, too, are in alphabetical order, but not according to the author's last name. They are given a letter, *B* (for "biography"), or the number 92. Then they are alphabetized according to the last name of the *subject* of the biography. If, for example, you want to read Gamaliel Bradford's biography of Robert E. Lee, you would look under Lee, Robert E. You would not find it under Bradford's name.

(3) Another section of the library is usually set aside for *reference books.* These include various types of almanacs, biographical reference books (such as *Who's Who*), encyclopedias, and the like. (See **R1d** for further discussion of reference books.) Because they are used so frequently, reference books ordinarily do not circulate.

(4) *Nonfiction,* or factual, books that may be taken out are grouped according to their subjects. Your library probably uses the **Dewey decimal system** for this purpose. This system was invented by the American librarian Melvil Dewey. He grouped nonfiction into ten major categories and gave a number to each, as follows:

000–099	general reference works
100–199	philosophy, psychology, ethics
200–299	religion, mythology
300–399	social sciences
400–499	language
500–599	science
600–699	technology (applied science)
700–799	the arts, recreation, sports
800–899	literature
900–999	history, geography

Within these broad divisions, there is further coding. For example, literature is 800. American literature runs from 810 to 820. American poetry is 811. If you were looking for a book of poems by the American poet, Robert Frost, you would find it under 811, followed by an *F* (for Frost's last name). After the main number, you will sometimes find decimal points. Books about American poetry in general, for example, are numbered 811.09.

Not all libraries use the Dewey decimal system. Some use the **Library of Congress system.** This divides books into categories according to the letters of the alphabet. A book on education, for example, would be found under the letter *L*. Since most secondary school libraries use the Dewey system, we will not discuss the Library of Congress system further here. You may find the latter in use in your local college library, however.

(5) In addition to books, your library probably contains *magazines, newspapers, and pamphlets.* It may also have a record collection and perhaps other nonprint materials, such as filmstrips, microfilm, and the like.

Magazines are in the **periodical section.** Current issues of magazines are usually on display. They are normally classified alphabetically according to the name of the magazine. Back issues of magazines may be stored near the current issues, or they may be elsewhere in the library. Current issues of newspapers are usually on a wooden rack. Depending on the size and resources of the library, back issues of newspapers may be kept on microfilm.

Pamphlets and papers that cannot be put on shelves are stored in what is known as the **vertical file.** This will usually be a metal filing cabinet. Articles on the same topic are put into manila folders and labeled. These folders are then alphabetized and filed appropriately. Always check the vertical file on your subject before you do a research paper. You will find that there are often current articles of interest on your topic filed here.

EXERCISE 1

According to the directions your teacher gives you, go to your school library or to a library in your neighborhood. Draw a floor plan of that library, showing its overall layout and the specific location of each important section. In your floor plan, be sure to label each of the items listed on the following pages. (The list appears below the sample map.)

Using the Library

Here is a sample map:

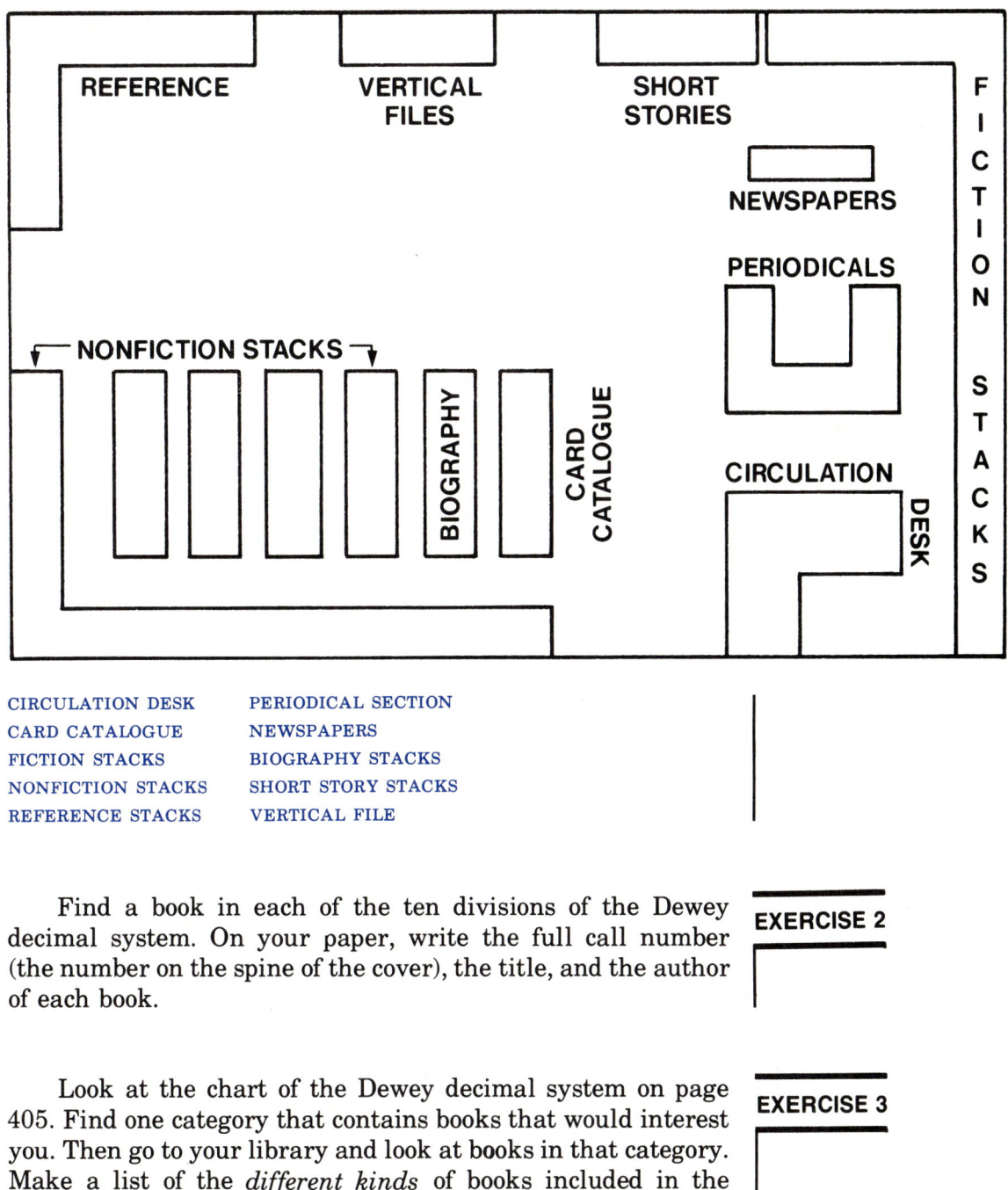

CIRCULATION DESK
CARD CATALOGUE
FICTION STACKS
NONFICTION STACKS
REFERENCE STACKS

PERIODICAL SECTION
NEWSPAPERS
BIOGRAPHY STACKS
SHORT STORY STACKS
VERTICAL FILE

EXERCISE 2

Find a book in each of the ten divisions of the Dewey decimal system. On your paper, write the full call number (the number on the spine of the cover), the title, and the author of each book.

EXERCISE 3

Look at the chart of the Dewey decimal system on page 405. Find one category that contains books that would interest you. Then go to your library and look at books in that category. Make a list of the *different kinds* of books included in the category.

Resources

EXERCISE 4

On your paper arrange the following books of fiction in the order in which you would find them on the library shelves. (When you are alphabetizing by title, do not use *a, an,* or *the* when they are the first word in a title.)

1. William Saroyan, *The Human Comedy*
2. James Thurber, *My Life and Hard Times*
3. Jack London, *The Sea Wolf*
4. Jack London, *Martin Eden*
5. Willa Cather, *O Pioneers!*
6. Richard Wright, *Native Son*
7. Edna Ferber, *So Big*
8. Howard Fast, *April Morning*
9. William Hoffman, *The Dark Mountains*
10. Willa Cather, *Death Comes for the Archbishop*
11. Richard Wright, *The Outsider*
12. Margaret Weymouth Jackson, *First Fiddle*
13. Pearl Buck, *The Good Earth*
14. Anne Tyler, *A Slipping Down Life*
15. Jack London, *The Call of the Wild*
16. Margaret Weymouth Jackson, *Elizabeth's Tower*
17. Willa Cather, *My Ántonia*
18. Anne Tyler, *Celestial Navigation*
19. Edna Ferber, *Show Boat*
20. Jack London, *White Fang*

R1b
Using the Card Catalogue

Learn how to use the card catalogue.

The **card catalogue** is a cabinet containing small drawers. Each drawer contains 3 x 5 cards, arranged alphabetically. Their purpose is to help you find the location of nonfiction books in the library. On the front of each drawer are letters which tell you what part of the alphabet that drawer contains. A drawer marked *R-SO,* for example, would contain all cards beginning with *R*. It would also contain all *S* cards up through *SO*. Thus you would find "Southey" in that drawer, but you would not find "Sports."

There are four basic types of cards found in the card catalogue. These are title cards, author cards, subject cards, and "see"/"see also" cards.

(1) *Title cards.* Often when you go to a library, you will know the title of the book you want. In that case you look in the card catalogue for the first word of the title. Suppose, for

Using the Library

example, that you want to take out *The Complete Book of Running*. You look in the file drawer that would contain the word "Complete." (The drawer might have something like *CO-DE* on its front.) If there are other books with "complete" as the first word in their titles, you would then go to "book," and so on. If the library has the book, you will find a title card. It will look like this:

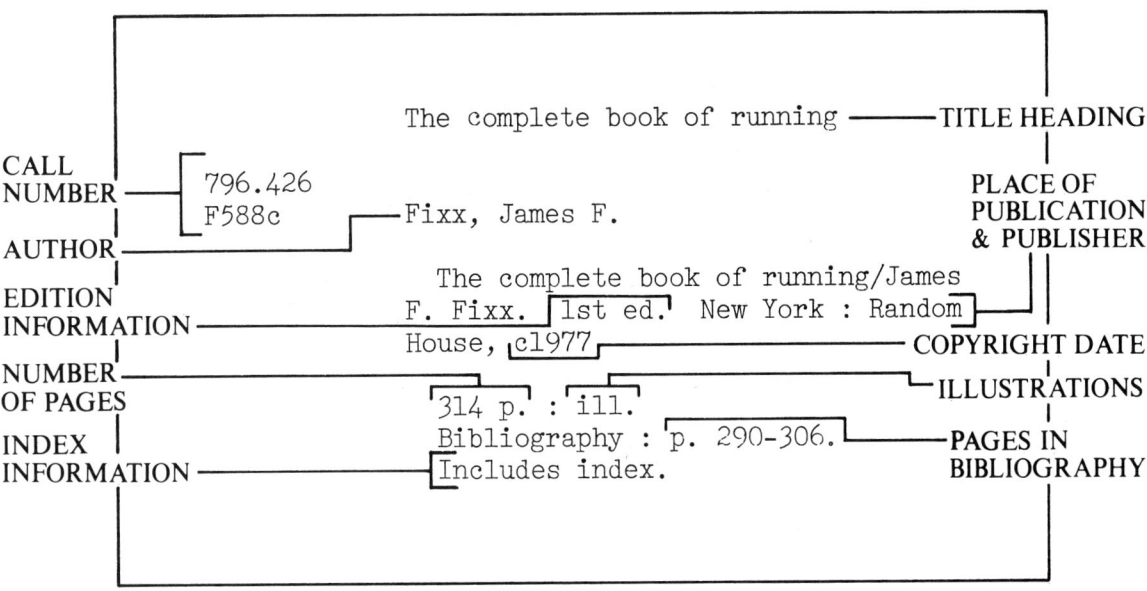

Notice the **call number** in the upper left-hand corner of the card. This tells you that the book is in the 700 section of the nonfiction collection. The other information on the card may not interest you in this particular case. But on other occasions, you may want to know such things as how recently the book was published and whether or not it has a bibliography and index. The name of the publisher will help you if you wish to order the book by mail.

(2) *Author cards*. You may have forgotten the title of a book you want but remembered the name of its author. Or you may have read a book by an author and wish to read more by the same author. In both these cases, you may look for an author card. You will find it under the author's last name. Under an author's name, you will find all books written by

her or him. You will also find all books written *about* him or her available in that library. They will be arranged in alphabetical order, by title. An author card looks exactly like a title card, except that the author's name instead of the title heading will appear at the top of the card.

(3) *Subject cards*. If you want to learn something about a subject but do not know the name of a book or an author, you may look for a subject card. If you are doing a report on a subject, you may also go to subject cards. Subject cards may be a little more difficult to find than title and author cards, for you need to find the correct key word. Suppose, for example, that you want information on jogging. You may not find a subject card labeled "jogging." But if you look under the subject "running," you will find a card, and you can probably find a book that will help you. The top line on subject cards contains the subject, usually in capital letters. (**Note:** Some catalogue cards may contain information about what is in the book.)

(4) *"See" and "see also" cards*. A "see" card directs you to another part of the card file. For example, if you were to look up "Pete Pomeroy" in the card catalogue of your library, you may find a card that looks like this:

```
Pomeroy, Pete (PSEUD.), see

Roth, Arthur J.
```

Using the Library

This card tells you that "Pete Pomeroy" is a pseudonym (pen name) for Arthur J. Roth. You would then look for information about this author under his real name.

"See also" cards direct you to additional information. Suppose you wanted some information about fishes. You could probably find a good deal if you looked at the subject cards headed "fishes." But in front of those cards, you might find a "see also" card like the following:

```
FISHES, see also

        Aquariums
        Tropical fishes
           (also names of fishes, e.g., Salmon)
```

This card tells you that you may find additional information about fishes after the subject cards labeled "Aquariums" and "Tropical fishes." Still further information might be found under the names of specific fishes.

EXERCISE 1

Look in your library card catalogue for author cards for each of the writers below. If you find a card, write the title of one of his or her books. Also write the call number of the book. Write these on your paper next to the name of the author. If you find no card, write "none" after the name of the writer.

1. Mari Sandoz
2. A. Conan Doyle
3. Margaret Walker
4. Jesse Stuart
5. Mario Pei
6. Paul Gallico
7. Richard E. Byrd
8. Helen Keller
9. Loren Eiseley
10. Margaret Craven

Resources

EXERCISE 2

Look in your library card catalogue for title cards for each of the books below. If they are in the catalogue, write the full name of the author (or authors) and the call number of the book. Write these on your paper next to the name of the book. If the book is not in your library, write "no" next to the name of the book.

1. *The Pigman*
2. *The Chocolate War*
3. *The Diary of a Young Girl*
4. *Mythology*
5. *The Guns of August*
6. *Sewing the Easy Way*
7. *The Complete Book of Skin and Scuba Diving*
8. *How to Play Better Tennis*
9. *Of Mice and Men*
10. *Nobody Knows My Name*

EXERCISE 3

Look at the subject cards in your library to find a book on each of the following subjects. If you find one, write its title, author, call number, and copyright date.

1. Field hockey
2. Cooking
3. The stock market
4. Stamp collecting
5. Juvenile delinquency
6. Extrasensory perception
7. Nuclear energy
8. Chess
9. Witchcraft
10. Farming

EXERCISE 4

Spend ten minutes browsing through the card catalogue looking at the kinds of information on "see" and "see also" cards. Copy all the information on one of each type of card and bring what you have written to class. Compare your discoveries with those of your classmates.

EXERCISE 5

Think of a topic that interests you. Look in the card catalogue for the subject cards under that topic. (Remember that you may have to look a little to find the right key word.) Count the number of cards under that topic and write it down. Then pick what seems to you to be the most interesting book that you have not read. Write on your paper its call number, title, author, date of publication, and any other information you consider important.

R1c

Using the Library

Use the *Readers' Guide* to find articles in magazines.

**R1c
Finding Magazine Articles**

The card catalogue for magazines is the *Readers' Guide to Periodical Literature,* known as the *Readers' Guide,* for short. This reference work indexes all articles, stories, and poems that have appeared in close to 200 magazines. It is published twice a month, except in February, July, and August—when it is published once a month. There is a bound cumulative volume published each year. To find out which magazines are indexed, look at the list in the front of each issue of the *Guide*.

The *Readers' Guide* has an author and a subject index (combined, not separate). There is no title index, except for stories. Below is a sample author index:

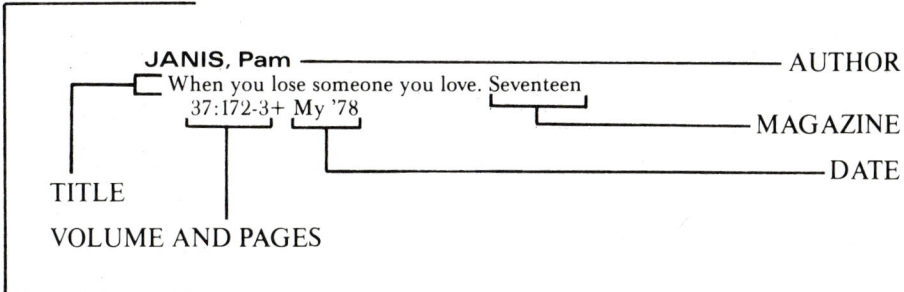

The plus symbol after the page numbers means that the article continues on later pages of the same issue. "My" is an abbreviation for May. The magazine name in this case is not abbreviated, but the names of many other magazines are abbreviated. At the front of the *Guide,* you can find a list of the abbreviations used.

Here is an example of a subject entry in the *Readers' Guide:*

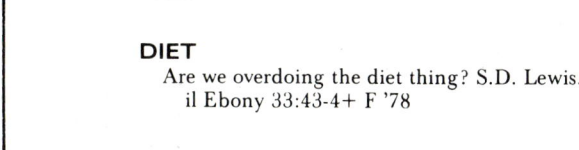

Notice that the subject is printed in capital letters—rather than the author's last name. Then come the title and the author. The abbreviation "il" tells that the article is illustrated.

Resources

Subject entries in the *Guide* often contain "see also" notes. Subheadings and expanded headings are also common. Here, for example, are all the headings under "HOUSES" in one of the August issues of the *Readers' Guide:*

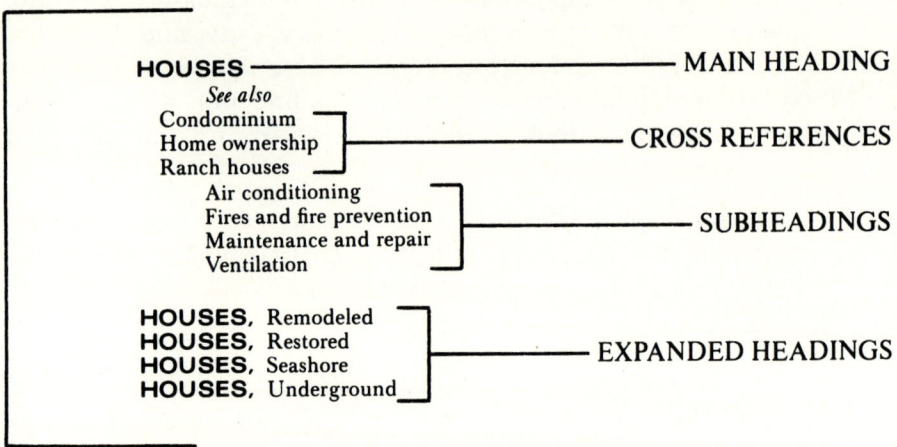

The advantage of such multiple headings is that they help the reader to find exactly what he or she wants.

At the back of the *Readers' Guide,* there is a book review section. This could be very useful to you if you wanted to know what others thought of a book you were considering reading or purchasing. Reviews are indexed by the name of the author of the book, followed by the book title. Here is an example:

> **Tyler, A.** Earthly possessions
> Ms 6:35-6 Ag '77. K. Bouton
> New Repub 176:35-6 My 28 '77. N. Delbanco
> New Yorker 53:130+ Je 6 '77. J. Updike
> Newsweek 89:75 My 2 '77. M. Jefferson

The reviews are all of Anne Tyler's novel, *Earthly Possessions.* The name of the magazine is printed first, followed by the volume number and the pages on which the review appears. Then come the month and the day—if the magazine appears more than once a month. The last entry is the reviewer's name.

Using the Library

EXERCISE 1

Consult the lists at the front of the *Readers' Guide*. On your paper, write the meaning of each abbreviation given below. Note that abbreviations for the names of magazines appear in a different table from the other abbreviations given in the *Guide*.

1. sec
2. tr
3. D
4. q
5. w
6. m
7. bi-w
8. jt auth
9. rev
10. Car & Dr
11. Bus W
12. Good H
13. Sci Am
14. Chr Cent
15. Pop Mech

EXERCISE 2

Consult the list of periodicals indexed in the *Readers' Guide*. Write *yes* next to the number of any magazine that is indexed in the *Guide*. Write *no* next to the number of any magazine that is not indexed.

1. *Motor Trend*
2. *Sports Illustrated*
3. *Language*
4. *Smithsonian*
5. *Stereo Review*
6. *Travel*
7. *Handyman*
8. *True Confessions*
9. *American History*
10. *Changing Times*
11. *Ladies Home Journal*
12. *Consumer Reports*
13. *Hudson Review*
14. *Hot Rod*
15. *High Fidelity*
16. *English Journal*
17. *Reader's Digest*
18. *Time*
19. *Circus*
20. *New Times*

EXERCISE 3

Pick a personality or a topic that interests you. Then look through several volumes of the *Readers' Guide* for articles on that person or topic. Select five articles that you would like to read. List those articles, giving complete information for each one. Be prepared to tell the class the title, author, magazine, date, and page numbers of each article. In other words, be sure you completely understand each entry.

R1d Using Reference Materials

Explore the reference resources of your library.

What is the world record for the 1500-meter run? Where is the Great Sand Dunes National Monument? How does one repair a leaky faucet? What chemicals are needed to develop film? What is the population of Zaire and where is it? Who wrote, "Success is counted sweetest by those who ne'er succeed"? You can find the answers to these and hundreds of thousands of other questions in the reference section of your library. Discover what kinds of books are there. Learn when and how to use them.

Resources

(1) *Almanacs.* An **almanac** is an annual publication containing information on current events. It also contains much statistical information, such as population figures, election results, average temperatures in major cities, and the like. Facts and figures about sports are also included, as are obituaries for the year. Probably the best-known almanacs are the *World Almanac and Book of Facts* and the *Information Please* almanac. Many newspapers also publish paperback almanacs each year. These are relatively inexpensive. An almanac is probably the best place to go if you are looking for a quick answer to a specific question.

(2) *Encyclopedias.* **Encyclopedias** consist of articles written on almost any subject you can name. The articles are typically written by experts in the field and therefore are generally authoritative. Keep in mind, however, that an encyclopedia article *surveys* a field. You would find even more detailed information in a book on the subject. For example, an encyclopedia might give you an excellent overview if you wanted to learn something about Shakespeare and his plays. But it would not give you the detail that a biography of Shakespeare would, nor would it give you very much information about any specific play.

The most widely used multivolume encyclopedias are the *Encyclopaedia Britannica,* the *Encyclopedia Americana, Collier's Encyclopedia,* and the *World Book Encyclopedia.* All of these have an index in their last volume. All also publish an **annual supplement,** which gives the most recent events and latest developments in various subject fields.

If you are doing a report on a subject, an encyclopedia is a good starting point. It will give you a bird's-eye view, and it may lead you to further information. Consider also using some of the more specialized encyclopedias you may find in your library. Here is a brief list of some of these:

Encyclopedia of World Art
Encyclopedia of Music
Scribner Music Library
McGraw-Hill Encyclopedia of Science and Technology
The Harper Encyclopedia of Science
Encyclopedia of the Social Sciences
The Book of Popular Science
Dictionary of American History
Worldmark Encyclopedia of the Nations
Lands and Peoples

(3) *Biographical Reference Books.* These books are devoted to the lives of well-known persons. Of course you can find some biographies in encyclopedias, but biographical reference books include more detail. They definitely cover a wider range of persons than an encyclopedia can. Generally, biographical reference books give factual details about a person—when and where born, where educated, and the like. They may also tell you what the person's contribution has been. They do not, however, try to judge that contribution; nor do they explain the person's character. For details of these sorts, you should go to individual biographies. Some useful biographical reference books are listed below:

> *Dictionary of American Biography*
> *Who's Who in America*
> *Who Was Who in America*
> *Who's Who of American Women*
> *Concise Dictionary of National Biography*
> *Current Biography*
> *The Junior Book of Authors*
> *Contemporary Authors*
> *Twentieth Century Authors*
> *American Men and Women of Science*
> *Grove's Dictionary of Music and Musicians*
> *World Biography*

(4) *Reference Books on Literature.* Books like those listed below give a wide range of useful information about literature and quotations from literature.

- General books on literature:

    The Concise Encyclopedia of Modern World Literature
    Reader's Encyclopedia of American Literature
    Cassell's Encyclopedia of World Literature

- Books of quotations:

    Home Book of Quotations—Arranged by subject
    Bartlett's Familiar Quotations—Arranged chronologically; alphabetically by key word

- Indexes (titles indicate contents):

    Books in Print—Three volumes: author, title, and subject
    Paperback Books in Print
    Cumulative Book Index
    Book Review Digest

Resources

(5) *Atlases.* Atlases contain maps and useful information about the cities and countries of the world. You may also find in your library some specialized atlases, such as *Hammond's Pictorial Travel Atlas of Scenic America.* This is an excellent book to consult if you are planning a vacation in the continental United States. The following are some good world atlases:

The Encyclopaedia Britannica Atlas
Goode's World Atlas
Hammond's Ambassador World Atlas
National Geographic Atlas of the World
Rand McNally Cosmopolitan World Atlas

EXERCISE 1 Explore the reference section of your school library. From each of the five categories given above, write the title of one listed book that your library has. Also write the title of one book in each category that your library has but that we have *not* listed.

EXERCISE 2 Number your paper from 1 to 10. After the number of each item below, write the letter that tells in which major type of reference book you would find the information, according to the following key:

    A. An almanac
    B. An encyclopedia
    C. A biographical reference book
    D. A reference book on literature (note that there are several types of these)
    E. An atlas

1. Specific figures giving the results of the most recent presidential election in the United States
2. A map of Japan
3. An authoritative article on scuba diving
4. A quotation on the topic "love"
5. The distance between Berlin and Moscow
6. A book review
7. The name of the person who said, "Those who cannot remember the past are condemned to repeat it."
8. The home address of a prominent writer
9. The origin and development of the game of chess
10. The titles of the books written by John Steinbeck

Improving Study Skills

UNIT REVIEW

Number your paper from 1 to 20. Find the definition in the right-hand column that matches each item in the left-hand column. Write the letter of that item on your paper next to the appropriate number.

1. a biographical reference book
2. Dewey decimal system
3. card catalogue
4. author card
5. an encyclopedia
6. The *Readers' Guide*
7. the stacks
8. "see also" card
9. "see" card
10. an almanac
11. Library of Congress system
12. vertical file
13. periodical section
14. subject card
15. subheading
16. subject index
17. call number
18. copyright date
19. an atlas
20. circulation desk

a. A cabinet containing 3 x 5 index cards
b. A card whose top entry lists a topic
c. The shelves where books are kept
d. A book or set of books containing authoritative information on a variety of subjects
e. An annual book containing facts and other statistical data
f. An alphabetized listing by topic
g. Place where magazines are kept
h. Place where pamphlets are kept
i. A card directing you to additional information
j. A card whose top entry lists a person's name
k. A method for classifying books by numbers
l. A method for classifying books by letters of the alphabet
m. Place where books are signed out
n. Year in which a book was published
o. A book containing data on well-known persons
p. A smaller division of a general one
q. A book indexing articles, etc., that have appeared in magazines
r. A card directing you to another part of the card file
s. A book containing maps
t. A series of numbers appearing on a file card, to help you find a book
u. A card whose top entry lists a title

R2 IMPROVING STUDY SKILLS

Build good study habits.

Good study habits and techniques are critical to success in school. They may also make the difference between moving ahead and staying in the same job later in life. Build good study habits now. Consider the following tips to help you improve your study habits:

Resources

- *Study in a quiet place.* It is true that some persons like a little noise around them. Some music in the background may not distract you. But give yourself a chance. You are *not* likely to study efficiently in front of a television set. If there is no quiet place at home, try to do most of your studying in a school or local library.

- *Study in the same place.* People—like writers—who spend a great deal of time on concentrated tasks often advise that it is best to work always in the same place. They do little or nothing else in that place. It is as if there were a sign—WORK ONLY. Perhaps you can find a spot in your home or room that you can reserve for study. Each time you are there, you will know it is study time.

- *Keep all necessary materials in that place.* Prolonged concentration is not easy for most of us. We will jump at almost any excuse for interrupting ourselves. If you keep pencils, pens, paper, a sharpener, books, and whatever else you may need for studying in your study place, you will have fewer excuses for interrupting your work.

- *Keep an orderly notebook.* You may prefer a separate notebook for each subject. Or you may devote a section of a larger notebook to each subject. Choose good-sized notebooks. Very small notebooks are all right for jotting down assignments, but they are not good for notes.

- *Use some abbreviations in taking notes.* Speed may be important, especially in taking lecture notes. When the same word or phrase comes up over and over, abbreviate it. For example, you could write AH instead of "American history" or "S" for "science" or "scientists." Use a plus sign instead of "and" and "w/o" for "without." Make up your own abbreviations for common words. List them in the front of your notebook so you do not forget them.

- *Read over your class notes from time to time.* There are many advantages to rereading your class notes. Perhaps a note will be unclear to you and you can talk to your teacher about what was said. You can underline or cross out material in your notebook on the basis of later lectures. Best of all, you will have a head start when a test comes. This will be especially advantageous to you if you are not the kind of student who crams well.

• *Budget your study time.* Make a list of what you have to study. Divide up your time appropriately. Be sure to give more time for the more difficult assignments, and do them while you are fresh. Crossing tasks off your list as you complete them will give you a sense of accomplishment.

Make sure that tests show what you know and what you can do.

Tests are an ever-present feature of modern life. The more you know about them, the better you will be able to handle them in a businesslike way. Remember the following general advice:

(1) *Always read instructions or directions carefully.* What exactly are you asked to do? Take time to read and understand the key words in the directions you are given.

(2) *Keep moving.* Do not allow any part or any item on a test to use up too much time. Do not allow yourself to become flustered by something difficult or confusing. Move on—return to the difficult item or the difficult part later if you have the time.

(3) *Use common sense about guessing.* Some tests encourage guessing. If only *right* answers are counted for test results, even wild guessing cannot hurt. If a test states, "Wrong answers will be penalized," wild guessing is not advisable.

(4) *Make some notes before answering essay questions.* Even though you may be under some time pressure, pause to think before you begin to answer an essay question. While you are thinking, jot down a few key ideas. Take a moment to put those ideas in some logical or chronological order. A few minutes spent in thinking are often worth fifteen minutes spent in writing hastily.

(5) *Allow time to proofread essay tests.* A comma where a period should be, a misspelled word, a "their" for a "there"—these may seem to be small things. But little errors like these make the writer appear careless or badly prepared. Take a minute or so before you hand in a test, and correct any errors you may find.

R3
TAKING TESTS

Resources

R3a
Vocabulary Tests

Know the different ways tests measure your knowledge of vocabulary.

Tests of vocabulary are very common. You have probably taken several of them already. They occur in batteries of tests from kindergarten through the graduate schools of universities. They are used in tests that are given to applicants for many different kinds of jobs. In almost all intelligence tests, the verbal part of the test measures vocabulary.

The most common tests that are used by colleges and universities for admission purposes include measures of the applicants' vocabulary. In general, students with the best vocabularies get the best grades in college. (Of course, some students with good vocabularies get poor college grades.)

The *Scholastic Aptitude Test,* which is published by the College Entrance Examination Board, is very widely used by colleges and universities in selecting the freshman class from the group of applicants. This test is commonly called the "S-A-T" and is frequently written as "SAT."

The SAT in recent years has used three kinds of test items to measure vocabulary. These sections are called: Antonyms, Analogies, and Sentence Completion. The verbal part of the SAT also measures reading comprehension. It gives five to seven reading passages, with about five questions for each.

① SYNONYMS

The most common vocabulary tests ask you to find synonyms. For a test word, you select from a number of choices the word that is closest to it in meaning. In each of the following examples, the correct answer to each test item has been circled:

A
1. rejuvenate   a. rejoice   b. connect   (c. make young)   d. identify
2. provisional   (a. temporary)   b. professional   c. careful   d. backward
3. fatigue   a. anger   (b. weariness)   c. introduction   d. judgment

② ANTONYMS

The Antonyms section of the SAT has directions similar to the following:

> DIRECTIONS: In each test item there is a word in capital letters followed by five answer choices. From these five choices select the one whose meaning is **opposite** to the meaning of the word in capital letters.

Try to work these four sample items before reading the discussion that follows them.

B   PLACID
- (1) calm
- (2) dirty
- (3) rancid
- (4) sanitary
- (5) stormy

C   SUBJUGATE
- (1) conquer
- (2) liberate
- (3) predicate
- (4) submerge
- (5) verbalize

D   LACONIC
- (1) clever
- (2) concise
- (3) lackadaisical
- (4) pedantic
- (5) wordy

E   EPILOGUE
- (1) catalogue
- (2) dialogue
- (3) monologue
- (4) prologue
- (5) travelogue

An antonym test makes us look for a word with the *opposite* meaning. Very often the author of antonym items will include a synonym among the answer choices. Notice *calm* in B, *conquer* in C, and *concise* in D. These are all synonyms for the word in capital letters in their respective items.

Tests often offer *false leads* to the examinee who does not know the meaning of a word. Look at Item C: *subjugate*. The word *submerge* has the same prefix as the test word: *sub–*. *Predicate* is used for those persons who may confuse *subjugate* with "subject." The word *verbalize* is also used, because some examinees may think *subjugate* comes from "subject" and *verbalize* may come from "verb." The correct answer for C is *liberate*.

Item E tests knowledge of prefixes. You probably know the meaning of several of the answer choices. Since an epilogue is the conclusion of a play or a novel, the correct answer is *prologue,* which is an introduction to a play or a poem. The prefix *pro-* is often used to mean *before* or *in front of.*

③ ANALOGIES

The Analogies section of the SAT has directions which are similar to the following:

DIRECTIONS: Each test item contains a pair of words in capital letters. Try to establish a relationship between these two words. Then from the five answer choices select the pair of words which bear a relationship to each other which is the same as that between the two words in capital letters.

This test involves more than a knowledge of word meanings. To find the relationship between the two words in each pair requires reasoning, which is absent in solving the Antonyms items. Try to solve the four samples before reading the discussion that follows them.

F REGICIDE:KING::
   (1) homicide:murderer
   (2) infanticide:baby
   (3) purified:water
   (4) regulation:rules
   (5) royalty:queen

G CHANGE:MUTATION::
   (1) frizzle:hair
   (2) ghoul:birth
   (3) litigation:lawsuit
   (4) range:mountain
   (5) repast:pioneer

H LIQUID:LITER::
   (1) distance:meter
   (2) mile:walk
   (3) solid:scale
   (4) water:ice
   (5) year:month

J DIAMOND:BASEBALL::
   (1) catcher:pitcher
   (2) court:tennis
   (3) emerald:football
   (4) gem:game
   (5) hit:strike

In Item F *regicide* means the killing of a *king.* To find the correct answer it is necessary to find a pair of words in which the first word means the killing of the second word. Although homicide is a killing, it is not the killing of a murderer. The correct answer is *infanticide:baby,* because infanticide means the killing of an infant, a baby.

The relationship in Item G is very simple. A change is a mutation. The two words are synonymous. The correct answer, then, must be a pair of synonyms. Litigation is a lawsuit; this is the correct choice. A mountain can be a part of a range, but the two words are not synonymous.

In Item H a measure for a quantity of liquid is a liter. Since meter is a measure of distance, that word-pair is the correct answer. A scale can be used to weigh a solid, but it does not measure a quantity of the solid. Walk and ice are not measures. Month is a measure, but it measures time and not a year.

In Item J a diamond is the place where baseball is played. The only word-pair with a similar relationship is *court:tennis,* because tennis is played on a court.

The author of these test items used various techniques to create the distracters. In some cases he used words that resemble the given pair or one of the pair. In other cases, he used words that were in some way related to one or both of the given pair. To work these items, be careful in determining the relationship that exists between the words in the given pair. Then express this relationship in a sentence that uses both words. Check each answer choice by substituting the word-pair in that sentence that expresses the relationship. For example, in Item F the relationship is: regicide is the killing of a king. The first answer choice on being checked would read: homicide is the killing of a murderer. In this way you often find the correct answer.

Remember to guess if you are not sure of the answer and if you think you can eliminate one or more of the answer choices.

④ **SENTENCE COMPLETION**

The directions for the Sentence Completion section of the SAT are similar to the following:

DIRECTIONS: In each of the following sentences one or two words are missing. Select the answer choice that fits the sentence best.

Resources

Try to solve the four sample items before reading the discussion that follows them.

> K The President _____ the problem and has come up with a list of _____ to deal with it.
>   (1) created . . . . laws
>   (2) dislikes . . . . officials
>   (3) is . . . . teams
>   (4) recognizes . . . . suggestions
>   (5) suggested . . . . regulations
>
> L We must _____ study the problem of pollution before it can be overcome.
>   (1) lethargically
>   (2) nefariously
>   (3) tacitly
>   (4) tersely
>   (5) thoroughly
>
> M The man sitting next to me was so _____ that I missed many of the show's good lines.
>   (1) corpulent
>   (2) garrulous
>   (3) opulent
>   (4) pious
>   (5) wan
>
> N While some paintings were inspired, others were _____, but all showed evidence of hard work and _____.
>   (1) dour . . . . humor
>   (2) ethereal . . . . frugality
>   (3) inane . . . . ingenuity
>   (4) ludicrous . . . . avarice
>   (5) ridiculous . . . . pulchritude

All of these items require a knowledge of the meanings of words in them as well as an understanding of the words' relationships with the rest of the sentence. To answer such items, it is generally best to read the sentence with each of the answer choices filled in. You can immediately eliminate those that make no sense or sound silly. Usually, however, the test is written so that all choices will *sound* good, but if you know the meanings of the words, most will not make sense.

The answer to Item K is (4), because the President can see that a problem exists and so he offers ideas for solving it. The answer to Item L is (5), for all other choices are ridiculous: *Lethargically* means "sluggishly"; *nefariously* means "wickedly"; *tacitly* means "silently"; and *tersely* means "briefly." The answer to Item M is (2), because *garrulous* means "talkative." If you do not know the meanings of some of the other answer choices, you should look them up in the dictionary. The answer to Item N is (3). The paintings ranged from inspired to worthless, but all showed the artist's hard work and cleverness in using materials.

I. SYNONYMS

In each test there is a word in capital letters followed by five answer choices. Select the one whose meaning is most nearly like the meaning of the word in capital letters. Write the letter of your choice in the space next to the number of the item.

SAMPLE TEST A

_____ 1. RESIGNATION
    A exclamation
    B indication
    C profession
    D signature
    E surrender

_____ 2. PHILATELIST
    A coin collector
    B map maker
    C philosophy teacher
    D songwriter
    E stamp collector

_____ 3. EXILE
    A banishment
    B costly
    C death
    D departure
    E foreign

_____ 4. IMPETUS
    A furious
    B incentive
    C misfortune
    D prayer
    E rash

_____ 5. ADVENT
    A arrival
    B breeze
    C holiday
    D opening
    E risk

_____ 6. BELLIGERENT
    A brief
    B dreamy
    C friendly
    D hostile
    E musical

_____ 7. DETERIORATE
    A improve
    B increase
    C lecture
    D plunder
    E worsen

_____ 8. FATIGUE
    A doom
    B end
    C overalls
    D plumpness
    E weariness

_____ 9. VITALITY
    A description
    B hunger
    C liveliness
    D love
    E sorrow

_____ 10. ULTIMATE
    A first
    B high
    C last
    D late
    E outside

Resources

II. ANTONYMS

In each test item there is a word in capital letters followed by five answer choices. From these five choices select the one whose meaning is most nearly opposite in meaning to the word in capital letters. Write the letter of your choice in the space next to the numeral that designates the number of the item.

_____ 1. MAGNIFY
    A build
    B destroy
    C increase
    D lower
    E shrink

_____ 2. TEMPORARY
    A cold
    B hurried
    C permanent
    D rural
    E shiny

_____ 3. INFINITE
    A adult
    B limited
    C little
    D polite
    E unending

_____ 4. SECEDE
    A fail
    B follow
    C join
    D lead
    E withdraw

_____ 5. UNIFORM
    A colorless
    B costume
    C general
    D identical
    E varied

_____ 6. ELOQUENT
    A creative
    B foreign
    C harmful
    D speechless
    E stingy

_____ 7. PAINSTAKING
    A burning
    B careless
    C fresh
    D healthy
    E husky

_____ 8. IMPARTIAL
    A entire
    B exportable
    C fully
    D secretive
    E unfair

_____ 9. OPTIMISM
    A baptism
    B humanism
    C hypnotism
    D journalism
    E pessimism

_____ 10. INTEGRITY
    A adolescence
    B dishonesty
    C exterior
    D fraction
    E superiority

III. ANALOGIES

Each test item contains a pair of words in capital letters. Try to establish a relationship between these two words. Then select from the five answer choices the pair of words which bear a relationship to each other which is the same as that of the two words in capital letters. Write the letter of your choice in the space next to the number of the item.

___ 1. DOCTOR:ILLNESS::
    A disease:cure
    B hospital:doctor
    C police:crime
    D sickness:medicine
    E surgeon:knife

___ 2. BRUSH:ARTIST::
    A book:librarian
    B needle:tailor
    C paint:painter
    D seeds:farmer
    E singer:music

___ 3. BULLET:ARROW::
    A bow:quiver
    B fast:slow
    C pistol:revolver
    D plane:stagecoach
    E song:melody

___ 4. MAY:YAM::
    A apple:pear
    B April:potato
    C can:tomato
    D carrot:August
    E top:pot

___ 5. EGGS:DOZEN::
    A butter:pound
    B buy:sell
    C chicken:meat
    D milk:cow
    E oranges:three

___ 6. HOE:HOSE::
    A garden:lawn
    B house:horse
    C land:water
    D rake:shovel
    E toe:tows

___ 7. AREA:SQUARE::
    A ball:round
    B circle:sphere
    C time:minute
    D triangle:meter
    E volume:cube

___ 8. THRIFTY:STINGY::
    A cheap:expensive
    B famous:notorious
    C miser:gold
    D saving:spending
    E wealthy:poor

___ 9. GIVE:TAKE::
    A borrow:lend
    B finish:end
    C seed:spring
    D story:tale
    E win:prize

___ 10. DRUDGERY:TOIL::
    A fun:play
    B history:science
    C like:hate
    D rowdy:boisterous
    E work:labor

Resources

IV. SENTENCE COMPLETION

In each of the following sentences one or two words are missing. From the five answer choices select the one that fits the sentence best. Write the letter of your choice in the space next to the number of the item.

_____ 1. Many persons find the _____ of rheumatism to be exceedingly _____.
- A addiction . . . . . helpful
- B affection . . . . . lengthy
- C affliction . . . . . painful
- D concentration . . . . . nagging
- E inflection . . . . . tender

_____ 2. The lieutenant who led his troops into the ambush was _____ by his _____.
- A deceived . . . . . children
- B honored . . . . . captain
- C praised . . . . . platoon
- D reciprocated . . . . . wife
- E reprimanded . . . . . superiors

_____ 3. After a long and heated debate, the Senate voted to _____ the Panama Canal Treaty.
- A defy
- B intensify
- C justify
- D purify
- E ratify

_____ 4. His _____ gray suit contrasted with his brother's _____ red pants and striped jacket.
- A colorful . . . . . bright
- B conservative . . . . . loud
- C dull . . . . . somber
- D expensive . . . . . dangerous
- E worn-out . . . . . burned

_____ 5. Her dancing was magnificently _____: she seemed to float through the air without _____.
- A awkward . . . . . charm
- B elegant . . . . . haste
- C fluid . . . . . water
- D graceful . . . . . effort
- E spirited . . . . . shoes

430

Taking Tests

_____ 6. The Earth's climatic balance is so _____ that hardly _____ changes could upset it.
      A delicate ..... perceptible
      B mysterious ..... plausible
      C rainy ..... noticeable
      D uneven ..... any
      E weak ..... responsible

_____ 7. If life is ever created _____, it will be done by an _____ scientist.
      A artificially ..... ingenious
      B intentionally ..... ignorant
      C purposefully ..... immigrant
      D scientifically ..... old-fashioned
      E secretly ..... insane

_____ 8. He wanted to see the game, but the cost of the ticket was _____.
      A alleviated
      B excessive
      C inconsistent
      D minimal
      E suppressive

_____ 9. _____ speakers use words that seem clear, vigorous, and _____.
      A Effective ..... alive
      B Honest ..... truthful
      C Interesting ..... dreary
      D Political ..... deceptive
      E Religious ..... impressive

_____ 10. After many years of destitution, the lottery winner needed considerable time to adjust to a new life of _____.
      A affluence
      B gambling
      C misfortune
      D moderation
      E popularity

Know the different ways tests measure your command of written English

R3b
Tests of Written English

Many different tests are used to measure the student's ability to write standard English. These tests have names such as *Test of English Usage, Test of English Grammar, Test*

Resources

of Language Expression, Test of Mechanics of English, and the like. The right or correct answer on such tests is the choice that is right for formal written English. Things to be marked wrong or incorrect will include problems of usage and mechanics, such as the following:

- informal or slang words;
- lack of agreement between subject and verb;
- nonstandard forms of verbs;
- nonstandard comparative or superlative forms;
- vague use or wrong form of pronoun;
- double negatives;
- sentence fragments;
- wrong use of comma;
- problems with capitalization;
- wrong use of the apostrophe.

In senior high schools these tests are usually included in a battery of achievement tests, which also measure reading and mathematics. Among the most widely used achievement batteries at this level are the California Achievement Tests (now called "CAT" by many users), the Comprehensive Tests of Basic Skills (CTBS), the Metropolitan Achievement Tests (often called "Metro"), and the Stanford Test of Academic Skills (TASK). In colleges, tests of English usage and mechanics of written composition are often administered to entering students to aid in placing them in the appropriate level of English classes.

The best way to find out if students have writing ability is to ask them to write an essay. Such tests are called **essay tests.** However, standardized tests use multiple-choice test items to measure some of the knowledge and skills that are *part* of writing ability. The following is a sampling of test questions that you may be asked to answer.

① PARAGRAPH REVISION

This kind of test asks the student to check a paragraph for usage problems or errors in mechanics. Portions of sentences in these paragraphs are underlined and numbered. The student is asked to mark each numbered phrase as follows:

- *U* for usage problem
- *P* for punctuation error
- *C* for capitalization error
- *NE* for no error

Taking Tests

R3b

Read the following example:

> A deadly <u>Drug, "angel dust"</u>, has other names on the
>   1
> street: <u>PCP</u>, rocket fuel, super joint, peace weed, etc. In a
>   2
> recent year it killed about 100 persons <u>and sends about</u> 4000 to
>   3
> hospitals. <u>It's effects on</u> users can be very violent. Some young-
>   4
> sters have died after using only a very little. Some have fallen off
> <u>cliffs, some</u> jumped off buildings, and some <u>drownded themselves</u>.
>   5   6

In answering test items of this type, remember what you are looking for: a punctuation error, a capitalization error, or inappropriate usage. For each item, first read the entire sentence. Then see if the underlined phrase contains any punctuation. If there is punctuation, ask yourself if it is the correct mark. If it is not, mark the item *P*. If there is no punctuation, ask yourself if it needs a comma, an apostrophe, quotation marks, etc. If it does, mark the item *P*.

If there is no error in punctuation, look for an error in capitalization. Is there a capital in the underlined section? Is it correctly used? If not, mark the item with a *C*. If there is no capitalized word, check each word to determine if one of the words should have been capitalized. If a capital letter is needed, mark the item *C*. If not, check for usage errors.

All sentences should be written in formal standard English. Check each word or phrase for informal English or slang. Look for verbs that do not agree with the subject. Check on the proper use of relative pronouns. Are the modifiers properly placed? Is the right comparative or superlative form of the adjective or adverb used? If the phrase contains an irregular verb, is the standard form used? If you find an informal or nonstandard use, mark the item *U*. If you can find no error, mark *NE* to show there is no error. Tests of this kind always include several items without any errors in them.

Here are the answers for the sample paragraph:

- In Item 1 the word *drug* should not be capitalized. The answer to Item 1 is *C*.
- In Item 2 the colon is correct punctuation. The drug's name, PCP, is properly written in capital letters. There is no error in usage. The answer, then, is *NE*.

Resources

- Item 3 has no punctuation and no capitals, and it needs neither a punctuation mark nor a capital. However, the verb *sends* is in the present tense. It should be parallel with *killed* because the two verbs form a compound verb. The word should be *sent*. This is a shift in usage. The answer is *U*.
- In Item 4 there is a punctuation mark, an apostrophe, and a capital letter. The apostrophe in *It's* makes the word a contraction of *it is*. Since we cannot say, "It is effects...," we know there is a punctuation error. The answer is *P*.
- The comma in Item 5 is right. It is used to separate the first two clauses in a series of clauses. There is no need for a capital, and there is no usage problem. The answer is *NE*.
- The word *drownded* in Item 6 is nonstandard. The standard past of the verb *drown* is *drowned*. The answer is *U*.

② BEST-SENTENCE TESTS

One test that measures writing ability lists three or four sentences, each saying roughly the same thing. The student selects the one sentence that is the best expression of that idea. Often the best choice is the most direct statement: brief and clear, with an active verb, with no misplaced modifiers, and with no confusing shifts. Look at the following four sample items and choose the *best* sentence for each one:

---

7 A I don't want no one to give me nothing.
    B I don't want no one to give me anything.
    C I want no one to give me anything.

8 F We should expect some wins and some losses in this tournament.
    G In this tournament some wins and some losses should be expected by us.
    H Some wins and some losses in this tournament by us should be expected.

9 K Skiing and to ride a toboggan are my favorite sports.
    L My favorite sports are skiing and to go toboggan riding.
    M Skiing and tobogganing are my favorite winter sports.

10 A With his feathers flying, the little boy caught the headless rooster.
     B Amidst a flurry of feathers, the little boy caught the headless rooster.
     C The little boy caught the rooster without a head with the flying feathers.

Answers:

- In Item 7, sentence A has three negative words: *don't, no one,* and *nothing*. The double (or triple) negative is non-standard English. Sentence B uses a double negative. Sentence C is most acceptable.
- In Item 8, sentence F is the most direct. It uses an active verb. It is better than the passive construction in G and H, which makes those sentences very awkward. Also, in sentence H the phrase *by us* is badly misplaced.
- Item 9 is a test of parallel structure. In sentence K there is a compound subject made up of a verbal noun and an infinitive. In sentence L there are two nouns following the linking verb *are* that are joined by the connective *and*. These are a verbal noun and an infinitive. Both of these compounds lack parallelism. Sentence M uses two verbal nouns to form a compound subject, making M the best choice.
- In Item 10, sentence A is written so that it sounds as if the little boy has his feathers flying. Sentence C appears at first glance to be more direct than A. It includes a subject followed by a verb and an object with modifiers. However, the two modifying prepositional phrases are quite awkward. *Headless* is shorter than, and it has the same meaning as, *without a head*. The best choice, therefore, is B.

③ **SENTENCE REVISION**

Some tests ask the student to look for a problem—punctuation, capitalization, or usage—in two or three parts of a single sentence. Parts of the sentence are underlined and numbered. The student is asked to label the problem, if any, in each numbered section. The student marks:

- *P* for a punctuation error
- *C* for a capitalization error
- *U* for a usage problem
- *NE* for no error

Try to find the problem in each underlined phrase of the following sentences. If there is no error, mark *NE* on your worksheet.

I'm not gone to do Bills paper route while he's away.
  11   12   13

By the time she was thirteen, she travels from Ocean to Ocean.
         14   15

Resources

Answers:

- In Item 11, the apostrophe correctly forms a contraction for *I am,* but *gone* should not follow *am.* The standard form would be *going.* Since standard verb forms are a usage problem, the answer to Item 11 is *U.*
- In Item 12, there is need for an apostrophe in *Bills* to show that the paper route belongs to him. The answer to 12, therefore, is *P.*
- In Item 13, the apostrophe is correctly used to make *he's* a contraction for *he is.* The period is correct for the end of the sentence. There is no error in punctuation. There is no capital letter in the underlined section, and there is no need for a capital. Because there is also no problem in usage, the answer to Item 13 is *NE.*
- In the second sentence, Item 14 has no error in punctuation or capitalization. It does, however, have a shift in tense. The girl *was* thirteen years old in the *past.* She *travels* shifts to the present. The answer to Item 14 is *U*—a problem in usage.
- In Item 15 the phrase *from Ocean to Ocean* probably means "from Pacific to Atlantic," or it may mean "from Atlantic to Pacific." We know only that she has crossed the United States. Since we cannot identify each ocean, we should not capitalize the words *ocean.* The answer, therefore, is *C* for capitalization.

④ **COMPLETION TESTS**

One widely used test of language expression provides paragraphs with several blanks. For each numbered blank, the student is given four choices. The student picks the choice that fits best. Sometimes the four choices are different forms of the same word. For other blanks the student must select the appropriate relative pronoun, or the proper comparative or superlative form of an adjective or adverb, or the right word to fit the context of the rest of the sentence. The following paragraph is an example of a completion test. Read the entire paragraph first and then go back to consider which of the four choices should fit into each numbered blank. Remember that the best way to select an answer is to read each sentence with its alternatives filled in. One choice should sound best in context.

Taking Tests

Backpacking has become one of America's ___16___ activities. ___17___ the summer vacation months, people of all ages can be found hiking along highways and byways, into the hills, along the beaches, in the national parks, and, ___18___, in the wilderness areas. It is in these wilderness areas where they can explore exciting new vistas, many that have been seen by ___19___ before them. However, if the growth of this pastime continues, there will soon be no ___20___ spot left in the country.

16	17	18
A exercise	F For	K especially
B health	G From	L moreover
C leisure	H Throughout	M nevertheless
D mountain	J When	N wildly

19	20	
A explorers	F scenic	
B many	G "undiscovered"	
C no one	H vacation	
D others	J wilderness	

Answers:

- For Item 16, you can eliminate *exercise, health,* and *mountain.* Only a few backpackers hike for the exercise or for their health, and many do not hike in the mountains. For nearly all it is a pastime. The answer, therefore, is C.
- The word needed to fill the blank in Item 17 must be a preposition. That eliminates *when.* The only appropriate choice is *throughout.* The answer is H.
- The best choice for Item 18 is *especially.* The two sentences that follow the sentence with Item 18 tell about the wilderness areas, which are very popular with backpackers. The answer is K.
- For Item 19, the clue to the correct answer is *new* in the earlier part of the sentence. If the vistas are "new," it suggests they may have been seen by *no one* before. The answer is C.
- The same idea leads to the answer for Item 20: "undiscovered." The answer is G.

Resources

⑤ MISSING TRANSITIONS

Some tests include a paragraph with numbered blanks to be filled by the right transitional expression. The missing link may be a coordinating connective or adverbial connective. For each blank the student selects the best word from the four choices. Read the following paragraph and select the best transition word for each numbered blank from the lists of four choices below the paragraph.

Dr. Starkhof was arrested after the attempt to assassinate Hitler. He proved his innocence conclusively and ___21___ escaped the death sentence. ___22___, he was sent to a concentration camp. ___23___ he was still alive when the Americans reached it, he died three months later.

	21		22		23
A	furthermore	F	Besides	K	Although
B	in addition	G	Fortunately	L	Because
C	luckily	H	However	M	Unless
D	therefore	J	So	N	Yet

Answers:

• The sentence containing Item 21 tells us that Dr. Starkhof escaped the death sentence because he was innocent. The word to fill the blank should be a word that means "consequently." So, the correct choice is D: *therefore*. The word *so* would also have been acceptable here, but it is not included among the four choices.

• The only appropriate word for Item 22 is *however*, answer H. The word *nevertheless* would also have been appropriate here.

• The answer to Item 23 is K: *Although*.

⑥ PARAGRAPH ORGANIZATION

Below are examples of test items that test the student's ability to develop a paragraph. Each item has a list of four sentences, numbered from one through four. The student is asked to find the order of these sentences that would make the best paragraph.

Taking Tests

R3b

13 1 Then I headed for my usual bench in the park.
      2 It was after dark when I left my aunt's house.
      3 Thinking of the fun I had had there years before, I sat until the clock struck ten.
      4 I walked to the nearest corner and crossed on the green light.
         A 1–3–2–4
         B 2–3–1–4
         C 2–4–1–3
         D 4–1–3–2

14 1 Most tourists visit there to see its Blue Grotto.
      2 These have a blue look, caused by the refraction of light as it passes through the water at the cave's mouth.
      3 The roof and sides of this grotto are composed of stalactites.
      4 A beautiful, rocky island near Naples is called Capri.
         F 1–3–2–4
         G 1–4–2–3
         H 4–3–2–1
         J 4–1–3–2

- To answer items like Item 13, consider the order in which each thing might happen. In what order would the four things that the author said he or she did naturally occur? What is the logical chronology? The author said he or she left the house, walked to the corner, entered the park, and sat on a bench. The answer to Item 13 is C: 2–4–1–3.
- Item 14 does not provide a time sequence as does Item 13. Each sentence, however, has a word in it that refers to something mentioned in a previous sentence. In Sentence 1 you can read the word *there* and the word *its*. These must refer to something in the sentence that comes before this one in the completed paragraph. Sentence 2 starts with *These*, which also points to something in the sentence that should come before it. Sentence 3 uses *this grotto,* which refers to a grotto that was mentioned earlier. Sentence 4 has no word that points back to an earlier sentence. The correct order for these sentences is J: 4–1–3–2.

Resources

SAMPLE TEST B

I. THANK-YOU LETTER

Read the following letter completely. Then go back and reread it carefully. When you come to a numbered, underlined section, look at the four answer choices whose number corresponds to that of the underlined section. Decide which of the four responses is the best choice. If you think that the underlined material is correct as it exists in the passage, mark the letter of the "No Change" response. If you think that one of the three alternative responses is the best choice, mark the letter of that choice. Write your choice in the space next to the number of the item.

April 17, 1979

Dear Grandmother,

    The <u>Swiss music box</u>[1] arrived in <u>todays'</u>[2] mail. <u>It's colors</u>[3] will go very well with my <u>bed-spread</u>[4] and draperies. You <u>knew to</u>[5] that I am very fond of Chopin. Thank you very much.

    I <u>can't hardly believe</u>[6] that I am 18 <u>years' old</u>[7]. In less than two months I will graduate, and soon I will be a college student at <u>Sutter community college</u>[8]. It is my plan to study nursing. My hardest course will be <u>english!</u>[9] You can see from this letter that my spelling and <u>grammer is</u>[10] poor.

    Thanks again for the lovely gift. Come to visit us soon.

Your loving granddaughter,

Sharon

Taking Tests

R3b

____ 1. A Swiss Music Box
        B Swiss Music box
        C swiss music box
        D No Change

____ 2. A today's
        B todays
        C tueday's
        D No Change

____ 3. A Its colors
        B Its' colors
        C Its collors
        D No Change

____ 4. A bed spread
        B bed spred
        C bedspread
        D No Change

____ 5. A knew, too,
        B new two
        C new too
        D No Change

____ 6. A can't hardly beleive
        B can hardly beleive
        C can hardly believe
        D No Change

____ 7. A year's old
        B years old
        C years-old
        D No Change

____ 8. A Sutter Community college
        B Sutter Community College
        C Sutter community College
        D No Change

____ 9. A english.
        B English?
        C English.
        D No Change

____ 10. A grammer are
        B grammar is
        C grammar are
        D No Change

II. LETTER OF PETITION

Read the letter on the following page completely. Then go back and reread it carefully. When you come to a numbered, underlined section, look at the four answer choices following the letter with the number that corresponds to that of the underlined section. Decide which of the four responses is the best choice. If you think that the underlined material is correct as it exists in the passage, mark the letter of the "No Change" response. If you think that one of the three alternative responses is the best choice, mark the letter of that choice. Write the letter of your choice in the space next to the number of the item.

Resources

1429 South 33rd Street
Salona, AZ 88242
June 4, 1979

Ms. Marcia Valdez. President
Salona School Board
City Hall
Salona, AZ 88240

Dear Ms. Valdez:

    This is a <u>petition from us</u>[1] fellows who attend <u>south Salona high school</u>[2]. We are all seniors who played on the football team last year. We object to the recent decision of the <u>Salona School Board</u>[3] to eliminate football from our school's sports program for next year.

    We <u>know of course</u>[4] that football is the most expensive sport. We believe that football can pay for <u>it's self</u> when the price of the tickets <u>are adequate</u>[5][6]. Many of our <u>friends, students</u>[7] and adults, and our parents have said they would be willing to pay more for a season ticket. If the student ticket price is raised to $6.00 and the adult ticket price is raised to <u>$12.00; would</u>[8] that not make football a <u>self-supporting</u>[9] sport?

    Please retain football as an interscholastic sport at our high school.

                                         <u>Most respectively</u>[10] yours,

                                         Senior Team members

Taking Tests

R3b

___ 1. A petission from we
        B petission from us
        C petition from we
        D No Change

___ 2. A South Salona high school
        B South Salona High School
        C south Salona High School
        D No Change

___ 3. A Salona School board
        B salona school board
        C Salona school Board
        D No Change

___ 4. A know, of course,
        B know (of course)
        C know—of course—
        D No Change

___ 5. A its self
        B its' self
        C itself
        D No Change

___ 6. A is adequate
        B be adequate
        C were adequate
        D No Change

___ 7. A friends' students
        B friends—students
        C friends (students
        D No Change

___ 8. A $12.00 would
        B $12.00—would
        C $12.00, would
        D No Change

___ 9. A selfsupporting
        B self supporting
        C "self" supporting
        D No Change

___ 10. A Most respectfully
        B Mostly respectful
        C Mostly respectively
        D No Change

III. PARAGRAPH ORGANIZATION

Each of the following test items has a list of four sentences, numbered from one through four. Read all four sentences and decide in which order these sentences would make the best paragraph. If you can find that order among the four answer choices, mark that choice next to the number of the item.

___ 1. 1 As she did, she remembered the man who had so lovingly tended these roses in the past.
        2 Bending over the bush of the yellow roses, she enjoyed the odor of the largest rose.
        3 She ambled slowly down the garden path.
        4 She let the screen door slam.
           A 1-4-3-2
           B 2-1-3-4
           C 3-2-1-4
           D 4-3-2-1

443

Resources

_____ 2.   1 It is actually a breakfast cake in a pie crust.
        2 The cake is made by mixing a variety of ingredients.
        3 Shoo-fly pie is popular among the Pennsylvania Dutch.
        4 This mixture is put into a pastry-lined pan and baked.
          A 1-2-4-3
          B 2-4-1-3
          C 3-1-2-4
          D 3-2-4-1

_____ 3.   1 Oberammergau is a village in southern Germany, famous for its Passion play.
        2 The next showing will be in the year 1990.
        3 It takes place only during the summer of the years that end in -0.
        4 This play shows the crucifixion and ascension of Jesus.
          A 1-3-2-4
          B 1-4-3-2
          C 4-2-3-1
          D 4-3-2-1

_____ 4.   1 It is an adventure narrative of a whaling voyage.
        2 It is generally considered to be his masterpiece.
        3 The object of this voyage was to kill Moby Dick.
        4 *Moby Dick* is a novel by Herman Melville.
          A 3-1-2-4
          B 4-2-1-3
          C 4-3-2-1
          D 3-4-1-2

_____ 5.   1 Next, clean the air filter.
        2 In the spring, check three critical items in the lawn mower: the oil, the air filter, and the fuel.
        3 Finally, check the fuel to be sure it is fresh; do not use fuel stored in the mower over the winter.
        4 Make sure the crankcase oil is at the full mark.
          A 2-1-4-3
          B 2-4-1-3
          C 4-1-3-2
          D 4-2-1-3

_____ 6.   1 One of them died when she was sixteen.
        2 Mr. Wilson also had two daughters.
        3 Carl was Mr. Wilson's only son.
        4 The other daughter, the elder one, lived close by.
          A 1-4-3-2
          B 2-1-4-3
          C 3-2-1-4
          D 3-4-2-1

Taking Tests

_____ 7. 1 The story of the used car that gave out on the way home from the lot is very common.
       2 Nevertheless, they seldom will guarantee a used car for more than 30 days.
       3 All used cars are worn machinery.
       4 Dealers stoutly maintain that such stories are gross exaggerations.
         A 1-4-3-2
         B 3-1-4-2
         C 3-2-4-1
         D 4-2-1-3

_____ 8. 1 We reached Dodge City in a howling blizzard.
       2 We stayed only long enough to replenish our food supply.
       3 Then we moved on toward Denver.
       4 The place was devastated.
         A 1-2-3-4
         B 1-4-2-3
         C 3-1-2-4
         D 4-2-1-3

_____ 9. 1 The water buffalo is found wild in several Asian countries.
       2 Domesticated breeds are highly valued for their flesh and milk.
       3 They are also used as beasts of burden.
       4 It lives in grassy swamps near lagoons and spends much time in the water.
         A 1-2-3-4
         B 1-3-4-2
         C 1-4-2-3
         D 2-3-1-4

_____ 10. 1 In practice, however, they are often written in a hurry and show a familiar bias.
       2 Editorials are a special form of writing used in newspapers.
       3 Sometimes they interpret the news; sometimes they give opinion about subjects of current interest.
       4 The judgments expressed in an editorial should be based on accurate knowledge of facts and on sincere belief.
         A 1-3-2-4
         B 1-4-2-3
         C 2-1-4-3
         D 2-3-4-1

ILLUSTRATION CREDITS

Page 6, 9: Jack Weaver. 20: (top left) Mike Mazzaschi/Stock, Boston; (others) Owen Franken/Stock, Boston. 33, 44: Jack Weaver. 61: Pedro A. Noa. 66: Jack Weaver. 68: (left) Irene Bayer/Monkmeyer; (center right) Bettina Cirone; (bottom right) Patricia Hollander Gross/Stock, Boston. 73: Jack Weaver. 74: (top and bottom right) Hugh Rogers/Monkmeyer; (bottom left) Daniel Brody/Stock, Boston. 80: (top) Peter Vadnai; (bottom) Joe Foldes/Monkmeyer. 85, 90, 93: Jack Weaver. 95: George Guzzi. 99, 102: Jack Weaver. 108: The Bettman Archive. 117, 133: Jack Weaver. 137, 170, Peter Vadnai. 172: United States Postal Service. 178: Jack Weaver. 182: (top) Ira Kirschenbaum/Stock, Boston; (bottom) Ellis Herwig/Stock, Boston. 189: (top) The Bettman Archive; (bottom) UPI. 199: Jack Weaver. 204: National Safety Council. 220, 227, 231: Jack Weaver. 245: George Guzzi. 263, 267: Jack Weaver. 269: George Guzzi. 290: Jack Weaver. 300: George Guzzi. 314, 319, 326: Jack Weaver. 333: Washington Post; Chicago Tribune; The New York Times. 336, 384, 385, 386: Jack Weaver.

ACKNOWLEDGMENTS

Doubleday and Company, Inc. for permission to reprint an excerpt from *Lilies of the Field* by William E. Barrett. Copyright © 1962 by William E. Barrett. Used by permission of Doubleday and Company, Inc.

E. P. Dutton for permission to reprint an excerpt from *All Men are Brothers* by Charlie May Simon. Copyright © 1956 by E. P. Dutton. Reprinted by permission of the publisher, E. P. Dutton.

W. H. Freeman and Company, Publishers, for permission to reprint an excerpt from "Fresh Water from Salt" by David S. Jenkins, which appeared in the March, 1957, issue of *Scientific American*.

Harcourt Brace Jovanovich, Inc. for permission to reprint excerpts from "Rope" from *Flowering Judas and Other Stories* by Katherine Anne Porter; and from *A Walker in the City,* by Alfred Kazin, copyright © 1951 by Alfred Kazin. Both reprinted by permission of Harcourt Brace Jovanovich, Inc.

Harper and Row, Publishers, Inc. for permission to reprint an excerpt from *The Miracle of Language* by Charlton Laird. Reprinted by permission of the publisher.

Harper's Magazine for permission to reprint an excerpt from "Son of the Catskills" by John Corry. Copyright © 1970 by *Harper's Magazine*. All rights reserved. Reprinted from the September 1970 issue by special permission.

Hodder and Stoughton, Ltd. for permission to reprint an excerpt from "High Adventure" by Sir Edmund Hillary. Reprinted by permission of the publisher.

Acknowledgments

Houghton Mifflin Company for permission to reprint two excerpts from *Silent Spring* by Rachel Carson. Copyright © 1962 by Rachel Carson. Reprinted by permission of Houghton Mifflin Company.

Young Kansas Writers for permission to reprint an excerpt from "Huck Finn's Crazy Box" by Bob Tedford, which appeared in the April, 1977, issue of *Young Kansas Writers*.

King Features Syndicate, Inc. for permission to reprint a series of *Flash Gordon* comics from 1939. Copyright © 1939 by King Features Syndicate, Inc. Reprinted with permission.

J. B. Lippincott Company for permission to reprint an excerpt from "Why Nobody Pets the Lion at the Zoo" from the book *The Reason for the Pelican* by John Ciardi. Copyright © 1959 by John Ciardi. Reprinted by permission of J. B. Lippincott Company.

Little, Brown and Company for permission to reprint excerpts adapted from "Snow" from *The Snow Walker* by Farley Mowat, copyright © 1975 by McClelland and Stewart, Ltd.; and from *The Reapers of the Dust: A Prairie Chronicle* by Lois Phillips Hudson, copyright © 1958, 1964 by Lois Phillips Hudson. Both reprinted by permission of Little, Brown and Company in association with The Atlantic Monthly Press.

Mankind Magazine for permission to reprint an excerpt from "The Great Buffalo Slaughter" by Norman B. Wiltsey. Copyright © 1968 by Mankind Publishing Company. Reprinted with permission.

McGraw-Hill, Inc. for permission to reprint excerpts from the *Reference Manual for Stenographers and Typists,* Fourth Edition, by Ruth E. Gavin and William A. Sabin; and from *Business English and Communication,* Fifth Edition, by Marie M. Stewart.

G. & C. Merriam Company for permission to reprint the entries "candidate," "itinerary," and "maverick" from *Webster's New Students Dictionary,* copyright © 1974 by G. & C. Merriam Company; and the entries "slim" and "larrup" from *Webster's New Collegiate Dictionary,* copyright © 1977 by G. & C. Merriam Company, publishers of the Merriam-Webster Dictionaries.

William Morris Agency, Inc. for permission to reprint an excerpt from *Return to India* by Santha Rama Rau. Reprinted by permission of William Morris Agency, Inc. on behalf of the author. Copyright © 1960 by The Reporter Magazine Company.

Organization of American States for permission to use an excerpt from "Cecilia Rosas" by Amado Muro, which is reprinted from *Américas,* monthly magazine published by the General Secretariat of the Organization of American States in English, Spanish, and Portuguese.

Acknowledgments

Oxford University Press, Inc. for permission to reprint an excerpt from *The Sea Around Us* by Rachel Carson. Copyright © 1950, 1951, 1961 by Rachel L. Carson. Reprinted by permission of Oxford University Press, Inc.

The Pennsylvania State University Press for permission to reprint "dandelions" from *The Paradise of the World* by Deborah Austin. Copyright © by The Pennsylvania State University. Reprinted by permission of The Pennsylvania State University Press.

Ramparts for permission to reprint an excerpt from "The End of the Ocean" by Paul Ehrlich. Copyright © 1969 by Ramparts Magazine, Inc. Reprinted by permission.

Random House, Inc. for permission to reprint two pronunciation keys from the *Random House College Dictionary*. Copyright © 1968, 1975 by Random House, Inc.

Scott, Foresman and Company for permission to reprint a pronunciation key from the *Thorndike-Barnhart Intermediate Dictionary* by E. L. Thorndike and Clarence L. Barnhart, copyright © 1971, 1974 by Scott, Foresman and Company; and the entries "fork," "canvas," "cap," "concord," "marshall," "anthem," "buy," "protective," "protective coloring," "itinerary," "maverick," "thimble," "microfilm," "Conestoga wagon," "ignition," and "polyglot" from the *Thorndike-Barnhart Advanced Dictionary* by E. L. Thorndike and Clarence L. Barnhart, copyright © 1973, 1974 by Scott, Foresman and Company. Reprinted by permission.

Charles Scribner's Sons for permission to reprint an excerpt from *The Night Country* by Loren Eiseley. Copyright © 1971 by Loren Eiseley. Reprinted by permission of the publisher.

Simon and Schuster, Inc. for permission to reprint an excerpt from *The Flammarion Book of Astronomy* by Camille Flammarion.

Skin Diver Magazine for permission to reprint an excerpt from "Autobiography of a Skin Diver" by Guido Garibaldi, which appeared in *Skin Diver Magazine*.

The Society of Authors for permission to reprint "The Ghost" by Walter de la Mare. Reprinted by permission of the Literary Trustees of Walter de la Mare, and The Society of Authors as their representative.

Wadsworth Publishing Company for permission to reprint sample business letters from *Communication in Business,* Second Edition, by Walter Wells. Copyright © 1977. Reprinted by permission of Wadsworth Publishing Company.

INDEX

a, an
  as noun markers, 60
  standard uses of, 268
  and *the,* 135-136
Abbreviations
  acceptable, 375
  exceptions to using, 375-376
  in dictionaries, 40
  initials for name, 375
  Latin, 375
  before names, 375
  with numerals, 375
Accusative case. *See* Object forms
Action words
  forms of, 56
  in sentences, 56-57
Addition coordinators, 111
Adjectives, 59
  and adverbs, 264-265
  common endings of, 76
  comparative, 75
  defined, 73
  degree; *see* Intensifiers
  and double comparisons, 264
  forms of, 75
  how to recognize, 73-76
  intensifiers, 75
  irregular, 265
  as modifiers, 73
  predicate, 97
  standard forms in comparisons, 264-265

---

*Page numbers in italic type indicate illustrations. Charts are identified in the Index.

Index

Adjectives (Continued)
  superlative, 75
  with linking verbs, 279
Adventures of Huckleberry Finn, The, 267
Adverbial connectives, use of semicolon with, 319-321
Adverbs, 59, 137
  and adjectives, 264-265
  charts for using, 279
  common endings of, 80-81
  defined, 79
  and degree, 81
  how to recognize, 79-82
  with -*ly* endings, 278
  meaning of, 79
  misplaced, 294
  place in sentence, 81
  standard formal English forms, 278-279
  with linking verbs, 279
Agreement
  of collective nouns and verb, 288-289
  of compound subjects and verb, 288-289
  of subject and verb, 253-255, 287-289
  of verb with subject having unclear plural, 288
ain't, 268
All Men Are Brothers, 183
Alone, 190
an, before vowels, 241
Anderson, Wm. R., 192-193
Antecedents. *See* Pronouns
Antonyms, 23, 25
  defined, 25
anywhere, 265
Apostrophe
  in contractions, 343-344
  in forming plural of numbers, letters, and words, 345
  in forming possessive, 344-345
  review of (chart), 309
Appositives
  defined, 131
  punctuation of, 312, 328
  using, 131-132
Articles
  a, an, 60, 241, 268
  as noun markers, 60
  the, 60, 135-136
"**Autobiography of a Skin Diver,**" 177-178
Auxiliaries
  guidelines for using, 258
  to indicate time, 298
  in standard English, 258
  three most common, 258

bad, badly, 261, 279
Baldwin, Hanson, 188-190
Baraka, Imamu Amiri. *See* Jones, LeRoi
Barrett, Wm. E., 226-227
be
  forms of, 241, 250, 254
  use with -*ing* verbs, 258
  see also Auxiliaries; Verbs
because vs. *being as, being that, on account of, seeing as how,* 267
being as, being that vs. *because,* 267
Berry, Adrian, 198
Biography, in library collection, 405
Book of Negro Folklore, The, 392

Book reports
  characterization, setting, and plot in, 225
  evaluation, 227
  guidelines for preparing, 226
  questions to answer in writing, 225-226
  theme in, 227
Brackets, 249
Business English and Communication, 210
Byrd, Richard E., 190

California Achievement Tests (CAT), 432
Capitalization
  of adjectives derived from proper nouns, 340
  of compass points, 339
  of the Diety, 339
  exceptions to using, 340
  of geographical features, 339
  of languages, 339
  of name, title, and rank of persons, 338
  of names of days, months, holidays, 339
  of nationalities, 338
  of political parties, 338
  of proper names, 337
  of religious names, 337
  review of (chart), 341
  of sentences, 337
  special uses, 338
  of specific names (buildings, documents, etc.), 339
  of titles, 338
  of trade names, 340
Card catalogue, library
  author cards, 409-410
  call number, 409

"see" and "see also" cards, 410-411
subject cards, 408-409
using, 408-411
Carson, Rachel, 203, 204-205
Case of pronouns. *See* Pronouns, functions of
CAT. *See* California Achievement Tests
Cause subordinators, 115
"Cecilia Rosas," 232, 399
Central idea, in original writing, 166-167
Choice coordinators, 111
Choice of Weapons, A, 154
Chronological order, 176-177, 188
Ciardi, John, 383
Classification of detail, 169-171
Clauses
adverbial, 115
defined, 110, 317
dependent, 114, 317, 324
independent, 111
main, 114
nonrestrictive, 324
noun, 120-121
punctuation of, 317, 323-324
relative, 118, 295
restrictive, 323
Clichés, 29
Clipped words, 273
Clues, to word meanings, 4-5
Colon, 348
review of (chart), 309
when to use, 334
Comma
with appositives, 312, 328
with coordinators, 317-318
and credit tags, 348
in dates, addresses, and measurements, 331
and dependent clauses, 323-324
exceptions to using, 318
with modifiers, 327-329
in page references, 331
and quotation marks, 348
review of (chart), 309
with sentence interrupters, 332
in series, 330-331
with subordinators, 323-324
Comma splice, 320
Communications in Business, 210
Comparative degree, 265
Comparison, 241
in descriptive writing, 183
in paragraphs, 156-158
using *-er* or *-est* in forming, 264
Complement. *See* Pattern Two Sentences; Subject-verb-object sentences
Composition
central idea, 166-167
chronological order, 176-177, 188
classification of detail, 169-171
imagination in, 229-236
outlining, 169-172
see also Paragraph development; Writing, original; specific type of writing
Compound words, 352
Comprehensive Test of Basic Skills (CTBS), 432
Compton's Encyclopedia, 388
Condition subordinators, 115
Connectives
adverbial, 319-321
coordinating, 111
defined, 83
how to recognize, 83-85
relative pronouns, 118
subordinating, 114-115
Consonants, sound spellings for (chart), 36
Content, of paragraphs, 146
Context, 4, 24-25
and word meanings, 4-5
see also Word clues
Contractions, 273
in informal language, 273
use of apostrophe in forming, 343-344
Contrast, use of, in paragraphs, 156-157
Contrast coordinators and subordinators, 111, 115
Coordinating conjunctions. *See* Coordinators
Coordination of sentence parts, 300
Coordinators, 111, 115, 317-318
commas with, 317-318
Correcting final manuscript
adding words or phrases, 374
changing paragraphs, 374
correcting words, 373
omitting words or phrases, 373
Corry, John, 396

451

Cousteau, J. Y., 180
Crane, Stephen, 5, 31
Credit tag, punctuation of, 348
CTBS. *See Comprehensive Tests of Basic Skills*

Dangling modifiers, 294-295
Dash
 review of (chart), 309
 when to use, 335
Declarative sentence. *See* Statements
Degrees
 of adjectives, 74-75, 265
 of adverbs, 81, 265
de la Mare, Walter, 382
Demonstrative pronouns. *See* Pronouns, pointing
Dependent clauses, 114, 317, 324
Descriptive writing, 181-183
Dewey decimal system of cataloguing, 405-406
Diagnostic Test
 for mechanics of writing, 310
 for using standard English, 242-243
Dialogue, using in narrative writing, 190-191
Dictionary
 abbreviations used in, 40
 alphabetical order in, 34
 biographical section, 35
 chart of sound spellings, 36
 contents of (chart), 33
 definitions; *see* word meanings
 diacritical marks, 46
 entry words, 34-35
 etymology; *see* word history
 explanation of entries, *41*
 finding words 34-35
 forms related to entry word, 34
 geographical section, 35
 guide words, 34
 homonyms, 35
 idioms, explained, 40
 kinds of, 32, 34
 phonetic spellings; *see* sound spellings
 as pronunciation guide, 45-47
 pronunciation keys, *48*
 sound spellings in, 35, *36*, 45-47
 stress signals in, 46-47
 use of, 32-50
 word division in, 35
 and word history, 43-44
 word meanings, 39-41
Direct object, 91
Direct quotation, 348
Division of words, 374
do
 use of in questions, 258
 see also Auxiliaries; Verbs
Double comparisons, avoiding, 264
Double-duty words, 135
double negatives, avoiding, 241, 266
Dragging and Driving, 197, 198
Durrell, Gerald, 183

Ehrlich, Paul, 205-206
Eiseley, Loren, 185-186

Ellipsis points (spaced periods), 349
"End of the Ocean, The," 205-206
Etymology. *See* Dictionary, word history
"Everybody's Sport," 159
everywhere, 265
Exclamation mark, 315
 and quotation marks, 348-349
Exclamations, 315
Expanding sentences, how to, 88-89, 91-92, 94-95, 97-98, 100-101
Explaining a process, 196-198
Explanation coordinators, 111
Exposition. *See* Explaining a process

Famous American Women, 192
Fiction, in library collection, 404-405
Figurative language, 28-29
Flammarion Book of Astronomy, The 154
Flammarion, Camille, 154
Folk speech, 303
"Footprint in Olduvai, A," 198
Ford, Corey, 5
Foreign words, italics for, 354
Formal vs. informal usage
 adverb forms, 278-279
 clipped words and contractions, 273

defined, 271
formal words (lists), 272, 273
guide to formal English, 281-283
guidelines, 272-274, 276-277
informal words (lists), 272
and pronoun case, 272-277
pronoun reference in, 291-292
slang, 274
"Fresh Water from Salt," 176
from, off vs. *off of,* 268
Function words
with adjectives, 75-76
with nouns, 60
with verbs, 69
Fused sentences, 320

Gann, Ernest K., 7
Garibalidi, Guido, 177-178
Geographical names
capitalization of, 339
in dictionary, 35
Gerund. *See* Verbal noun
"Ghost, The," 383
good, well, 265
Gottlieb, Annie, 207-208
Grammar
coordination and subordination, 114-115
sentence building, 87-123
word classes, 60-61, 64-65, 67-70, 73-76, 79-81, 83-84
"Great Buffalo Slaughter, The," 199-201

Greek words
prefixes, 15
roots, 11-12
Guide to formal English, 281-283
Guide to manuscript revision, 238
Guide words, in dictionary, 34
Guidelines
for assuring good appearance of written papers, 373-374
for avoiding nonstandard English, 266-268
for avoiding sentence fragments, 311-312
for checking agreement of subject and verb, 287-289
for conducting interviews, 393-396
for descriptive writing, 181-183
for distinguishing between confusing word pairs, 368-370
for explanatory writing, 196-198
for expressing personal viewpoint, 390
for forming plural nouns, 244-245
for forming verb tenses, 244-245
for improving spelling skills, 357
for improving study skills, 419-421
for letter writing, 210-212, 220-221
for narrative writing, 188-191
for outlining a paper, 169-172
for persuasive writing, 203-204
for preparing informational talks, 388
for preparing summaries, 222
for punctuating dependent clauses, 323-324
for punctuating elements in series, 330-331
for punctuating modifiers, 327-329
for punctuating quotations, 348-350
for recognizing formal and informal words, 272-274, 276-277
for taking tests, 421-422
for using abbreviations, 375-376
for using adverbs, 278-279
for using apostrophes, 343-345
for using auxiliaries, 258
for using colons, dashes, and parentheses, 335-336
for using hyphens, 352-353
for using italics, 354
for using numerals, 376
for using pronoun reference, 292
for using question and exclamation marks, 315
for using singular and plural verbs, 253-255
for using standard adjectives and adverbs, 264-265
for using standard pronouns, 261-263
for writing book reports, 226

453

Guidelines *(Continued)*
  for writing paragraphs, 146-147
  for writing short papers, 166-167

Halsey, Maxwell, 208
Handbook Key, back
have
  with perfect verbs, 258
  see also Auxiliaries; Verbs
High Adventure, 147-148
Hillary, Edmund, 147-148
Homonyms, 35
"Huck Finn's Crazy Box," 397-398
Hudson, Lois Phillips, 193-195
Hyphens
  in compound numbers and words, 352
  in fractions, 352
  in groups of words used as adjectives, 353
  with prefixes, 352-353

Idea, central, in composition, 166-167
Idioms, explained in dictionary, 40
Imperative sentence. *See* Requests
"In the Presence of Whales," 184, 207-208
Indefinite pronouns, in formal English, 283
Independent clauses, 111
Indirect object of verb, 100-103
Indirect quotation, 349
Infinitive phrase, 124
Infinitives
  defined, 124
  as modifiers, 124
  phrases, 124
  as subject, object, and predicate noun, 124
  using, 123-124
Informal English
  adverbs, 279
  clipped words and contractions in, 273
  pronouns in, 276-277
  word choice in, 272-274
  see also Formal usage
-ing **and** *-en* **verb forms,** 127-129
Intensifiers, 97
  adjectives, 75
  adverbs, 82
Interrogative sentence. *See* Questions
Interview, how to conduct, 393-396
Intransitive verbs, 88
Introduction, in preparing talks, 175
irregardless **vs.** *regardless,* 266
Irregular adjectives, 265
Irregular verbs, 67, 241, 249
it, **orphaned,** 292
Italics
  for emphasis, 354
  exception to using, 354
  for foreign words, 354
  for single letters and words discussed as words, 354
  for technical terms, 350
  for titles of complete works, 350, 354
it's, its, 344

Jenkins, David S., 176

Jones, LeRoi, 190-191

Knowles, John, 159

Language
  criteria for use, 240
  formal and informal, 271-286
  sources of, 2-3
  see also Nonstandard English; Standard English
Language in Action
  basic sentence patterns, 99
  common noun endings, 61
  figurative expressions, 29
  speaking informally, 273
  spelling reform, 360
  taking a survey, 395
  using adjectives, 76
  using apostrophes, 346
  using capital letters, 346
  using coordinating and subordinating connectives, 117
  using the dictionary, 44
  using nonstandard English, in literature, 267
  using verb endings, 72
  word meanings, 6
  words that deal with numbers, 13
Language, figurative
  defined, 28
  forms of, 28
  vs. literal, 28, 29
  metaphor, 28
  personification, 28
  simile, 28
Latin
  prefixes, 15
  word roots, 11-12, 51-52

learn vs. *teach,* 267
leave vs. *let,* 267
Lessing, Doris, 190
Let's Drive Right, 208
Letter writing
   addressing envelopes, 212
   appearance of letters, 209
   block form, 210, *214*
   business letters, 210-219
   folding and inserting letters, *213*
   guidelines for, 210-212, 220-221
   indented form, 210, *215*
   parts of, 210, 211
   personal letters, 220-211
   purposes, of business letters, 216-219
   sample letters, *210, 211, 212, 214, 215, 216, 217, 218, 220*
Library, card catalogue in. *See* Card catalogue, library
Library of Congress cataloguing system, 406
Library, how to use
   almanacs, atlases, and encyclopedias, 418
   biographical collection, 405
   circulation desk, 404
   Dewey decimal cataloging system, 405-406
   fiction collection, 404-405
   finding magazine articles, 413-414
   finding materials, 404-406
   layout of, 404, *407*
   Library of Congress cataloguing system, 406
   main divisions, 404-406
   nonfiction collection, 405

   periodical section, 406
   Readers' Guide to Periodical Literature, 413-414
   reference materials, 405, 417
   stacks, 404
   using card catalogue, 408-411
   using reference materials, 415-418
   vertical file, 406
lie, lay, 282
Life on the Mississippi, 4, 51
like, as, 282-283
Lilies of the Field, 226-227
Lindbergh, Anne Morrow, 31
Linking punctuation
   commas, 317-318
   semicolons, 319-321
Linking verbs, 94, 97
   use of adverbs with, 279
London, Jack, 188
Look-say-write word attack, 357

McCutcheon, John T., 304
MacPherson, Tom, 197, 198
Manner subordinators, 114
Mannes, Marya, 7
Manuscript preparation
   abbreviations, 375-376
   appearance, standards for, 372-376
   handwritten papers, 373
   how to correct, 373-374
   margins, 373
   title, 373
   typewritten papers, 373

   word division, 374
Manuscript revision guide, 238
"Map words," 57
Markers
   for adjectives, 75
   for adverbs, 82
   for nouns, 60, 65
   for verbs, 69
Meanings, dictionary, 39-41
Mechanics, of writing
   Diagnostic Test for, 310
   end punctuation, 311-312, 315
   guidelines for, 335-336, 348-350
   inside punctuation, 327-328, 330-332, 334-335
   linking punctuation, 317-318, 319-321, 323-324
   punctuation marks (chart), 309
   spelling, 356-361, 363-366, 368-370
   spelling improvement guidelines, 357
   standards for appearance of manuscript, 372-376
   using abbreviations, 373-376
   using apostrophes, 343-345
   using capital letters, 337-341
   using hyphens, 352-353
   using italics, 350, 354
   using numerals, 376
   using quotation marks, 348-350
   word division, 374
Metaphor, 28
"Metro." *See Metropolitan Achievement Tests*

Index

Metropolitan Achievement Tests ("Metro"), 432
might have vs. *might of,* 370
"Mind over Matter," 180
Misplaced modifiers, 294-295
Modifiers
  adjective, 73
  appositive, 328
  dangling, 294-295
  dashes with, 335
  introductory, 328-329
  misplaced, 294-295
  nonrestrictive, punctuation of, 327
  in Pattern Four sentences, 97-98
  in Pattern One sentences, 89
  position of, in sentence, 294-295
  prepositional phrases, 328
  verbal, 128
most, almost, nearly, 283
Mowat, Farley, 178-179
Muro, Amado, 232, 399
Murphy, Robert, 188

Narrative writing, 187-191
Nautilus 90 North, 192-193
Night Country, 185-186
Nominative case. *See* Subject forms
Nonfiction selections, in library collection, 405-406
Nonstandard English
  ain't, 268
  being as, 267
  being that, 267
  connectives, 267-268
  defined, 243
  double negative, 266
  examples, 243, 248, 250, 254, 255, 258, 261, 262, 263, 264, 265, 266, 268
  how to shift from, 266-268
  incorrect forms of *be,* 255
  irregardless, 266
  learn and *leave,* 267
  off of, 268
  on account of, 267
  seeing as how, 267
  them vs. *these, those,* 261
  this here, that there, 261
  use of *a, an,* 268
  without, 268
North to the Orient, 31
Noun clauses, 120-121
Noun markers
  articles, 60
  noun-making endings, 13, 61
  pointing pronouns, 60
  possessive pronouns, 61
Noun, verbal, 129
Nouns, 59, 60
  collective, 288-289
  common, 60
  common endings of, 61
  guidelines for forming plurals, 244-245
  how to recognize, 60-61
  irregular plurals, 244
  after linking verbs, 94-95
  markers for, 13, 60-61
  in Pattern Three sentences, 94
  plural forms, 60, 241, 244-245
  plurals of nouns ending in *f* or *fe,* 245
  proper, 60
  use with numbers, 245
  used as verbs, 129
Nouns, possessive (chart), 345
  forming, 344-345
nowhere, 265
Number
  of nouns, 60, 241
  of pronouns, 65, 262
Numbers
  forming plural of, 345
  when to use numerals, 376
  words dealing with, 13
Numerals. *See* Numbers
Nyad, Diana, 180

Object forms, of pronouns, 275
Object of verb, 91-92
  defined, 91
  indirect, 100-103
off of vs. *off, from,* 268
on account of vs. *because,* 267
Oral language. *See* Speaking to groups
Organizing written materials
  adding details, 181-183
  choosing and supporting central idea, 166-167
  classifying information, 169-171
  outlining, 169-172
  summarizing, 222-223
  writing topic sentences, 148-149
  see also Paragraph development; Writing, original
Outlines
  guidelines, 169-172

sentence outline, 172
topic outline, 171
Outlining, 169-172

Paragraph
defined, 145
developing comparison and contrast, 156-158
gathering material, 146-148
giving examples, 153-156
giving reasons, 159
sample paragraphs, 146-148, 149, 154
topic sentences in, 148-150
Paragraph development
chronological order, 147
topic sentence, 148-150, 157
using known facts, 146
using observation, 147
see also Composition; Writing, original
Parallel structure, in sentences, 300
Parentheses
review of (chart), 309
when to use, 335
Parenthetic elements. *See* Sentence interrupters
Parker, Dorothy, 5
Parks, Gordon, 154
Participial phrase, 128-129
Participles
dangling; *see* Dangling modifiers
defined, 127
past, 127
phrases, 128-129
present, 127

using, 127-129
Parts of speech. *See* Word classes
Passive transformation, steps in, 106-107
Past participle. *See* *-ing* and *-en* verb forms
Pattern Five Sentences, 100-101
Pattern Four sentences, 97-98
Pattern One sentences, 88-89
how to expand, 89
modifiers in, 89
Pattern Three sentences, 94-95
how to expand, 95
Pattern Two sentences, 91-92
how to expand, 92
Period
in complete sentences, 311
and quotation marks, 348
use with coordinators, 318
Periodical section, in library, 406
Personification, 28
Persuasion, 203-205
"Philistinism and the Negro Writer," 190-191
Phonetic spelling, 45
see also Dictionary, as pronunciation guide; Sound Spellings
Place subordinators, 114
Plurals
irregular, 244, 245
of nouns, 60, 241, 245
after numbers, 245
of numbers, letters, and words discussed as

words, 345
of pronouns, 65, 262
Poetry, writing, 229
Porter, Katherine Anne, 233-234
Positive form. *See* Adjectives, forms of
Possessive
first and second, 344-345
forming, 344-345
of nouns, 60, 241, 344-345
of pronouns, 65, 241, 262-263, 345
Predicate, defined, 88
Predicate adjectives, 97
Predicate nominative. *See* Nouns, after linking verb
Predicate nouns, 94-95
Prefixes, 11, 14-15
defined, 11, 14
hyphen with, 352-353
Latin and Greek, 15
list of, 15
Prepositional phrases, 85
misplaced, 295
punctuation of, 311, 328
Prepositions
common, checklist of, 84
defined, 84
how to recognize, 83-85
in phrases, 85
as subordinators, 117
Present participle. *See* *-ing* and *-en* verb forms
Pronoun case, 275-277
object forms (chart), 275
subject forms (chart), 275
Pronoun reference,
points to remember, 291-292
Pronouns
formal, 276-277
forms of, 64-65

Pronouns *(Continued)*
 functions of, 65
 indefinite, 283
 informal, avoiding, 276
 how to recognize, 64-65
 person, 64
 plural, 65, 262
 pointing, 241, 261
 position in sentence, 65
 possessive, 65, 241, 262-263
 reference, vague, 292
 relative, 118
 -self, 241, 262-263
 singular, 65, 262
 test for agreement of subject and verb, 254, 255
 third person, 253
 unnecessary shifts in case, 297
 use after *than, as,* 276
 using standard forms, 261-263
 who, whom, 276-277
Pronunciations, in dictionary, 45-47, 48
Proofreading. *See* Correcting final manuscript
Prose models for writing, 185-186, 193-195, 199-201, 205-206
Punctuation
 apostrophe, 343-345
 capitalization, 337-341
 colon, 334, 348
 comma, 317-318 323-324, 327-329, 330-332
 of complete sentences, 311, 315
 dash, 335
 end, 311-312, 315
 exclamation mark, 315
 hyphen, 352-353
 inside, 327-328, 330-332, 334-335
 italics, 350, 354
 linking, 317-318, 319-321, 323-324
 parentheses, 335
 period, 311
 question mark, 315
 quotation marks, 348-350
 review of (chart), 309
 semicolon, 318, 319-321, 331
 and sentence fragments, 311-312
 see also specific marks
Purpose subordinators, 115
Purpose, writing for a
 book reports, 225-228
 descriptive, 181-183, 185-186
 dialogue in, 190
 explaining a process, 196-198, 199-201
 guidelines for, 181-183, 188-191, 196-198, 203-204, 222, 226
 imagination, place of, 229
 influence of reading on, 221-222
 letters, 209-221
 narrative, 187-191
 persuasive, 203-205
 prose models, 185-186, 193-195, 199-201, 205-206
 summary, 222-223
 technical terms in, 198

Question mark, 315
 and quotation marks, 348, 349
Question transformations, mechanics of, 104-105
Questions, 104
 use of *do* in forming, 258
Quotation marks
 in direct quotations, 348, 349
 exceptions to using, 350
 and indirect quotations 350
 order of, 348-349
 and punctuation of credit tags, 348
 and technical terms, 350
 and titles, 350
 use of single quotation marks, 350
Quotations
 how to change, 349
 how to shorten, 349
 indirect, 349
 punctuation of, 348, 349

Random House Dictionary, The, 48
Rau, Santha Rama, 147
Readers' Guide to Periodical Literature, how to use, 413-414
Reading, influence on writing, 221-222
Reapers of the Dust, 193-195
Red Badge of Courage, The, 31
Reference
 of pronouns, 291-292
 vague *it, they, this, which, you,* 292
Reference books
 almanacs, encyclopedias, 416
 atlases, 418
 biographical, 417

Index

in library collection, 405, 415-418
on literature and quotations, 417
Reflexive pronouns. *See -self* pronouns
regardless vs. *irregardless,* 266
Relative clauses, 118, 295
punctuation of, 324
Request transformations, mechanics of, 104-105
Requests, 104
punctuation of, 311
Result coordinators, 111
Return to India, 147
R.M.S. Titanic, 188-190
Roots, of words, 11-12
"Rope," 233-234
Ross, Walter S., 7
Roughing It, 202
Rules
basic spelling, 363-366
exceptions, coordinators, 318
for using capital letters, 338-341
for using commas with coordinators, 317
for using semicolons, 319-320
for word division, 374
see also Guidelines

SAT. *See Scholastic Aptitude Test*
Scholastic Aptitude Test (SAT), 422
seeing as how vs. *because,* 267
Semicolon
review of (chart), 309
in series, 331

use with adverbial connectives, 319-321
use with coordinators, 318
Sentence building, 58
using connectives in, 110
using coordination in, 111
using noun clauses in, 120-121
using relative clauses in, 118
using subordination in, 114-115
Sentence fragments
appositives in, 312
dependent clauses, 312
kinds of, 311-312
prepositional phrases, 311
verbal phrases, 312
Sentence interrupters, 131-132, 327-328
punctuation of, 332
Sentence patterns
basic, 58, 137
how to adapt, 103-106
S-LV-Adj pattern, 97-100, 102
S-LV-N pattern, 94-96, 102
S-V-IO-O pattern, 100-103, 107
S-V-O pattern, 93, 96, 97, 102
S-V pattern, 88-90, 97, 102
see also Pattern One, etc., sentences; Sentences
Sentence shifts, unnecessary
to the passive, 298
in person, 297
in time, 297-298
Sentences

active, 106-109, 298
appositives in, 131-133, 327-328
as basic tool of communication, 56
capitalization of, 337, 338
combined, 110-123
and comma splice, 320
complete, 87-103
coordination in, 111
coordination, of parts, 300
defined, 56, 87
fused, 320
how to adapt, 58
how to expand resources of, 123-133
infinitives in, 123-124
modifiers, 328
noun clauses in, 120-121
object in, 91
parallelism in, 300
within parentheses, 335
participles in, 127-129
passive, 106-109, 298
patterns; *see* Sentence patterns
predicate, 88
relative clauses in, 118-120
review of (chart), 58
simple, how to adapt, 103-109
subject in, 88
subordination in, 114-116
verb in, 88
Sentences, topic, 148-149, 159
Series, punctuation of, 330-331
Shifts within sentences
from nonstandard to standard English, 226-268

Index

Shifts *(Continued)*
  to the passive, 298
  in person, 297
  in perspective, 297-298
  in time, 297-298
  unnecessary pronoun, 297
Short paper, preparing
  central idea, 166-167
  chronological order, 176-177
  "echo effect", 175-176
  gathering material, 163-164
  guidelines for, 166-167
  outlining, 169-172
  related points, 161-163
  title and introduction, 175
  transitional expressions in, 176-177
should have vs. *should of*, 370
Silent Spring, 203, 204-205
Silent World, The, 180
Simile, 28
Simon, Charlie May, 183
sit, set, 282
Slang, 274, 303
"**Snow**," 178-179
Snow Walker, The, 178-179
somewhere, 265
Son of the Catskills, 396
Speaking to groups
  expressing personal viewpoint, 390
  preparing brief talk, 387-388
  using the body, 385
  using the face and hands, 384
  using the voice, 381
Spelling
  adding *-ly, -ness,* or *-ful* to words, 366
  adding prefixes to words, 366
  basic rules, 363-366
  commonly misspelled words, lists of, 358-361
  confusing pairs of English words, 368-369
  contraction of *have*, 370
  double-vowel words, 364
  doubled consonants, 364
  ei and *ie* words, 363
  guidelines for improving, 357
  silent *-e* words, 364, 365
  suffixes with similar or alike sounds, 370
  y-ending words, 365
Sound spellings, 35, 45-46
  chart of, 36
Standard English
  defined, 243
  examples, 248, 250, 254, 255, 258, 261, 262, 264, 265
  how to shift to, 266-268
  irregular verbs (chart), 249
  number of verb, 253-255
  overview (chart), 241
  plural forms of nouns, 244-245
  use of auxiliary verbs, 258
  using standard adjectives and adverbs, 264-265
  using standard pronouns, 261-263
  verb tense, 248-250
Stanford Test of Academic Skills, (TASK), 432
Statements, 87, 88
  changing to questions, 104-105
  punctuation of, 311
  see also Sentence patterns; specific kind of sentence
Steinbeck, John, 7
Stewart, Marie M., 210
Stoddard, Hope, 192
Storytelling, 187-191
Study skills, guidelines for improving, 419-421
Subject forms, of pronouns, 275
Subject—linking verb—adjective (S-LV-Adj) sentences, 97-100, 102
  use of *-ly*-ending adverbs in, 278-279
Subject—linking verb—noun (S-LV-N) sentences, 94-96, 97, 102
Subject—verb—indirect object—object (S-V-IO-O) sentences, 100-103, 107
Subject—verb—object (S-V-O) sentences, 93, 96, 97, 102
  and *lay*, 282
  use of *-ly*-ending adverbs in, 278-279
Subject—verb (S-V) sentences, 88-90, 97, 102
  and *lie*, 282
  use of *-ly*-ending adverbs in, 278-279
Subordinating conjunction. *See* Subordinators
Subordination, in sentences, 114-116, 117, 122
Subordinators, 111, 114-115, 117, 323-324

Index

punctuation of, 323-324
Suffixes, 11, 17
  defined, 17
  list of, 17
Summary
  example, 223
  how to prepare, 222
Superlative degree, 75, 265
Synonyms
  defined, 23-24
  shades of meaning, 24-25

Taking tests. *See* Tests; Tests of written English; Vocabulary tests
Talks, brief
  expressing personal viewpoint, 390
  informational, 388
  preparing, 387-388
  preparing commentary, 391
TASK. *See* Stanford Test of Academic Skills
teach vs. *learn,* 267
Tense, 67-68, 70, 248-250
  auxiliary in perfect tense, 69
  shifts in, 297-298
  standard verb forms of (chart), 249
Test, Diagnostic
  for mechanics of writing, 310
  for using standard English, 242-243
Tests
  California Achievement Tests (CAT), 432
  Comprehensive Test of Basic Skills (CTBS), 432

  guidelines for taking, 421-422
  Metropolitan Achievement ("Metro"), 432
  pronoun, for agreement of subject and verb, 254, 255
  sample tests, 427-430, 440-445
  Scholastic Aptitude Test (SAT), 422
  Stanford Test of Academic Skills (TASK), 432
  vocabulary, 422-431
  of written English, 431-445
  see also Tests of written English; Vocabulary tests
Tests of written English, 431-445
  best-sentence tests, 434-435
  completion tests, 436-437
  missing transition tests, 438
  paragraph organization tests, 438-439
  paragraph revision tests, 432-434
  sample test, 440-445
  sentence revision tests, 435-436
that kind, those kinds, 281
the, 135-136
these, those, 261
they're, their, 344
this kind, these kinds, 281
this, that, 261
this, which, vague, 292
Thorndike Barnhardt Dictionary, 40, 41, 48, 49
"Through the Tunnel," 190

Time subordinators, 114
Titles, capital letters for, 338
"To Build a Fire," 188
Topic sentences, 148-149, 157
  exercises for, 150-153, 155-156
Transformations, 104-109
  active to passive, 106-107
  defined, 104
  questions, 104
  requests, 104-105
Twain, Mark, 4, 202

Underlining in manuscript. *See* Italics
unless vs. *without,* 268
Using the right word, 21-32 *see also* Words, specific

Verb markers
  auxiliaries, 69
  be, 69
  have, 69
  -fy, -ize endings, 69
Verbal nouns, 129
Verbal phrases, punctuation of, 312, 328
Verbals
  dangling, 295
  defined, 123
  infinitives, 123-124
  nouns as, 129
  participles, 127-129
Verbs
  active vs. passive, 107, 108
  agreement with subject,

Index

Verbs *(Continued)*
253-255, 287-289
auxiliary, 69, 241, 248, 258
and collective nouns, 288-289
common (chart), 70
defined, 67
-ed forms, 248-250
-en forms, 127-129
forms of *be,* 241, 250, 254, 255, 258
guidelines for using, 248-250, 253-255, 258
how to expand, 92
how to recognize, 67-71
indirect object of, 100-103
infinitives, 123-124, 127-128
-ing forms, 127-129, 258
intransitive, 88
irregular, 67, 241, 249
linking, 94, 97, 279
markers, 69
object of, 91-92
past tense, 248, 255
in Pattern One sentences, 88, 89
perfect tense, 248
plural, 253
present tense, 248, 255
regular, 67, 241
singular, 253
standard forms of (chart), 249
tense, 67, 70-71, 248-250
third person, 241, 253
time in, 248-250
transitive, 91-92, 93
Vocabulary
learning new words, 4-5
sources of, 2-3
using words, 10-12
see also Word building; Words

Vocabulary tests, 422-431
for analogies, 424-425
for antonyms, 423-425
for completing sentences, 425-427
sample tests, 427-431
for synonyms, 422
Voice
active, 107
passive, 108
Vowels, sound spellings for, 36

Webster's New Collegiate Dictionary, 34, 40
Webster's New Students Dictionary, 49, 50
well, good, 265
Wells, Walter, 210
Whispering Land, The, 183
who, whom, 276-277
who's, whose, 344
"Why Nobody Pets the Lion at the Zoo," 383
will have vs. *will of,* 370
Wiltsey, Norman B., 199-201
without vs. *unless,* 268
Word building, 10-20
building blocks, kinds of, 11
Word classes
adjectives, 73-76
adverbs, 79-82
classifications, major, 59
connectives, 83
nouns, 60-61
prepositions, 83-84
pronouns, 64-65
review of (chart), 58
verbs, 67-71
Word clues
and comparison and contrast, 5
and example, 5
and explanation, 5
kinds of, 4-5
and situation, 4-5
Word division
doubled consonants, 374
one-syllable words, 374
prefixes, 374
suffixes, 374
Word history, 43
Word meanings, 11-12, 14-15, 17, 43
clues to, 4-5
Word resources, 2
Word roots, 11-12
Latin and Greek, 11, 51-52
list of, 12
Words
antonyms, 25
building blocks of, 10, 11
choosing right word, 21-32
concrete, 22, 23
core meaning of, 11
dealing with numbers, 13
division of, 374
double-duty, 135
function, 60, 69, 75-76
homonyms, 35
meanings, 9, 19, 39-41
in sentences, 59-73
specific vs. general, 21-22
synonyms, 23-25
uses of, 2
World Book Encyclopedia, 388
would have vs. *would of,* 370
Writing, mechanics of. *See* Mechanics of writing
Writing, original
book reports, 225-227
central idea in, 166-167

Index

comparison or contrast, 156-157, 183, 198
connecting parts of, 175-177
descriptive, 181-183, 185-186
explaining a process, 196-198
expository; see Explaining a process
gathering material, 146-148, 163-164
giving examples, 153-154
giving reasons, 159
guidelines for, 166-167, 181-183, 188-191, 196-198, 203-204, 222, 226
how to revise, 273-274
and imagination, 229-236
letters; *see* Letter writing
manuscript revision marks, 238
narrative, 187-191
observation in, 147
outlining, 169-172
paragraphs, 145-161
persuasive, 203-205
poetry, 229
prose models for, 185-186, 193-195, 199-201, 205-206
for a purpose, 180-209
and reading, influence on, 221-222
short papers, 161-180
storytelling, 187-191
summarizing, 222-223
technical terms in, 198
topic sentence in, 148-149, 157
transitional expressions in, 176-177
using contrasts, 157

Written sentences
checking agreement of subject and verb, 287-289
compound subject in, 288
modifiers, position in, 294-295
and pronoun reference, 291-292
shifts in perspective, 297-298

you, they, vague, 292
"You've Got to Learn," 188

HANDBOOK KEY

Chapter 1		WORDS	1
	W1	Learning New Words	4
	W2	Word Building	10
	W3	The Right Word	21
	W4	Using the Dictionary	32

Chapter 2		SENTENCES	55
	S1	Words in a Sentence	59
	S2	The Complete Sentence	87
	S3	Adapting the Simple Sentence	103
	S4	Building Combined Sentences	110
	S5	Expanding Our Sentence Resources	123

Chapter 3		COMPOSITION	141
	C1	Writing the Paragraph	145
	C2	Writing a Short Paper	161
	C3	Writing for a Purpose	180
	C4	Writing a Letter	209
	C5	Writing and Reading	221